FREDERIC MANNING

An Unfinished Life

Also by Jonathan Marwil

The Trials of Counsel: Francis Bacon in 1621
A History of Ann Arbor

FREDERIC MANNING

An Unfinished Life

JONATHAN MARWIL

Duke University Press
Durham, N.C.
1988

To the memory of my brother Michael

Published in the United States of America
by Duke University Press, Durham, North Carolina

ISBN 0-8223-0803-7

Library of Congress Cataloging-in-Publication Data

Marwil, Jonathan L., 1940–
Frederic Manning.

Bibliography: p.
Includes index.
1. Manning, Frederic — Biography. 2. Authors, Australian — 20th century — Biography. 3. Authors, English — 20th century — Biography. I. Title.
PR9619.3.M267Z78 1988 823'.912 [B] 87-15708
ISBN 0-8223-0803-7

Contents

I always swore to everyone that Private 19022 could, if he would, write greatly; but I never dreamed that time and the man would produce anything like this.

T. E. Lawrence, 1930

Introduction

In January of 1930 the English firm, Peter Davies, published *Her Privates We*, "a record of experience on the Somme and Ancre fronts, with an interval behind the line, during the latter half of the year 1916". Its author, said to be a well-known man of letters "already distinguished in another kind of literature", signed himself "Private 19022". Reviewers praised the novel as the most accurate and moving portrayal yet rendered of the common soldier, and the reading public, though awash in war books, quickly made it a bestseller. Mingled with respect was the mystery of who was responsible for a book hailed as superior to *All Quiet on the Western Front* (1929) — the standard by which other accounts were judged — and its numerous epigoni.

The question was soon answered. On 26 February a story in the *Daily Mirror* identified Frederic Manning as the author. To many readers the name meant nothing, and so the month-long guessing game ended in a fizzle; to those familiar with Manning's work the news offered a more difficult puzzle: how had a literary figure hitherto valued for refinement written such a knowing and searing book about men in war?

Twenty years before, at the age of 27, Manning had published *Scenes and Portraits*, a book of philosophical dialogues whose sensibility and style, at once sceptical, ironic, and chaste, announced its author a legitimate heir to the classical traditions of Anglo-French letters. Critics then and later proclaimed the work a classic, imagining that it would soon be a fixture in every serious library. Admirers praised its style and marvelled at its intelligence and wit. Many spoke respectfully as well of its learning, for Manning seemed no less at home with the first and thirteenth centuries than he did with the nineteenth, reinforcing the impression left by the publication of his narrative poem, *The Vigil of Brunhild* in 1907, that he was disposed to look to other eras for inspiration and materials. Subsequent collections of poetry published in 1910 and 1917, while containing poems with a manifestly contemporary resonance, did not change this impression. Nor did his 1923 biography of Sir William White, director of construction for the Royal Navy from 1885 to 1902. Commissioned by the subject's family and intended for a professional audience, *The Life of Sir William White* was obviously a labour of necessity and had been followed in 1926 by a more congenial undertaking: a long introduction to an edition of Epicurus. The appearance, therefore, of a novel by an author whose imaginative efforts had hitherto been limited to short forms, usually of an historical character, a novel that Arnold Bennett described as "full of horrors, cruelties, stupidities, [and] grossnesses", was a striking anomaly. And for those able to read it in its unexpurgated version — which appeared simultaneously but was sold necessarily by subscription and under the title *The Middle Parts of Fortune* — a shocking one as well. For Manning's privates walked through his pages ridiculing each other for being "cunt-struck" and grousing that those back home "don't care a fuck 'ow us'ns live". Readers seeking explanation for so dramatic a shift in literary mode and decorum were to be disappointed. Manning would eventually acknowledge his authorship but in public spoke little of his achievement.

Or of much else. He lived in great privacy, away from London and literary connections, guarding his delicate health and preferring the company of his own thoughts. He declined invitations to give lectures, and "fled" to Italy when the war novel came out. His productivity, moreover, was small, a half dozen books in a career of 30 years, spaced in a way that suggests the amateur's habit of picking up his pen only when it suits him. T. S. Eliot, an admirer, saw him accurately as a writer "without ambition for notoriety". Numerous writers have espoused a similar lack of ambition; few have lived it so successfully.

But in the absence of popular notice Manning enjoyed considerable esteem among his peers. Illustrious contemporaries besides Eliot wrote in superlatives about his work, and the man who first guessed the identity of Private 19022, T. E. Lawrence, did so (he claimed) because he had read *Scenes and Portraits* "at least fifty times". Of special importance was Ezra Pound, whose respect for Manning's prose knew no bounds, and who in 1920 tried unsuccessfully to coax the New York literary magazine *Dial* into publishing serially an historical novel Manning had been working on for a decade. Thirty years later Pound was still interested in the unfinished manuscript, but efforts to publish it came to nothing.

What Pound, Eliot, and Lawrence found in Manning were talents and values they cherished. In range and depth of learning he was at least their equal, despite only six months' formal schooling, and he shared each man's absorption in the principles and aesthetics of classical culture. Eliot, in eulogising this "early and valued" contributor to his journal, *Criterion*, could have been thinking of himself when he praised "a style of writing, and a frame of mind, suited to a more cultured and better educated age than our own". What age Eliot had in mind he did not say, but he believed that some of Manning's work, not least his assorted criticism, would stand the tests of time and fashion. So too did Pound, Lawrence, and many others.

Indeed, as early as 1909, on the basis of *Scenes and Portraits*, Manning was being hailed as one who would be "remembered in literature when people talk of the masters". Less enthusiasm had greeted his early verse, but the promise of his prose, strengthened by his prewar reviews for the *Spectator*, was sufficient. Comparisons were frequently made to Matthew Arnold and Walter Pater, neither of whom had accomplished so much so early. And virtually overnight his opinion had begun to carry weight with the literary establishment. "I am sending you," he wrote to poet and novelist Henry Newbolt in November 1909, "a small volume of poems, by my friend Ezra Pound, which contains some good work. The Ballad of the Goodly Fere, Sestine for

Ysolt, and Song of the Virgin Mother, seem to me particularly fine.'' When that favour was performed no one would have wagered that Pound's fame would one day far outdistance that of the man he honoured with Yeats as being his ''First licherary'' companion in England.

But after such early promise Manning's career sagged, and he slipped almost entirely from public notice. A writer of whom much was expected became a figure of marginal interest. *Her Privates We* revived Manning's reputation. Its achievement, both as fact and art, was an abrupt reminder to contemporaries of his extraordinary endowments. It was widely read, and as a novel generally considered to be the best of the English war novels. That categorisation, however, eventually narrowed its importance and confined its readership, so that despite having written a second classic, Manning as a literary figure has been ignored.

Coming so late and followed by so little — he published before his death in 1935 only an additional sketch for a new edition of the dialogues — *Her Privates We* urges certain questions. Some confine themselves to Manning's life, others reach beyond. How, for example, does one explain the author of *Scenes and Portraits* composing what Hemingway later recommended as the most candid book about men in war? Why was a writer respected and befriended by some of the great modernists so long content to labour in older modes? Why was *Her Privates We*, like the earlier *Scenes and Portraits*, followed by years of faltering productivity? What explains the privacy that wrapped itself around Manning's life and sanctioned his neglect even while he lived? These and other questions engage issues of influence, choice, and success with which every serious writer must reckon, and every serious commentator subsequently discuss. In the case of Frederic Manning, a writer who so obviously succeeded and yet so obviously failed, the asking of them takes on a special importance as well as a special poignancy. Answering them has been a difficult and lengthy process.

It began on a summer day in 1976 when I walked into the Houghton Library at Harvard to read Manning's letters to the painter William Rothenstein. At the time I was indulging an attack of superfluous curiosity. I had read *Her Privates We* and found it unlike any other book I knew on the Great War. Although cast and advertised as a novel it does not fit comfortably into any genre, and its point of view, that of a gentleman ranker self-consciously distanced from both officers and enlisted men, is unusual. Efforts to learn something about its author had been largely wasted. Even some standard reference works did not mention Manning, and those that did had little to say beyond that he was born in Australia and had lived most of his life in England, principally in the small Lincolnshire village of Edenham. The one informative article I had come across referred to the manuscript letters at Houghton,* and being nearby on a vacation trip I took a day to examine them. I certainly did not anticipate writing anything about Manning. I had just published a book on Sir Francis Bacon and was reading my way through a series of seventeenth-century histories with the aim of writing a book about their authors. The day in Cambridge was to be merely an interlude.

The letters to Rothenstein, starting with their exquisite calligraphy, well justified the detour. The small, softly stroked letters formed clean straight lines, separated by spacings so wide as to seem wasteful. An immediate and recurrent image is of Manning poised over a sheet of paper, pen in hand, sensing that a work of art, not just a message, begins as soon as the ink touches the white surface. No summary of the letters' contents would be fair, except one that stressed their intelligence, generosity, and modesty. They discuss art, religion, and war, the common ground of the two friends' interests and experiences, but their tone reveals deeper affinities. Even without Rothenstein's replies the reader knows that these were men who respected and were kind to each other, and who valued what they shared. Manning often reaches out to Rothenstein and his family as if wanting to be drawn within a circle of love and responsibility that his solitary life could not provide. He also, however, keeps his distance, protecting behind the concern and sweetness of his address a privacy that Rothenstein did not challenge. Finally, the writer of the letters has a habit of stepping outside himself, the vulnerable figure of experience, so as ostensibly to take a more accurate reading of things. One letter, fully quoted, will suggest their interest; it was written from the Somme in October of 1916.

> 19022 Pte Manning H.Q. Coy
> Signals Section
> 7th K.S.L.T.
> 31. X. 1916
>
> My dear Will,
> You will make me bankrupt of thanks. At present we are four men and a dog in a dug-out — the dug-out being the reconstructed cellar of a shattered house: the dog is suffering from a slight shrapnel wound and shell shock, and the men are very grateful for a cigarette — yours in this case. The weather is horribly wet, and there is a great deal of shelling. I am acting as a relay runner between the trenches and brigade. At first I took up my quarters in a comfortable dry barn, until Fritz began dropping shrapnel and high explosive around it. I stood it all night — some very close, and then migrated to this damp but healthier refuge, during the first lull. It is not pleasant to hear a whole iron foundry being hurled thro' the air. I stand it better when I have something to do.
>
> I can't tell you how much I look forward to seeing you at Stroud, when the tempest and the whirlwind have passed, and there is time for the still small voice to make itself heard; and yet, curiously enough, even here the mind is free. We become more or less indifferent to what is going on about us, and to consider it all as tho' we were, in a sense, only spectators of an incredible madness: this, even while the same madness infects our own blood. I am horribly dirty, and there is a smear of

> wet clay on the top of the page, but these are merely the inherent accidents of our life, and you will forgive them. Dirt, misery, and madness are the realities of war. We are cooking our dinner now over an improvised brazier, and the damp wood has filled the dug-out with smoke that stings the eyes — there's one thing that matters in war time. I am generally on duty from 12 midnight until 6 a.m. and it means a couple of long walks, on a road which is continually shelled. We are supposed to go in pairs, but so far I have always gone alone, and it is a curious sensation. I am not ashamed to say that I have felt fear walking beside me like a live thing: the torn and flooded road, the wreckage — mere bones — of what were living houses, and I have always felt the character or personality of a house; absolute peace of the landscape and indifferent stars, then the ear catches the purr of a big shell, it changes from a purr to a whine and then detonates on concussion. Another comes, then a third. After that a short space of quiet. Sometimes, as I have said, I feel fear, but usually with the fear is mingled indifference which is not pious enough to be termed resignation.
>
> 1.XI. 1916
>
> We have been relieved, but we don't get much rest from the noises of the guns. I must try to sleep through it. Good night, my dear Will: thank you for your kindness, and my love to you all.
>
> Yours always affectly
> Fred

These letters spurred my curiosity. That autumn I read Manning's other works and began to catch glimpses of what I took to be the real figure entangled within the public and private personae, and to hear the voice behind the words, the nuances of feeling and intention that words can only mark. I also sent off letters to several libraries and individuals whom I thought could provide biographical information. The results exceeded expectations. Yale had the run of letters to Pound as well as a handful to Newbolt; Texas, a batch to the writer Richard Aldington dealing with their secret collaboration on the writing of the White biography; and Mrs T. S. Eliot acknowledged possession of *both* sides of an extended correspondence with her husband. In addition, two of Rothenstein's children volunteered their help, as did the librarian of the *Spectator* in identifying Manning's unsigned reviews. Most welcome, though, was the letter from Manning's niece and literary executor, Miss Eleanor Manning of Sydney, whom I had been trying to reach for several months. Twice I had written, and as I opened her letter I was anxious: Why had she not responded earlier? Would she approve of my inquiries and offer help? Was she already assisting someone else? All worries were quickly dispelled. "I am delighted to hear of your interest in my uncle. . . I shall certainly do anything I can to help you in your research. . ." Subsequent letters would reveal that she had barely known her uncle and doubted having any useful papers, but for the moment I was happy just to be in touch with someone in the family. The contact bestowed an imprimatur on my search and brought me closer to Manning himself.

No longer was he an interest of the left hand. And there were signs that he was becoming important to others as well. Poet and critic Donald Davie had recently called for "the recovering" of Manning and Allen Upward as matters of "great urgency" if the Edwardian milieu in which Pound had written was to be rightly understood, and I heard that a professor at Amherst, Richard Cody, was already on the trail. Reading Davie I was pleased; news of Cody made me feel as if someone had walked into my house and laid claim to my possessions. For I had begun to feel not only that special satisfaction that emerges from championing the lost and the neglected — be they causes or writers — but also a certain proprietary impulse. No one else, I had been assuming, knew or cared about Manning to the degree I did; he was mine.

As it turned out, his life was mine. A phone call to Cody determined that he had in mind a literary essay and was neither interested in specifically biographical questions nor optimistic that evidence to answer them could be found. This allowed each of us space, and later the opportunity to chat and exchange articles. We both avoided suggesting that Manning had been a major twentieth-century writer, but agreed that he had written two brilliant books — one of them a masterpiece of its kind — and deserved more than casual notice. For myself, I was growing confident that there was sufficient evidence to reconstruct his life and career. If I was right, at least some of the puzzles and incongruities surrounding him might be explained. And his story, for all its idiosyncrasy, was sure to illumine an epoch in English letters.

In March of 1977, therefore, I went East for a week, spending two days in the Beinecke Rare Book Library at Yale. Compared to the red-brick, colonial Houghton, which has the appearance and tone of a private eating club, the massive, sepulchral Beinecke looks as if it were intended to commemorate its holdings, not merely house them. Walking into it for the first time I felt myself in the scene from *Citizen Kane* where a reporter visits a tomb-like library in search of the identity of "Rosebud", the apparent key to Kane's life. Manning's life was then still a tissue of mysteries, so that I was happy to gain from his letters (as well as from Pound's letters to his own parents) basic information concerning friendships and projects, tastes and sensibility. Only later, and halfway around the world, would I discover that in Manning's life too there had been a "Rosebud", a mother of enduring significance.

On the same trip I stopped by St Martin's Press in New York, which was soon to co-publish with Peter Davies the first commercial edition of *The Middle Parts of Fortune*. As an unannounced and unknown visitor, I caused some surprise among the people at St Martin's, but since they knew virtually nothing about Manning, they graciously accepted the information I could give them. Some of it prompted an immediate trans-Atlantic phone call about copyright, and some was later used in preparing the book's dustjacket. St Martin's warm reception reinforced my missionary zeal, and soon after returning home I received an offer to write a brief article on Manning for a literary supplement. This gave me an opportunity to pull together what I thus far knew and to appreciate how much I did not. It also made me realize that a figure who increasingly occupied my working hours, and increasingly stayed in my mind beyond them, demanded a book rather than simply an article or two. It was a conclusion that had been growing in my mind until I could no longer ignore it.

Thus I laid aside my project on seventeenth-century historians and began planning a summer trip to England. More letters were sent to people who had known Manning and to institutions that might have a record of him, and in reply came information and invitations. One letter, from the publisher John Murray, promised a rich treasure. It disclosed an archive containing folders of correspondence with Manning relating to all but one of the five books he had published with the firm. Access simply required a few days' notice and the payment of a small service fee.

I also pondered exactly what sort of book I should write. A conventional biography did not seem appropriate for a little-known writer, most of whose work was not even readily available. And there might be difficulties finding a publisher for such a book. A friend suggested doing it as a novel, but that struck me as a problematic and evasive strategy. If the story of Frederic Manning contained the interest and significance I thought it did, why should I need to invent? And could I? Writing fiction had never been an ambition of mine and a botch was apt to come of my first try. No, a book on Manning would have to stay within the familiar boundaries of fact and inference.

Within those boundaries were, however, other opportunities, and I finally decided to let my search for Manning organise the narrative. Since I needed to make several extended journeys to discover the facts of his life, the book would follow my movements, reading at times like a travel diary or detective story as its subject gradually emerged into view. The strategy risked preciousness but was not without precedent. I did not aim to reveal myself as Boswell had chosen to, nor had Manning's life the exotic flavour of Corvo's, but these and other examples gave credibility to my method. Besides, I thought, readers might enjoy watching how the story of a man's life is assembled from scratch.

What follows is what I had in mind to do back in 1977. My stay in England that summer began with a pilgrimage to St Mary's Catholic Cemetery in north-west London, where after two hours of tramping around in the rain I finally found Manning's grave, his name all but erased from the bevelled stone. From there my search widened, as I looked for papers, visited the places where he had lived and, most fascinating of all, talked to people who had known him. One of these was Lady Cynthia Sandys of Himbleton Manor in Worcestershire, who was in her eightieth year when I interviewed her one afternoon. We sat first in her large garden and then, when rain threatened, moved into the parlour of her Victorian home, a cavernous brick structure where cobwebs and dust enjoyed certain territorial rights and memories drifted through empty rooms meant for large families and continual guests. How many elderly people, I caught myself wondering, inhabit such houses in the English countryside, remembering a past crowded with voices, leisurely afternoons, and innumerable servants who made it all possible? Over tea Frederic Manning was recalled by Lady Cynthia with affection and intensity, so that it seemed at moments as if he were a tangible presence, perhaps idling in another room waiting to be asked in.

The next summer I went to Australia and found more than I had expected, beginning with the extraordinary helpfulness of the Manning family. Eleanor Manning had pledged her assistance to a stranger, and she lived up to her word far beyond what I had reason to expect. I also spent a couple of days on a dairy farm outside Melbourne talking with Ivor Woolmer, who had worked as a servant for Manning in the early 1920s before emigrating to Australia. "Chick", as everyone called him, was a man I liked immediately, though, unlike most of my informants, it was his will to remember, not memory itself, that needed prodding. For decades he had been burying his English past, so that real effort on both our parts was needed to force his memory to send up images that had shape and colour. But in the end I think our talk, interrupted though it was by milking and haying and watching the Wimbledon tennis matches on television, proved at least as valuable for Woolmer as it did for me.

Three years later, in the summer of 1981, I returned to England. By then a draft of the book was in hand, yet questions and leads remained. I found several more people with long memories and visited places missed on the earlier trip. To some I was invited, notably Beauforest House in Oxfordshire, where I talked to William Rothenstein's son, Sir John Rothenstein, about his and his father's relationship to Manning, and Newbuildings in Sussex, where I had hoped to trace Manning's connection with the Blunt family, but where all I found were some wonderful William Morris tapestries. To other places I went unannounced. One of these was The Node, an estate in Hertfordshire that from Manning's letters I knew he had visited often in the 1920s and 1930s when it belonged to someone named Carl Holmes. Who Holmes had been was a mystery, and so I decided to stop at The Node to see if its present owner could be of help. Much to my surprise I found all kinds of memories and traces of Holmes. It turned out he had been an American who had settled in England after the war, and spared no expense in creating a most unusual estate. Among other features it boasted:

Item: A dairy modelled after the one built for Marie Antoinette at Versailles and having the largest thatched roof in England.

Item: A Japanese garden designed by a professor from the Imperial School of Gardening in Tokyo and constructed by workmen specially brought from Japan.

Item: Bathrooms of English, Turkish, and Japanese design, reflecting the successive nationalities of Holmes' wives while he lived at The Node.

In all this there was no evidence of Manning, though I did learn that Holmes had gone back to America and might still be alive. I eventually found him on Long Island, but by telephone realised that there was little point in my going to see him. Though alert and wishing to help, his memory of those days was very poor — "stinking" was how he described it. All he could recall was that Manning had been "a nice chap" whose handwriting was difficult to read, and whose books were too "highbrow" to get through. I was disappointed, but solving the mystery of Mr Holmes had been its own reward.

Finally, in June of 1985, when the manuscript had already entered the publishing process, I flew to London for the sole purpose of reading Manning's letters to Eliot. Previously they had been withheld by Mrs Eliot; now she was to make them available. Unfortunately I was not shown all of them, but those I did see — about two-thirds of the total — clarified the relationship between two men who were, in several ways, very much alike.

Much about Manning has probably eluded me. He was an elusive figure even to his friends, with whom he shared few of the details of his life. I tried to look in the right places for clues, and steadily sent off letters, ultimately in the hundreds, to people whom I hoped might be able to help. Usually I received apologies for ignorance, and once got back my own letter, unopened, with a single word scrawled on the envelope: "Deceased". Then there are specific pieces of the puzzle which I have not located, search though I did. Chief among them is Manning's correspondence and papers, which were stored in Harrods Depository at the time of his death. Presumably they were taken out — Harrods now has no record of them or their removal — but what happened to them is a mystery. How different an impression they might have given me can only be guessed at; but having the letters of his friends and acquaintances would have told me much about him. And, predictably, my research ran into accidents and roadblocks, people and institutions who had casually destroyed what traces of Manning they once possessed, or who refused to share them.

But in the end there has been enough to write a book about a man who deserves one, not only for his own achievement but for the role he played in English letters. Manning touched important lives in important ways; his work, his mind, and his values commanded the admiration of peers now regarded as giants. And if, as it seems, his long allegiance to the agendas of High Victorianism stymied his progress as a writer, that makes his story worth telling for its cultural meanings. The tale of how Yeats and Pound found their way out of the 1890s has often been told; perhaps as important is the story of a writer who did not, until very late. For what he accomplished as well as for what he did not, and, too, for the insights his unusual career offers into a richly tangled literary milieu, Frederic Manning merits attention.

Influences

Chapter One

I never wanted to go to Australia. A country even more recently settled than my own, a continent three parts desolate, the place seemed sterile, its people genial, athletic, faceless. Not even when I began to investigate Frederic Manning's life did I look forward to a trip down under. Perhaps his own neglect of his homeland encouraged my indifference; I cannot be sure. I gradually realised, however, that I would have to go, at least to Sydney. Only there would I be able to increase the meagre book-found knowledge that I had of his youth and family background.

Thus, in April of 1978, I began making plans for a trip in June, expecting that a stopover in New Zealand — a place I had always yearned to see and which was now the home of some old friends — would be the highpoint of my journey. Two letters, however, sweetened my outlook on Australia. Since August of 1977, when I had met his brother Victor in Edenham, Lincolnshire, I had been trying to establish contact with Ivor Woolmer, who operated a dairy farm near Alexandra, 80 miles north-east of Melbourne. A former servant, I supposed, could tell me a great deal, if only about the habits, moods, and preferences, of Manning's daily life. But several letters to Woolmer had gone unanswered, and I was beginning to think that he had died, or had chosen a purposeful silence, when at the end of May a cheery message finally arrived.

> Dear Mr. Marwil,
> I guess you will almost have despaired of getting a reply to your letters, but here we are at last. First of all, my apologies for not having answered your three letters

> earlier. We have had a very busy time on the farm during the last six months owing to unusually dry conditions. We supply a certain amount of milk under contract to Melbourne all through the year. This necessitated quite a lot of irrigation of pastures during the summer months and long hours of toil. There are no fortunes in dairy farming, but it helps to keep the family together, and it is a way of life that appeals to many people.
>
> As regards your inquiry in connection with Fred Manning. I will give you what information I can in that respect, but my knowledge of his literary undertakings and achievements was very limited. True, I was with him for three years, but at the age of 15 to 17 years is hardly the period when one is thirsting for knowledge...

While the rest of the letter mainly told me things I already knew, I discounted Woolmer's supposition that he could be of little help. His answer indicated a clear, if cautious, intelligence, and face-to-face questioning, I imagined, might unlock his memory.

The second letter came from the National Library at Canberra, informing me that they had recently obtained a substantial number of letters Manning had written to James Griffyth Fairfax between 1907 and 1914. Fairfax had been an important friend in Manning's life; how important I did not yet know. They had met in England while Fairfax, scion of the family that owned the *Sydney Morning Herald*, was a student at New College, Oxford. Like Manning, who was four years his senior, Fairfax had literary ambitions, and before the outbreak of World War I he published four volumes of verse and frequently reviewed for the literary magazines. But it was not a notable career, certainly not as notable as his record in the war, during which he was four times mentioned in despatches. Such commendation no doubt helped him win a seat in Parliament in 1924 as the Conservative member from Norwich. By then Fairfax had married and published three more books of poems and translations. Henceforth his pen would be less active, but Manning's death stirred him deeply and inspired an elegy drenched in grief and nostalgia.

In Memoriam

For F. M.

(22: 2: 35)

I said this to myself when the word came
That you were — if you ever could be — dead,
Grieve not that Death has drawn from that torn scabbard
The incorruptible and shining blade:
Grieve not that Time has poured with hated hand
The last grains through his glass of mortal hours.
Grieve not for this or that; gladly remember
How we were young together, laughed, drank wine,
Wrote verse by reams, and talked the late stars pale
Into the dawn, with question and surmise;

The poem stumbles on to speak of separate wars, and of times together later in Lincolnshire.

Sitting once more where books climbed ceiling high,
While through the window on that English lawn
Stooped the low branches of the mulberry-tree
Where Kim would crouch for hunting — how long since!

The final lines, bereft of grace and imagination if not of feeling, resume the determination not to grieve.

Feeling that with you all at last is well,
Peace in a starry space, and no more pain;
And those we both loved eager to welcome you.
Dead, will you take my greeting to those dead,
And say, "To live is not the lightest doom."

That poem and dedications to Manning of several other poems — including "Birthday Ode" To F. M. July 22, 1908 — revealed Fairfax's fondness for his friend, but until the letter from the

National Library arrived I had too few details to grasp firmly the importance of their relationship. And it had been very bad luck that Fairfax died less than a year before I became intrigued with Manning. Canberra was added to my itinerary.

Even in the age of jet travel a journey from the United States to Australia is taxing. For almost 24 hours you are either strapped into an aeroplane and given intermittent feedings, or you wander in bright music-padded airports that compound the time-and-place confusion. During a brief stopover in Auckland, New Zealand, there was a rush to the duty-free counter, prompted as much by the need to escape the confines of the plane, which by now resembled a gigantic bedroom, as to take advantage of the bargains. When the plane finally touched down in Sydney, the cabin was sprayed by agricultural officials before we could disembark. Then, groggy, dishevelled, and disinfected, we went our separate ways, with a better appreciation, perhaps, of what steerage passage to the colony had been like.

I was met at Sydney airport by Eleanor Manning and her friend Dot, with whom she had lived since her father's death in 1962. Eleanor was very much a lady of the old school, someone for whom good taste and manners are the embodiment of virtues, not merely smoothing gestures. With her fresh complexion and lively eyes she looked younger than her 70-odd years, and at moments her glance and voice held a striking innocence. Much of her adult life she had worked in the Girl Guide movement, rising finally to the post of president. Dot, on the other hand, was a rough-hewn, tweedy woman who since retiring as a school teacher had spent most of her days challenging the Sydney golf courses. She, too, had never married and was a blunt advocate of the traditional values. Both women, though poised and outspoken, were actually quite shy, so that during the car ride into the city conversation did not come easily. When I was dropped off at my hotel an invitation to dinner that night was extended. Politeness called for the offer, but I sensed that Eleanor wanted to take the measure of this unexpectedly young man — "I thought you would be much older" — so curious to learn about "Uncle Fred".

More than hospitality, I needed help. Frederic Manning had gone to England in 1903 to pursue a career as a writer. The shape of that career was visible enough, as was the rhythm of the life he led. But the first 21 years of his life were almost a blank. I knew that his father, Sir William Patrick, had been an important figure in Sydney financial and political circles, serving as mayor for four terms; that Frederic had been a sickly child and attended school for only a brief period; and that in 1898 he had been taken to England, where he stayed for two years, by a man who was to play the crucial role in his subsequent development, Arthur Galton. Obviously, I needed more information about his childhood and early youth, not merely for itself but for what it could disclose about the adult patterns of work as well as behaviour. Eliot had suggested in his obituary that illness and an excessive fastidiousness accounted for Manning's small output. Both were factors, but as explanations they were insufficient. Many writers have struggled with illness, and at least as many have been harsh critics of themselves. Why had Manning not cleared these hurdles? Then, too, I was convinced that *The Middle Parts of Fortune* was a unique, powerful book for reasons other than Manning's own war experiences or the particular concerns of his art. These mattered of course, but so, I thought, had his personal odyssey. Thousands of soldiers could have written *All Quiet on the Western Front* — a reason why the book has always drawn some sneers — or, for that matter, most of the other well-known war novels. The same cannot be said for Manning's, for it manages not only to convey with touching immediacy the ambience of a soldier's life — and in that achievement has many worthy competitors — but quietly demands of its readers that they view the experience of war in contexts larger than itself. In that perspective, *The Middle Parts of Fortune* is virtually alone, and there had to be reasons.

That evening I took a taxi out to Eleanor's home in Point Piper, a small exclusive harbourside suburb of Sydney. The house itself, in which Eleanor and her sister had been raised, was a modest, comfortable dwelling which looked out over Rose Bay, one of the many inlets contributing to Sydney's remarkable beauty. When I entered the house I immediately saw hanging on a wall the portrait that William Rothenstein had painted of Manning during Manning's first visit to England. Fred, wearing a frock coat, is seated stiffly on a chair, silk hat resting on his knee, looking very much the smug dandy. In his autobiography Rothenstein tells how this particular commission came his way:

> One day a stranger came, a young Australian, who wished to be drawn. Frederic Manning was his name; he admired the poets and writers I knew, Max especially, and since I had drawn so many poets, he had sought me out. He was an attractive youth, a little precious and frail, looking wise for his years. I found him to be very intelligent; he came almost daily, then he disappeared. Manning had no money it transpired; he believed his father would pay for the drawing I did of him, and for other extravagances; not so his father. And now he was afraid lest I might take proceedings against him. I reassured him, his father would pay some day; if not, what matter.

Examining the drawing, I sensed that the boy's urgent wish to be revealed by the hand that sketched admired writers had unduly influenced the artist himself; there is a great deal of pose in the picture but not much person, which perhaps explains why Rothenstein did not recognise him when they met again several years later.*

The portrait was a surprise; I had thought it lost. A further surprise came when Eleanor, after offering me a drink, casually handed over several letters of her uncle's dating from the 1930s that she said she had found that afternoon. Up to that moment I had been under the impression that she had no relevant papers. In 1962 her father, Henry — Harry to family and friends — had made a formal bequest to the Mitchell Library in Sydney of those of his brother's papers that he then held, and after his death

Eleanor had supposedly passed on to the Mitchell whatever else came into her hands. Altogether there had not been much: most importantly a series of letters from T. E. Lawrence, the holograph of the war novel, and miscellaneous letters and reviews concerning Manning's work. Eleanor's sudden discovery of these letters "at the back of a drawer" demonstrated that houses have a way of concealing things. Skimming the contents of the letters while sipping a drink and trying to hold up my end of the conversation, I began fantasising about boxes of letters yet to be discovered. Manning must have written hundreds to his family over the years. Could it be that Harry, when sorting the materials for his donation, had overlooked a cupboard or, more likely, deliberately held back private correspondence thinking that it was not the business of scholars? The only thing to do was to ask permission to look through the house, a request that was graciously approved for the next day. Eleanor was sceptical that I would find anything of importance, but like her father she was ready to assist any efforts to make Frederic Manning better known.

The rest of the evening went splendidly. A perfectly cooked roast chicken and a bottle of Australian wine set a relaxed mood for our talk. Eleanor could actually tell me very little about her uncle. She had been away from Sydney during his long visit home in 1933–34, and when he had come back in 1925 for three months she had seen him only a few times. About other members of the family, however, she was quite helpful, as were her sister Pat and cousin Bill, whom I would visit later in their homes near Cootamundra. Their memories, together with the few family papers that survive, gave me some sense of the family in which the future writer had grown up. To be sure, oral evidence of the sort I collected is suspect. The anecdotes I heard usually had either the smooth rounded character of a polished stone, or were handed to me as vague crumbly things that dissolved under the slightest pressure. Everyone told me the truth as they recalled it, or recalled being told it, but the stories frequently served a purpose. I was seeking facts but was handed judgements, and not always those of the speaker. The odour of ancient animosities and affections permeated the tales I heard of opportunities and oversights, successes and failures; in brief, I was given the processed material of human memory. The public record of newspaper and archive was less mythical, but except about Fred's father, of little help.

William Patrick Manning was born in Sydney in 1845, the son of John Manning, a baker who had emigrated from Cork some years before. The story is told that as a boy William played marbles with a wealthy schoolmate so as to win enough money to buy an arithmetic book. As symbol the story rings true, for it would be a shrewdness in managing money that would bring him riches, influence, and community esteem. That and the appearance and demeanour of a gentleman, which impressed his contemporaries. "His dignity," wrote a journalist in 1906, "is such that no one has ever had the temerity — except perhaps in his schooldays — to give him a nickname." He went to work at 16 as a clerk in the office of P. N. Russell & Company, a Sydney engineering firm. Subsequently he was employed by the Colonial Sugar Company for many years, and from there went to work for W. W. Billyard, the agent for a number of English investors. As a public accountant William Patrick honed the skills needed to manage money and men productively. In time he became the managing partner at Billyard, a director of several insurance companies, and a leading figure in Sydney banking circles. Not the least of his investor clients was Peter Nicol Russell, his first employer, who entrusted Manning with his own Australian investments when he decided to leave Sydney and live in England. Success at finance begat political interests, and election in 1887 to the Sydney City Council, on which he would sit for 12 years. For almost four of those years (1891–94) he served as mayor, and his brother aldermen's unusually copious letter of thanks when he left office expressed particular respect for his efforts during the economic crisis of 1893, "a period of commercial depression more acute than any the colony has hitherto

William Patrick Manning in mayoral robes, c. *1891*
(William O. Manning)

experienced". A more visible mark of esteem came in the form of a knighthood bestowed by Queen Victoria in 1894. He had impressed a recent governor of New South Wales, Lord Jersey,* with his conduct as mayor, and as one newspaper suggested, "the fact that he represents Lord Rosebery, the Duke of Manchester, and several other wealthy capitalists no doubt had some influence." Indeed, rumour had it that he represented more "absentee capital" than any other agent in Sydney.

His political life also encompassed a term in the New South Wales Legislative Assembly (1893–94) and periodic appointments to governmental commissions. In 1891 he served as chairman of a New South Wales Royal Commission looking into Chinese gambling and immorality, and charges of bribery against members of the police, while in 1892 he was a member of a Royal Commission appointed to examine the military service of New South Wales.* He also had a long and very active role in promoting the cause of Australian federation. In Sydney there were few more hearty champions of the great cause, and fewer still who could claim to have been "intimately associated" with the movement from its inception. He was a key member of the Australian Federation League, chairing its earliest meetings,* and the newspapers of the 1890s carried reports of many speeches he gave in support of its aim. But Manning's protectionist principles in Sydney's free trade environment seem to have undercut his other campaigns for elective office, and he never gained the ministerial post that friends and associates believed he merited. Other interests also took up his time. For almost a quarter of a century he served as president of the Sydney Philharmonic Society, and for 20 years he was a Fellow of St John's College of the University of Sydney. He was, in addition, an observant Catholic and served his church well with his advice and his charity, so well that in 1903 he was made a Papal Chamberlain.* Evidence that the honour sprang from service rather than piety comes from the pen of his literary son: "My father," wrote Fred in 1908, "does not care two straws for orthodoxy, but has a vague notion that orthodoxy is what he thinks himself."

When William Patrick died in 1915 he was eulogised as an exemplary public citizen. He had done many good things for Sydney, and despite one or two attempts over the years to question his probity,* his reputation remained untarnished — no mean accomplishment in the snatch and gouge of the city's political life in those days. As a father, he may have been less successful: a little too busy, and a little too dominating to win the hearts of his children. At least that is the suggestion implicit in Fred's appraisal of him in 1915. "He had little sorrow or disappointment. . . He had the content that comes from a single and complete nature." Years later, toward the end of his own life, the son would speak of his father as a "very just man". There are no warmer words; nothing that suggests love. Respect and admiration were felt, even perhaps a touch of the wistful jealousy that artists — wary of their complex natures — occasionally feel for the bourgeoisie. Otherwise, a sense of distance, if not detachment, except for those moments when fathers like William Patrick loom up in the dreams and imagination of their sons.

Honora Manning, known always as Nora, was portrayed to me as being very much the opposite of her husband. Irish-born (County Clare), short and stout in figure, easily swept along by her emotions, and deeply religious, she is vividly remembered by her grandchildren because she lived until 1940. William Patrick, by comparison, is a shadow in family memory. "Emotional" was a favourite anchoring term in descriptions I heard of Nora; Eleanor's cousin Bill Manning confided that during an audience with Pope Pius XI, arranged by Fred in the early 1920s, she was so overcome by her feelings that she broke into uncontrollable sobbing and had to be taken from the room. Whether or not the story is true — and her granddaughters insist that "Granny" had too much decorum to allow "*that* to happen" — it is consistent with the accepted image. An earlier tale reveals another side of her. At Government House the Mannings dined off Limoges china that had the Governor's initials stamped in gold on each piece. Such a splendid service, Nora felt, belonged also in the home of a Lord Mayor (or former Lord Mayor — the date of the occasion is lost) and so she promptly ordered a set with the initials W. P. M. It remains in the family today. As wife to the mayor Nora performed the duties expected of her. She gave teas, sponsored charities, arranged balls, and appeared elegantly dressed — often in brown, her favourite colour — at the innumerable functions that mayoresses need to attend. Yet she seems to have been a woman who could enjoy only in private the opportunities of affluence and position. A society columnist praised her ever present "kindly" smile, but noted that after a year of engagements Nora was "still very nervous in public". Her obituary suggests that she never gained a public identity except as wife and mother:

> Lady Manning, widow of the late Sir William Patrick Manning, who was five [*sic*] times Mayor of Sydney, and a member of the Legislative Assembly, died in Sydney yesterday. Lady Manning was the mother of the Attorney-General, Sir Henry Manning, and of the late Frederick [*sic*] Manning, the author of "Her Privates We", about which "The Times" said: "Any similar book on a former war would have taken its place as a classic of its kind."

As wife and mother, however, this unsophisticated woman is recalled as a formidable figure in her own right and a worthy helpmate to the husband she adored. Wise and energetic in domestic matters, she managed the children with bountiful affection and the sagacity that chooses not to take notice of all that it sees. Duties as wife to an important figure took her frequently away from home, but a preference for being near her children is signalled in the spring of 1895 when she stayed behind in Sydney instead of accompanying William Patrick to England for several months after he had given up his mayoral office. According to all accounts, her favourite child was Fred — and he remained bound to her throughout his life. After her husband's death she frequently journeyed back and forth to Europe, usually with at least one daughter in tow, seeing her son in England or

Honora Manning, c. 1891 (William O. Manning)

travelling with him on the continent. She never, it is reported, quite got on with the wives of the sons who married and had, aside from a passion for horse racing shared by all the family, few interests or even personal friends in Sydney. During her last years she made weekly pilgrimages (followed by hours of weeping) to the graves of her husband and children, half of whom predeceased her. "She came to live as much for the dead as for the living", sighed one of her grandchildren, who suggested that Nora's Irish heritage might account for the ritual. Shortly before his own death Fred wrote a letter to his brother William which speaks a deeper truth, one realised from a more significant attachment:

> Another point that always worries me if I fail to appreciate her point of view is that old people always become so lonely; it is so difficult to get into touch, or to keep in touch with them, they cease to have the same interests as younger people have, and they are all prone to blame others for not understanding them. And really it is not their fault. If I show any lack of patience I am always very self-reproachful after it, because I usually find in the long run that the failure to understand is as much on my side as on the other. Their failure is generally as much physical as anything else. It is a melancholy time of life, at the best. Lady Mexborough, who is seventyish, sent me a Xmas present of some silk handkerchiefs today and with it a letter saying she was going off by herself for Xmas: "I am no lover of Xmas and its attendant horrors" she writes; "and family reunions are just rubbish to me — and sadness." You see that illustrates what I mean — "Just rubbish and sadness." It is rubbish, I suspect, simply because of the fact I have noted above, the isolation which comes with age and is an inseparable part of it; the failure of interest, the disillusion, the lack of any common ground even with one's children: that makes it all just rubbish — and sadness. I suppose the sadness redeems it from cynicism, if one recognizes it.

Through that passage rushes a sympathy unsullied by self-interest or sentimentality.

Besides Fred, there were seven other children, with a spread of 17 years between them, creating what amounted to three generations within the household. Tales of the five boys having to walk to appointments and parties because their father denied them the tram fare suggest that they were not indulged. Like many rich men who have risen from poverty, William Patrick evidently believed that if he practised frugality with his children they would duplicate his success. It was not to be. All but one, Harry, who enjoyed a distinguished legal and political career climaxing in his tenure as Attorney-General of New South Wales (1932–41), led anonymous lives. William and John (known as Jack) both took up the law but it was their early prowess in sports — Will as the best amateur rider in New South Wales, Jack as captain of the Australian Rugby Union football team — which has been remembered; that and their not speaking to each other for years although they worked in the same office. No one today can recall what prompted the split. Then there was Charlie, the youngest son, who lived alone at Longreach in Queensland managing a sheepstation for most of his life. He, too, had his finest hours on the playing fields, being remembered by cricket fans as "one of the outstanding school batsmen of his time". Like Jack and Fred, he had a drinking problem.

Of the girls there is even less to be said. Beatrix, the youngest of the children, died unmarrried at the age of 37 while on a visit to Paris in 1924, and is vaguely remembered as being lively and fun — perhaps merely the result of her being the "baby" of the family. Edith, the middle sister, became an alcoholic in her forties, and henceforth was a burden and shame to the family. The eldest girl, Félicie, born in 1870 and always called Dot, was also the eldest child and alleged to have been not much loved by most of the others. Her caustic jest that "small boys should be brought up underground" may explain why. As a young woman she often served as her father's escort or hostess at functions Nora did not attend, and in 1895 it was she who

Manning's sisters: (top) Beatrix, (bottom) Edith and (top right) Dot (Eleanor Manning)

Manning's brother Harry (Eleanor Manning)

accompanied her father to England. Early responsibilities seem to have given in her poise as well as a taste for independence, for as an adult Dot lived apart from the family, unlike Beatrix and Edith, and for a brief time before World War I she wrote brisk literary reviews reflecting a distinctly feminist outlook for the women's page of the *Sydney Morning Herald*.*

Sad as this sketch of the children may seem, all was not friction and failure. A few achieved success and there are signs of caring and help. Dot, for example, travelled out to the Queensland bush during a steaming summer when she was past 70 to nurse Charlie for several weeks; Harry, his daughters told me, tried always to keep the others linked and to offer aid when it was needed; and Fred, at least in his letters, displays a quiet fondness for the brothers and sisters he seldom saw. Admittedly, my impression of them rests on a trifling amount of paper evidence, a score of photographs, and the memories of three of their children. Still, there is no ignoring the conclusion that despite the comfort and opportunity in which the Manning children were raised, several of their lives were disfigured by loneliness and alcohol. Why this happened is impossible to know. The dynamics of family life are regularly misperceived by the members themselves; the next generation, not to mention outsiders, will find them barely scrutable. And perhaps the explanation does not even lie in what they were to each other. As the biographer of only one of them, my responsibility to the rest was limited, though I am not sure that further searching would have produced a clearer — or different — portrait. For as I gazed at the pictures of the children, the early commercial cameos of elegantly frocked boys and girls, the proud family snapshots of the young men as soldiers and fathers, the occasional passport photos so brutal in their dead-eye austerity, I was struck by the facial characteristic common to all: the long thin-lipped mouth, inherited from their father, sealing each face as if to proclaim secluded lives.

I returned to Point Piper the next morning ready to find

treasure. For more than eight hours I rummaged through the three-storey house, searching through cabinets and closets, examining the contents of dozens of boxes, peering at albums of photographs, and scanning the numerous shelves of books. Family wills, private letters, confidential memos: all were scrutinised, their secrets opened after many years. I was ransacking a house. I was also violating lives, and with little shame or finesse. Not surprisingly, most of what I found belonged to Harry Manning's life and career; it had been his house, and he had led the sort of life that generates scrapbooks. Eleanor sat by patiently, identifying papers and photographs, ever eager to tell me something about "Dad", of whom she was enormously proud and, from what I learned of him, rightfully so. He had been a very able lawyer and politician, a public servant whose wisdom and tact — like that of his father — had served the community well. He had evidently also been a very warm human being.

Toward the end of the day Eleanor, obviously intrigued and a little startled by a mode of scholarship that resulted in dust-blackened clothes and legs cramped from constant squatting, said smilingly to me, "Jon, you should have been a detective." The remark was kindly meant; there was, it seemed, even a hint of pride in her own efforts. Still, I felt like a snoop. Perusing personal papers in the house from which they have sprung is not like reading them in a library.

I also felt like a relic hunter, a familiar sensation to most biographers. Quite apart from letters and papers, I was searching for the mute residue of Manning's life, for tangible traces of his existence. A pen, a cigarette case, even a special book or household bauble would have satisfied. The remnant might not be able to speak, but at least it would provide a physical link. We value mementoes in our personal lives because they persuade us that someone important, though distant or even dead, has not altogether gone from us. Things have a special potential for stopping time, for igniting remembrances. The biographer, almost always a stranger to his subject, cannot use these vestiges to invoke memories; instead, he seeks them out as a means of access into a life. Words, however plentiful, precise, or intimate, establish only certain forms of proximity; a man's possessions may tell more about him than his letters. As it turned out, the search of the house uncovered several such clues; scarcely enough to satisfy my fantasies of the previous evening, but valuable nonetheless.

There was, for example, a sketch of a woman shown looking out to sea. Obviously a hasty effort, it was of no interest except for the writing at the bottom: "Drawn by Conder at Dieppe Feb. 1898 in my sketchbook, Ryllis Hacon." "Conder" was Charles Conder, the English-born artist who spent many years in Australia. So far as I knew he and Manning had never met. Ryllis Hacon, on the other hand, had been a good friend of both Manning and Conder. As Amaryllis Bradshaw she had been an artist's model, sitting for several painters including Rothenstein, who thought (with good reason) that she looked "like a Rossetti", and whose brush performed a special service for her beauty. A pastel he did of her was seen by Llewellyn Hacon, a wealthy barrister interested in the arts. An introduction to the model was requested; Rothenstein obliged; Hacon immediately fell in love; and Ryllis Bradshaw became Ryllis Hacon. This had all happened more than a decade before Manning settled in England and became acquainted with the Hacons. Once he did, a close friendship evidently developed, for besides being a guest on more than one occasion at their home, "Oversteps" on the Dornoch Firth in Scotland, he dedicated ("To LLE and Ryllis with my love") the volume of poems he published in 1910. Other than that I knew hardly anything about the friendship, and could only guess as to how the Conder sketch landed in the Manning home. But it certainly qualified as a meaningful relic.

Then there was the elegant edition of Milton's sonnets, with two inscriptions on the same page. One reads, "Edith Manning 8 March/98", the other — in a different hand, but not Fred's — "Fred Manning 11th December 1900". The thought behind the transfer is suggested by lines inscribed on the following page, presumably by Edith, for they are in the same hand as her name.

Fred Manning

No more the grecian Muse unrivalled reigns
To Britain let the nations homage pay
She boasts a Homers fire in Miltons strain
A Pindars rapture in the lyre of Gray

The verse is a not quite exact copy of William Mason's epitaph on Gray in Westminster Abbey. Its presence in this volume points to the expectations that the family already had of Fred, expectations that the gifted youth himself shared, as Rothenstein's account of their first meeting reveals.

An inscription on a vest pocket Catholic prayer book ("W. P. Manning, London, July 1909") announced another important fact about the Manning family: they were, like so many Australians of their day, Janus-faced in their sympathies. They enjoyed the success and standing they knew in Sydney, and yet were drawn to England. It did not matter that William Patrick had been born in Sydney, or that his wife had come from Ireland; England was "home". Trips were common, not merely to consult on business or to taste the pleasures of a richer culture, but to reconnect with some vital essence that was not transportable. When I visited Eleanor's sister Pat in Cootamundra, she showed me a diary that listed important family events — births, marriages and so on. The most common entry, however, seemed to be the various departures and arrivals of family members as they steamed back and forth to England on the Orient Line. With such migratory instincts it was easy for a son to become an expatriate.

A small leather-bound King James Bible, complete with colour maps of the Holy Land, roused my interest much more than did William Patrick's prayer book. I found it tucked away in a bookshelf, its boards tied together with pink twine quite faded by the years. Eleanor had never seen it before. On the frontispiece, in the bold script of Arthur Galton was the following:

Fred Manning 1897
πολλαὶ μὲν θνητοῖς
γλῶτται μία δ'ἀθανάτοισιν

"Among men there are many languages, in heaven only one." A worthy aphorism, fashioned by Henry Carey and used as the motto for an early nineteenth-century polyglot edition of the scriptures. Though the gift of a Bible is as common as the passing of salt, this particular Bible had something important to say. In 1897 Catholic families in Sydney, and elsewhere, did not countenance the King James version. Presumably the Mannings were not fearful that their son would be weaned from the faith. Indeed, they must have understood and supported the gift-giver's purpose: that Fred immerse himself in the graceful periods that had inspired and disciplined English writers for generations. He was already showing signs of a literary bent and a better tutor than Arthur Galton could hardly have been found in Sydney. At least the Manning family would have been inclined to think so, and no doubt so did the boy himself. A serious, well-educated Englishman of good family, a man of letters and taste who had time on his hands and a passion to instruct, Galton was ideal. And so began a relationship that would end only at Galton's death a quarter of a century later, and even then persist in memory and instinct. For though Fred Manning would grow into a writer and intellectual respected in his own right, there would always be in his life and work the imprint of Arthur Galton. His influence was profound, and, as often happens in such cases, at once liberating and constricting. Without Galton Fred Manning might have ended his days in Sydney, a charming dilettante living off his father's money while escorting his mother through her long widowhood. Without Galton he might also have become a major writer, realising sooner than he did a vast potential for pulling his art from personal memory and experience rather than myth and history.

Arthur Galton belongs in a novel. He may possibly already be in one, for as Ezra Pound would later remark to his mother, he seemed to know "everyone since the flood", including most of the later Victorian literary illuminati. Pound's statement was only slightly hyperbolic. Galton managed to become acquainted with numerous people of talent and influence, and in most cases to win their respect. Moreover, his personal odyssey, while not marked by the trials that tempt epic poets, would certainly provide fine material for a novelist.

Born in 1852 to an old Worcestershire family, he was the eldest son of Herman Ernest Galton, an army officer until service in the Crimea ruined his health, and Mary Abercrombie Duff. Among his relations were the eugenicist Francis Galton, the Duke of Fife, and other titled personages. Further back there was a strong Quaker connection through the Barclays, and a line to the noble Dutch family of Schimmelpenninck. But these were distant names to the small boy raised at Hadzor House by his loving grandmother, Isabella Strutt Galton, whose influence on him was enormous.

> Thou mad'st me love all Nature's ways,
> Thou mad'st me truth and beauty see,
> From thee I learnt to give my days
> To poetry

These lines come from a ten-page elegy that Arthur composed and privately circulated in 1885, eight years after her death.* The poem — partially inspired by Matthew Arnold's "Thyrsis" — is a soggy mixture of love, remembrance, and lingering sorrow, an exercise in catharsis rather than poetry. But as such it is revealing, as autobiographical verse anxious to be faithful to feeling often is. The stanzas testify to an engrossing and exclusive relationship, of the sort that cripples even while it is nourishing.

The boy attended schools in nearby Leamington and spent two years at Cheltenham (1868–70) before going up to Clare College, Cambridge, in 1873. There his religious beliefs came unravelled. He had always dreamed of becoming the "rector of my old home" but now found himself drawn to Roman

Catholicism. In April of 1875 he took the decisive step at the Jesuit church in Farm Street, London. A serious break with his family followed, including the withdrawal of support for his education and exclusion from his father's will, and he soon was "practically banished" from home. For the next ten years he tried to find a life in the church. He spent time at the Brompton Oratory in London, and later at Oscott College near Birmingham, where he took orders in 1880. A photo of him in clerical garb shows a resolute unsmiling face, revealing nothing to the camera except determination. His hair is already turning grey. For a brief time he served a parish at Windermere — a place he loved and returned to often — but he did not enjoy the duties and went back to Oscott to teach and study. By 1885 his reading had persuaded him that conversion had been a mistake:

> But that I held to any sort of Christianity, and continued to use and enjoy the Bible, I owe entirely to Matthew Arnold. I began to read him in 1882; first his prose, and then his verse. For several years I read him over, and over, and over again with growing delight and profit; until, so far as I was able, I had possessed something of his mind and methods. He taught me how to think, and how to write. He undoubtedly saved me from leaving the papal church a blind and blank materialist, thoroughly and violently anti-Christian; and his gentle influence tended me through the next few years, until I was mellowed for a process of reconstruction.

So wrote Galton in 1900 when he published *Rome and Romanising*, an account of his experiences in the Catholic Church. Stitched together from articles earlier published in the *National Review,* it is a far less engaging autobiography than the Oxford scholar Mark Pattison's *Memoirs,* a book Galton cherished for describing so well "the case of so many of us". But recognising a peer scarcely compares to admitting a master, and the fulsome tribute to Arnold openly declares a discipleship that was earnest, orthodox, and lifelong. It was not that Arnold introduced him to cultures and writers hitherto unknown or unvalued by Galton. Greece and Rome were already signposts in his consciousness, and as a youth he had developed a "passion" for all things French, loving not only the language and its literature — "I could read French almost as soon as English" — but also the "absorbing drama" of French history. Rather it was Arnold's values and charm, the modes of his thought and style, that appeared as true answers to a man long troubled. Once rescued, Galton could not praise his saviour too highly or too often, and after Arnold's death in 1888 he assumed the responsibilities of a votary, writing essays and at least one poem celebrating the greatness of "a king of words". Two of these essays he later reprinted in *Two Essays upon Matthew Arnold with Some of his Letters to the Author* (1897), the letters being mainly concerned with the disciple's literary efforts and a mutual passion for dogs. (When Arnold's dachshund Kaiser died, Galton sent him another, Hans.) And until his own death Galton maintained a correspondence first with Arnold's widow, and later with his sister, remembering always to send a note on the anniversary of the revered poet's death. "The fifteenth of April shall come and shall go many times, before it ceases to dawn upon a group of mourners who are inconsolable."

Having forsaken the Catholic Church, Galton decided to finish his education, this time at Oxford. He went up to New College in 1886 and though he was to take his degree in history (1890), he devoted his time and energies to the Classics. Some effort, however, was spent extending his literary ambitions. Even before Oxford he had published *Urbana Scripta: Studies of Five Living Poets; and Other Essays* (1885)* — amongst which was a glowing piece on Arnold as a poet — and during his years at what he termed "the natural home of humane letters" he contributed reviews and essays to London periodicals, most notably *The Century Guild Hobby Horse*, an elegant quarterly with high aesthetic and intellectual pretensions.* In 1887 he published *The Character and Times of Thomas Cromwell*, a volume he described in the preface as "a critical essay rather than a history", and which he dedicated to

My Master in Criticism
And Therefore
in
The Highest Function of History
To
The Artist
Whose Style is
My Delight and My despair
To
MATTHEW ARNOLD
I
Dedicate
This Essay

Arnold found this to be "strong, too strong", but gentle urgings to tone it down were lost on the grateful follower, who had once thought to send the poet some ivy from the grave of "Thyrsis".

Galton's Oxford years were marked by the friendships he made, such as with Walter Pater, "a very dear friend of mine", whose work he admired despite serious reservations about its style. When Pater died, Galton publicly eulogised him as "better and more interesting than his books. He had the rare virtue to be a scholar without pedantry, and an author without conceit." Correspondences were also struck up with other great men, including William Gladstone and John Addington Symonds, to whom he would send copies of his articles and books. But more energy went into befriending his peers at Oxford. Though almost twice the age of most of them, he easily won their affection and respect, particularly from those with literary hopes. Chief among these were Lionel Johnson and Laurence Binyon, both of whom would later make reputations as poets and critics and, in Binyon's case, as a translator of Dante and an expert in oriental art as well. To each Galton served as supporter and critic, encouraging their muse, sharing their dreams, and commenting on their work. "I like," he wrote to Binyon about a poem, "its directness, and the simplicity of construction, and the punctuation. It wants, perhaps, to have some of those felicities of phrase, which heighten Matthew Arnold's austerity into a work of genius." With Johnson, a superb Latinist, Galton could also share his love for Roman literature, and in the autumn of 1890 he would depend on the 23-year-old youth to correct the proofs of his introduction to an edition of Thomas Gordon's translation of Tacitus that he was preparing.* Galton's willingness to assist reflected more than simple good will. Raised by a grandmother, rejected by his family, and salvaged — so he felt — by the example and kindness of Arnold, his own development was testimony to the value of affective and nurturing guardians. Although he seems to have had little capacity for intimacy — his letters rarely ask for or offer anything more than news and opinions — he had concern and sincerity, and these are winning attributes in the eyes of the young. Both Binyon and Johnson acknowledged their esteem: Binyon in the obituary he would eventually compose for *The Times*, and in his decision to keep Galton's letters when destroying most of his other correspondence;* Johnson in the several poems he dedicated to his friend, as well as in the dedication planned for a book of essays on Walter Pater that was never published, "To Arthur Galton whom Oxford gave me for my best friend and companion in the study of letters."

After Oxford Galton went on, in a somewhat desultory way, with his literary career. He continued to contribute to the *Hobby Horse* — even living for a time at 20 Fitzroy Street, the house shared by the staff — and wrote reviews for the scholarly *Academy* as well as for other periodicals. Whatever he wrote was marked by its learning, vigour, and clarity. A classicist to the core, he found in the ancients and the eighteenth century those models of form, sanity, and precision by which he judged all writing. To his mind, an author unfamiliar with the great tradition of Western literature could not expect to create anything of value, and those poets and prose writers who would not school themselves in that tradition but depended on "transient feelings" to nourish their art would produce only slop and sentiment. "Really, Dickens is intolerable: his people are not human, his writing is not literature, his work is not art." Writers of his own day, like H. G. Wells, often received similar spankings. Galton's writings also have a touch of humour, though he rarely practised the smiling irony he loved in Voltaire, Ernest Renan, and Anatole France, all great favourites of his. Perhaps it was because the man himself seems to have lacked a sense of play; perhaps it was simply because he was plagued by a chronically bad stomach. His classical taste and exacting standards extended even to the fine points of composition and format. One of the appealing qualities of Gordon's translation of Tacitus had been its "scholarly punctuation", and his own edition would have included those touches, "which add so much to the seductive and sober dignity of an eighteenth-century page" — turn-over and "bounteous capitals" — if the printer had only heeded "my entreaties". Still, Galton was no mere pedant. He had a scholar's knowledge of the things that interested him, a seriousness about literature that was not pretentious, a distaste for critics who strutted their "smartness" rather than aiming for "simplicity and enlightenment", and, sometimes, a keen insight into the authors and issues that came under his pen for review. Here he speaks of seventeenth-century England: "Among its defects we must note a strange want of humour, and perhaps, therefore, of sincerity: defects in which the King [Charles I] is still the best representative of his time; and springing from both of these is a curious prolixity, a strange kind of affectation."

If he had had the chance, Galton would have departed the "evil age" in which he found himself and gone to live in the eighteenth century, probably in France.* However, there too he would doubtless have elegised upon a vanished purity, for the moralist, by condition, cannot be satisfied. Lacking a time machine, all Galton could do was to remove himself spatially from the annoyances of modern life. He hated London for its dirt, its noise, and its bustle; city life troubled his dyspepsia and made work impossible. And so he moved to a small house near Bowness on Windermere, where along with his dachshund (one of several he would own), and his Horace and Tacitus, he would find that rural contentment of which the ancient poets had so sweetly sung.

When away from Windermere he was often visiting his uncle, Robert Duff, who lived at Fetteroso Castle near the Kincardineshire coast, just south of Aberdeen, and who for almost 20 years had sat in Parliament as the Liberal member for Banffshire. In the spring of 1893 Gladstone appointed Duff to succeed the Earl of Jersey as Governor of New South Wales and arranged that he be given a knighthood to bolster his prestige. Duff, in turn, asked his nephew to accompany him as his private secretary, and Galton accepted. What "tempted" him is not clear. It may have been the salary of £400 per year, a large sum in those days; or Sydney's benevolent climate, which must have appealed to a man with a delicate constitution; or simply the desire to try his hand at more worldly pursuits. Though bookish, Galton had long been interested in politics, and valued those who served their country. While at Oxford he had belonged to the New College Home Rule Society, and in *English Prose from Maundeville to Thackeray*, a volume of selections he had edited in 1888, the choice of passages had often been governed as much by his own Liberal political views as by the shape and texture of the authors' sentences.* Whatever the motive, at 40 years of age — a point at which many have taken inventory of accomplishments, ambitions, and time — Arthur Galton, together with his uncle and aunt and several of their children, set sail for Sydney. In the private secretary's trunk were volumes of his favourite authors, together with copies of his own writings and testimonials from such worthies as Arnold, Pater, Gladstone, Symonds, Leslie Stephen, Bishop Stubbs, and Oscar Wilde.* Awaiting was a colony allegedly miffed at getting as governor a freshly dubbed knight instead of a seasoned peer, and a mayor ready to lend the new governor and his party whatever assistance and comforts lay within his powers. There was also a precocious boy, presumably informed of the impending arrival, but entirely unaware that he was soon to meet his mentor.

Education

CHAPTER TWO

Forty years after a man's death is not a favourable moment to begin collecting facts about his childhood. The hard evidence has usually long since disappeared, and so too have his siblings and friends. From nieces and nephew I expected to hear passed-down tales of the young Fred Manning, but I dreamed also of finding at least a few traces of him. Why Harry, especially at the time of his donation to the Mitchell Library, had not set down his memories of his younger brother was a question with an easily imagined answer: no one had asked him. If someone had, the result could have been very enlightening, for a "Retrospect" of his own schooldays at Riverview College that Harry wrote in his last years reveals a memory quite intact.

Manning's own references to his childhood are rare, which is not surprising in a man noted for protecting his privacy. Early in the war novel, Bourne — a character obviously based on Manning himself — recalls "playing again a game of his childhood though not now among rocks from which reverberated heat quivered in wavy films." And in March of 1930, when rumour held that he was the novel's author, he gave a guarded interview in which he mentioned his early frailty and how his education had depended on private tutors. Otherwise silence, as if childhood, like Australia, were a distant, forgotten place.

One curious and recurrent discrepancy adds a touch of mystery to his silence: on several occasions he misrepresented his age. In 1913 when asked by the Chicago-based *Poetry* magazine to submit a brief biographical sketch he wrote that he was born in Sydney "on July the 22, 1884", and when joining the army in 1915 he once more gave 1884 as the year of his birth. Moreover, in the records of the Sydney Grammar School, which he attended for three months — the extent of his formal schooling — he is listed as being 14 years of age in October 1897.* Whether this last mistake was his own, his parents', or a clerical error cannot be determined from the records themselves. And, finally, there is real confusion about his age in the 1930 interview. The reporter wrote — presumably on the basis of what he was told — that Manning "left Australia at thirteen and came to England, to live in Lincolnshire." In fact, Manning was nearer 16 when he first visited England, and he did not settle in Lincolnshire until he was almost 22.

From my first searches, I had assumed July 22, 1882, to be his birthdate. That was the date offered by most reference books — notably a 1912 Australian biographical dictionary.* Still, I had also found references to 1884 and 1887, and so when I came to Sydney I was determined to find proof of his birthdate. Even if I could not penetrate the recesses of his mind and personality, I could at least set straight the elementary facts of his life.

A visit to the New South Wales Registry of Births, Deaths, and Marriages did not settle the question. Despite an 1856 law requiring all births to be registered, Frederic Manning was not listed, and his parents had neglected as well to have officially recorded the entry into the world of several of his siblings. My other hope was parish records; surely the Mannings had not failed to baptise their offspring. And so I spent the better part of a day going from one church to another and leafing through their registers. Finally, at the Church of the Sacred Heart in Darlinghurst Road, I found a baptismal record: Frederic Manning had, indeed, been born on July 22, 1882, and on August 26 he had been baptised, with Harry and Edith Manning as witnesses. Not a glamorous discovery; simply a necessary one.

What then to make of those misrepresentations, and do they even matter? Fibbing about one's age is a common peccadillo, and I could easily imagine why Manning had been tempted: vanity in the case of the 1913 sketch for *Poetry* — after 30, poets lose a certain bloom; and when joining the army, what might be termed nervous prudence — in 1915 volunteers much beyond 30 risked rejection if, like Manning, they looked to be frail. And the error in the school records could simply reflect a parent's desire to ease the difficult adjustment from home to classroom, just as the interviewer's mistake could be charged to his own carelessness rather than to Manning's wish to tinker with his past. All reasonable, even probable, explanations; a biographer who probed further might be ridiculed for creating, in Swiftian terms, the problem that is not.

Yet I remained uneasy about those explanations. Early in my research I had learned that Manning had had a serious drinking problem which he managed to conceal from many of his friends. While dissembling about one's age is not like hiding a serious weakness, I was not sure that they were altogether unrelated phenomena. Had there been other situations where Manning had misrepresented himself to the world? Were, indeed, his desire for privacy and his oft-noted reticence about himself more complicated matters than they seemed to his contemporaries? I was not optimistic that I would ever learn enough about his personal life to answer these questions, but as the search went on a part of me was alert to other evasions and concealments.

Frail and precocious: that is the lingering family memory of the young Fred Manning. From an early age he was afflicted with bronchial asthma, a condition shared by his father and at least one brother (Harry). But Fred's case was significantly more acute. He was kept from school, played no sports, and, as often happens with asthmatics, was greatly indulged — at least by his mother and apparently also by his older sisters, Dot and Edith. With his three older brothers away at boarding school much of the time, the needs and whims of illness — perhaps especially in a youth shining with intelligence — were lovingly catered to. It was only natural, therefore, that the boy would grow up with an exaggerated sensitivity to the state of his health and the expectation that others would share his concern. His early letters to Fairfax contain many accounts of how his body has let him down. "The thundering air has given me neuralgia." While migraine sufferers might sympathise with the complaint, it must nevertheless be seen as a symptom of a highly sensitive constitution, one as easily unbalanced by emotional upsets as by attacks of actual disease. Our bodies always stand ready to be accident victims of our minds; in Manning's case collapses were frequent. His susceptibility to illness was remarkably high; beyond, indeed, what might even be expected of someone who suffered from a frustrating and fear-inducing condition like asthma. Galton's comment to a mutual friend when Manning was accepted into the army in 1915 makes the point, and not unkindly: "The doctors all passed him as sound; so that he must realise that all his ailments were imaginary or nervous, and this will be a great advantage to him."

His schooling was at home. Jesuit tutors came to the house at 35 Bayswater Road, Rushcutters Bay, and Dot, according to family lore, played a role in his early education. A dozen years his senior and the most intellectual of the other children, she would understandably have taken an interest in the younger brother so eager to learn. Fred seems usually to have had a book in his hand, and when his parents, fearing for his eyes, once tried to curb his reading he took himself and his book under a table covered by a cloth that hung to the ground. Or so, years later, he told Ivor Woolmer. It is a good story, foreshadowing, like the one about his father playing marbles, the life-purpose of the man. His love of music was no doubt born during these early years, encouraged, one suspects, by his father's connection with the Philharmonic Society. And then there were vacations in the country, periods when the family would go to the Blue Mountains, a 60-mile train ride from the city. There in the mountains whose colour Mark Twain thought made the blue of the sky look "pallid and unwholesome, whitey and washed out", and whose clean air would have eased the strain on an asthmatic's lungs, the boy experienced a special freedom. Decades later he still recalled "with delight" the hours he had spent horseback riding among the trees and gullies. In Sydney there was a fine house, numerous books, and a steady parade of interesting people to see and meet* — Mark Twain, who charmed Sydney as a lecturer, or Sarah Bernhardt, for whom the Mannings gave a reception while she was on one of her tours — but in the country Fred could be like any other boy.

Precisely when and how he first met Arthur Galton is not recorded. One story that I was told had it that they were introduced when Galton heard the 12- or 13-year-old Fred giving a lecture in Greek:* an anecdote needing, I suspect, radical pruning before one would come to its real shape, if it had one at all. The boy might already have known Greek, but who would have been the audience for such a declamation? More prosaic circumstances probably attended their introduction to each other, for Galton, as the Governor's secretary, had a myriad of official and social opportunities for seeing the mayor and his family. Moreover, Galton would have appeared, in his own right, as someone the boy should know, for he had quickly established his intellectual credentials in Sydney. He gave public lectures on such topics as "The Military Art of the Romans, as Illustrated by the Wars of Caesar", "The Life and Times of the Duke of Marlborough", and (of course) "Matthew Arnold"; wrote book reviews and obituaries of significant writers for the newspapers (as well as adapting one of his *Hobby Horse* essays for the maiden issue of *Cosmos*, a literary periodical); and even made it into the gossip columns. During a formal ball he was seen reading a Greek Homer in "a quiet corner", which both impressed and tickled Sydney society. Galton's uncle, however, proved to be more seriously maladroit. The role of governor was largely a ceremonial one, but Sir Robert Duff mismanaged even the few substantive problems that came his way, and had he not suddenly died in March of 1895 he would very likely have been replaced.* As it was, his nephew, having tired of the "petty distractions rather than occupations" that filled his days — and of his uncle's bumbling as well — had resigned his post the previous July to accept an appointment from the outgoing Premier, Sir George Dibbs, to continue "the compilation of the

History of New South Wales''. When the new government cancelled the appointment, Galton applied unsuccessfully for a professorship at the University of Adelaide.* After that he stayed on in Sydney, writing for the newspapers and cultivating the many friends he had made. He lived at 7 Roslyn Gardens, Elizabeth Bay, very near to the Mannings, and it was apparently during this period that he befriended the young prodigy.

Years later there was still a sense of wonder in Galton's recollection of the youth. "He was then [*c.* 1895] a very delicate little boy, with an astonishing amount of reading, and a tact for literature which was more astonishing than his knowledge." Family tradition records that Galton became Fred's tutor. While there may have been such an arrangement, it is equally likely that as a frequent visitor to the Manning home Galton exercised a steering influence rather than committing himself to a formal duty. The boy obviously had talent; he might even have genius: what he needed was the kind of energetic guidance that Galton was so willing to give and which, in the eyes of the boy and his parents, he was so finely equipped to give. They would have viewed Galton as a scholar and a gentleman whose learning was remarkable, whose writings were respectable, and whose confidence in himself was considerable. He had no hesitation in telling people of his success as a teacher at Oscott: "I had a certain sympathetic power over my pupils and my classes, which made them enthusiastic, and which kept them orderly. I was not only the most popular master at Oscott, in my time, but the best disciplinarian." And he prided himself particularly, with some reason, as being valuable to those with literary tastes. "I have trained myself into a keen sense for the niceties of form, both in verse and prose; and a reader of that kind, however poor his other endowments may be, can be of some use to even the greatest writers." Galton wrote those lines in 1895 to Sir Henry Parkes, five times Premier of New South Wales, who had sent him some of his poems to read. Young Fred Manning had as yet no literary works in need of criticism, but a preceptor such as Galton — "a lover of our literature at once enthusiastic and discreet'', Pater had written of him — does not come along every day.

Except for the gift of the Bible, tangible evidence of the mentor's influence during this period is lacking. But we may assume that Galton encouraged the boy's thorough grounding in the classics, stimulated his growing love for French culture, lectured him in the literary values he had long cherished (''What we require now is not a romantic Wordsworth, but an austere and rigorous classic''), and drummed into his mind the wise lesson about writing that he often read to the world at large: good prose results when ''a writer condescends to think clearly, to stick to the point, and to express his ideas in the plainest, the simplest, the most direct and unpretentious way.'' Galton would naturally have pressed Fred to read Arnold, and would have insisted that he study Milton, the poet who had transformed the ''great style'' of the ancients into English. To a Sydney audience Galton once presented Milton as being important ''especially to people in Australia''. He would have also urged the study of Horace, whose verse he tirelessly quoted in his own writings. In time both Horace and Milton would become favourites of Manning, and one of his early compositions would be an ode* to the author of *Paradise Lost*. Of course, resemblances in taste are only mute witnesses to influence, but when they are numerous — and more will appear — they are convincing witnesses. And if Galton did not deliberately foster the youth's religious scepticism, said to have been already strong by the time the two met, his example, and perhaps his steady praise for Voltaire, Renan, and Anatole France, who formed their own ''apostolical succession'', may well have encouraged it.

Strong bonds of another sort were forged between the two. Galton was not a warm man, certainly no Mr Chips; but his ministrations won the affection of those he advised, be they aspiring youths or ageing amateurs. Young Fred Manning was no exception, and if besides growing to respect Galton he transferred to him some of those feelings a boy normally reserves for his father, it would have been altogether natural. Galton represented the life of the mind and the society of writers and intellectuals, both of which would have fascinated a boy with so much reading and knowledge. The boy's father was shrewd, sensible, and not without respect for culture; his championship of Sydney as the "first city of the Southern Hemisphere" incorporated a vision of its citizens engaging "in all matters of culture relating to art, literature, science, and music". But Sir William Patrick was also a man with little time for books, less appreciation for subtleties and ambiguities, and no patience at all for talk about realities other than those of the here and now. An earnest and sympathetic teacher might well take his place as a model.

One other family member may have developed strong feelings for Galton. Edith Manning, who would have been 20 in 1895, is vaguely remembered as having been in love with a man who had been a priest; possibly it was Galton. In a letter from Galton to Binyon there is certainly the suggestion of a romance while Galton was in Australia: "Nunc scio quid sit amor...and so I linger on; but what will come of it, I know not." A tantalising clue — no more. Perhaps this early disappointment — whether or not it involved Galton — had something to do with the sadness of Edith's life, but that is a conjecture beyond research.

As he grew older Fred Manning grew stronger, strong enough for his family to consider formal schooling. In October 1897 he was enrolled at the Sydney Grammar School and took a place in Mr McBurney's form in the languages division. His attendance was marked by frequent absences, and after the Christmas holidays he did not return.* By then another plan seems to have been made for his education: he would go to England and attend Winchester. Galton's hand can be seen in this strategy, for though not a Wykehamist himself, he knew that the school was the traditional place to prepare for New College, whose grey halls were the ultimate goal of the plan. It may be that the term at Sydney Grammar School was a deliberate first stage, a chance to have peer experience and to become accustomed to the discipline and pressures of a school situation. Whatever the case,

Arthur Galton, c. 1893 (Omar Pound)

the prospect of going to England would surely have excited the boy. Already he lived primarily inside books, few of which had anything to do with his native land, and many of which supposed him to be — or want to be — an Englishman. Winchester and Oxford must have been tingling prospects, the latter long since made familiar by Galton's rhapsodic talk of it. And guided by his mentor, who was himself returning to England, Fred could look forward to visiting places and meeting people that had hitherto been only names.

Galton was no less eager to be leaving Australia. He had made many friends and earned more than a few good memories, but five years of what he viewed as provincialism, impoverished scenery, a noisy and corrupt politics, an ignorant public opinion, and a venal press had wasted his patience and further greyed his hair. Let cousin Francis, he sometimes mumbled to himself, come out and study what happens to an isolated population with an originally suspect gene pool.* The climate, admittedly splendid, was not transportable, but everything else that he found to his liking, including the tonic for his stomach which had earned from him a grateful testimonial ("I have used the preparation called Yaala for some weeks, and it has given me a complete relief from Dyspepsia of very long standing") might be had back in England. Even the friends* he had made were the sort to travel "home" at some point. England also held out the hope of a new start for Galton. His recent letters to Gladstone had talked of a revival of interest in religion, after years of wandering following his disillusionment with Catholicism. "Waiting, reading, and pondering", he wrote in March of 1897, had established perspective; answers and dedication would come in time. The key, he thought, to restoring his faith would be the Old Testament, and so he had begun to study Hebrew. He even talked of taking Anglican orders and offering himself to "the service of our own church". Like most sojourns in the wilderness — Galton's view of his time in New South Wales — this one had not ultimately been wasted.

The two did not leave together. Galton went ahead in late

January, 1898, so as to spend some time in Ceylon with his brother Ralph, a planter. On the day he left Sydney, there appeared a savage notice of the Arnold volume ("one of the silliest ever published") in the *Freeman's Journal*, a local Catholic newspaper. The attack would not have shaken his faith in the value of his testament to Arnold, especially as he knew himself to be unloved by at least some of Sydney's clerical community ever since he had written critically of the Church in general and Cardinal Manning in particular two years before in a review of Purcell's revealing *Life*.* Subsequent to that review the former Secretary to the Governor had been for some time the "pet aversion" of another Catholic paper, the *Catholic Press*. He had handled the abuse levelled at him by never troubling to answer it, a tactic, he felt, which "neither Hume nor Gibbon" could have improved upon. Now, as he was departing and readying himself to become a Protestant clergyman, it seemed as if his enemies were throwing one last spear. Before too long Galton would be giving their English counterparts even more cause for anger.

Fred's departure came almost two months later, on March 23, aboard the *India*, one of the newest ships of the P&O line. Standing at the rail that early autumn day he undoubtedly was eager to be off. Indeed, like most travellers about to leave on a great adventure, he had already gone. At noon the *India* pulled free from the wharf at Circular Quay and was guided out through the harbour to the sea. Left behind were family tears and last cautions; ahead was the rendezvous with Galton in Colombo and soon the journey to England.

After two days of talking and searching with Eleanor, I was ready to attack the resources of the Mitchell Library. Some of Harry's donation had been xeroxed and sent to me the year before; the rest awaited my personal inspection. I also wanted to learn more about the public career of the elder Manning, and hoped to find traces of Galton. Evidence of William Patrick Manning was not hard to come by, and a later visit to the Town Hall supplied more, as well as a glimpse at the Council Chamber where for so many years he had argued the cause of the city he loved. Galton was also easy to track. It was at the Mitchell that I found copies of some of his public lectures, together with several of the articles he had written for the press, including a lengthy obituary of his uncle that was carefully confined to the career "not of his Excellency Sir Robert Duff, but of the Right Hon. R. W. Duff, MP". And it was there that I went through the volumes of Parkes' correspondence, bemused to watch Galton acting as critic, go-between (with the publisher Kegan Paul, another old friend), and praise-singer. "No better English has been written in Australia," he claimed in a preface he wrote for the English edition of a small volume of Parkes' letters after the old man's death, "than the English of Sir Henry Parkes." Knowing what I did about Galton the whiff of condescension was obvious.

But as the days passed and the lode at the Mitchell Library ran out, I grew anxious to leave Sydney. Waiting for me were Ivor Woolmer, Eleanor's sister and cousin, and the Fairfax letters in Canberra, which promised to be extraordinarily valuable. Thus, I called a halt to library work and on a Friday morning boarded a plane for Melbourne. There I had a six-hour lay-over, followed by a two-and-a-half-hour bus ride out to Alexandra, which I did not reach until almost ten o'clock at night. As the bus pulled into the station lot I saw outside my window a man who had to be Ivor Woolmer, so close a resemblance did he bear to his brother Victor whom I had met the year before in England. At no previous moment in my search had I felt as excited; a few steps away was a link to Manning that made papers and relics seem momentarily trivial. When the door opened Woolmer stepped aboard and said hello to the driver, who was evidently a friend. Then, turning to the seats, he found me smiling at him with hand outstretched.

Ivor Woolmer turned out to be a quiet, still man, with a smile as guileless and sweet as a child's, and a nickname (Chick) to match. He had worked hard all his life, and at 70-plus years was beginning to bend. Yet despite a weak heart he was still up

Ivor Woolmer, 1978 (author's collection)

before six every morning taking care of his cows with the help of his wife Jessie and their two sons. We stayed up late that night drinking tea and eating cookies in the kitchen of his house, with Chick talking about his boyhood in England, his time with Manning, and his subsequent years in Australia. England and Fred Manning had been long ago, and after a time I began to worry that I had come far for very little. Chick wanted to be helpful, and was certainly pleased that I had come to talk to him, but his answers to my questions were often hesitant and not very illuminating. Suspecting that perhaps I was being too aggressive in my questioning and that what he might have to tell me was logjammed with the material of his own life, I decided to cut off my inquiry until the next day. Chick himself hoped he would be able to remember more then, and I resolved to be patient.

Saturday morning belonged to the cows. I watched as the swaying herd trundled up the short hill to the barn, there to be fastened to plugs that would drain them of milk in a matter of moments. I wondered if the cows preferred the swift consistent touch of machines over warm hands and a nearby body. A city boy's question, and one that I dared not ask. After breakfast I helped Chick and his oldest son, Jack, with the feeding of the stock. Bumping along on a trailer behind a tractor we tossed out bales of hay to the cattle, who moved with surprising speed to catch a supplement to their regular diet of grass. It was interesting to watch father and son work together, both of them silent men, expert at their chores. They belonged to the herd as thoroughly as men could to any work. The younger son, in his late teens, obviously was not wedded to dairy farming. He was a competent hand but he always wanted to be finished so that he could go and have some fun.

In the afternoon Chick and I returned to Fred Manning. This time memory was more responsive; the previous evening's barrage of questions had stirred his subconscious. Images of the mature writer emerged, not always clear and sometimes in fragments, but with an accuracy I did not doubt. All were of the years 1923–25, when Manning lived at Buckstone Farm in Surrey.

> Manning standing in the garden watching Chick dig. He is, as always, well dressed, his suit cut a bit large. He carries a walking stick, and in the other hand a cigarette. The two casually chat. Manning is fond of a garden but will not work in it. Except for walks in good weather, he never exerts himself. There is a slight swagger in his gait.
>
> The ground floor study, where Manning spends most of his time. Books — too many books, Chick thought — are stacked all around the room, and fill the sitting room as well. Here Manning reads, writes, eats, and

plays chess with Chick, or sometimes with a Captain Charteris from a nearby farm. He also plays a lot of patience. Today he is sitting at his desk, pen in hand, trying to finish a review.

Upstairs in Manning's bedroom. By the bed stands a table on which a candle will always burn through the night. (Witness to a common fear of asthmatics that death will approach while they are asleep?) But now daylight floods the room, as does the smell of brandy. Manning is stretched out on the bed, seized by one of his sporadic drinking fits. The housekeeper, Kate Lynn, also brought from Edenham — for Manning is not comfortable with strangers — is standing nearby with Chick. Kate has summoned a doctor because this time Manning looks bad. Her alarm proves unnecessary, and in a few days everything will be fine. Weeks, perhaps months, will pass before the next episode, during which time Manning is apt not to touch alcohol.

Again in the study. Chick has had a blowup with someone and is threatening to leave Buckstone. Manning likes the boy and tries to persuade him to stay. He offers to include him in his will if he will remain. In a day or two Chick's anger passes and life in the house goes on as before. When Chick finally does determine to leave, to try his luck in Australia, Manning gives him money toward his passage and some clothes.

A bright spring day. Charlie Manning is in England and has been visiting his brother for a couple of weeks. Today he has hired a Rolls-Royce run by a local taxi driver to take him and Chick to Ascot. Manning will not go with them. He frequently bets on horses but goes no nearer the track than a phone call to his bookmaker, Enticknap, in Woking. As the car pulls away Manning waves goodbye and walks back into the house.

We broke off late in the afternoon, both of us more satisfied than we had been the night before. I sensed, however, that I still had not heard from the bottom of Chick's memory. As he talked about Manning he seemed to keep him at a distance, as if unwilling to let the ghost enter his home. Greedy for more information but now taught the value of patience with this man, I was content to let another night's sleep do its work. There would still be time to talk before I returned to Melbourne the next afternoon.

Before supper Jack Woolmer and I drove several miles to a nature reserve in the hope of spotting some kangaroos. As we left the car and walked to the edge of a large clearing, the clouds that had hovered for most of the day broke apart and a golden vaporous light enveloped the field. Little of the vegetation was familiar, and my sense of disorientation was increased by the total silence of the place. Even the birds were quiet, as if in awe of the peculiar light suffusing the area. It took me a few moments to catch sight of the kangaroos, but as my eye adjusted to the light and the terrain it became obvious that there were dozens of them within a hundred yards of me, with more arriving from beyond a distant line of trees. Jack theorised that there was probably a water source that was attracting them. The combination of the dying light, the muted colour of the vegetation, and the grace of the kangaroos themselves, whether moving or still, was mesmerising. I had come upon a kind of primeval tableau and for a quarter of an hour or more Fred Manning was gone from my mind. Here was the Australia of exotic and threatening landscapes, the Australia that urged generations to think of England as home.

Only when it was too dark to distinguish the animals any longer was I ready to leave. Though at the time I regretted not having my camera with me I later was glad of my oversight. What stays in the mind of that scene is the sharper for having no copy.

The next morning farmwork and giving his guest a tour of a local dam project, the Eildon Weir, preoccupied Chick's attention. Not until the noonday meal did our conversation return to the past, and this time it centred on his youth in Edenham, and especially on the time when he had had to leave school and go to work. He had evidently been a very good student, but there had been many mouths to feed in the Woolmer family and Chick's father had not seen his way clear to paying fees for an able-bodied 14-year-old boy to continue his education. As Chick recalled what had obviously been a disappointing, even wounding decision, he stared into his teacup, his body tense.

"I wanted badly to go on with school, but it was not to be."

He had then worked briefly on a farm before going to Surrey as Manning's servant, and after that he moved to Australia. He had not gone back to England at the time of his father's death, nor had he returned years later when his mother was ill. Mention of his mother snapped the tension of his body. Tears started down his cheeks and by now only half-aware of my presence he looked up at his wife:

"I should have gone back, Jessie."

"Now, Chick, you know you couldn't. And your mother, she understood."

I now better understood Chick's difficulty in talking with me. I had wanted to disinter a period in his past that raised issues better left buried. He naturally imagined that had he been able to go on with school his life would have taken a different turn. Instead of years of hardship capped by a late and modest prosperity, there might have been an early and continuing success. He was by no means a bitter man, but if prodded — and what else had I been doing that weekend? — he could not help but reflect on what might have been. I also suspected that his willingness to accompany Manning to Buckstone Farm may have been bound up with a desire to get away from home; distance and hard times had then kept him from returning, as had perhaps a lingering disaffection, albeit one softened over the years by a sense of guilt.

I pressed no further questions. As Chick waited with me out on the highway for the bus to Melbourne, there was a marked warmth in his manner, and an invitation to return which seemed to be more than a glib courtesy. Visiting the past had not been easy or comfortable for him, but it had loosened feelings. I sensed that I was not the only one to have gained something from the weekend.

My next stop was Cootamundra, a country town in the midst of the great rolling pastoral lands of New South Wales. It was a six-hour train trip from Melbourne, and much of the ride was through a landscape given over to sheep. They were everywhere, meandering about or nibbling at the grass, their historic role in the Australian economy made clear in a way words and statistics did not convey. Pat Dickson met me at the station. She was several years younger than her sister Eleanor Manning, but strikingly similar in looks and carriage and, as it turned out, in her abilities as a cook. Raised in Sydney, she had lived in the country since marrying Graham Dickson and had come to love country life. The Dicksons kept sheep, and the next day I would clumsily assist Graham in dipping some of his flock. A fair exchange for hospitality and a distinction that probably few biographers can claim.

Like her sister, Pat had no substantive memories of her uncle and no physical evidence beyond a copy of *Kim* given to her on his long visit home in the 1930s and a sumptuous edition of *Don Quixote* that apparently had belonged to him as a boy. Cervantes' classic was a book much cherished by Manning, hailed in his critical writings, and invoked in *The Middle Parts of Fortune.* It may, therefore, have been a special gift, accompanied by more than the usual courtesies. If so, what was said had long been forgotten, as was the giver himself. Pat's talk centred on her grandmother and the aunts and uncles she had known.

By comparison, Bill Manning, Pat's cousin, who lived a few miles away with his wife Dora, was a treasure trove of information. As the son of Fred's eldest brother Will, he was now the oldest of the surviving Mannings, and with his wavy white hair and bushy eyebrows he resembled the late American labour leader, John L. Lewis. Bill had the greatest interest in family history and had managed to collect a number of artifacts. While I was interviewing him he frequently rose from his chair and went into his study to fetch some family memorabilia: a photo album, the documents naming his grandfather (William Patrick Manning) as a Papal Chamberlain, even a cigarette case which he said had belonged to Fred. His memory included one or two images of his grandfather — "tall", "dark", "eyes like a Spaniard, very dark brown" — and some stories of his uncle Fred that he had heard from his father. In one of them Fred is supposed to have gone for a day to Riverview, the school his brothers attended, but hated it so much that he never went back. Perhaps this was true, though existing records at the school did not verify it. Another story had Fred mistaking some angry cats for burglars trying to enter the Manning home, and proceeding to throw a water jug at them from the bedroom window. And then there were Bill's own memories, derived largely from the ten days Fred had stayed with him and his wife in 1933: of Fred making an apple pie which he then threw away because it was not "good enough"; of Fred tearing up a story after Bill and Dora had praised it, also because it was not "good enough". Often during our conversation Bill, and sometimes Dora, would comment on how "lazy" Fred had seemed to be when he stayed with them. He never exerted himself and seemed happiest when lying in the sun, undisturbed by the sounds of cows, dogs, and maids.

There was an unmistakable note of condescension in most of what Bill told me. Fred had not been a beloved uncle; indeed, Bill himself never once referred to him as "uncle". It sounded more as if he were speaking of an errant boy. And Bill seemed a little too fond of hyperbole — it was from him that I heard of Nora Manning's breakdown in front of the Pope. I could not, however, simply dismiss his versions of the past. From other sources I already had hints of Manning's indolence, and in their obituaries of him both Eliot and Rothenstein referred to his self-defeating "passion for perfection. . .almost indistinguishable from a passion for destruction of his own work." As uncharitable as Bill's recollections were — it seemed not to matter (or be remembered) that Fred Manning had returned to Australia in 1933 partly to recover his health — they had a certain plausibility. After all, Chick Woolmer had not worked for an energetic and productive writer during those three years in Surrey.

While Bill and I were talking, his son Joe, who lived nearby and raised horses, came into the house, accompanied by a gigantic dog that immediately took possession of a sofa. For a moment I was stunned, though not by the dog: it was as if Fred Manning had walked into the room, so close was the resemblance that Joe bore to the photographs and descriptions I had thus far come upon. There was much the same face, the same dark olive complexion, and the same size and build, except that Joe was a bit more thickly set. Bill, on the other hand, bore no resemblance to Fred. I later mentioned the likeness to Pat as we drove back to her house, and after I showed her a couple of pictures of her uncle she too was fascinated by the resemblance. Unfortunately, I never had a chance to talk to Joe alone. Had there been time, I would have looked for other similarities. Could this odd passage of genes, I mused, have stopped at the design of the flesh?

My last evening in Cootamundra I sat up late talking with Pat. At our feet lay Jock, the family shepherd; he and I had determined at first meeting that we were friends. Everywhere I went and with everyone I met rapport was easily established. Though I came as a stranger poking through family heirlooms and memories, I was treated as a guest-friend with whom, it seemed, almost anything could be discussed. By the same token, I would be asked to clear the table, take out the garbage, or assist in the dipping of sheep. Of course I made every effort to put my hosts at ease, and both the Australians and the English are very hospitable. But that did not fully explain why I was treated so well. Another reason gradually became clear: what I sought from people quickened a sense of their importance and thoroughly legitimised the human desire to tell one's own story. What I met with is what interviewers from the age of the epic singers to the present day oral historian have encountered.

In the morning Pat drove me to Canberra, a city that still reflects its origins as a capital built to plan. Buildings, roads, and parks are neatly organised in a pristine aesthetic whole, and a visitor is apt to feel that the city does not belong to its inhabitants but is on temporary loan from the architects. On Friday afternoons the airport is awash with people escaping to Sydney or Melbourne for the weekend. Almost all of my time in Canberra was spent in the Australian National Library examining Manning's letters to James Fairfax as well as other Fairfax materials, and at the Australian National University talking to scholars working on the multi-volumed *Australian Dictionary of Biography*. The letters to Fairfax were as valuable as I had hoped they would be.* In no other correspondence had I seen Manning so open, so willing to talk of himself — of his feelings and values as well as of his literary projects and ambitions. ''Jimmy'' was someone with whom he was ready to share the concerns and anxieties of his personal life, or at least some of them. With most of his other correspondents, including Rothenstein, he was more selective, composing his messages within the assumptions of friendship but careful, it seems, not to expose his life to excessive curiosity or concern. But with his reticence came a ready wit. He would amuse his friends if he would not always inform them.

I did not learn much from the people at the university since my knowledge of both Fred and his father — each of whom was to have a niche in the *Dictionary* — already far surpassed what was needed for an entry. But one item in their folders, a clipping from the Sydney *Bulletin* of October 15, 1903, was new to me. It announced that Fred Manning would soon go to ''live awhile in the land of the Vatican, macaroni and anarchists'', and that the London publishing firm of Heinemann & Son ''has accepted a book of his.''* I knew of no such book and neither, it turned out, did Heinemann. What the book might have been, or whether Manning had sent it to another publisher, I was never able to discover. There may have been no book at all. Nevertheless, the notice was important for what it revealed about his movements and the development of his ambition. Between 1898 and 1903 the choice of becoming a writer had been made. The notice also underlined the significance of the most valuable find that I had made in Eleanor Manning's home: a black notebook containing some early literary sketches in Fred's hand.

Between March of 1898, when Fred Manning left Sydney, and September 1900, when he was brought home by his parents — his father having decided that he was "doing nothing definite, and had better go back to Sydney with him" — there is little evidence of his life. He did not attend Winchester or matriculate at New College, nor did he spend all of his time with Galton who, after being received back into the Church of England by the Bishop of Carlisle, became a curate at St Martin's church, Windermere in December 1898. But though the traces of Manning's whereabouts and activities are meagre, they are nevertheless evocative of his future.

Writing to Fairfax in 1908 Fred mentioned having "read [Cyrano de] Bergerac's Voyage to the Moon in /99 at Florence. Berenson had it." A provocative memory, one possibly including Galton, who had met Bernard Berenson at Oxford in 1888 and had seen him again after returning from Sydney. Italy was a natural place for the boy to visit, and Galton would have been a sympathetic and informed guide. He had gone there first in 1880, "with my head full of Gibbon" and with Rome, as befitted a recently anointed priest, his primary destination. That he subsequently departed Rome "much less papal than I had entered" is understandable given the tension between his calling and his literary inspiration. But Rome as a city, and the Italian towns, such as Perugia and particularly Assisi — "our last classic" and home of "one of Nature's truest, tenderest sons" — with their "close mingling of the ages", always cast a charm over this lover of the past who regularly condemned "the havoc of restoration" and the "ruin of modern improvements aiding the work of time and decay". Small wonder, therefore, that it was Piranesi's Rome that Galton cherished, and that he became a collector of the engravings, eventually accumulating one of the finest collections in England. His pupil also fell in love, though at least as much with the city's galleries as with its ruins and memories. Manning would grow to love Rome as a connoisseur, and in the 1920s he would visit for weeks and months at a time. He even thought of settling there permanently. No other city gave him quite the same sense of belonging — despite his wry observation that "no man was a Roman until he was dead".

Another anecdote I found in a letter written to T. E. Lawrence in 1932. There Manning talks of having been taken by Max Beerbohm, at the age of "about 16", to a performance of G. B. Shaw's *You Never Can Tell,* during which George Street and A. B. Walkley — critics of the day — discussed with Beerbohm how to save Shaw from "undeserved neglect".

> The result was a series of articles in The Saturday [Review], Blackwood's, and The Times which were, I think, effective. Earlier *Candida* had been a success; but after the production of You Never Can Tell to which I refer, Shavianism became a cult...I assisted at the birth of a vogue.

This reminiscence of a heady occasion reinforces the impression that the youth, owing largely to Galton's connections, enjoyed singular opportunities during his time away from Australia. Not every day included a Beerbohm or a Berenson, but Fred Manning was circulating in a milieu where his cleverness was appreciated and where dreams of a literary career could easily have been born. Thus the bold visit to the studio of Rothenstein, the artist known for having "drawn so many poets". Fred was young and unpublished, a poet only in expectation, but he sensed his metier. Rothenstein, in granting his request, bestowed on him a kind of authenticity. However shallow the portrait, its subject was pleased. Of the many visions I have of Fred Manning, one of the most tempting is of his going up the gangplank of the ship that would take him back to Sydney, clutching this souvenir. But

William Rothenstein's portrait of Manning, c. 1899
(Pat Dickson)

reality will not have it that way. Rothenstein retained possession of the picture at least until the mid-1920s.*

The last item of information about these years in Europe, though less glamorous, may be the most important. For a time — how long I could not discover — the youth lived with the Reverend G. Edward Willes (1844–1901) at Calverton, a tiny hamlet in Buckinghamshire that may well have seemed then as it does today to have survived from another era. How he came to stay with Willes, a simple country parson who never married and left no papers, remains a mystery, but not so the purpose of his stay. In applying for a commission during the war, Manning identified Willes as the person he "studied under. . . with a view to matriculating into New College". Life in the rectory was presumably quiet and bookish, the days following the amiable rhythm of rural clerical life, the twice daily post often providing the greatest excitement. There is not likely to have been anyone in the hamlet who was, except in age, the youth's peer. It probably did not matter to him very much as long as there were excursions to London and elsewhere. Besides, he had grown used to living with "people much older than myself". He told Fairfax in 1908 that this had "always" been his situation, an exaggeration which does not distinguish between a family environment where he was the object of special attention, and circumstances where he lived as the ward–companion of an older man. When he mentioned this to Fairfax he was apologising for his rather avuncular "way of talking". The experience of living with adults overly sensitive to one's cleverness (and frailty), while being deprived of peer companionship, will generally have consequences. What they were in Manning's youth, aside from being "spoilt" and escaping "many a deserved whipping" as he later acknowledged, is beyond guessing. But as he grew older there appear those signs of emotional retardation commonly found in cosseted, highly valued children.

"Ill-health", of what nature or duration the record does not say, prevented his going to New College. His father's decision that he should go back home, therefore, was "just". At least that is how Fred viewed it in 1932. Whether the 18-year-old Fred Manning, who had now tasted some of the delights of the larger world, was quite as philosophical can reasonably be doubted. For what was there to go back to? The youth was in limbo: he had no profession, he had had no formal schooling, and he had no ambition except of the sort that fathers distrust and bankers will not support. He was also too delicate and too inexperienced to go wandering. And so he went back to Sydney on board the P&O liner *Himalaya*, along with his parents who had been in England on a six-month holiday. When he arrived back he found that home was now "Tusculum", a spacious Italian-style residence at 83 Macleay Street, Potts Point, that is still standing. In its day it was an elegant house with a fine view, but now it is a drab building, hedged in by its neighbours, shrinking from a world no longer dazzled by its form and pretension.

The glimpses I had gleaned of Manning's life during his visit to England were few; yet single matches struck in a dark room can outline form. Hardly more of him is visible during the three years he was back in Sydney. No letters survive from this time, and the only later reference is to a "Xmas Camp" held at Broken Bay with Harry and some friends. The group had apparently gone to this picturesque area north of the city because of its reputation for good fishing. In addition, there is a brief essay on Ibsen published in the Sydney *Daily Telegraph* shortly after Manning's return from England. There my matches run out, and in feeling my way around the darkened room I found myself relying on those trusty allies of the biographer, "perhaps", "probably", "may", and "likely".

For example, it is possible that during this period he visited Canada, for Chick Woolmer later wrote to me that he recalled Fred's talking about such a visit.* This may, on the other hand, have occurred sometime in 1905 or 1906, or even before his first visit to England; all that Chick remembered was a funny story about it that Manning used to tell. Less mysterious, but hardly clear, is the story of a friendship that is said to have developed between the youth and Lawrence Hargrave, one of the pioneers of flight. A journalist who had obviously known Manning wrote shortly after his death that from his "early years he was convinced of the possibilities of aviation and, though he could not himself participate, was a close friend of Lawrence Hargreaves [sic]". Born in 1850, Hargrave lived in or near Sydney for most of his life, and there is some circumstantial evidence that might link him to the Mannings,* and particularly to a boy 30 years younger but on easy terms with older people. I am tempted to place Fred Manning as a spectator at one of Hargrave's numerous tests with box kites, watching as the clumsy mechanism lifted off long enough to prove flight possible. And perhaps he was. Perhaps flight held a special fascination for one so imbued with his own constraints. But if his excitement was only that of all boys (and most men), it was nonetheless real and deep. Shortly before the war he actually went up in a plane, an experience that a friend thought had "stirred up his brain nicely". It comes as less of a surprise, therefore, to learn that the first unit he tried to enlist in during the War was the Royal Flying Corps, because, as he told a friend, "I like flying."

Seemingly more conjectural is the kind of reading he did during these years. There are no booklists and no later references, but there really needn't be. Galton's instruction and Manning's own instincts had by now formed tastes that were to be lifelong; it is only a question of when a particular author was taken up. We may be sure that he was continuing to read in the classics, and by now (1900–03) in the ancient philosophical tradition. He had the kind of reflective and sharply analytical mind that is drawn to philosophy, and the dialectical element in much of his writing, while traceable to several influences, reflects a mastery of Plato equal to that of many dons. The Epicureans touched him most deeply, however, and his early critical writing for the *Spectator* shows a fine appreciation of their most complete spokesman, Lucretius. We may also be certain that Manning was adding to his already extensive knowledge of the English literary tradition, perusing authors recommended by Galton but looking, too, at others, such as Landor, Peacock, and Hardy. And since he had been recently in Italy, it is fair to assume that he was now polishing his Italian and reading Dante, the poet whom he would later think of translating in collaboration with Ezra Pound.

But I suspect that the greater portion of his reading hours was spent with French authors: Montaigne, Racine, La Fontaine, Voltaire, Mérimée, Renan, and Anatole France were particular favourites, and the last two, he told Fairfax in 1907, were part of his "constant reading". His attraction to the classical (and sceptical) is obvious from his writing; he found the "romantic subjectivity" of a Chateaubriand no more to his taste than the "chaotic enthusiasm" of a Shelley. (Mérimée, he would argue strenuously in a late essay, had been inappropriately labelled a "romantic".) Critics of Manning's early work had no trouble spotting the Gallic influences, and one of the friends he was to make in England, Olivia Shakespear, waggishly suggested that he "used the English language as a medium for writing in French." He was "quite unconscious" of the "imitation", though evidently not displeased by the charge, and never embarrassed by his forthright Francophilia.

In brief, while living at "Tusculum" Manning may well have read as much as if he had been at Oxford. The fact that his plans to attend the university collapsed never seems to have bothered him, nor did he develop that scorn for formal education sometimes found in autodidacts. Galton's affection for Oxford would most probably have forestalled such an attitude, and later Manning's friendship with C. S. Shadwell, Provost of Oriel, editor of Pater, translator of Dante (and friend of Galton), would make Oxford "seem a mother" to him. What his real mother thought of her son's increasing learning is not known, though pride would have been among her feelings, and perhaps too some concern for where it would all lead — which concern leads us back to Eleanor Manning's home, and the notebook I found there: the decisive piece of evidence from those three years back in Sydney.

Two hands had written in it, though much of the volume is as clean as when it came from the stationer. There were several literary sketches by Fred, including pieces of stories and poems, snatches of dialogue from a play, and the opening thrusts of a couple of essays. One witnesses that scepticism he is recorded to have already drifted into, a scepticism of doubts and questions rather than rejection. In its phrasing and irony the compositon falls short, understandably, of the masters he was then reading:

> To exercise one's imagination in speculating upon the existence of God is always a thankless task, and also unpleasant in itself, leading as it does to mere uncertainty, or something worse. But one's vanity must suffer as well, for the evidence is never conclusive and the premisses themselves are always unsound so after a great deal of labour one must be content either with lamenting the incapability of one's mind to solve the problem set, or remain satisfied with the rather vague ideas we have discovered on our way.

None of these efforts is finished and most have the smug tone usual in juvenilia:

> The Jewish religion is merely sanitary.
> The Christian religion is merely superstitious.
> All religions are essentially selfish.

All of the fragments seem to date from the period 1901–03, for there are references to the "late Queen" (Victoria died in 1901), as well as to the "celebrations" inaugurating the Federation of Australia (January 1, 1901). The heading on what would be the title page offers a whimsical purpose:

> The Wisdom of Childhood
> written for the education of Old Men
> by a youth;
> and Printed chiefly by the
> most inattentive Editors for the edification
> of a Community of Fools

Below are Fred's initials and, further down the page, three attempts at a formal signature — a common identity exercise. The other few pages of writing contain Harry's jottings about legal cases of later years. The book had evidently first belonged to Fred, and was presumably left behind in 1903 on his second departure from Sydney. His brother later picked it up to use for making notes. On a few of its pages are drawings by Fred, usually of heads and always viewed from the side. The one exception to this is an awkward rendering of a figure lying in bed. He is drawn frontally, facing the viewer through the vertical bars of the bed frame. Even if the model, seemingly imprisoned by the bed, was someone else, this drawing could be an early representation of the youth's awareness of how illness had restricted his life.

No publisher would bother with these fragments. Though foreshadowing later themes and strategies, as well as the irony that would mark his outlook and style, they have no literary value. Yet as the tracks of a youth flushed with recent flattery, taking his first hesitant steps as a writer, they are the stuff of which biographers dream. It is not important that the pieces are few and crude. Contemporaneously Manning was producing the polished Ibsen essay in the *Telegraph.* Presumably his first published criticism, it offers much despite its superior tone. Ibsen the satirist is congratulated for understanding the "essentials to civilization, and the hollowness of it all". His tragedies, structured like the "static theatre of the Greeks", begin with the vision that the greatest of all the evils bred by civilisation is "boredom". It is a theme Manning himself will touch upon in *Scenes and Portraits.* But a more significant foreshadowing occurs when Manning speaks of one of Ibsen's disciples, Maurice Maeterlinck:

> He writes, as his master does, of the closing of inimical powers around his poor human puppet. "Pelleas! Pelleas!" cries Melisande, as Death enters; the echoes mock, and, with the last breath we hear King Aker, "She was a little being of mystery, like everyone else."

King Aker's lament will be heard again in Sergeant Tozer's reflections on Bourne's death at the end of the war novel. "There was a bit of mystery about him; but then, when you come to think of it, there's a bit of mystery about all of us." The life as well as the outlook of the novelist are felt within that sustaining vision.

It was only a matter of time before the inevitable was accepted by all parties. Fred had "no taste" for any of the conventional occupations open to him in Sydney, and in July of 1903 he reached his twenty-first birthday. He had to apply himself to something, for he was not so frail that he could retire to a couch and lead the life of an invalid. His own wish was to "work seriously" at literature, and aside from whatever doubts his father and mother might have had about such an ambition there was no compelling reason to forbid his trying. That he should return to England — stopping in Italy on the way — was in every way proper. There was to be found the stimulus, the peers, and the publishing opportunities he would need. There, too, was Galton, ready to take the aspiring writer in hand: to have him live with him, to coax and discipline his talent, and to intervene where he could to try to ensure success. England did not promise fame, but for someone like himself to undertake a literary career in Australia, Fred would have argued, invited frustration. He was no poet of the bush, but one who raised his eyes to Helicon. In Sydney a poet might speak of Horace as "the Patron Poet of wise bachelors" — but did a critic dare to quote him in Latin? Had not a few years before all the French as well as the Latin quotations been excised from the article Galton adapted for *Cosmos*?* And did not most Australian writers at one time or another in their careers feel the lure of England?* The conclusion was obvious: he had to go to the place where serious literature was a tradition and where there was an audience to appreciate it.

How different from five years before must have been Fred Manning's excitement as he prepared to leave for England again. Earlier he had gone expecting to see a world that conformed to his imagination; now he hoped to persuade that world to recognise his talent. Earlier he had listened while literary men talked of making reputations; now he hoped to be the subject of their talk. Earlier he had asked an artist to do his portrait; now he dreamed of a day when he would be sought after as a subject. Earlier he had boarded with an obscure clergyman in order to prepare for futher schooling; now he would lodge with a man of letters and would himself work at the literary craft. In brief, the youth must have sailed from Sydney aglow with ambition, looking only straight ahead. Behind was a land to which he felt small attachment — he would not see it again for twenty years — and a family that had accepted his need for leaving. He also left a smiling photograph, which I found among his brother Harry's papers. An expression of humorous watchfulness plays on Fred's face, as if waiting for someone to guess the answer to a riddle he has posed. And as in all the photographs and drawings of him, the mouth is shut tight. Beneath the image is an inscription that framed, at least for himself, the significance of his departure:

> your ever
> 23/9/03 Frederic Manning
> *Cras ingens iterabimus aequor*

"Tomorrow we shall cross again the vast sea." In Horace, a copy of whose works later went with him to war, the context of the line divests it of risk, adventure, even futurity; it is only a fact. Detached from the ode, however, and fixed to the picture the words resonate with challenge and purpose.

After my stay in Canberra, Sydney with its swarms of people and motley buildings was a welcome sight; it was a city, not an architectural panorama. During this last leg of my Australian journey I stayed at Point Piper. The third floor of Eleanor Manning's house became mine, and from the window I had a spectacular view of Rose Bay. I could also see "Arn", the house that the Mannings had moved to in 1905 and where they lived until William Patrick's death in 1915. Smaller, and without the

Manning at 21, just before his departure for England
(Eleanor Manning)

regal flourish of "Tusculum", it had served the needs of a family half the size it had been ten years before. Now only the daughters lived with their parents.

My final days in Sydney passed quickly. I was usually in the Mitchell Library searching through old newspapers and magazines, filling in as best I could the story of the Manning family and looking for fresh clues about Fred himself. One day I ordered up the holograph copy of the war novel and, like any scholar or layman privileged to see a text as it was written out by a respected writer, I felt both awe and excitement. I also was impressed by the sheer beauty of the pages. Even corrections and interlineations, which were remarkably few, could not mar the impact of that precise and graceful handwriting. It gave the manuscript a feeling of greater aesthetic wholeness, and made me think of the hours Manning must have spent as a youth perfecting a skill as rare today as it seems irrelevant.

Evenings were spent with Eleanor and Dot, who were always eager to hear of the day's find. Eleanor in particular was now entirely caught up in the quest and no favour I asked of her was refused. She was also anxious that I should be introduced to some interesting friends of hers, so that one evening she arranged a dinner party where I met the editor of the *Sydney Morning Herald*, Guy Harriott. He was a fascinating man, a shrewd and experienced journalist, and ready to talk about Fred Manning. Aside from family members he was the only person I met in Australia who had read the war novel in either form. Having already been told by Eleanor something of Harriott's experiences in World War II — as a correspondent covering the Italian invasion of Greece in 1941, he had been in the thick of the fighting, earning a mention in Greek despatches as well as the praise of his editor — I was not surprised that he knew the book. A couple of days later I visited him in his office where he let me see the morgue file on Manning. It was thinner than I had anticipated, even thinner than Harriott had. He made up for it, however, by talking to me at length about Australia, encouraging me to see more of it. By this time I no longer needed encouragement. I had come to Australia only to find Manning, but soon my indifference to its landscape and people had been replaced by curiosity and affection. So much so that I was talking already of coming back.

One afternoon a day or two before leaving Sydney I stopped by a bookstore in Pitt Street that specialised in war. Browsing, I found no copy of the new edition of *The Middle Parts of Fortune*, though the shelves held an ample collection of novels. An inquiry to the manager brought an unexpected reply: he had never heard of the book or its author. I would have expected such a response in a general bookstore, but not here. Casually suggesting that it was a book he and his patrons might enjoy, I left the shop. From there I walked to Hyde Park — many of the names on a Sydney map mimic London — to have a look at the ANZAC War Memorial, an imposing structure built to commemorate the war dead of New South Wales. As I sat on a bench behind the memorial watching birds skim over the water of a reflecting pool and enjoying the quiet of the scene, I knew that nothing of Fred Manning was here either. He had chosen to go to war with an English county regiment, and he had survived. Even had he perished, he might not have wished his memory to be honoured within this shrine. It was no accident that in the previous weeks I had found so little evidence of him. Early and deliberately he had detached himself from his homeland (though not his family), opting for an English identity and a literary career suitable to that identity. He never wrote about Australia — even the notebook sketches, if they have a locale at all, take Italy as their setting — and he never seems to have felt the tug on his sympathies familiar to expatriates. He ignored Australia, and he is largely ignored there.

With these thoughts I left Australia. I did not go directly home, but stopped off briefly in New Zealand to see my friends, who had emigrated from America two years before. Now they were separated, and in listening to both parties speak of their pain and confusion, I was removed from my preoccupation with Manning. Or thought I was. For on a bright Sunday afternoon, standing alone on the verandah of what had once been my friends' happy home in Whangaparoa, high up over the ocean rolling in below, I saw two children riding bareback on horses along the beach. Instantly I was reminded of the single specific childhood memory that Manning granted an interviewer, of riding in the Blue Mountains, and I realised, watching the children far below swinging along with abandon, why that particular memory had been offered.

Success

Chapter Three

The first Sunday in October, the year is 1904, the place Edenham, in the south-west corner of Lincolnshire, a hundred miles north of London. People are filing into St Michael's church, a modest stone structure, portions of which date back to the thirteenth century. Flowers, corn, and fruit decorate the interior of the church, for today is the harvest thanksgiving service, long a tradition in Edenham and other rural parishes. The sermon preached is "Cast thy bread upon the waters", but harvest celebrations date from long before the Christian era so St Michael's, on this particular Sunday, also evokes a pagan setting. The worshippers, few of whom know about Demeter or Persephone, have come from the hamlets of Grimsthorpe, Elsthorpe, and Scottlesthorpe, as well as from Edenham proper, which contains some 500 souls. It is a congregation made up of country people: ruddy, practical men not quite comfortable with Sunday dress and long sitting but aware of their place on the sabbath, as on the other days of the week; hardworked, strong-looking women, attentive to a ritual soothing at least in its familiarity; and children, fidgeting, their minds spinning ahead to afternoon games, their faces innocent and bored, their hands in some cases already showing the stains of farm work.

At the front of the church is the pew of the Earl of Ancaster, patron and impropriator of St Michael's, who normally attends services with his family when he is in the area. When he is away, the numerous plaques honouring his family that are affixed to the walls remind those in attendance of his importance. Though the earldom is new (1892), the family (Heathcote–Drummond–Willoughby) is old, reaching back through the earl's father to Sir

Gilbert Heathcote, one of the projectors of the Bank of England in the early eighteenth century, and through his mother to Walter de Bec, a twelfth century worthy. At 74 years of age the earl is a dignified, aristocratic-looking gentleman, well-known for his business ability, his devotion to the Conservative Party, and the care with which he looks after his estates and tenants. All the land in Edenham is his, and his holdings in England, Wales, and Scotland together total more than 150,000 acres, making him one of the principal landowners in the United Kingdom. Besides his home at nearby Grimsthorpe Castle, he has seats at Normanton Park in Rutland and Drummond Castle in Perthshire. For many months of the year he is absent from Edenham.

Conducting the services on this Sunday is the new vicar, Arthur Galton, who also serves as domestic chaplain to the Ancasters. Galton has been in the parish only a couple of weeks, hardly enough time to have become familiar with his flock. As yet he has performed neither a baptism nor a marriage; in a few days he will read his first burial service, for an infant boy who lived but 17 hours. Galton has come to Edenham after a stint as chaplain to the Bishop of Ripon. Now 52 years of age, he has arrived by a circuitous route at the station he dreamed for himself as a boy: vicar of a country parish. He is a thin, ascetic-looking figure, his thick hair gone almost white, his body still prey to digestive disturbances and, increasingly, to rheumatism. But his energies and enthusiasms have not diminished. Since returning to the Anglican Church he has become one of its most ardent champions. In the last five years articles and books have flowed from his pen, their titles revealing as much as need be said about them: *The Message and Position of the Church of England, Our Attitude Towards English Roman Catholics and the Papal Court, Rome and Romanising*, etc. Though tolerant of Catholicism and sympathetic to its adherents,* the former convert and priest has become fiercely anti-papal, and these writings, composed in a crisp, pungent style and benefiting from their author's own experience in the church as well as from his considerable historical knowledge, have given him a new standing, evidenced by his selection the preceding year as the Jowett lecturer.* This lectureship had been founded in 1897 to honour the memory of the Master of Balliol and, like his predecessors, Galton was expected to urge the study of religion through the use of the highest critical standards. His topic for the course of eight lectures, "The Influence of Modern Thought and Knowledge on Theology", further suggests how his interests have been redirected. He is still the Arthur Galton who worships the memory of Matthew Arnold, delights in the classics, and extols the eighteenth century, and of late he has been collecting materials for a memoir of Lionel Johnson,* but a style and scholarship that did not serve literature or history with any brilliance have now found an excellent use. Galton has all the parts of a born polemicist; anger, knowledge, sarcasm, and a fund of personal disillusionment; and in religion there is ample opportunity for combat. His new parishioners, however, do not pay much heed to his role as a *fidei defensor*. To them he appears a learned and well-spoken parson who gives promise of being an efficient and caring shepherd, despite his brusque manner.

When the service concludes the congregation goes back up the aisle to the front doors and, after greeting each other and the vicar, file out into the yard, where moss-green grave markers and several ancient wide-spreading cedars of Lebanon meet their view. Across the lane that runs along one side of the church is the schoolhouse, the social as well as the educational centre of the village. Down the main road lies the Five Bells, the public house where twice yearly the earl treats his tenants to a supper. Sitting just behind the church is the vicarage, a rambling Georgian structure with room enough for a large family. Ivy runs up its walls and a carpet of lawn stretches from its front down to a sunken garden. Like the church, the vicarage is in need of repair. Otherwise, there is no building of note in Edenham. To travellers in this part of the country *Kelley's 1905 Directory to Lincolnshire* recommends only St Michael's as being worthy of pause. The mention is brief, and few travellers would have been persuaded to stop, much less go out of their way. And, indeed, a detour is needed to get to the village, which is not on the road to anywhere except to Grimsthorpe Castle. A quiet village, Edenham is invisible to all but its inhabitants, whose private lives are its only history.

Absent from St Michael's that day is Fred Manning. Had he been inclined to attend church he would have had to go several miles to find a Catholic service, but it is not likely he would have chosen to. He enjoys the ritual for its aesthetic qualities, but he is indifferent to the doctrine and generally contemptuous of priests, particularly — like Galton — the Irish sort.* Formally still a Catholic, his personal beliefs now approximate the Epicurean vision of the Gods captured in a poem he knows well, *De Rerum Natura*:

> Forever calm, serene, forever far
> From our affairs, beyond all pain, beyond
> All danger, in their own resources strong,
> Having no need of us at all, above
> Wrath or propitiation.

So on this Sunday he might burn some incense in his room — a favourite habit — and open a novel, or take a walk around the village that is as yet new to him. To a villager who has chosen to busy himself in his garden that morning rather than go to the service, the strolling youth would be an intriguing sight. Slight of build and very well-dressed, his long tapered fingers perhaps clasping a book to read should he decide to rest awhile, he might seem a little out of place in this most rural of English counties where the pronunciation of the very elderly preserves eighteenth-century habits of speech.* A few minutes conversation would reinforce the impression. The youth is not of native stock, possesses the air and manners of a gentleman, and seems to have no specific purpose for being in Edenham. He is pleasant enough, certainly, with a wide smile and an engaging wit, and he praises the quiet, unhurried pace of rural life, but there is about him a delicate, nervous quality. It is easy to guess that he is living at the vicarage. Less easy to determine is his age. He looks 16, but his conversation and demeanour make him seem twice that.

At 22 Frederic Manning has the sophistication that culture and travel provide, as well as the innocence and self-concern common to sheltered, inexperienced youth. He also has the ambition to be a writer, and in bucolic Lincolnshire, under the eye of Arthur Galton, he has found the ideal place to work. Or so it seems.

I did not go immediately to Edenham when I arrived in England in 1977. Too much of Manning's (and Galton's) life had to be researched in London. But after ten days of libraries and offices I was eager to go north. And so early one morning I took a train to Cambridge to see G. R. Elton, the doyen of Tudor studies, whom I had first met seven years before. Then I had been an English historian in the making, now I was something else, and while talking to the scholar who had refurbished the reputation of Thomas Cromwell, Henry VIII's key minister, I did not mention Galton's "essay" on Cromwell, dedicated to Arnold. Elton turned out to be less sceptical of my quest than many others had been, perhaps because he himself had tracked more than a few mysteries, perhaps merely out of kindness. I sensed that after my fling with Manning I would be welcomed back to the fold.

The next afternoon I rented a car and drove through a rainstorm to Bourne, a market town three miles from Edenham. Seven centuries earlier Robert Mannyng, the poet, had lived and worked there. That fact, together with the myth that Charles Kingsley had written part of *Hereward the Wake* at Edenham vicarage, gave the area a slight literary odour.* Upon reaching the town I checked into the Angel Hotel, and then dashed across the street to a public phone to make some calls. One was to Manning's doctor in his later years, another to his landlady during the final months of his life, and the last to the Reverend G. T. Roberts, the current vicar of Edenham, who invited me to the vicarage the next day.

It is about a seven-minute car ride from Bourne to Edenham via the West Road, and before one comes within its boundaries the tower of St Michael's stands out. Built on the highest ground in the village, the church exists now almost more as a monument than as a place of congregation. Even in Galton's time, religion had lost much of the impetus that had gone into the building of it. Nonetheless, I was anxious to go through it, and through the vicarage as well. However few reminders of Galton and Manning there might be, I wanted to obtain a feeling for the structures in which their shared lives had been spent.

Reverend Roberts was a round-faced, pleasant man who had taken orders late in life and thoroughly enjoyed his pastoral duties. He guided me through the church with that special pride men of God have in their sanctuaries, making sure that I appreciated the antiquity of certain of its parts and every so often pointing out small niceties of workmanship. In the vestry were the baptism, marriage, and burial registers, richly bound in calfskin, their parchment pages neatly filled with the vital records of the parishioners' lives. The tour of the vicarage was necessarily more perfunctory; it had been lived in by too many vicars since Galton to retain vestiges of his and Manning's habitation. Regarding them, Roberts was understandably ignorant; no gossip, evidently, had passed through his predecessors. A year or so earlier, however, prompted by a visit from Richard Cody, he had placed a note in the parish newsletter asking for recollections of Manning. The response had been meagre; one respondent clearly had a bad memory, the other had since gone completely senile. Roberts saved me from despair by mentioning that there was one man in the village who he thought could help. And so I met Victor Woolmer.

Long retired, he lived across the street from the church in a tiny cottage, occupying his days mainly with woodcarving and gardening. I spent two hours talking with him, my pencil ready to catch any significant word or silence. Though he was 79 years old, his mind was clear, and in a soft precise voice that I would hear again the following summer, he spoke warmly of a man he had come to know after World World I, and whom he had liked very much. Galton, too, remained a sharp image in his mind, and one story about him was told with obvious glee. One day two women found a bone in the churchyard, and worrying lest it be of human origin (and thus a disturbance of a grave), sent it to the Bishop of Lincoln. A few weeks later Galton began his Sunday service by announcing that "the bone found in the churchyard was a mutton cutlet, probably taken there by a dog." With this line, Woolmer began chortling. I could muster only a smile, out of politeness. I also sensed that the old man's laugh had come from long ago.

Life in the vicarage before the first war was comfortable, although by today's standards a little primitive. There was no indoor plumbing until 1912 and electricity did not reach Edenham until after World War II. But with day girls to do the chores, a live-in housekeeper to cook the meals and attend to common domestic needs, and a gardener to see to the grounds which Galton had much improved, the residents of the vicarage were well taken care of. Each had his own study on the ground floor, with Manning's, the smaller of the two, having a set of French doors opening on to the lawn:

> Through my windows the song of birds pours in
> And the sunlight on to my table streams.

These lines from an early poem evoke a happy scene, yet on many more days the weather would block both sun and song. Galton's study was lined from floor to ceiling with books, many bearing his bookplate on which was stamped the words, "Gaudet Luce". At his death the greater part of the library went to London for auction, and a story was passed down that what was shipped weighed seven tons. Also in his study was a small stand on which sat an open volume of Piranesi drawings.* Every morning, with the regularity of a man winding a clock, Galton would turn a page. He might also be heard scolding one of the help, for he was very difficult to please and servants generally did

Edenham Vicarage, c. 1914 (Eleanor Manning)

not stay long in his employ. Today, of course, no country vicar could afford so much help, but in those days wages were low and vicars like Galton often augmented their modest incomes with the proceeds from their writings. Galton also presumably had an arrangement with Manning for a share of the household expenses, while the extensive repairs and improvements he made in the vicarage during his tenure were probably financed in part or in whole by the Earl of Ancaster. Like almost everything in Edenham, the vicarage belonged to him as well.

Though quiet and remote, Edenham was not cut off from the world. Twice daily the post brought newspapers, magazines, books, and most important of all, letters. Manning did not share Galton's passion for writing article-length letters, but he could easily devote the better part of a day to his correspondence, describing occasions, judging books and writers, and enumerating the particulars of his health, topics natural to a youth taking hold of a new world. The letters were an outlet, too, for humour, their whimsy and irony confirming that smiling visage in his farewell photograph. Visits to Bourne were probably fairly frequent, especially on Thursday market day, for Edenham was too small to have many shops. Bourne was also where the nearest doctor could be found, though most of Manning's maladies, as well as Galton's aches and pains, were outside a physician's power to heal. Beyond Bourne were people and places of importance, like the Hacons in Dornoch, or the Gascoignes (the family of Lady Sandys) in Yorkshire; but London, easily reached by train, was where Manning was usually to be found when he was outside Edenham. "Town" beckoned and repelled him; it was "the most attractive place in the world", and yet it "trample[d]" one's spirit. Like Galton, he could not bear the clamour and the crowds. "I'm not a gregarious animal; and people who move about in herds seem to me no better than shadows of each other, without any ultimate reality." Nonetheless, several times a year he went to London, despite the jolting effect it had on his nerves. He sought to break the pattern of living in "this hermitage", as well as to see friends such as Lady Russell, the widow of his father's first employer, a Mrs Key, an old friend of Galton's, and Olivia Shakespear and her daughter Dorothy, who in 1914 would marry Ezra Pound.

As was the case with many of his friends, the Shakespears entered Manning's life through Galton, for Olivia was the cousin of Lionel Johnson. She was a beautiful woman, with a ready wit, wide culture, and literary ambition. Between 1894 and 1910 she wrote six novels, one dedicated to Lionel and all of them now as forgotten as they are difficult to find. She also wrote articles and reviews, and at least one play. None of her work, however, has secured her a reputation; nor has her family tie to Pound. No, if the sonorous name and patrician features are familiar at all it is due to her relationship with William Butler Yeats. For a short time in the 1890s and perhaps again in 1903 she was his mistress — she is the unhappily married "Diana Vernon" of Yeats's *Autobiography* — and subsequently she was his friend and treasured correspondent, the person he called "the centre of my life in London". In Manning's life she did not play so glamorous a role, but as his often described "belovedest aunt" she was someone of great importance, someone he depended on. At least as early as 1905 he was sending her drafts of poems and stories to read, and in 1909 he dedicated one of the sketches in *Scenes and Portraits* to her. Moreover, his few surviving letters to her, which are mainly about his writing, further point to a relationship built on intellectual respect.* But his gift to her, later, of the manuscript of *The Middle Parts of Fortune* suggests deeper feelings, going back, perhaps, to afternoon teas at the Shakespear home in Brunswick Gardens, Kensington, in the early years of the century, when the shy young writer, long used to being attended to, could enjoy good talk of books and authors and sense himself enfolded in a familiar but now seldom felt feminine concern. Was it merely coincidence that the three people, except for Fairfax, whom he should single out in 1907 as his London "friends" were women, and all of them old enough to be his mother?

Dorothy Shakespear was both part of that comfortable setting, and possibly something more besides. In 1904 Manning knew her as an 18-year-old girl who painted watercolours, read the fashionable poets, and whose face had a softer, mellower beauty than that of her mother. His earliest surviving letters, whimsical, self-conscious notes about his work and himself, are to her.

Edenham, Bourne, Lincs.
December the Second, 1905

My dear Dorothy,
Oh! such a tragedy has happened! Cats were created by the devil, they are possessed by the devil whose name is Legion; they have no morals, no manners, no respect for the property of others or the inspirations of the Muse. Let them be anathema maranatha! I left the cat in my room for a moment — but I cannot tell you, it is 'immonde' it has no parallel in history — when I came back I found it scratching at a bundle of papers — and on investigation I found — but it is impossible to tell you. The Book of Valiance had to be taken away and burnt, a book the world has been waiting for since its creation...

Whether Dorothy thought his wit tedious is unknown, just as we do not know what she thought at the time of the poems he sent her — one as a "peace offering" for some undescribed sin. Did she suspect that this "entertaining, nervous character" who came to her parents' home wanted to say more than he could? Probably not, if her impersonal recollections 60 years later of him reflect her earlier awareness. Certainly as time went on all that Manning acknowledged toward her was the sort of binding, passionless affection that comes of long association. "I have known you half of my life," he writes in 1914 when congratulating her on the engagement to Pound, "and have grown fond of you." If his feelings ever ran deeper, they may be concealed in the romantic poem "Canzone" which he published in 1910 and dedicated to her.

In his first half dozen years at Edenham Manning established himself as a writer of extraordinary promise. "The principal hope for English prose literature," wrote a reviewer of *Scenes and Portraits*, "lies in the fact that Mr Manning writes." Less demanding praise greeted his poetry: "After reading his poems we expect a good deal," commented Percy Lubbock. As a critic himself Manning quickly won the kind of respect that promised a future ranking him with Arnold and Pater. At least St Loe Strachey, the editor of the *Spectator*, suggested as much. "I must just write a line to thank you for your two admirable reviews, the one on Shelley and one on French verse. They are two as fine pieces of criticism as have passed under my editorial pencil for the last 20 years." Besides glowing words there were cash prizes — almost, that is. In November of 1911 a committee composed of Henry Newbolt, Edmund Gosse, Maurice Hewlett, and J. W. Mackail, all noted literary figures, voted unanimously to give Manning the first Edmond de Polignac literary prize for *Scenes and Portraits.* Unfortuately for Manning's wallet and general reputation, the decision had to be rescinded and the prize given instead to Walter de la Mare when the committee discovered that *Scenes* had been published prior to the date set by the rules.* Manning took his bad luck gracefully. So gratifying was the "compliment" paid his work that if "I were to slap my pocket I should not miss the money [£100] a bit."

To be sure, his early work was known only to those of culture and taste, those who recognise influences and hear echoes. This was Milton's "fit audience...though few", and the audience for which Manning deliberately wrote. But he had also, since 1909, been working on an historical romance, "The Gilded Coach", which he anticipated would achieve a popular success. He dreamed of its rivalling in quality Thackeray's *Henry Esmond*, and of its selling as well as the historical fictions of Newbolt and Hewlett. If the fates continued to be kind, then financial reward might be added to critical respect.

Even young writers with talent, however, need help in launching a career. Galton, appreciative of that reality and well-practised in it, did everything he could. He offered suggestions as to what to write about, criticised Manning's drafts, appealed to publishers on his behalf and, in the best tradition of literary assistance, informed the public of what they were missing. "As Mr Manning has said so wittily and eloquently in the most inimitable of his *Scenes and Portraits*..." So Galton noted in a review for the *Spectator*, and it would seem from the dates when each man began writing for the magazine — Galton in July 1909, Manning five months later — that the mentor may have had a hand in his protégé's being taken on. Galton also kept the young writer to his task: "Perhaps if Mr Galton is in an amiable mood," Manning wrote to Fairfax in June of 1907, "I may be able to get a day in town; but at present he is annoyed because the poems should have been ready for the publisher." The poems referred to were shortly thereafter submitted to John Murray by Galton who, in a seven-page letter, strongly urged their publication.

> I want you to consider this batch of poems, not as an isolated volume, but as the beginning of what I hope will be a fruitful career. It is never safe to prophesy, especially about literature; but I cannot help feeling

> confident that if Fred Manning can get the necessary start, he will soon find a public to which he will appeal successfully. For these reasons, I am very anxious he should get a start; and no introduction to the public would please me so much as one under your auspices.

So enthusiastically did Galton go on to argue his case that Henry Newbolt, the reader to whom Murray referred the poems and Galton's brief, felt his "first duty" was to advise the publisher "as *advocatus diaboli*".

Galton wanted Manning to succeed because he believed in the youth's "great promise", just as he had believed in the promise of Lionel Johnson and Laurence Binyon and exerted himself on their behalf. Nothing that he did to assist Manning would, indeed, surprise anyone familiar at all with the nitty-gritty of literary life. And if Galton occasionally mused that Manning's eventual fame would justify both his literary values and his efforts, that would only prove him human.

A vexing difficulty in writing about Manning was finding his early work. Before *The Vigil of Brunhild* (1907) he had had "things accepted" according to Galton, both prose and verse. One was the Ibsen article, but what were the others? Two earnestly delicate poems in *The Outlook*, a respectable weekly of the day, were all that the standard bibliographical indices revealed.* To discover his other alleged works — how many there might be I did not know — took patience and luck. I was aware of "a picture of life seen through the eyes of an organ grinder's ape" because T. E. Lawrence had mentioned it in a letter to E. M. Forster in 1927, but no index knew of the piece, at least not by any title I could invent. Nor did I know if this piece was early or late. I decided therefore to go through all the volumes of *The Outlook* on the hunch that Manning might have submitted prose as well as poetry. One afternoon, well into the tedious chore, I came across an unsigned sketch that seemed to fit what Lawrence had described in his 1927 letter.

The Organ Monkey

The organ-grinder, with his degenerate Italian beauty, stands in the busy roadway, near the wet kerb, and mournfully grinds the "Lost Chord". At the end of a string, squatting on the pavement, is the organ-monkey. The Italian smiles insinuatingly at the nurses and mothers of the children collected to watch the little animal. The monkey wears a gay red coat, and occasionally, in answer to a twitch of his string, cuts a caper, and squats again on the greasy kerb. He fixes his eyes on each bystander in turn, and the world of half-human recollection shining in them is uncanny. What is this thing that has come to pass? Not so long ago he swung from giant tree to giant tree, with a troop of comrades, chattering all the time, or hung by his tail from some giddy branch, doing innumerable gymnasium exercises of his own invention...But how is all this gone and known no more, and what is this place where the ground is cold and wet and greasy?

The great roar of the unknown place is terrible, and the dreary grinding from the box his master carries dazes his ears, accustomed to sounds far other than this. The sun is dropped out of this new world, and grey twilight closes him in...Yet sometimes one who has been an exile, or one who has seen the "dim, rich city" and the immemorial forest, passes by; and for a second the monkey-eyes and the human ones meet in a passion, an agony of sympathy. For in a foot of shivering monkeyhood may be the appeal of all the exiles of the world, and on the nights of these few white days come dreams of the giant trees and the giddy branches where he swung and chattered; and in the midst of the dark garret rise the white towers of a forgotten palace, where the brothers of his memory run across the marbles laid for the knees of courtiers.

[July 16, 1904]

If this (condensed) sketch is not actually Manning's work, it could have been. A mind reflecting on its experiences, engaged in a dialogue with others or itself, will appear often in his prose and poetry. Hence the portraitist character of his work, and its ruminative, philosophical cast. *The Vigil of Brunhild* describes a warrior-queen looking back on her tumultuous life; 23 years later what would distinguish his war book from battalions of others would be its preoccupation with the soldiers' efforts — like that of the monkey — to understand "this thing that has come to pass". The drama that is to be found in his imaginative work is drama of ideas rather than of action.

Another feature of "The Organ Monkey" bears Manning's signature: its empathy for the monkey's plight. When "the monkey-eyes and the human ones meet in a passion, an agony of sympathy", we may question the expression but we believe that something actually felt is being described. Such empathy, and sympathy, was a notable part of his work, as it was a notable part of his life. No doubt his own frailties made him sensitive to the pains and perplexities of others. A poem written a few years later, which is strikingly reminiscent of the early sketch (and Blake's "Tiger"), has the writer witnessing his own dilemmas in those of a bush-baby, or galago, a small African primate.

To a Bush-baby

Little one, so soft and light,
Haunting silent, darkened ways,
In the shadow of the night,
Thee I praise.

Such an elf as danced of old,
Light as thistle-down or froth,
By Titania's throne of gold,
Little Moth.

What strange fate linked thee and me,
In this world of hope and fears?
Surely God hath sheltered thee
From our tears.

Hands thou hast, and eyes that seem
Troubled, by some pain obscure,

As though life were but a dream,
        Nothing sure.

Is thy tiny spirit vext,
As our own, by vague distress,
Haunted, by our life's perplext
        Weariness?

Wondering, at all the strange
Loveliness of lapsing days;
Change that passeth into change,
        Rain or rays?

Little hands that cling to me,
Helpless as mine own, and weak,
What in this world's mystery
        Do we seek?

Two other early works eventually came to light, neither of great merit. They told me something about Manning's tastes and sensibility, especially his fondness for irony, but I received them more as the reward of my industry than for their intrinsic value. The first I found by combing through several years of the *Westminster Gazette*, a paper that regularly published literary pieces and that I knew was read at the vicarage. Manning's contribution, "An Interlude", is a very brief sketch of a conversation between two men meeting after a long time. Their talk can have amused few readers, for Manning presses too hard on his material, forcing his humour with the kind of self-congratulating cleverness common to the novice writer:

> I ceased to wonder what had happened to him in the last two years; before such a man time sinks into its proper insignificance. He has a natural gaiety of manner, a kind of boyishness, that is almost immoral in a world in which, after all, time is money and one continually grows older. He was not even reminiscent, in itself a monition of age; he talked of the present with an ingenuousness that was almost irritating. For myself, under a mask of politeness, I am profoundly inquisitive.

In that last phrase there was something of himself, and in the piece as a whole echoes of the tone of the letters he was writing to Dorothy Shakespear at the same time. The other piece, "The Sacrament of Death", came to me by accident as a result of an inquiry to a library on a different matter. I already knew of the story's existence from a reference to it in one of Manning's letters to Dorothy Shakespear, but a search of several periodicals where it might have appeared had ended in the suspicion that it was never published. When I obtained from the library what was obviously a proof copy, with a single marginal correction in Manning's hand, I was surprised, but I remained unable to find evidence of its publication.

The story of "The Sacrament of Death" takes place in sixteenth-century Madrid, and concerns an attempt by a priest, Angelo, to assassinate the King of Spain by means of a poisoned communion wafer. Already suspected because of his sympathy for condemned heretics, Angelo's design is discovered and he is himself killed while celebrating mass. In the confusion, the wafer is accidentally given to a young girl who had earlier been reproached by the priest for teasing the herd-boy who is in love with her. When the boy hears that she is dying, he runs into the city to be with her:

> And the boy fell on her face, kissing away the tears from her wet eyelashes, kissing her cheeks, her neck, aye, and the white globular breast which the torn nightgown disclosed. And she held him by the neck with her white arms, while the old man and woman hid their faces in their long thin hands, lest they should intrude their gaze on things too sacred to see.

The tale owes much to a number of nineteenth-century storytellers, not least among them Prosper Mérimée. "The Sacrament of Death" has not the control of Mérimée's work, but in subject matter and tone it can claim cousinage — which is only fitting, for Manning (like Galton) was a passionate enough admirer to chastise Lytton Strachey in 1912 for ignoring Mérimée in his *Landmarks of French Literature* and constant enough to be still celebrating his virtues in an article he wrote for Eliot in 1927:

> His reserve is simply that of the well-bred man towards a world which he knows, for which he has something of pity and contempt. He neither asked for its sympathy nor admitted it to his confidence. He does not bore us with the story of his life, gloze away his own incompetence by revealing to us how excellent were his motives and intentions, how deceived he had been in his friends, how fatally misunderstood by the world. On the other hand he is not a lunatic automaton traversed occasionally by a *crise des nerfs* to whom life is only a nebula of intangible dream and ineffective desire. He is not that pathetic spectacle, an artist in need of an interpreter. He seems an enigma to our modern world only because he was perfectly sane.

Such a tribute, almost a defence, suggests a felt resemblance, and is of the kind that is often more revealing about its author than its subject.

Besides these pieces, the only other early work my search turned up were some brief letters to periodicals. They were usually about current affairs, though one, printed in *The Outlook* in November 1905, discussed "the symmetrical resemblances in the leading ideas of Gobineau and Matthew Arnold", and another ably seconded a letter by Galton in a squabble over the impact of the Civil Constitution of the Clergy (1790), which set about establishing a French national church.* There may, of course, be other stories and sketches hiding away in hard-to-find periodicals, or grinning anonymously from pages I have already scanned. There is, however, only so much time for collecting, and when the quest is for youthful efforts perhaps only so much reason.

Edenham, Bourne, Lincs.
December the Fifth, 1907

My dear Dot,
I heard from Murray this morning that Brunhild will be published tomorrow; it is rather an advantage that it should have been delayed a week, as it is more likely to be reviewed in an adequate way than if it had appeared in the rush of Christmas books last week. I enclose some press cuttings announcing its appearance. I shall send you the reviews and may want some of them back, as I cannot afford two subscriptions to the press-cutting agency. AG has been dining, sleeping, and breakfasting at Grimsthorpe since Monday, he comes home for lunch; while he is away the workmen are pulling the house down over my head, and have made a large hole in the wall opposite my bedroom door. It is a nice amusement for the winter.

The Vigil of Brunhild was Manning's first book, and he took the pleasures that such an occasion bestows, including sending happy notes to friends like Dorothy Shakespear. The tempo of life picked up — "I have been living in a whirlwind," he wrote to Fairfax — and complimentary reviews together with congratulatory letters began arriving daily in the post. He could laugh at the house being pulled down around him, and for a time his "maladies" disappeared, leaving him "very cheerful and robust". He was now a book-poet, not just a youth who had occasional poems tucked in magazines. And he was a poet who had dared an unusual subject, for the Brunhild of his narrative was not the better-known Brunhild of the Nibelungenlied but a sixth-century Merovingian queen who conducted a long and bloody feud with Fredegonde, the paramour of her brother-in-law, Chilperik. Brunhild's was a tangled career of love, murder, revenge, and ambition, redeemed by its supposed commitment to establishing political order where for so long there had been only anarchy. Never before had a British poet taken her as a subject, doubtless because few English readers would have recognised her. To prepare readers of *The Vigil of Brunhild,* therefore, an historical "Note" extracted (untranslated) from Lavisse's *Histoire de France*, was placed at the end of the poem. As a final flourish Manning added an observation worthy of Anatole France: "Though I lay claim to no historical accuracy, the story as I present it is, probably, as near to the truth as any other vision. History is not a science: it is prophecy looking backward, and no doubt is often as far from scientific truth as the more conventional mode of prophecy."

More significant comments occur in Manning's three-page introduction to the book. Brunhild, he explains, is "essentially a figure of tragedy", but he has deliberately eschewed her as a "subject of dramatic action" and instead has chosen to portray her looking back on her life as she awaits a grisly execution. Her visions, told to a priest who has come to shrive her, reveal a passionate life and an extraordinary will. She has followed her heart and has no regrets; old and friendless, she sounds a note of triumph.

> "Ye, who are sheltered from the world, O priest,"
> Spake Brunhild, mocking him, "have time to pause
> Ere your minds fix the measure of pure truth
> And perfect justice; but our windy life
> Loses no time on niceties: for me,
> I gave such justice as I look for now;
> I swung a hammer on mine enemies,
> To forge the world anew unto my mind;
> My cause was justice in mine eyes, and those
> Who stood against me, enemies of God.
> Lo! I have failed of all my purposes,
> And age has come upon me like a cloud;
> And these old shoulders groan beneath the shame,
> The bitterness, the burden of defeat:
> Yet I have seen the star, where others saw
> Only the froth and spume of angry storms."

Manning saw in her more than the scarred warrior, the eager

lover, or the Queen who insists that beyond her passions there was a dream to raise

> An empire on the ruins of the old,
> Whose seat should be the Rhine.

His Brunhild has a mind that, while easily mocking priestly casuistry, does not lose hold of its faith, or its self-awareness.

> But answer, priest:
> I, who wrought wisely through long weary years
> To build a kingdom, where was turbulence,
> And mould a civil state out of this strife,
> Come at the last unto a shameful death;
> While Fredegonde, who wrought for her own lust,
> Died peacefully: has God been just to us?
> Bow not thy head; bear with my bitterness:
> Though God desert me in mine hour of need,
> Yet shall I carry a firm heart to death;
> Nor blame him, nor blame other than myself,
> Who never trusted other.

She also has tenderness, and an understanding of love — not merely the love of woman for man, but of mother for child, and of sister for sister. Manning elects — contrary to Lavisse — to make the murder of Brunhild's sister Galswintha, by her husband Chilperik, the pivot of the feud.

> And Galswintha's page, wild-eyed and tremulous
> Telling us how, as soft as evil dreams,
> Hilperik and his harlot crept, by night,
> Into the shadowy chamber where she lay,
> Her sweet, frail body nestled close in sleep:
> Sleep, that alone drove sorrow from her soul;
> And he, the hairy hound, leaped on her bed,
> Kneeling on those twin breasts of ivory,
> And crushed the slender throat in his huge hands!
> "I think I swayed a little; and I know
> That something seemed to burn up all desire,

Leaving me rigid, filled with winter frosts:
For I remembered how, when we were young,
And shared one chamber in the donjon keep,
When she awoke, and felt the darkness, thick
And fearful, on her sunshine-loving eyes,
First she would call to me, and then, grown brave
At her own tongue's sweet music, cross the floor
To creep into my bed, and cling to me,
Telling me how she dreamed that she was dead."

All this was in keeping with Manning's wish to illuminate a "complex psychology". Having selected a subject all but unknown to literature, a story one of his sources termed a "strange mixture of romance and tragedy", Manning opted for a portrait of a soul revealed through dialogue, rather than a tragedy of circumstances and actions. Brunhild is a figure akin to Cleopatra and Lady Macbeth, but her fate interested Manning far less than her spirit — a spirit he deduced from the historical record and from the experiences of his own sensibility. He realised, he told Fairfax, that he had winnowed her story until she became "a figure in a void against a background barely suggested": but that, by choice and by instinct, had already become characteristic of his art. Understandably, the obscurity of his subject and the focus of his poem placed a burden on his publisher. How much of a burden, and how it was dealt with, became clear when I visited the offices of John Murray in August 1977.

I sat for the better part of two days in the Murray offices at 50 Albemarle Street. Like many English business and professional offices, there was an informal, almost domestic tone to its operations. Much of the furniture could have slipped unnoticed into a drawing room; the pace of work and talk was, by American standards, leisurely, and phones rang at comfortable intervals — a sign of the willingness still to transact business by letter. I was seated at a small table dating possibly from the time Murray had moved into its comfortable offices (1812), and in the middle of both the morning and afternoon I was served a cup of tea. Only one other person occupied the spacious room, an editor who was ready to answer an occasional question but who was otherwise busy with his own concerns. Stacked on my table by previous arrangement were several thick folders, looking as if they had been untouched for decades. In them were the correspondence and assorted papers generated by four of the five books Manning published with Murray. *Brunhild* had formed the opening chapter of a long association.

On the advice of his reader, Henry Newbolt, Murray had decided to publish the narrative poem by itself and await public response before determining what to do with the rest of the poems Galton had sent to him. Manning's poetry, Newbolt thought, was "interesting and often beautiful", and its "promise" obvious: "he has gone much further than most men of 24." But he wondered if Manning would "ever take hold of the public: at present he does not touch life closely enough for that." In his letter Galton had acknowledged that Manning would have to "find a public to which he will appeal", but for poetry that rivalled the work of Yeats in both thought and words — and, Galton further claimed, which had been praised by Yeats, Binyon and "other writers" — an audience would surely be found. Neither Newbolt nor Murray was as sanguine. The reader could detect only "echoes" of Yeats in Manning's poems, while the publisher, better at numbers than he was at sounds, appreciated that "a poem by an unknown writer has an uphill fight to encounter." Manning was a worthy venture, but his poem was not going to sell itself.

All parties, therefore, set about gaining an audience for *Brunhild*. Several hundred postcards bearing a photograph of the author and announcing the book were posted by Galton and Manning to friends, booksellers, and newspapers in England and Australia. It was hoped that the mailing would arouse at least a "moderate demand", although Newbolt doubted that Manning's countrymen would read anything but "doggerel anecdotes about horses, and sentimental pothouse ballads". Murray also delicately suggested to Galton that the poet "give the book away fairly widely to his friends'' so as to increase the chances of ''making it popular''. Galton had already thought of this tactic:

> We had intended to give copies away judiciously to people who are capable of helping the book in magazines and newspapers; men like Gosse, & W. C. Courtney, of whom I know a fair number, either personally or by correspondence.
>
> I think Mr Manning will be justified in distributing 40 or 50 copies in those directions. We are making out lists, and we will send for copies as we get them off.
>
> If necessary, the number so distributed can be increased.
>
> I am ordering copies from the four or five booksellers with whom I deal regularly, so as to get it circulated in various directions.
>
> I think we may rely upon good notices and a fairly abundant sale in Sydney.
>
> I am giving the book away as Christmas presents; and begging the recipients, if they like it, to do the same.

It was only natural that Galton should take charge: he knew how books got sold and noticed, and he had the contacts to make that knowledge work for Manning. Five hundred copies, the size of the printing, may seem like a small number of books to dispose of, but poetry did not sell much better eighty years ago than it does today, especially if it was by an unknown writer.

As anticipated, *The Vigil of Brunhild* needed all the help it could get. Sales went slowly, particularly in Australia, occasioning some unusual merchandising practices. One exchange of letters in the file was between Murray and Mrs Caroline David, of Sydney, wife of the well known geologist, Edgeworth David, who was then on an expedition with Shackleton in Antarctica. It seemed that Mrs David, with her advance copy in hand, had marched around to local bookstores to see if they had *Brunhild* in stock, only to find ''sleepy owls'' who gazed at her ''blankly''. Would Murray, therefore, send her a dozen copies so that *she* might distribute them? Murray obliged, but asked that she keep the transaction a secret, since trade custom required publishers to go through booksellers exclusively. Two months later the redoubtable Mrs David told Murray that she planned to read the poem before the Women's Club of Sydney, which had a membership of 300, in the hope that the reading would make the book "go". Seventy ladies showed up, half of them allegedly with copies already in hand.*

A copy that made its way to America carries a different story. It is on the shelves of the Sterling Library at Yale, and was the gift some years ago of the novelist Frederic Prokosch. On the first page is an inscription by Manning that has the tone of a parent discussing a less favoured child.

> To Gertrude Kurath
> 27. II. 1932
>
> This poem was written when I was about 20 years old, three or four years before publication. I lived then at Edenham in Lincolnshire. As to what I think of it now . . . a poem records the traces of an experience, it is not the experience itself, tho' it may evoke in other minds a similar experience: it is an analysis between two syntheses. To me, therefore, it is bound to be less than the experience itself; and I consider principally its technical characteristics.

Gertrude Kurath is the sister of Frederic Prokosch, and was now living a couple of miles from my own home! When I discovered her proximity I immediately phoned, imagining letters and reminiscences — all to be obtained without having to compose a letter or board an airplane. I was too hopeful: she had never heard of Fred Manning and could not remember ever seeing the book. That left her brother, who had apparently asked for the inscription and then never delivered the book to her. But my letters to him went unanswered. What I was left with was an inscription, another instance of Manning's disguising/confusing his age — he was 22 when he came to Edenham, and does not mention the poem before 1907* — and fresh evidence of how small his fame was: a signed and inscribed book sat on an open-access shelf.

It is quite safe where it is. Years might pass before a pair of hands would approach, and they would probably come only in order to dust. If anyone actually took the book down from the shelf, it would like as not be a scholar rather than a casual reader. For narrative poems belong to another era; the vogue for them had already passed when Manning found himself having to comment on his own contribution to the genre. Even in 1907 one reviewer sighed at yet another "of those needless, well-built, uninspired, smooth-flowing Tennysonian renderings of medieval subjects which young poets inevitably make". As that opinion came from Australia it may not have pricked Manning's ego, and would have been as babble to Galton. English critics caught "Arnoldesque" lines as well as "Tennysonian renderings" — the latter comparison annoyed Manning — but they were generally kind to the poem, and certainly did not judge it to be an anachronism. Why should they? Manning was hardly alone in turning out such poems. A few of the critics, though, balked at its lack of passion and "virility"; a barbarous time in history, to their minds, needed to be treated with more "dramatic force". A defence of Manning was provided by James Fairfax in a review he wrote for the February 1908 issue of *The Isis*, an Oxford literary magazine. The poem's "tranquillity", he argued, was due to the nature of the medium: "poetry tends to soften, and an imaginative treatment to render not less impressive, but often fortunately more remote." From poetics his argument went to conscience: "In conclusion, it is a book worthy of the attention of that scholarly and leisured audience, which surely, if anywhere, should be found in Oxford." Fairfax may have coaxed some of his peers to read the poem; but he had already done Manning the much greater favour of introducing his work to a London acquaintance, Mrs Eva Fowler.*

Eleven years his senior, Eva Fowler became Manning's "most loyal and most generous friend". Except for his mother, he

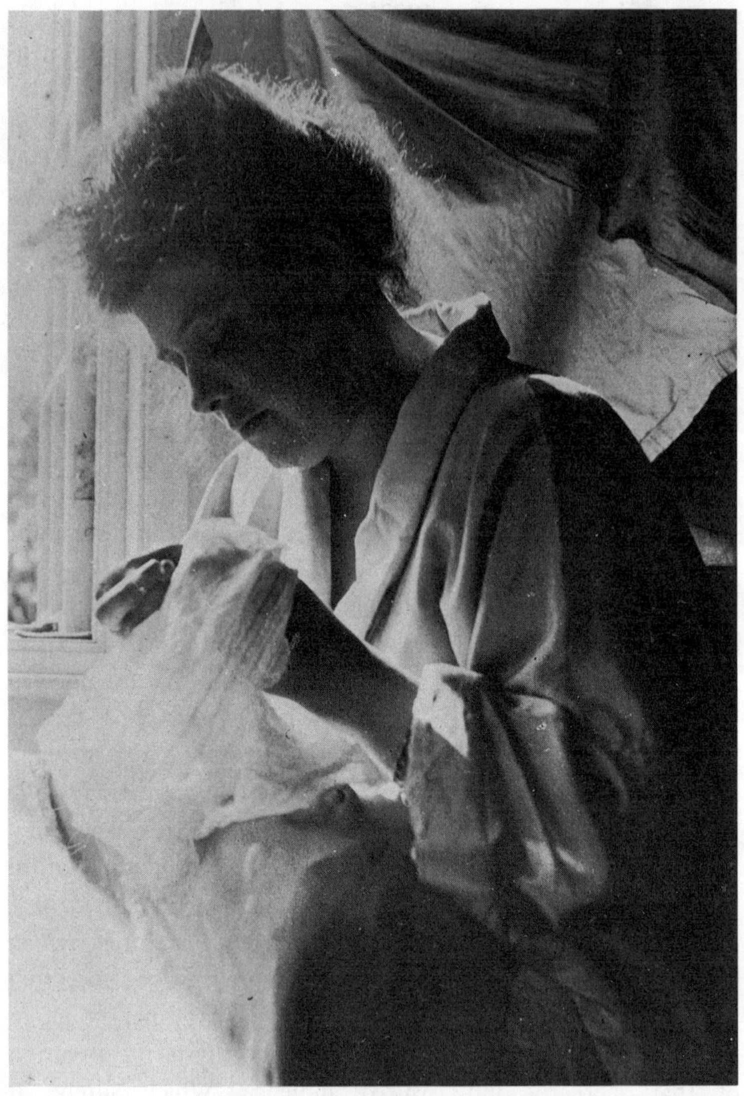

Eva Fowler, c. 1910 (Eva Focke Sumner)

spoke of no one else with such active affection. But then everyone loved Eva Fowler. Born in California of German–Mexican parentage, she grew up in Honolulu where her father, Paul Neumann, practised law, advised the Spreckles sugar interest, and served as attorney-general to Liliuokalani, the last queen of Hawaii.* In 1890 Eva married Alfred Fowler, then a junior member of John Fowler & Co. of Leeds, the family business, which made steam ploughs sold all over the world. When the Fowlers eventually settled in London, Eva began opening her home, first in Knightsbridge and later at 26 Gilbert Street, Mayfair, to a varied collection of artists and writers. Pound was a frequent guest and so too was Yeats, who conducted many experiments in automatic writing at "Daisy Meadow", the Fowler country home near Brasted in Kent.* To one and all Eva Fowler became "Aunt Eva", who behaved less like the mistress of a salon and more like a woman concerned for the welfare of talented people she genuinely liked. Childless, without pretensions, and a woman of discriminating taste — Olivia Shakespear thought her the "most fascinating woman" she had ever met — Eva treated her guests as if they were her family. "Willie," she once addressed Yeats, "shall I take the egg off of your tie or will you?" Photographs of Eva Fowler seem to catch her truly: a large, handsome woman, often dressed in loose flowing robes, with an open, benign countenance promising warmth. She was once drawn by Sargent, who had trouble capturing the expression he wanted until a gramophone record of Hawaiian music was played in the background. The likeness that Manning cherished was a simple photo of her, bent over her sewing in a pose and light reminiscent of a Vermeer painting.

Her husband, known to everyone as "Taffy", was sometimes sceptical of Eva's friends. Rabindranath Tagore, he complained, always looked "grimy". He thought better of Manning, however, and in the years following Eva's death welcomed him to 26 Gilbert Street. Their talk would have been of the world rather than art, for Taffy was decidedly less intellectual than his wife. Golf and butterflies, a collection of which he kept under glass in his dressing room, were his great pleasures. A big, burly man, who in his hunting clothes exemplified Edwardian well-being, he once trekked into Addis Ababa with the intention of selling steam ploughs to Menelik, the Emperor of Ethiopia. The story of that journey is marvellously recorded in a series of letters written to Eva and, eager raconteur that he was, Taffy often described the journey and Menelik's subsequent difficulties with the tractors he ordered.* Pound heard the tale, probably more than once, and stitched it into his 18th cnto. As familiar with the tale were Eva's three younger sisters, all of them attractive, married, and well known to Manning. Each would have a poem dedicated to her by him as did both the Fowlers. But it was "Mrs Taffy" who really mattered, who read his work with a "delicate sensibility", who devoted many hours to typing his poems and stories, and who was always concerned with his well-being. "Tell Mrs Fowler," he wrote to Fairfax in December 1908, "that I shall soon be well again; I don't want her to fret about me."

Much of my information about the Fowlers came from a niece and namesake, Eva Focke Sumner, an elderly widow living in Honolulu. Our correspondence began in the spring of 1979.

> I was most interested to hear you are writing a book about Frederic Manning as I knew him well. I lived with Alfred & Eva Fowler at 26 Gilbert Street during the first world war and had been over there every summer before that. I was in Paris studying music (piano & violin) when the war broke out and my parents wired to proceed to England as quickly as possible...
>
> Why don't you write me any questions you may have and I will be glad to answer them — if I can! I am now 81 years old so am getting forgetful of course but those dear people are very clear in my mind.

And questions I sent, dozens of them, in a stream of letters that brought prompt answers spilling over with information and enthusiasm. I had tapped into a delicious desire to reminisce.

> I hope these answers have helped you a bit. There is so much more I could say about Eva and Taffy. They are so very dear to me in my memories. Grandmother Fowler was so wonderful to her, never having seen her and Taffy only writing that she was Paul Neumann's daughter and very lovely to look at. No mention of whether she was black or white! And the Hawaiian Islands were in those days [1890] a rather remote and uncertain quality!

Having also known many of Manning's other friends, some quite well, Eva Sumner was able to provide identities where I had only names, or worse, mere initials. In addition, she sent me the few of Manning's letters that had survived the heat and wet of Honolulu, numerous photographs of the Fowlers — including two in which Eva Fowler is holding the Bush-baby that inspired Manning's poem — and several pages of transcriptions from a diary she had kept between 1914 and 1917.

	1915
July 2nd.	Daisy Meadow. Said goodbye to Sig.
July 3rd.	Mrs, Shakespeare and Mr, Yeats came down and I walked to Brasted station to meet them.
July 5th.	Read to Mr, Yeats for a while. He has nicknamed me "The Infant".
July 6th.	Uncle Taffy came home and says Sig is tired out and probably leaving on Saturday.
July 7th.	Mr, Yeats went home, of course forgetting to put his shoes on!
July 30th.	Fred met me at Edenham, Bourne. It is lovely here.
July 31st.	Went for a walk with Fred and Mr, Galton in the afternoon.
Aug. 1st.	Walked a little in the morning and went to church in the evening.
Aug. 2nd.	Fred and I came back to D. M. [Daisy Meadow] via London.

''Sig'', or Siggy as he was often called, was David Sigismund Don, an early beau of the diarist, and another youthful friend of Manning.* He, too, visited Edenham, and in the late 1920s would become the personal pilot to the Prince of Wales. Manning, like many shy and reserved people, evidently found it easy to establish rapport with the young, often the children of his adult friends. His letters and random comments indicate, moreover, that he often gave them freer access to himself than he did their parents. Eva Sumner managed to find only three of his letters, all written when Manning was almost 33 and she 16, and all willing to entrust important feelings to the recipient.

Edenham, Bourne, Lincs.
24. II. 1915

My dear Evchen:
...Don't be foolish: I loved what you wrote to me of Walter's [Rummel] cantata. You needn't think that you write ''nonsense'', when you write what you really think or feel about things; and if it is ''difficult to say what you mean'', you may at least give me credit for enough imagination to guess. But you don't appreciate me, which isn't unusual.

Sig has relapsed into his customary silence, as far as I am concerned, so I suppose he is in good health and spirits. When one lives alone in a wilderness, one is always thinking of his friends who are never thinking of him. At least that's my experience, and it forms a cynical commentary on all protestations of friendship. Would you believe it? I know half a dozen people who will love me with the utmost devotion for five minutes and then forget that I exist for weeks. ''One cannot keep Heights which the soul is competent to gain,'' and there is always bread and butter to be thought of even outside of Berlin. I'm the only man of leisure I know; everybody else is too busy about a thousand trifles, for the greater part of life, even to have time to think. And half of them are busy because they don't dare to think. The other half? Well, with them business is a bad habit.

Don't argue and say: "a habit, but not necessarily a bad habit." All habits are bad habits, a truth I'm never tired of telling people. Business is Business, you'll hear people say; but from what I have heard and seen of it, business is robbery. Oh, Eva, when you marry go away into the country where you can have a garden, and where your mind won't feed like a parasite on conversation and plays. A book isn't so atrophying to the mind, as one's imagination has to help the words. And never get busy, you only gather more and more momentum, until the speed makes you giddy. Well, if you think all this is lunacy, you may know that the Greek word for "a private gentleman", a man who didn't have any profession or business, was "idiotes", whence we get our word idiot. If a man doesn't live like a thousand other people he's odd and eccentric. You know that "Blessed are the peacemakers" and "Blessed are the poor in spirit" etc. But I add to 'em "Blessed are the lonely for they have created their own world."

This letter is like a good *toque* — made out of nothing. Much love to you all (if you have any time for it.)

yours in the odour of sanctity

Fred

Young people other than Eva and Siggy also found Manning to be a sensitive and caring friend. Rachel Rothenstein recalled to me how kind he was to her when visiting her father's house; and her brothers, John and Billy, each had his own reasons for liking and trusting their father's friend.

Manning's affectionate concern for young people differed from the concern of Galton who, despite his desire to assist the young, managed to keep his distance, sharing little of himself. Eva Sumner had one typically sermonising letter from Galton, written a few weeks after Manning had entered the army. It reveals a willingness to amuse, but is devoid of intimacy; indeed, the letter reads as if it were addressed to an anonymous person:

Nov. 10, 1915

My dear Eva,
Thank you for your note. I came back into a frozen house, and found the hall stove was giving no heat. Though the anthracite coal makes no soot, damp and dirt from the roof had lodged in the flue, and were baked into cement; and my stupid girl had not the sense to get it cleared at once, but waited and did nothing while the walls were drinking in cold. For several days I could not get my study up to 50°. However it is all right now, and the house has become genial.

I am expecting my new prints from the framer. The frieze will fit in exactly where I wanted it, without moving anything except the hat stand, which will do better in a different place.

Fred writes in good spirits. If he keeps well, the hard exercise will do him a lot of good.

The cat is well, but I don't think he can hunt as he used, so he is more [illegible] at dinner, and he looks very bored when he is out. It is a pity he won't learn to be moral, and then he could spent most of his time before my fire, but it is not safe to leave him in a room alone, and there is always a risk if he is in the house at all. His stupidity costs him a great many uncomfortable hours; but all stupidity has to be paid for by somebody, not always by the stupid person unfortunately

Galton looked for artistic and intellectual promise in youth; Manning searched for special charm and understood vulnerability. When he went to war and was surrounded by young men dying, he honoured them in the only way he could:

The Face

Out of the smoke of men's wrath,
The red mist of anger,
Suddenly,
As a wraith of sleep,
A boy's face, white and tense,

Convulsed with terror and hate,
The lips trembling...

Then a red smear, falling...
I thrust aside the cloud, as it were tangible,
Blinded with a mist of blood.
The face cometh again
As a wraith of sleep:
A boy's face delicate and blonde,
The very mask of God,
Broken.

Back in 1908, however, the war was still far away, and Manning was busy at the task of being a writer. To read his letters in the 18 months following the publication of *The Vigil of Brunhild* is to find him engulfed in projects: "Stheneboa", a dramatic poem; "Theseus and Hippolyta", a lyrical poem; "Judith", a narrative poem; "Man and Nature", apparently a long philosophical poem with a classical setting. That his poetry should find its bearings in antique myths and symbols was understandable. However much they had been used, they seemed to be forever renewable, perhaps especially to a poet who could jest about "seeking for a classical parallel" to the "constancy" of two white pigeons who had died together in a water-butt. Mockery has a way of freshening the vision. But with the exception of "Theseus and Hippolyta", none of these poems was to be finished. Increasingly Manning worked on the prose sketches that would become *Scenes and Portraits,* and his daily regimen, as he described it for Fairfax, seems disciplined, almost spartan:

> My day being taken up with a variety of work, all equally clamorous for immediate expression, I have been obliged to get up at dawn and take my exercise then. Yesterday I walked four miles in the rain before seven o'clock, and then had my bath and breakfast, after which I did not move from the table, except for lunch, until six o'clock; when I walked another three miles.

But other letters indicate that days when he walked seven miles and sat at his work almost without cease were rare. Along with accounts of his writing and reading, which in the summer of 1908 included a chapter of Tacitus every day,* there are reports of bodily breakdowns. In February 1908 he thinks his "maladies have left him for a time"; in May a "lame back" keeps him from writing much; in July a "hurt hand" leaves him scarcely able to hold a pen; in September "my stomach is rotten, my nerves and indigestion ditto"; in November "all my teeth ache, and I have been awake all night." All of these afflictions — and there were others — were described for Fairfax, and embroidered with whimsy:

> The text of this letter should be: "and God smote the Egyptians with a sore plague of flies". What myriads of them we have you could scarcely believe; and one has stung me in the eye so that I cannot see. . . For your own sake I am glad that you are not here, with a half-blind host, morbidly fretful and depressed, unable to read or write or even to talk intelligently. I could lie down quite cheerfully on the flat tombstone of John Pell: Gent. and of Mary, ye Wife of ye aforesaid John Pell, which is just outside the dining-room window, and wait for the parish to bury me.

No death wish here, but neither is the conceit without significance. Manning was an easy prey to injury and illness, and what someone else would brush aside as of no account he experienced as debilitating. His acute sensitivity to his body's vulnerability complicated and exaggerated his response to any kind of breakdown, which meant that the shock to his psyche from accident or disease was often prolonged and enervating. He was keenly aware of how "this stupid body of mine and all its clumsy apparatus get in the way of my own and other people's enjoyment of life"; he sensed, he could admit to Fairfax, that at times he was a "nuisance". But his letters, for all their insights and self-reproaches, suggest that his depressions were not exclusively the result of his body's betrayals and nature's assaults. In the autumn of 1908 he was under a good deal of pressure.

Brunhild had been only a modest critical success, and a less than modest commercial success if one counted only the disinterested purchasers. While Manning professed indifference to popularity, he could hardly expect to establish a reputation as a writer if he found no audience at all. A lot, therefore, was resting on the volume of prose sketches: "I shall be quite broken-hearted if it is not a success."

More troubling, perhaps, than the ordinary pressures of being a young writer was his situation at the vicarage, a situation that would have nurtured melancholy thoughts even in a more self-possessed personality. Put simply, it was a lonely existence. Galton was there to talk to, at least much of the time, but a middle-aged man lacking a penchant for intimacy could not provide the companionship that Fred Manning needed. Neither could the village lads he talked to during his walks or over a pint of ale at the Five Bells. They were friendly enough, but their lives and his were so utterly different that they had little to share. And his friends in London and Oxford and Scotland were of small use to him in Edenham, not even when he sat down to talk to them on paper: "The art of letter-writing, I suppose, is the art of being intimate, but letters to me always convey a sense of estranging distance, and I can only put out a few tentative hints as to what I mean." Like the kept youth of mythology, Hylas, the subject of one of his early poems, Manning was sometimes overwhelmed by the longing for contact:

> A desire to mix with man
> To gather in the vintage, tread the grapes
> With laughing, naked, boys in the great press...

Edenham was a pleasant village on an April morning, with "the garden full of daffodils and bullfinches, and the fields of sheep and lambs...as delightful as children, playing all manner of games, and having hurdle races over the troughs", or in high summer, "the garden full of nightingales" which "babble all night", and Fairfax and himself lying under the mulberry tree smoking cigarettes in total "abandonment to the moment". It was at those times that he could advise friends like Eva Sumner to "go away into the country". But more often Edenham was a damp grey cloister of a place, and the young writer would be lying in bed, nursing some illness and thinking of his friends going happily about their affairs, too busy to be thinking of him. Or he might be suffering a hangover, for even in his early years in England he was drinking. How serious the problem was is difficult to say, but it was serious enough for Galton to go to the Five Bells and ask the publican to limit the amount he served to Manning. This was told me by Rose Walpole, who had been a day girl at the vicarage early in Galton's tenure. In her 90th year when I talked to her, she had forgotten more than she could remember, but her mind was clear about the memories that remained. When I asked her at the beginning of the interview to tell me what first came into her mind when I mentioned Fred Manning, she said at once, "He drank too much." Of course, she went on to say, many of the villagers in those days were heavy drinkers, but Manning — whose drinking was "common knowledge" in the village — was less able to hold his alcohol. Was his drinking chronic, kept under some control by his living with Galton, or was it intermittent as Chick Woolmer remembered it, binges brought on, perhaps, by specific pressures? I have no evidence to settle the question, and the pattern may well have changed over the years. More certain, however, is the likelihood that his instinct for privacy was reinforced by the need to hide from his friends and the world what he (and Galton) did not want them to know.* Manning was a shy and private person, but shyness can be intensified by guilt, and privacy used to avoid discovery. And living in a "hermitage", one is well screened.

When I went to Edenham in 1977 I came upon another memory. A Mrs Hill, who had also been a day girl at the vicarage sometime before World War I, reported that Galton "would not let me go into Mr. Manning's room alone. He used to draw. Rather rude some of them were." The black notebook later found in Sydney verified that Manning sometimes did make sketches of semi-naked women. There is nothing unusual in that, and nothing strange in Galton's effort at propriety. Nor should we deny Manning his lust, disciplined, even repressed, as it must have been while he lived at the vicarage — which Eva Fowler once called the "monastère". Was there, though, never a courtship during these years? Perhaps, but for the most part Manning's eroticism was apparently channelled into his poetry:

> Theseus followed his prey
> As a lean hound follows the fleet
> Quarry: the dusty way
> Smoked with the speed of his feet.
> She was swift; but he burned in the chace:
> He was flame, he was sandalled with fire,
> Hungering after her face,
> With a fury, a lust, a desire,
> As a hound that whines for the blood
> Of the hart flying winged with fear;
> And she yearned, and she longed for the wood,
> Seeming far from her still, though near,
> And she strained, and she panted, and pressed,
> With her head flung backward for breath,
> And the quick sobs shaking her breast,
> Agonised, now, as by death,
> Fearing utterly, fighting with fate,
> Stumbling. And swifter behind,
> With a love made hot by his hate,
> Strained he pursuing. The wind,
> Lifted, and played with the fold
> Of her chlamys; and showed made bare
> The swift limbs shining, as gold
> From sunlight, and streamed through her hair
> As wind in a cresset of fire,
> As tresses of flame in the night,
> While she fled, desired, from desire,
> Till the brakes hid the flame from his sight.

Throughout his life Manning seems to have been a man who loved from afar, if not entirely in his head. There are no good proofs of a romantic attachment to a woman. The evidence in the case of Dorothy Shakespear is too slight to alter this view; perhaps, indeed, she was treated as a sister because of Manning's affection for her mother. When he speaks of women in the abstract he alternates between amused condescension ("Ce n'est pas necessaire qu'une femme aurait de l'intelligence, puisque elle est très silencieuse") and the cynically respectful ("Women never give their true reasons for doing anything; they have too much practical wisdom"). Such attitudinising may be no more than a cultural reflex, but in Manning it seems to have been part of a lifelong ambivalence: on the one hand, he had an overwhelming trust in (and attraction to) mothering figures, and on the other, a great hesitation and shyness about women as potential romantic partners. Bourne, in *The Middle Parts of Fortune,* speaks of women as a "mystery", and tells us that he "always treated" them with "a little air of ceremony". Manning never married nor, apparently, did he even come close. He may have contemplated marriage to one of his older spinster friends, a woman by the name of Polly Barry whom he met in Ireland in 1918, but again the evidence is too slight — merely a rumour — to warrant more than a suspicion. Comments about love and marriage in his letters never refer to a specific person, and their brevity together with their whimsical tone protect their author against speculation. If not uninterested, he was at least extremely cautious. In a letter to Rothenstein in 1918 he claimed that marriage had always seemed a "desperate adventure, even for the young", and implied that now, at age 36, it would go beyond "the boundaries of courage". To another friend a few years later he lamented, "I'm an unlucky man: when I think of the innumerable young women who have broken my heart it makes me cautious." Who these "innumerable young women" were is a mystery, perhaps because he pined after them in silence. A romance requires two parties and normally leaves whispers if not stories; a broken heart such as the one Manning describes can be a solitary matter.

Which raises the question frequently asked when I mentioned to people that Manning and Galton lived together: Was there a homosexual bond?* Almost certainly not. Their domestic arrangement was originally prompted by mutual respect and economic considerations. In time, deep dependencies developed, as one might expect between two people who live under the same roof for many years and share mutual tastes, common friends, and similar values. And naturally their attachment would have been further solidified by those two powerful forces: convenience and inertia. But though their household could be compared in some respects to other well-known intellectual cum domestic partnerships of the era — Ricketts and Shannon come to mind — there is no evidence of the libidinous in the relationship between Galton and Manning. Of course, proving a negative, especially one involving sexual activity, is next to impossible, but the absence of any contemporary gossip together with the backgrounds and personalities of both men strongly urges the conclusion that theirs was a friendship solely of the mind and spirit.

And even within those realms it was not complete by any means. Galton probably cared as much for Manning as he did for anyone, with the exception of his grandmother. But despite his array of friends and correspondents, Galton was a man who lived very much to himself, possesssing a limited insight into people and an even more limited sympathy for their dilemmas. Close as he felt himself to Manning, how well did he understand his protégé's anxieties? A more primary question would be — how much did he *care* to understand? My guess is that on neither question would Galton do very well; but then according to his lights, why should he? He was Manning's mentor, not his confessor or his mother. Besides, Galton had many other tasks to perform at Edenham besides watching out for Manning. There were his pastoral duties; his own writings, which included new books in 1905 (*The Appeal of the Church of England*) and 1907 (*Church and State in France 1300–1907*) as well as articles and reviews for a variety of periodicals; his extensive correspondence, in which the letters often go on for a half-dozen pages (Lionel Johnson used to complain about the "whole folios, on great yellow paper" he was expected to answer); and his reading, perhaps the most time-consuming occupation of all. Days would go by when the two men hardly saw each other, and in later years they often did not take their meals together. The vicarage was certainly spacious enough to accommodate two separate existences, so that lives which never ceased to be intertwined might for long periods seldom cross.

Guests, though, were shared, and over the years many came. One was Albert Houtin, a French priest who visited Edenham in October of 1907 while in England for a conference. Houtin was a principal figure in Modernism, a largely clerical movement among Catholics, particularly in France, who believed that the dogmas and traditions of the church should be subjected to scholarly and rational scrutiny. He and Galton had begun to correspond earlier in the year when Galton, having read some of the Frenchman's books, sent him a few of his own, notably his "little apologia", *Rome and Romanising* (1900). Houtin's visit to Edenham was a singular success. He found Galton "un homme maigre, sec, alerte, de manières très distinguées, d'un esprit extrêmement cultivé", and the two had much to share besides their disdain for "Vaticanism". Houtin was also greatly impressed with Manning, who showed him *Brunhild* in an "incomplete form", and a correspondence started up between them that would continue until Houtin's death in 1926. For Manning, Houtin was less important as a figure of religious controversy than as a kind and learned Frenchman who took a keen interest in his work and was always ready to perform a favour. The first of many such favours was his willingness in June of 1908 to read and criticise in draft form one of the sketches Manning was working on, and to allow its author to dedicate it to him.* The request was granted, improvements suggested, and the opinion born that Manning was a writer whose talent and erudition promised comparison with Walter

Pater.* That was not only Houtin's view but the judgement of a number of critics when *Scenes and Portraits* appeared in April of 1909.

Scenes and Portraits made Frederic Manning's reputation, and for 20 years it would be the book people associated with his name. Virtually overnight he was transformed from a poet who composed "interesting" verse into "undoubtedly a new force in English letters". This opinion, like the first, came from the pen of Henry Newbolt, who once again had been asked by John Murray to read Manning's work. The critics agreed with Newbolt. "Caviar", one of them respectfully labelled sketches rich in learning, charming in their ironies, and almost seamless in their construction and style. Such praise drew readers, and persuaded John Murray to consider publishing a volume of Manning's poems, "though, under ordinary circumstances, we do not care to bring out poetry." Standard practices, which allowed for a book-length poem, had to be compromised to hold on to an "exceptional" author, especially as it was bruited about that other publishers were "very keen to get him". Although Manning's books were never likely to produce the earnings of a Byron, from whom the house of Murray had reaped huge profits, they at least seemed certain to shed glory on the firm. Things did not turn out so, though in 1909 it was taken for granted that a remarkable performance like *Scenes and Portraits* promised many encores.

Even today the book, composed of six sketches ranging in length from 40 to 60 pages, and in time from ancient Babylonia to the early twentieth century, is impressive. The reader would not guess its author to have been only in his middle twenties, so controlled and knowing, so full of *sagesse*, are the skilfully wrought sketches. Each is set at a historical moment when traditional beliefs are under challenge and each pivots on a colloquy involving actual or archetypal historical figures. Talk is the essence of these "studies", as Manning himself called them. It fashions their structure, their meaning and, in most instances, whatever drama there might be. Three of the sketches have virtually no narrative impulse: "At the House of Euripides", a symposium in which Socrates, Euripides, and Protagoras consider whether and how the Gods exist; "At San Cascino", a rambling political conversation between Machiavelli and Thomas Cromwell which uses Dante as a text and is subtly prophetic of later events at the court of Henry VIII; and "The Paradise of the Disillusioned", in which the ironical sceptic Ernest Renan and Pope Leo XIII meet in one of the "many paradises" after the Pope's death (1903), and find that their views are more congenial than their earthly postures suggested.

The other three sketches resemble conventional short stories, though even in them conversation provides the focus. "The Friend of Paul" portrays an ageing Roman of Epicurean sympathies who, upon hearing of the death of Seneca, recalls some early encounters with Paul. St Francis is the subject of "The Jesters of the Lord", in which we see how miracles arise from coincidences and how permission for a new religious order is extracted from a busy pope. And, finally, the most ingenious tale, "The King of Uruk", describes how a king who senses the vanity of all accomplishments plays a crucial role in formulating the story of Adam and Eve. In 1930 E. M. Forster called it "perhaps...the most exquisite short story of the century". Others might demur at the superlative, but the matter and language of "The King of Uruk" — as with several of the other pieces — are shaped with rare precision and delicacy. Another admirer of the story, Ezra Pound, claimed nine years after he read it that he could "quote from memory" its opening paragraphs.

The King of Uruk

> When Merodach, the King of Uruk, sate down to his meals, he made his enemies his footstool; for beneath his table he kept an hundred kings, with their thumbs and great toes cut off, as living witnesses of his power and clemency. When the crumbs fell from the table of Merodach, the kings would feed themselves with two fingers; and when Merodach observed how painful and

> difficult the operation was, he praised God for having given thumbs to man.
>
> "It is by the absence of thumbs," he said, "that we are enabled to discern their use. We invariably learn the importance of what we lack. If we remove the eyes from a man we deprive him of sight; and consequently we learn that sight is the function of the eyes."
>
> Thus spake Merodach, for he had a scientific mind, and was curious of God's handiwork; and, when he had finished speaking, the courtiers applauded him.

The recurrent theme of these stories is that religion, like any other ideology, is an expression of subjective ideas. Man seeks and defines his God(s) and his ideals as they suit his changing needs, while whatever forces lie beyond our ken exist, as Socrates was once told by a prophetess, "in a way which is peculiar to themselves". It is a motif designed for irony, and Manning has a fine time presenting his little comedies, several of whose smiling, sceptical principals seem like both examples for and copies of their creator's wit. The tragic mode is intentionally avoided, though sorrow and death are not absent from the situations described. Nor is the fun intended to leave religion in ruins. Faith and doubt are as old as man, and as answers to an instinctive, endless quest, both can be admired. In Manning's preface he bluntly laid down his principles, ending with an apposite simile.

> There are in reality only two religions on this little planet, and they perhaps begin and end with man. They are: the religion of the humble folk, whose life is a daily communion with natural forces, and a bending to them; and the religion of men like Protagoras, Lucretius, and Montaigne, a religion of doubt, of tolerance, of agnosticism. Between these two poles is nothing but a dreary waste of formalism, Pharisaism, "perplexed subtleties about Instants, Formalities, Quiddities, and Relations", all that bewildering of brains which comes from being shut up in a narrow system, like an invalid in a poisoned and stifling room.

Reviewers for several religious papers naturally fell upon these sentences as dangerous heresy. But the portraits of Paul and St Francis were drawn with respect and, in the case of the latter, with great affection.* Belief may be founded on illusion, but if so it is an illusion that comforts man and possibly civilises him. Manning recognised his own need to "trust something", as he told Fairfax in the same month as the book was published, "whether in ourselves or beyond ourselves I do not know — which seems to tell us that we are all one, that in spite of all revolt on our parts, we do what we were sent here to do, and that we are not wasted." These midnight thoughts, written on hearing of the death of Eva Fowler's youngest sister, Lillie, formed part of the personal "creed" which inspired, I suspect, the sympathy that is so interwoven with the irony of this book.

Several gifts are required to write dialogue in the mode of Manning's choice: a sense of history, a skill in dialectic, and a very good ear. Characters have to sound like their writings (or their reputations) but they ought not to speak like quoted texts. At times Manning failed and there is no life or rhythm to the conversations; more often he succceeds. Here is Serenus, the Roman Epicurean, recalling his first contact with Paul:

> He ceased, drew the curtain to again, and came towards me. Through his incredible ugliness there shone a majesty of power, fascinating, enchanting, wooing me with its strength and flame-like intensity. His hands were cold from the ledge of the window, and as they took mine a thrill ran through me. The other men looked at us quietly, as if they were conscious of some crisis, and of some antagonism between us. Paul looked at the manuscript upon my knees, and smiled.
>
> "What are my words to you?" he asked.
>
> "I have also thought of these things," I answered him.
>
> "Yes; it is not the thinking of them that is strange, but what do they mean to you? What does our law mean to you? What does our mystery mean to you?

> Nothing. You are given over to vain imaginations, the conceits of the mind. You have no humility, no faith. Your great possessions have turned your mind. Until the blow fell upon you, you had imagined that you were secure through life. You have put your trust in perishable things, and they have fallen through your fingers like water, like dry sand. What have you left sacred in the world? Your wisdom has made a desert about you, a desert where there is no God. What have you to hope?''
>
> It was as if he mocked me, pitied me, understood me. He made me cold toward him; and at the same time my sorrow flooded me.
>
> ''What is my trouble to you? I can bear it alone,'' I said harshly. ''The things which you have written I have read in our own philosophers.''
>
> ''You have found nothing else in me, which was not in them?''
>
> ''Nothing.''
>
> A gloom spread over his face, the light which had illuminated it died out, leaving only the smouldering fires of his eyes, which burned dimly. He dropped my hands. The others turned away their eyes and shifted uneasily.

Easy as it might seem to transform Paul's epistles or for that matter Machiavelli's advice into dialogue, Manning did not assemble his dialogues with scissors and paste. The people and attitudes he recreated were thoroughly familiar to him through substantial study. Tone and texture, therefore, are usually convincing, even when a character had to be largely invented:

> Adam broke in upon my thoughts as a prophecy, a promise. He was in his first manhood, almost still a boy, and represented, in consequence, an earlier stage of evolution. He seemed, in fact, half child, and half animal. He had the stature of a man; he was well-built, muscular, giving one the impression of an immense but

> graceful strength, of easy movements. His features were handsome, but unlike those usual in our country; the nose was a little rapacious, the mouth cruel, but his eyes were full of dreams. It was the face of one who looks towards distant horizons, having the immense calm of the desert, and full of sleeping energy. Youth softened it, and lent it a delicate charm; but in age it will be terrible. And suddenly I heard a sullen voice saying: "This is my garden."

So abrupt and yet so logical are Adam's words, when one views him as a wandering adolescent, distrustful of visitors to his "pleasant valley". But though Manning's characters speak as we imagine they could have, they also talk as he wished them to. Verisimilitude, the obligation of the artist, mattered less than right opinion, the object of the philosopher. Here Bagoas, the uninvited guest to Adam's garden, explains to the King of Uruk his estimate of the value of the Epic of Gilgamesh:

> "I deny," he said, "that it has any truth as an historical document. It is valuable, historically, as an instance of the narrow limits of human knowledge in the age which produced it. That is all its value to the historian. Its value to the theologian is different. He finds in it the first concrete expression of man's relation to God, as he understands it. The truth may be veiled in a mist of fable and metaphor, but he feels it to be there. At the same time, he gives it an extended sense, and interprets it in a larger spirit than that in which it was originally interpreted. It means to us at once something more and something less than it did to the ancient world; for religion is not a definite revelation of an eternal truth, but the contemplation of the unknown from the sum of man's experience. It is consequently susceptible of infinite developments and extension, it reacts to every new discovery of science; and its chief glory is that it is part of man's daily life."

In the Preface, Manning named Renan as the "principal

influence'' on the book, and it may look as if he thought to show his respect for Renan by writing a part for the estimable savant in the last study — except that debts of influence are never repayable and usually, as Manning himself understood, are impossible even to ''gauge'' to their ''full extent''. Renan's humane scepticism, his cleansing irony, his love for the play of ideas, his lucid and glowing style, all appealed to Manning because they resembled qualities and tastes he sensed and cultivated in himself. He, too, wished to write only ''pour des lecteurs intelligents, et clairs''. Renan was a kindred spirit, a cherished and comfortable *maître*, whose values were admired and absorbed, whose works were recommended to friends, whose ideas and strategies were sometimes borrowed, but whose judgements had, nevertheless, sometimes to be challenged. ''I do not think that Renan's verdicts have influenced my treatment of St Paul. Renan has a natural prejudice against 'ce laid petit Juif'.'' No self-respecting writer wishes to be thought an epigone, nor, perhaps, even a disciple.

Other influences included Pater, whose attempts at historical portraiture Manning knew well, and the early editions of whose works he recommended to Murray as a ''desirable'' model of book design for *Scenes*; W. S. Landor, whom Manning briefly thought of writing about when he was finished with *Scenes*; Plato, to whom Manning admitted a specific theft in his preface; and Anatole France, some of whose works were so admired by the young writer as to be worthy of imitation.* The list could be extended — in many ways *Scenes and Portraits* is a book of echoes — but these were the masters of the philosophical dialogue/study, that respected if rarified tradition which Manning sought to extend. And naturally there was Galton, to whom was dedicated ''The King of Uruk'', and who at the end of the Preface is thanked for ''his example and conversation''. Those simple words acknowledge an immense debt, compounded in this instance by Galton's careful reading of all the sketches while they were in manuscript, particularly the dialogue, ''At San Cascino'', that drew upon his own early scholarship. And we may also assume that Manning's views on the evolutionary character of religious belief had been reinforced by hearing Galton often dilate on the theme, "God speaks not only at sundry times, but in divers manners." But authors have other than intellectual debts. Manning expressed his on the book's dedication page: "Matri Carissimae."

Among the Manning papers in the Mitchell Library is a scrapbook of several dozen reviews of *Scenes and Portraits*, most from English newspapers and periodicals, and clipped for the author by an agency. Yellowing, creased, some of them torn, they are tangible evidence of the instant respect the book earned, and of the efforts — made once again by the interested parties — to discover Fred Manning's "audience". As part of the campaign Murray had eventually persuaded G. P. Putnam to distribute 250 copies of the book in America. But despite favourable reviews in Boston and Philadelphia, transatlantic readers ignored it. A year later Putnam still had 206 copies on hand, prompting their London representative to report plaintively to Murray, "Is not that awful? I don't know that there is anything more to be said, except that the book is a good one. I shall always maintain that." Copies were also dispatched to Australia, and sympathetic reviewers in Sydney and Melbourne made much of what mattered little to the native son.

> This book was placed in my hands as the work of a Sydney man, Mr Frederic Manning, the son of Sir William Manning, a young man we used to be fairly familiar with in Sydney. . . I read that book from cover to cover in one day and concluded either that Frederic Manning did not write it, or, that there had arisen in Europe a great Australian, whose name would become as familiar as household words in all the reading world, some day.

Amidst the chorus of praise there were occasional doubters. One or two of the pieces were "obscure", the irony was "too abundant", the book was "a little too literary" and "twenty-five years out of date''. Such chidings did not bother an author now celebrated by *The Times,* the *Edinburgh Review,* and the *Mercure de France.*

Nor did they bother Galton. The ''competent reviewers'' were all treating Fred ''as a classic'', and that was all that counted. A friend of Galton's, Alfred Fawkes, had been particularly kind in his notice for the *Edinburgh Review*: ''Since Mr Arnold, there has been no such ironist in this country.'' Had Galton thought of his protégé bending so mighty a bow? Why not? Had Arnold received such praise by the time he was 27? In Galton the hard flame of pride and ambition was burning brightly, and already, as the first reviews were coming in, he had sent off a copy of the book to a French publisher urging its translation. On the basis of sales, however, a translation would not have been warranted: in three months time only 500 copies of 1000 printed had been sold or given away. But Galton was not of course thinking of demand in terms of quantity, and neither was Manning. ''My aim in writing,'' he told his publisher, ''is not to supply ephemeral literature to the circulating libraries.''

Henry Newbolt had already hummed the same tune in his reader's report when he predicted that the audience for the book would be limited to that ''dwindling class who are rich enough to have education and leisure, but not rich enough to spend their time in motor cars.'' Fairfax had been thinking of the same people two years before when he had suggested Oxford as being the natural audience for *Brunhild.* Although the prose book sold distinctly better than the poem, there were no signs that Manning's art would ever appeal to an audience much larger than a coterie of friends, critics, and scholars. These, luckily for serious authors, are the people who keep books and reputations alive by talking about them. Unsold authors may fret and suffer; but if they are not discussed, they vanish. In the summer of 1909, Manning was in no danger of that fate. He was an author read, talked about, and flattered, one asked to lunch by important figures and invited to dine with London literary societies. The photograph of him that appeared beside one of the reviews of his book shows him smartly dressed in a three-piece suit with wing collar, his hair short and carefully parted, his face very serious — a solemn missionary of the word, like so many other Edwardian writers. He thought the photo "rather good", but the review "lamentable", especially the biographical section where "they have taken two years off my age. I am still young enough to feel that as a slight." Soon enough he would feel differently.

Finishing the book had also brought about a change in spirit.* He now felt himself to be in "rude health", and was no longer "irritated and depressed." Edenham remained an isolated spot, which Fairfax was regularly implored to visit; letters were still a "medium" which had "many disadvantages". But the strain of prolonged, concentrated work was behind him, and the days, as he told Fairfax at the end of May, were now largely taken up with "getting reviews and letters, and answering letters, and arranging about going to Town in three weeks". This was to be no ordinary trip to London. A letter had recently arrived saying that his father and younger brother Charlie were on their way to England. Manning was pleased, but less than he might have been: "I am very disappointed that my mother is not coming with them." Nonetheless, having to be in London for an extended period would give him a chance to see friends, and perhaps to talk with Murray about a novel then gestating in his mind: "a romantic, fantastic, quasi-historical long story about a French Cardinal, an abbé, and a boy who go to the Court of Rome in the seventeenth century." One of the reviewers of *Scenes* had referred to the sketches as "condensed historical novel[s] of the highest type". Manning now planned to stretch his reach, confident of his choices and focus as an artist. However ambivalent he felt about his situation at Edenham, he had no doubts — especially after the critical enthusiasm for *Scenes* — about the kind of books he should be writing. He experienced neither any urgency nor temptation to find subjects in his own world and, given the influences working upon him, he could hardly have been expected to.

It had been two years since he had seen his family — his parents and Beatrix had visited England in the spring of 1907 — and in that time he had become a respected author. Of no apparent concern to him or his parents was a story recently spread around Sydney by "an ecclesiastic" that *Brunhild* was to be put on the Index and that William Patrick, "ashamed of his heretical son", had bought up all the copies in the city. If in some way the poem had embarrassed his parents, then *Scenes and Portraits* would have undone them. But there is no evidence of any such embarrassment. And the scrapbook of reviews in the Mitchell Library — some of which would have been shown to his father when they met in London, others of which would have been sent to Sydney later — surely contributed to the parental feelings that are reported. "I met his father," Norman Lindsay wrote to Fairfax in September 1910, "and he seemed proud enough for his son — a rare instance in these radical days." So, we can be sure, was his mother. And it probably was of her — given his disappointment at her not coming — as well as of the soon to be seen father and brother that Fred Manning was thinking as the train carrying him to London in June 1909 sped across the flat Cambridgeshire country. Or, like any traveller, his mind may have been in a book, caught happily in a world of someone else's making.

Hard Passages

Chapter Four

In October of 1909 a young American poet living in London wrote to his mother in Philadelphia about his travel plans.

> Tomorrow I go up to Lincolnshire to stay...with Manning & Arthur Galton. Galton is an old friend of Matthew Arnold, & has known about everyone since the flood. Both Manning & Galton will be useful in discussing the opening chapter of the book, as they probably know their Latin literature much better than I do.

It was a profitable visit for Manning as well, for during it he wrote one of his finest poems, "Persephone", which appeared in the December issue of the *English Review*.

> Yea, she hath passed hereby, and blessed the sheaves,
> And the great garths, and stacks, and quiet farms
> And all the tawny, and the crimson, leaves.
> Yea, she hath passed, with poppies in her arms,
> Under the star of dusk, through stealing mist,
> And blessed the earth, and gone, while no man wist.
>
> With slow, reluctant feet, and weary eyes,
> And eye-lids heavy with the coming sleep,
> With small breasts lifted up in stress of sighs,
> She passed, as shadows pass, among the sheep;
> While the earth dreamed, and only I was ware
> Of that faint fragrance blown from her soft hair.
>
> The land lay steeped in peace of silent dreams;
> There was no sound amid the sacred boughs,
> Nor any mournful music in her streams:

Only I saw the shadow on her brows,
Only I knew her for the yearly slain,
And wept; and weep until she come again.

The January 1910 issue carried a reply by the American poet.

Be sped, my Canzon, through the bitter air!
To him who speaketh words as fair as theirs,
Say that I also know the 'Yearly Slain'.

Since the days when shepherds played their pipes in competition on Attic hillsides, poets have been answering each other in verse. Between these two the dialogue took a variety of forms, and was to be rich, witty, long, and acrimonious. So were many of the friendships of Ezra Pound.*

They had met in January 1909, these expatriates from "half-savage" lands "out of date", and immediately found value in each other's work. Pound liked *Brunhild* "quite much", and thinking to do its author some good wrote a notice of it for an American magazine. "I feel sure that I shall get nothing but thanks from such of you as through my measured praise are led to reading him." Caution was dispelled when he recommended the "quite beautiful" "Persephone" to Ford Madox Ford, the editor of the newly formed *English Review,* as it had been in his response to *Scenes and Portraits*. In a letter to his mother he described the volume as "a stupendous work", conclusive proof that its author "realy [*sic*] writes". For his part, Manning quickly discerned Pound's talent, and having the wider contacts Pound was seeking in his first months in London, he did what he could to help him. He introduced him to Laurence Binyon, and sent a copy of Pound's *A Quinzane for this Yule*, a 28-page pamphlet of poems and prose, to the influential Newbolt, hoping that he would like the poems "as much as I do". Although Manning had some reservations — "I wish Pound were not fond of these irregular cadences. . . the effect would be greater if used in blank verse" — from the first he held the young American's poetry in high esteem.

Each also discovered in the other a useful fund of learning. While Pound profited from Manning's (and Galton's) knowledge of the classics, Manning owed to his new friend an increasingly appreciative awareness of French troubadour poets. Then too they shared a ready and sardonic wit which they enjoyed directing at those contemporaries whom they judged less gifted than themselves. Pound wrote to his mother in March of 1910 that "we are the generation, or at least the only significant writers under thirty." Often he and Manning turned their sarcasm on one another, scribbling parodies of each other's work, and poems lampooning each other's "frailties & vanities". One of Manning's parodies, "The Ballad of the Goodly Hair", is a fine spoof of Pound's "Ballad of the Goodly Fere". The opening stanza will suggest why Pound, who once called parody the "best criticism", always spoke of it with admiring delight:

> Ha' we lost the goodliest hair o' all
> For a barber upon the spree?
> Who would ha' thought that a pint too much
> Would mean such a lot to me!

More than 50 years after this was written, Pound slipped (consciously?) the title of another of his friend's parodies, "Chocolate creams, who has forgotten them?" into the brief Preface he wrote for a book of his own early poems.* By then the reference was as lost to readers as was Manning himself.

Alongside these amusing thrusts there were frequent disputes, even bitter quarrels, for on "most matters" they disagreed. From the beginning Pound's sneers at Milton offended Manning, and when they tired of that disagreement they argued over the relative merits of individual troubadours, over the language to be used in translating medieval verse, over the "reality" of Greek prosody, over the value of Remy de Gourmont's philosophy — and so on. Given each man's dedication to the craft of letters and well-tempered sense of his own value, explosive disagreements were inevitable. Friends hearing their quarrels were shocked by some of the exchanges, for both men had the claws and the will to reach the other's *amour propre*. Though Manning had little of Pound's hair-trigger aggressiveness, when provoked — and Pound's "conceit" regularly provoked him — he could flick derision and scorn with expert aim. "He [Pound] is not as other men are. He has seen the Beatific Vision, which is an extenuating circumstance." As for Pound's manner, anyone familiar with his work — and his daughter's portrait of him when angry ("It seemed as though he were visibly fighting a wasp nest in his brain") — will easily understand how caustic he could be in argument. Yet the next day or the next week the wounds would close and the two men would resume their discourse, as sure of each other's worth as they were alive to each other's shortcomings, and as easy with each other's person as two tightly strung temperaments can be. "In fact," Pound wrote home in March of 1910 after an evening at the Fowlers where apparently he and Manning had argued once more, "our friendship is as firmly grounded as could possibly be desired."

When Pound visited Edenham in October 1909 he found his friend busy with "The Gilded Coach". "I am moving about like Gulliver in a Lilliputian world of my own creating. It is spread out on the table as I write, and is populated by a host of enchanting little people in seventeenth century costume." In time, he would find his little people a stubborn and unmanageable lot, as had Gulliver, but for now he was pleased with their company. There was Jean-Marie-Adhémar, Archbishop of Velay, the hero of the romance — if one can designate as a hero an ageing sceptic who loves his ease and has gained at the age of 69 an undeserved reputation for saintliness; Madame de Sainte-Claire, the Archbishop's niece who, taking advantage of her uncle's indolence, has for 18 years managed his life and her own affairs with an all too obvious skill; the Abbé Bigne, Velay's chaplain, who has an eye for beauty, a taste for books of a decidedly unreligious character, and a passion for piquet; and Louis XIV, portrayed here as a man of many graces and even more calculations who, wishing to exploit the Archbishop's reputation, pressures the reluctant cleric to undertake a secret mission to Rome.

> "The mere fact that you stand aloof from all parties, that you are a mediating influence, will give more than usual weight to your opinion; and the Holy See is bound to take into consideration the great reverence in which you are held by my people, more particularly by those to whom questions concerning dogma are of secondary importance, if not entirely negligible. There is the advantage of your position: you will be able to command more respect than our unaccredited agents; and, on the other hand, your action will not be binding upon us as any action through the usual diplomatic channels would be. We are confident that your mission will have valuable results, and that you will be able to convince the Holy See as to the direction in which their true interests lie. At Rome the truth is too often obscured by the blind prejudice of rival factions."
>
> "At Rome, Sire," said the Archbishop, simply, "there is never any question of truth, but only of authority."
>
> The King rose from his chair.
>
> "I am partly of your mind, Monsieur," he said, as the Archbishop stooped over his hand. "M. de Lionne will discuss the business with you now."

How this mission was to develop we shall never know. All that remains of years of effort is a 100-page typescript now resting in the Mitchell Library in Sydney.

In the autumn of 1977 I sent a copy of the typescript of "The Gilded Coach" to St Martin's Press in New York. The president, Tom McCormack, had expressed an interest in seeing it and feeling myself to be Manning's posthumous agent as well as his biographer, I was hoping he might publish it. Too short to be a book by itself, the fragment could be published, I thought, with some of Manning's other writings and possibly a selection of his letters. I reasoned that if *The Middle Parts of Fortune* sold at all well for St Martin's Press, the publisher might be happy to exploit the renewed interest in Manning, and that this in turn would create an audience for a biography. My fantasy was shortlived.

> The script does have its own special qualities but my judgment is that there isn't anything that we can do with it. The style is interesting but a bit of a throwback, displaying a kind of Watteau-like prettiness, which in the event is probably not inappropriate — but it's certainly not the Frederic Manning that we currently know.

As I read the letter I smiled at what McCormack's reaction would have been had I sent instead *Scenes and Portraits.* But he was right: the Manning of the war novel spoke in a different voice. He did so not because he had become a different person, but because he had a different purpose and was using different materials, the materials of actual experience.

When Manning lived at Edenham before the war he wrote from books for bookish readers. The past — real and mythical — provided the settings, the textures, and often the inspiration for his writing, as they did for many of his contemporaries. Of course inspiration might also be found in the matter and moods of his own life, but the historical mode was sanctioned by a rich literary tradition, one to which he had been carefully bred and to which he felt himself a legitimate heir. The habit of turning to other times and persons also nicely suited a diffident, withdrawn personality, disinclined to reveal himself. Signs that the future of prose and poetry might lie elsewhere were ignored or scorned, as well they might be, for a tradition still capable of inspiring fine work, and some of whose greatest exponents were barely cold in their tombs, was not to be lightly abandoned — and certainly not by a young writer watched over by a true believer in that tradition. Indeed, it is only a slight exaggeration to say that *Brunhild, Scenes and Portraits*, and "The Gilded Coach" were all

Galton books. Not that the older man could have written any of them, nor that he took any credit, but they were all written with his approval, support, criticism, discipline and, not least, his "conversation", which quite possibly implies a role in their conception. "Quand on étudiera le génie de Manning," Albert Houtin later wrote, "on y trouvera Galton. Il lui donne toute."

The alternative creative sources open to Manning were his memories of Australia and the life around him at Edenham. The former was inconceivable; the latter marginally useful. While he was sensitive to the patterns of rural existence and fitted its sounds and colours into many of his lyrics, he did not look upon the village people and events as anything more than a source of amusing gossip to fill up his letters to Fairfax. The little comedies that he reported, as well as the little tragedies that occurred but went unreported, did not have sufficient resonance — at least not until *Her Privates We* had become a great success. Then he began thinking about a novel centring on village life, a novel that he thought might "shock" people with its realism quite as much as had the war novel. No trace of the work remains; no word of it may have been written; it may have only been a passing fancy. But in 1932, with Galton long since dead, poems about the Middle Ages becoming musty even to their authors, and pride in the handling of his own memories naturally leading through to ambition, Manning sensed that his future might depend on materials once shunned.

Ezra Pound's letters home during his early years in London reveal, among other things, how he survived so that he might create. It is a story of small economies and careful strategies, not the least of which was knowing when and how to press for infusions of cash from home. Bizarre though his later economic theories may have been, from the beginning Pound knew how to make ends meet, and more. Whether Manning was similarly adept is difficult to know, since there is little evidence of his getting and spending. One fact, though, is certain: from the time he settled in England in 1904 he received a regular allowance from his family. How generous, the record does not indicate. Living at the vicarage would have required only a modest income, somewhat more than would have been needed had he gone on living at home in Sydney, but probably less than if he had attended New College. He would have paid no rent, while the cost of food, fuel, and servants (all presumably shared with Galton) would have been low. In 1904 a pound of butter or a dozen eggs could be had in Bourne for a shilling. Clothing, travel, books, and incidentals could have added up to a considerable figure, but the evidence of Manning's tastes and activities suggests otherwise. His wardrobe was of high quality but small, he stayed with friends (or family) on his trips to London, and he could use Galton's library as his own. In all, I would guess that at least during his first years in England Manning required £150–£200 a year, most, if not all of which, was presumably covered by his allowance.

Both father and son, however, must have hoped that his writing would eventually pay, and that his dependence on an allowance would slacken. A hint of this expectation may be present in a letter Manning wrote to Fairfax in November 1908.

> I sent Mrs Fowler Newbolt's letter, which is full of very high praise [for *Scenes*], and I had intended to send it on to you; but as this is the Xmas mail to Sydney I shall appease my father with it; otherwise he might be distressed at the book not coming out this year.

As it turned out *Scenes* paid better than *Brunhild,* but not as well as Manning had hoped, and even less than he felt the demand for the book had promised. For Murray had distributed the type before Putnam took its 250 copies, so that the firm was caught short when domestic orders kept coming in and had to publish a new edition. By the time the book was available again the demand had faded, and Murray did not, to Manning's mind, properly advertise the new edition. Twenty years later he was still nursing his annoyance at what he thought had been a major miscalculation — as well as what he thought of as Murray's unfair accounting practices, which made the first edition absorb some of the costs of the second. But in 1909 the larger question was how a writer with a small audience could make a living. It is not hard to imagine the sort of discussion that ensued when his father arrived in London that summer. As a "just" parent William Patrick Manning would have been pleased with his son's success; as a man with a "single and complete nature" he might have insisted on a greater effort to earn money. Whatever was said or assumed, the fact is that in December 1909 Fred Manning began to review regularly for the *Spectator*, at £3 per article, no doubt reinforcing the pride Norman Lindsay saw in his father nine months later. In good business fashion, he soon began to keep a ledger of his earnings. On its front page, quoting Edward Fitzgerald's translation of "Omar Khayyam", he showed that he could be his father's son.

(con molto expressione)

Some for the glories of this world, and some
Sigh for the Prophet's Paradise to come:
Ah take the cash, and let the credit go,
Nor heed the 'booming' of a distant drum.

The *Spectator* was the most widely read political weekly of the Edwardian era, with a circulation of 20,000, a sizeable number of whom were rumoured to be men of the cloth. Its politics were conservative and ultra-patriotic, and it regarded itself as a watch-dog of the public interest. This regard took many forms, from its campaign for strengthening the auxiliary military force after the embarrassments of the Boer War, to its refusal in June of 1911 to accept advertisements for the *English Review* because of a "mischievous" article by Frank Harris that had appeared in a recent issue. To personify the *Spectator* is almost necessary, for at that time it was the weekly creation of one man, St Loe Strachey, whose blue pencil skimmed every line that appeared, changing many, and who clearly relished the task of replying, often at length, to the many letters printed in the magazine's letter columns. These were frequently throat-clearing pronouncements by individuals who chose, in the older fashion, to conceal their identities behind pseudonyms like "Civis", "Senex", "Scotus Viator", or "Oútis". The last of these, when carefully printed in Greek script, veiled Galton. (Others who hid behind that well-worn pseudonym, first taken by Odysseus, were content with anglicised script). After the letter columns came several pages of book reviews, always anonymous. History, politics, and literature were the mainstays, and the level of reviewing was high by any standard.

The *Spectator* was a very respectable journal for which to write, and it paid well. Manning seems not to have minded (or to have been the victim of) Strachey's editorial habits. His inaugural review was a sharp dismissal of a book by Frank Harris on Shakespeare — "His tone towards previous students of Shakespeare is objectionable: if he could not revere them as his masters, he might have tolerated them as his precursors" — and in the next four and a half years he wrote 48 more pieces. Work on "The Gilded Coach" limited the amount of reviewing he did, and for a period in 1911 when he was bogged down in the novel and impatient with the quantity of dull and bad books sent his way, he became delinquent. "Half a dozen books, mostly rubbish, are lying on the floor, simply rotting there when they should have been reviewed a month ago." Strachey, "very anxious", according to Manning, that he continue as a reviewer, quickly agreed that he could "pass over" books not to his liking. And so the reviewing went on. Though Manning complained that it was not "worthwhile" and that it interfered with his own work, he could not, he told Fairfax, "afford" to give it up. There may have been an increasing psychological value as well — finished tasks sometimes numb the anxieties arising from grand but unrealisable projects.

Strachey had good reason to hold on to Manning, for besides being dependable in his tastes he often wrote superb reviews. Sent a new edition or a critical study of an English author between Langland and Hardy, Manning would produce an essay that was usually more than a hurried response to a quickly read book. He had the quality looked for most in a critic, a finely discriminating sensibility:

> In *Tess of the D'Urbervilles* the whole of the reader's attention is focussed upon a single aspect of life, and that aspect is reflected in a single person. Considered apart from Tess, Alec D'Urberville and Angel Clare are purely superficial characters. It is only in their relation to her, only when we see them bathed in the light of her own consciousness, only in so far as she turns from one to the other of them, that they interest us. On the other hand, Tess herself is an almost entirely passive character. She interests us, not by what she does or says, but entirely by what she feels, entirely by her capacity for suffering. To understand such a nature *il faut s'abêtir*, as Pascal said; it is spontaneous, instinctive, moody; it lacks both the control of will and the control of reason. It is one of the simplest organisms, in which the nerve-centres are not localized, but spread over the whole surface of the body, and in which thought is practically identical with sensation. It is essentially feminine. The passivity of her character is so firmly insisted upon by her author, in his eagerness to retain our sympathy, as in some measure to defeat his end, for in order that our sympathy with her should be complete we must realize her own responsibility.

Precision is apparent throughout that passage, a precision of thought, of feeling, and of language. No less apparent in these reviews is their learning. Manning had absorbed the English critical tradition right down to the work of his contemporary, A. C. Bradley; he had at his fingertips the essential classical texts; and he could deploy, as the quote from Pascal indicates, his loving knowledge of French literature and history to good effect. He also had compassion. Stupid and conceited writers like Frank Harris asked to be pilloried, and silly books like George Saintsbury's *A History of English Prose Rhythm* (1912) deserved to be scolded ("a critic has little heart for pointing out that the book teaches us nothing, that it begins with a misunderstanding and ends without yielding any profitable results"), but sometimes he had qualms.

> I have just got off an article on Stevenson, which has been sitting like a nightmare upon me for two months. I cannot honestly praise his work, and yet there is something in the man's fortitude, and personal charm, which appeals strongly to me. As it is, I have sent in a hostile, and slightly contemptuous review of the *Letters*, which I am half-inclined to hope Strachey will not print, tho' if I were asked for my opinion again, I could not conscientiously say other than I have said. It is absurd in me to attach so much importance to a review, which will probably not have the smallest influence; but somehow or other I always feel a reluctance to criticise such things harshly. I have a sort of respect for human endeavour, human vanity, and human failure even, as being after all common to the whole of mankind.

Like most confessions, that one looks for approval, and Fairfax undoubtedly gave his. So should we, even if we suspect an extra kindness is being given Stevenson for being a fellow martyr to a weak body. Though Manning had, in Pound's words, "his more envenomed moments", he usually spoke and wrote with a high and gentle tolerance. A part of him winced when he had to use the knife in a review. Other critics, like Pound, cut with enthusiasm.

Poetry was the substance or subject of nearly half the books Manning reviewed. As a practising poet and a serious student of prosody, he talked of his craft with splendid confidence and zeal, gradually defining his own poetics and urging his readers to see verse as crafted artifice and yet to sense it as a living, fascinating presence: "As we have said before in these columns, a poem may be extremely complex in itself, like the organ of sight; but the result of its organic complexity must be a greater simplicity of function.'' His reviews show him ready to discuss almost any aspect of poetry: whether it be a poem's parts, such as metrics, the poet's role as the agent of analysis between the experience he would recover and the experience he projects, or (a pet concern) how a poem should be viewed — ''as a single and continuous movement''. His detailed criticism of specific poems and poets owed much to Aristotle's definition of poetry as a ''representation of life''. A belief that poety should grow out of ''actual or potential'' experience was the litmus test he unswervingly applied: Meredith pales in comparison to Browning because he ''is never sufficiently direct in his vision of reality''; Coleridge's inability to finish such poems as ''Kubla Khan'' was due in part to his material not having been ''drawn from reality''; reams of Swinburne are ineffectual because the poet's ''inspiration'' knew only ''certain exquisitely chosen aspects of reality''; the defect of formal poety, like that of Carducci, is that it does not arise directly or spontaneously from experience; Francis Thompson is a ''true poet'' because his experience ''entered into his poetry''; William Morris is a great poet because his work is ''rooted...in reality''. ''Reality'' as a critical standard easily accommodated the historical mode of Manning's own imaginative work. To sense a contradiction would be to confuse genre with aesthetic intentions and capacity. Into the vanished people of his poetry and prose Manning sought to breathe life as he knew it.

Readers of the *Spectator* would have had little difficulty with Manning's standards, however much they might have disagreed with some of his specific assessments. For the most part they shared his classicist sympathies, his belief that literature should be disciplined and that it should concern itself with the ''essential and normal'' conditions of life. Some might also have agreed that Wordsworth, Coleridge, Shelley, and Byron were neither ''consistently nor sufficiently artists'', and that their impact on later nineteenth century poetry was to be deplored. Galton certainly did; he had been arguing the point for years. The views of Galton are echoed in many of Manning's critical judgements, though to compare their actual writings on the same author is to recognise at once the difference between the pupil's subtle criticism working within a text and the mentor's crude opinion working from without. Manning was also unsympathetic to the stress laid on the "accidental and the exceptional" in recent "realistic" literature. Balzac, for example, he detested, because the Frenchman had strained his characters of any humanity and of any claim on our sympathy. "He makes me feel the need to be sprinkled with Hyssop." And so while his review of the *Comédie humaine* contains some shrewd comments he finally dismisses the enterprise because of its "superficiality, its extravagance, its remoteness from life". There is a fine irony in that last phrase, though Manning probably did not see it.

Despite a sometimes cloying fastidiousness, many of Manning's *Spectator* pieces read well today. He wrote about the things he knew, and if his notion of "reality" seems occasionally an abstraction, he always wrote with a clear sense of what his values were. So too did another reviewer for the *Spectator* during those years, Lytton Strachey (St Loe's cousin), whose reviews make Manning's look sluggish, even dull. Strachey always strove for colour and grace in his writing; his charm as a reviewer is in his style. By contrast, Manning's aim was to inform and analyse; in content and tone he sounds like a scholar. And as is so often the case, each man's defects sprang from his virtues: Strachey is liable to disappear in a cloud of metaphor, Manning to stumble into a thicket of pedantry. The two apparently never met except in print, when Manning reviewed Strachey's *Landmarks in French Literature* (1912). Otherwise they were strangers, who drew on a common source of necessary income. Bloomsbury was a long way from Edenham.

To the other Edenham reviewer, St Loe Strachey sent books on the classics, history, and literature, and Galton occasionally submitted unsolicited pieces on theological and ecclesiastical subjects, one of which sparked an angry exchange with Hilaire Belloc.* In most of his articles Galton cited either Horace or Arnold for support, sometimes both, and rarely did he deny himself a short sermon on modern life and letters. He would criticise sloppy prose and the neglect of eighteenth-century literature, but more often he attacked Socialism and the rule of "King Demos". Usually he would support his argument by drawing classical parallels:

> Rome, again, can teach us that the culmination of militarism and of national rivalries is not all unmixed good; that a ruined agriculture is the precursor of all other ruin; that Socialism in many of its forms has actually been tried, and that it drained the State of industry, of energy, and of virility; that it is dangerous, and in the end disastrous, to encourage the unfit at the expense of the fit and thrifty; that it is a very false economy to pillage and penalise the wealthy in the supposed interests of the poor; finally, that a bureaucracy, is the worst of human plagues, especially when it is a theological persecutor as well; and that the tax-gatherer was more destructive to the Roman Empire than all the barbarians together.

Two years before he began writing for the *Spectator*, Galton had been "incubating" a volume of parallels between "our times and the age of Augustus". He never took the book beyond the planning stage, but he enjoyed the necessary reading for it, and the columns of the *Spectator* offered the right pulpit from which to deliver the fruit of his study. His fears were the fears of the magazine's average reader, and Strachey was "delighted" to publish so eloquent a spokesman. "Galton is being recognised as a prophet," Manning told Fairfax, "which is the role I always assigned to him." By "prophet" he meant someone with "a profound criticism of life to offer us". Today some readers would share that view; many others, I suspect, would be dismayed by the condescension of Galton's criticism and by an insensitivity bordering on prejudice. As a critic of his times, Galton usually sounds like a learned, aristocratic scold. He probably would not have much minded the characterisation, and

Manning's respect for his mentor's views reflects his own conservative predilections.

Manning thought of himself as "a Tory", as someone who respected tradition, favoured strong government, disliked party politics, and distrusted humanity in the "mass". He had no patience for the "cant" and "futility" of prewar liberalism, he "really hate[d] European democracy", he scorned "sentimentality" in discussions of British imperialism, and he deplored the levelling impulse of socialism, "which has got to consider mankind in the lump, and the lump is detestable."

These opinions appear in letters from Manning to Fairfax and Pound. Similar views can be found in his prewar imaginative and critical writings. *Scenes and Portraits,* notably the dialogue between Leo XIII and Renan, testified eloquently to a conservatism that saw "the laws which govern society [as]... essentially natural laws", while the hero of "The Gilded Coach", who "revered only one maxim of political wisdom, '*Quieta non movere*'", was intended to be a kindly embodiment of them.

> He had come to believe that progress was a chimera, that the welfare of society resulted from its moral condition, of which political action was merely an effect;...M. de Velay's ideal of government was aristocratic, as he reasoned that the genius of humanity was only found in a certain number of individual minds...

Manning's conservatism is even more strikingly evident in an unsigned essay, "Greek Genius and Greek Democracy", published in the *Edinburgh Review* in 1913. There he argued that the "reality" of Periclean Athens — a city riddled with class conflict and superstition and where, "as elsewhere, genius was a solitary and an isolated force" — bore faint resemblance to the "idealist" image rendered by many scholars, and ill deserved to be a model for Britain.

> For us there is nothing to emulate in the annals of Athenian democracy; its political and religious fanaticism should be as hateful to us as it was to Socrates, to Thucydides, to Plato, to Aristotle, and above all to Xenophon, the truest aristocrat in Athenian life and letters. These men were Athens' sternest critics; and it was because their qualities were lacking in the State as a whole, and neglected by it, that the adventure of Athenian democracy ended in ignominious failure.

Manning, Fairfax, and Pound, and for that matter Galton, were cultural and political elitists, intellectuals wont to sneer at the crowd and at those politicians and artists who curried its favour. Yet in Manning's voice there is rarely heard Galton's apocalyptic pronouncements or Pound's rage. Instead there is deliberate, philosophical detachment, as ingrained as it was cultivated. Thus, during the miners' strike of 1912 he wrote to Aubrey Herbert, an MP and recent acquaintance, that "if the miners decline to supply coal to the country, the country should decline to supply food to the miners". That logic may sound harsh, but it derives from principle rather than from fear or vindictiveness. And his summary comment about the strike — "it is awfully interesting to watch" — reflects a concern managed by intellect rather than passion. It also looks ahead to the time when he will write "a profoundly democratic book" about the common soldier.

> 22. vii. 10
>
> My dear Manning
> You will see in the Chronicle a review of your *Poems* from my pen. I am furious with them for putting my name to it. It is a rule of mine never to review Murray books. I broke the rule at their invitation because I was proud to tell the truth about your work; but it is dreadful to have one's weakness so openly shown. However — it is done.

The writer of that letter was C. E. Lawrence, an editor at

Murray; the occasion was the very slow sales of a collection of Manning's poems that Murray had published the month before. Manning had offered them to Murray in January, while still disgruntled over what he thought of as the publisher's clumsy handling of *Scenes*. He hoped that the book of verse would "revive the circulation" of the sketches. But *Poems*, his third book in less than three years, was faring the worst of all.

Lawrence had meant well. Two weeks earlier he had received a note full of threat and disappointment from Manning. "I do not think I shall ever publish another book of verse: or another book of prose unless the Romance pays when that comes out." Lawrence had done what he could privately to console Manning: "It is far too early for you to be putting your Muse into a Nunnery"; but the temptation "to tell the truth" publicly about a book and a poet he judged "truly golden" was obviously too much for his usual scruples. The resulting review, published the same day as Lawrence sent his apology — and Manning's 28th birthday — was about as exaggerated in its prophecy as it was in its praise:

> . . . this volume is a casket with several shining jewels, diverse, many-hued, brilliant. Mr Manning, with his *Scenes and Portraits* and these *Poems*, has proved himself one of the victors of the future. These volumes, we predict, will be worth more than their nominal value in the days to come.

Poems cost me $25; *Scenes*, despite being periodically judged as a "minor classic", $45 — hardly the prices fetched by "victors".

Poems contains much competent verse by a poet willing to try his hand at a variety of forms and metres. While most of the poems seem to date from the previous year or two (including "Persephone", now titled "Kore"), at least one, "Ad Cinarem", was written in 1905, when it accompanied a letter to Dorothy Shakespear. Homage to respected masters is paid by imitation, and in one instance by direct statement.

A. C. S.

April 10th, 1909

Ah! the golden mouth is stopped,
That so sweet was with its song,
Bright, and vehement as fire.
Grieve we, as a star had dropped
Out of Heaven's singing throng,
For the lord of our desire...

Swinburne, despite Manning's reservations about some of his work, meant much to the poets of Manning's generation. James Fairfax also composed a eulogy for him, which is worth mentioning only for its link with Manning.

Epistle to F. M.

Death of A. C. S., 10th April 1909

Whether upon the hills of Bourne
With drooping wings your Muses mourn,
Or southward on this azure coast,
My broken music falters most,
I know not — for we both must grieve
When these, the master-spirits, leave
Void the house of ancient song...

Fairfax was not to prove, as his countryman thought he might, to be the heir of Swinburne: "You really are the only one who can hope to match his music, and perhaps surpass it." But as a steadfast, admiring friend, who believed in Fred Manning's destiny and was willing to bear his miseries, he was exemplary.

By far the longest and most ambitious poem in this collection is "Helgi of Lithend", a dramatic monologue of some 600 lines spoken by a Viking chieftain who has survived into a Christian world and is now near death. Unafraid of what is to come and contemptuous of a present in which "swords rust in peace", he looks back on a life of war and passion without regret.

What are ye women doing? Get ye hence,
Nor weary God with prayers. But when I die,

J. G. Fairfax, c. 1910 (author's collection)

Lay me not there among the peaceful graves
Where sleep your puny saints. I would go hence,
Over the loud ways of the sea again,
In my black ship, with all the war-shields out,
Nor, beaten, crawl unto the knees of God,
To whine there a whipped hound. Yea, send me forth
As when I sought rich lands, and glittering gold,
And warm, white-breasted women, and red wine,
And all the splendour and the lust of war.

As with the Merovingian queen Brunhild, Manning means us to focus on the character in the act of contemplation rather than to become absorbed in the details of bed and battle. Shrewd as well as strong, thoughtful as well as wilful, Helgi is a cunning warrior who knows how to set an ambush for his enemies, and a perceptive consort who realises that the woman he took as "kingly spoil" and who then bore his children continues even in old age to remember the man she first loved — the man Helgi had to kill to keep her. And though he mocks Christian values, his own paganism is no mere superstition.

I have little wit;
I only know that in the looms of time
God's will moves like a shuttle to and fro.
I have heard him in the waves, and on the wind;
I have seen his splendour shine among the swords,
Soften the eyes of women, light and smile
On a child's lips; and know his presence there
Where all the waves stream eagerly to lick
The sunset's bloody splendours. Balder, the bright
Beautiful Balder, whose eyes hold our hope,
Who hath made love a light, and life a song,
In all men's eyes, and on their lips, who hath sown
The fields of heaven thick with golden fires,
As men sow corn: and forges in this flame,
Of life, with ringing blows, a strong man's soul
As swords are fashioned, keen-edged, straight, and blue,
How shall I die dispraising thee, whose praise
Comes, laden with the blown scents of the spring,
Opening dewy eyelids of bright buds,
And brings the swallows?

The poem was dedicated to Alfred Fowler, who had not swung an axe in his career, but who had crossed many a "fickle sea" in quest of gold.

Dynamic, wilful figures who seize from life what they want and are indifferent to death and custom alike have provided material for poets and pleasure to audiences at least since the time of Homer. Besides Brunhild and Helgi, Manning also tried his hand at Stheneboa and Judith, the latter of whom he cast aside upon learning that T. Sturge Moore had already written a verse play about her. We might also include his Theseus and Hippolyta, who are portrayed first slaughtering each other's comrades and then going off on a chase that culminates in a rape. Did such characters appeal to Manning because of the tedious routine of his own existence? The question is worth asking, for a poet's choice of subject, however much influenced by convention, also arises from the conditions of his own life, including his fantasies. All too aware of "this stupid body of mine", Manning may well have derived a special satisfaction from working with characters who had no limitations and who observed no limits. This speculation finds support in a daydream he reported to Fairfax: when war threatened in 1912 he had "visions of myself trailing a puissant pike, in Pistol's phrase, spilling my blood, what little I have got". Despite the disarming irony, the intention was serious, and soon enough he would have his chance.

The shorter poems in the collection more directly express his feelings. Quiet, at times almost dreamlike, they pursue the age old themes of love, longing, and the transience of life. Many have a bucolic setting, though Manning rarely particularises it; we could as well be in Greece as Lincolnshire. And though their affection for the rural is real, and at moments tangible, they dwell primarily, as Manning told his publisher, on "the informing spirit which is to be found in the aspects of nature".

The Pool

My soul is like a lake, whose waters glass
  Stars, and the silver clouds which uncontrolled
  Sail through the heavens, and the hills which fold
Its valley in a peace, tall reeds, and grass,
And all the wandering flights of birds, that pass
  Through the bright air; and, in itself, doth hold
  Naiads with smooth white limbs and hair of gold:
So is my dreaming soul. And yet, alas!

It holds but visions, unsubstantial things,
Transient, momentary; and the feet
Of winds that smite the waters, blur the whole,
Shattering with the hurrying pulse of wings
That crystal quiet, which hath grown so sweet
With fragile reveries. Such is my soul.

The soul, usually characterised as a delicate, hermetic thing, is frequently addressed and described in these lyrics.

In the soul of man there are many voices,
That silence wakens, and sound restrains...

The soul's privacy is both assumed and guarded; aloneness is its inevitable condition. In that respect, some of these poems have a modern sensibility, though so self-conscious and wistful is their tone and so chiselled their construction that we may easily overlook its presence.

Butterflies

Fluttering, haphazard things,
Delicate as flowers ye fly,
Wandering on airy wings,
Creatures of a tranquil sky,
Born for one brief, golden day,
Dying ere the roses die.
Butterfly of colours gay
Flutter in capricious flight,
Hover in thy wanton play,
Gather honey of delight!
Not such harvest as the bee
Carries to his hive at night.
Night shall keep no place for thee,
Death at dusk shall mock thy wings,
So our poor souls seem to me
Fluttering, haphazard things.

Both "The Pool" and "Butterflies" were part of a group of 22 poems gathered under the sub-heading "Les Heures Isolées" and dedicated to Eva Fowler. The title came from a passage in a tale by Henri de Régnier that Manning chose to quote in full.

> Tout homme à s'expliquer se diminue. On se doit son propre secret. Toute belle vie se compose d'heures isolées.

Those words register perfectly the taste for solitude and the practised reticence of Manning's life. Had he not followed so well the advice of Epicurus, "live unknown", he would have been less a mystery to his contemporaries and to us.

In December of 1977 Richard Cody sent me the article he had written for the *Newsletter* of the Amherst College Library. The emphasis, reflecting its author's scholarly interests, was on Manning the poet. Using "Kore" as a text and Eliot and Pound as whipping boys, he argued that Manning's early poetry deserved a better fate than the "modernists" or their "untiring allies and apologists in the academy" might allow. I obviously had reason to cheer Cody's defence of our shared subject, and I enjoyed the swipes he took at the Goliaths of modern literature. I also inwardly bowed to his knowledge. Cody had a command of the English poetic tradition that I did not possess; with seeming ease he had found the late Romantic texts to which "Kore" was a cousin. But as much as I envied his expertise, I could not share the pleasure he took in these early poems. They were well made, yet they had little magic or weight. I agreed with those contemporary critics who had suggested that Manning's technical skills were noticeably in advance of his inspiration. Even "Kore", a good poem and the poet's own favourite, could not make a serious bid for greatness.

Though *Poems* sold poorly the critics were not to blame. If less than enthusiastic, they were at least respectful. There was enough accomplishment and promise to sustain Manning's reputation as a writer to be watched. What he and his friends next expected from his pen was "The Gilded Coach". But this book, conceived as a work of the left hand, was proving troublesome.

When he had begun the romance in the summer of 1909 he thought he would have it finished by the following summer. He had written all of *Scenes* in little more than a year and expected that a book of similar length would take no longer. By August of 1910, however, it was still a long way from completion. "Next May", Ezra Pound was told, it would be done. May 1911 came and went without a finished manuscript, and it was clear that Manning was in trouble. The book was growing, but "slowly", and "otherwise as I would wish". Friends who read instalments praised what they saw and waited patiently. So too did editors at Murray, who shared the author's hope that with this book he would finally capture the general public's interest. But months passed, and the hitherto fertile and dependable writer made slow progress. He was engrossed in the work — "I have no head for anything but M. de Velay's journey to Rome", he told Fairfax in June of 1912 — but far from finishing it. In the autumn he began planning a long stay in Paris where he hoped to finish. "Some of the first chapters need retouching, as they seem to me to be not quite in line with the last part," he wrote to Henry Newbolt in December 1912. He went to Paris in March 1913 and had just begun (with Houtin's assistance) to look for an apartment when he came down with the flu. After a few days he thought it "wise" to return to Edenham. It was now nearly four years since he had conceived the project, and though he seems to have had a more or less finished draft, he was displeased with it. May 1913 found him in a state of uncertainty about what he had written thus far, and so, he told Pound, he was "sedulously pulling it to pieces, and sedulously putting it together again." It had become a "nightmare". He began sending chapters to Pound for comment — "it is awfully good of you to bother about it" — who in turn apparently alerted the editor of the *Smart Set*,* then in London looking for manuscripts, to the novel's existence. Nothing came of the contact with the American magazine, and whatever suggestions for revision "il miglior fabbro" made were no doubt discussed at length when the two poets spent several days together at Daisy Meadow in late July and early August. More months passed, and though Manning's confidence sometimes cracked, as did the patience of his friends, he continued to think that he would finish.

What went wrong? His letters offer a number of excuses, beginning with the time he gave to nursing his disappointment with Murray's handling of *Scenes*: "I feel," he wrote to Newbolt in November of 1909, "no inclination to proceed with my romance for the present, as this business has left me rather disheartened." Then there was time taken up by his *Spectator* work, time he gave to Harry and Beatrix when they visited England in 1911, and time lost to illnesses (though during one he wrote half a chapter). All of these interfered with a writer who, like most writers, could not work "without quiet and freedom from interruptions". Then there were his (and Galton's) high standards. Quick to cast aside what he deemed unworthy, he may well have burnt work which other writers would have rushed to their publishers. And, finally, it is reasonable to assume that there were periods when drinking left him unfit to work. Numerous though these obstacles were, however, I suspect they are not sufficient explanation for the delay of "The Gilded Coach". That, as is often the case with unfinished books, probably should be looked for in the particular resources of the writer and the demands of the project itself.

Put simply, Manning was working in a genre ill-suited to his instincts and, possibly, his talents as a writer. He was not a storyteller, and both his poetry and his prose reveal only a rudimentary concern with how to construct a narrative. What inspired his pen was the vitality of character and, even more, the vitality of ideas, so that the surviving 100-page fragment of "The Gilded Coach" consists mostly of fine-drawn portraits and clever colloquies. He was, it should be no surprise, writing a novel that in its strategies and concerns resembled *Scenes and Portraits*: characters are delineated more for their point of view than for themselves; dialogue is rich in moral and philosophical comment; the narrator is preoccupied with his own and his characters' reflections; and underlying all is a commitment to irony. Such novels are written, and 20 years later Manning would write one in *The Middle Parts of Fortune*. But "The Gilded Coach" asked too much of his inventive powers.

Thus far he had worked in smaller forms: the poem, the sketch, the article; things that could take rough shape in a day's work. "Kore" was written in one day during Pound's visit to Edenham. A novel asks for greater creative stamina, and for greater patience. Moreover, aside from his lyrics, almost all of Manning's imaginative efforts had been organised around known historical or mythological figures. This was not the case with "The Gilded Coach", which mainly employed characters of his own invention. Some actual historical figures (Louis XIV, for example) were portrayed in actual historical settings, but their roles were minor. The task now in front of Manning was to create a number of imaginary people and to keep them talking and moving through a variety of situations in a coherent and engaging manner. It was natural that he should think that he could do it: many a novelist has trained himself on the short story, and Manning had already written a 60-page narrative poem. But the conversations of *Scenes* and the monologue of *Brunhild*, while indicating his exceptional skills as a "symposiarch", had demanded only very specific kinds of imaginative effort and had hardly tested at all his architectural talent, or his endurance. A novel is more than scenes and portraits, just as a painting is more than figures and space. Without a compositional sense (or energy) adequate to the form, the parts will not come together.

Nor will they if the writer questions the value of the enterprise. "The historical basis has been a great bore," he informs Fairfax in November 1911, "as everything and especially Versailles, was in a state of flux in 1670; and the Cardinals die like flies." By itself this is an insignificant gripe; recalled later when Manning announces in 1912, "I aint a realist. I am what

Miss Austen called an imaginist,'' or much later, in 1927, when he tells his publisher, ''Sometimes I wonder whether the recovery of historical detail for the sake of recreating a period is worthwhile because its use is only implicit,'' and the casual complaint of any historical novelist becomes another clue as to why this particular novel was never finished. Frustration with the effort gradually drained him of inspiration, and ultimately led to his questioning not only the project itself but the mode of his art. In the prewar years Manning had every reason to be writing a book such as ''The Gilded Coach''; in the 1920s, with *Scenes* a memory, Galton in his grave, and Manning himself a more experienced if still very private individual, he could acknowledge doubts of the most profound and consequential sort: had he wisely measured his literary talents?

While struggling with the novel and churning out reviews for the *Spectator,* Manning continued to write poetry. He published mainly in the *English Review*, the *Spectator*, and the new American magazine, *Poetry*. Pound, as the English correspondent for *Poetry*, encouraged the editor, Harriet Monroe, to print his friend's work, though with markedly restrained enthusiasm. ''It would [do] no harm to have four or five pages of him.'' To Pound's developing tastes, Manning was now only ''important'' as a prose writer. However, the most ambitious poem that Manning undertook in these prewar years, ''Demeter'', which he described as ''a long semi-dramatic or semi-choral'' poem, and which he never finished, stirred Pound's respect. What interested Pound was the wide variety of classical metres used in the poem, and he informed its author that it was the ''only poem'' he had ever written — forgetting for the moment his praise of ''Kore''. He then proceeded to congratulate Manning in print, singling him out as one of the few poets ''seriously concerned with overhauling the metric, in testing the language, and its adaptability to certain modes''. Manning thought it likely that Pound took little pleasure in the poem except as an ''experiment in rhythm'', and he was probably right. But for himself it was a return to a myth that evidently held a special appeal. Demeter was a natural subject for a writer in his circumstances: he had the fields and seasons of Edenham as witness to the goddess' role, and her grieving for her daughter snatched away to another world may have struck a deeper chord in his life. "Demeter Mourning" is one of the fragments he eventually published from the never-completed poem, and in the opening stanza he seems to be doing what poets often do, remembering in the act of imagining:

> I have seen her in sorrow, as one blind
> With grief, across the furrows on soiled feet
> Pass, as the cold gray dawn came with cold wind,
> Gray as fine steel and keen with bitter sleet,
> Beneath the white moon waning in the skies:
> And I grew holy gazing in her eyes.

A vision less chaste inspired another poem from this period, a poem rejected by the *Spectator* for "being improper". This lone reference to a seemingly bizarre incident appears in a letter from Dorothy Shakespear to Ezra Pound (14 March 1913) that unfortunately fails to name or describe the offending poem. Though none of Manning's published verse is noticeably prurient by the standards of his day, lust was a passion he knew how to describe, and little of it was needed to offend St Loe Strachey's sensibility. Only the year before Strachey had led a crusade to persuade Parliament to pass a law against "indecent" literature, and in June of 1911 he had closed the pages of his magazine to advertisements for the *English Review* because it had published and was eagerly promoting an article by Frank Harris suggesting that women as well as men be allowed to sow their "wild oats". On the latter occasion Manning had sided with Strachey, arguing in a letter to the *Spectator* that a periodical was under no obligation to advertise ideas to which it was opposed. But for Manning, trade ethics were not to be confused with censorship of the artist, and, in 1912, persuaded that "art has no morality", he vigorously opposed Strachey. Any new statute on obscenity, he wrote, was bound to be vague and therefore "mischievous and unjust". Furthermore, for Strachey and his supporters to insist that they did not intend to establish censorship was "almost Sophoclean" in its irony.

> I regret his attitude and that of the gentlemen with whom he was associated, because with the best intention and with a conspicuous sincerity they are advocating a course which if persisted in will make literature subject to administrative torpor, and liable at any moment to be sacrificed to the clamour of a narrow and intolerant faction.

Responsible editor that he was, Strachey printed Manning's elegant rebuke. But one wonders if his subsequent rejection of the "improper" poem was influenced by the common suspicion that the defender of immorality might also be a creator of it. On the other hand, Manning might very well have transgressed conventional standards with a poem that has not survived. Years later would he not deliberately break custom and have his soldiers talk like soldiers even while knowing that he would only be able to print their language in a subscribed edition? Art and memory, though, he would not compromise, and the words with which he closed his 1912 letter to the *Spectator* defined perfectly his intentions in 1929.

> I am persuaded that the great majority of us write our books without taking into consideration either the incompetent Puritan or the incompetent sensualist. Both seem to us entirely irrelevant. But if we have to choose between them, we cannot do better than recall Renan's words: '*Mieux vaut un peuple immoral qu'un peuple fanatique.*'

Avant-garde contemporaries of Manning said it differently, but no better.

In July of 1912 Fred Manning turned 30. He was now a "respected" literary figure, if not a well-known one. Earlier in the year Pound had asked him to chair his lecture on Guido

Cavalcanti but Manning had turned him down with characteristic diffidence: "Have I the presence? Would my name command any, even the smallest measure of respect?" To those who knew his work it would, but their numbers had increased very slowly. He had not published a book in the last two years, and the notes and drafts on his desk promised nothing soon. The novel was still a long way from being finished, and "Demeter", which he planned to ask Murray to bring out in a volume by itself, had also become problematic. Pound, convinced that his friend was the "one man who understands Persephone and Demeter", offered advice, but the poem Manning envisioned continued to elude him.

Compounding the frustration with his work was his dissatisfaction with his life. "Villainous" colds and 'flus continued to plague him, and while trying to forget his "own diseases", he had now begun to feel "a few twinges of Galton's rheumatism". But at least as demoralising as his ailments were his fits of loneliness. His response to a house party in early August 1912 at the home of Aubrey Herbert — a poet as well as a politician — is revealing:

> I enjoyed my visit to Pixton immensely, and feel ten per cent better. That sort of country gets into one's blood. I am tired of living in a hermitage; one seems to get inhuman dwelling alone, and old, immensely old.

The phrase "dwelling alone" says much about how his life with Galton had developed. After eight years together they had each their own work, their own routine, and their own vacations. Mutual friends are communicated with in separate correspondences (in which Galton speaks of "Fred" and Manning of "Mr Galton" or simply "Galton"), and they show great respect for each other's privacy. They have, in brief, plumbed the depths of an essentially tutelary companionship, and while it has filled significant spaces in their lives, for Manning at least it is not enough.

Why did he not leave Edenham? If he ever asked himself that

question he left no answer, and if friends asked it they have left no record. In any case it would be surprising to find that it was a question Manning seriously pondered. He was rooted to a mode of life that he could not imagine altering. The rhythm and solitude of a rural existence seemed essential to him as a writer; the isolation he complained about one day he depended upon and celebrated the next. It also seemed essential to what he deemed a civilised life, a life, as he explained to the young Eva Sumner, not consumed with "business", "a thousand trifles", and endless chatter. His was the Epicurean ideal, a quiet life, "frugal et austère", its leisure used to contemplate the ways of man and God. When he told a friend that he led a life given over to "idleness and philosophy" he did not think it necessary to apologise.

And then, of course, there was Galton, the dominant figure in his development during the last 15 years. If Manning no longer consciously thought of himself as a pupil or ward, it was not because his dependency on the older man had measurably lessened. It did not matter that they had their own schedules or that they had long since probably discovered as much about each other as they could want to know. Galton was still the rudder in Fred Manning's life, and would remain so until his death. As the stronger personality, he needed only to be himself to keep Manning at Edenham. Years of being watched over and praised by adults had not developed in the younger man either the habits or desire for independence. When he was about to leave for Paris in March 1913 Manning wrote a letter (in French) to Albert Houtin informing him of his arrival and describing himself as "un petit enfant" who is both excited and fearful about adventuring "dans un autre monde". Deep down he knows he will be okay once he has been in Paris a few hours, "mais pour quelques âmes l'inconnu cache toujours des perils". The letter has significance beyond its immediate occasion, for it suggests why leaving the familiar life of the vicarage would have been so difficult. To have gone away would have been to venture into an unknown far more threatening than Paris.

And so he went on living at Edenham, experiencing twinges of desperation, but for the most part thinking himself content. The advantages of country living were many, and loneliness, too, had its rewards: "Blessed are the lonely for they have created their own world." The vicarage over the years had been much improved: there was now a bathroom, a remodelled kitchen, and a fresh coat of paint; and though in 1911 Galton had appropriated for his study the large room downstairs formally used as a dining room, Manning's space was comfortable enough. In the village he was a familiar figure, but he maintained his privacy; and if he had any status, it was that of a gentleman. And like a gentleman, he still depended on a private income.

Before the war his writings do not seem to have realised more than £60 a year, hardly enough to cover both his household obligations and personal expenses, yet sufficient when combined with his allowance.* But a three-month vacation in Paris promised to tax his resources, and thus in the autumn of 1912 he tried to get several poems into print and wrote for the *Edinburgh Review* the essay challenging the idealist view of fifth-century Athens. When he mailed out one batch of poems for publication he joked that they would one day be known as "Poems for an Overcoat". But there was more wit than want to the comment, and whatever shortages he experienced were presumably made up by his father, who in the same year made out a will in which Fred, treated the same as his dependent sisters, was generously provided for. While expected to earn what he could, and apparently conscientious in his attempts to do so — he tried unsuccessfully in the autumn of 1911 to get a position as a regular reviewer for *The Times* — he would not be allowed to become needy.

The pattern of life at the vicarage was occasionally broken by visitors, but if Manning wished to see his friends he had to go to London. Increasingly the Fowlers, along with Eva's sisters and their children, had become a family to him, and he prized the week or two he spent with them during the summers at Daisy Meadow.* It was not the house itself, nor its pleasant setting in woods near the top of a hill, that made him look forward to his visits, but the chance to be at play with people who cared for him and whom he liked. These people included Fairfax and Pound, who would often be invited at the same time.

Relations with the latter continued to be alternately sunny and stormy. In January 1914 they combined with Yeats in arranging a testimonial for Wilfrid Scawen Blunt, whose poetry and politics had scandalised many of his Victorian contemporaries. At the last moment Manning could not make it to the lunch held at Blunt's home in Sussex, and so his face is missing from perhaps the most famous literary photograph of the Edwardian era. His absence also set off a nasty quarrel with Pound "through the post" a few weeks later. Much tinder had been waiting for this spark. "I have been cranky and irritable," Manning wrote to Pound, "for the last 18 months, and feeling pretty wretched inside. The Blunt episode was only a determining factor. 'Phasellus Ille' hurt my feelings, and what I should have taken before as mere ragging had a different significance afterwards." "Phasellus Ille", the Pound poem to which Manning refers, satirises a "papier mâché" figure whose

> mind was made up in "the seventies",
> Nor hath it ever since changed that concoction.

While ostensibly having someone else in mind, the poem could easily have been used to tease Manning. News of Pound's impending marriage to Dorothy Shakespear, however, persuaded Manning to seek a truce.

3.III.1914

> My dear Pound:
> A good deal of ill feeling has developed between us lately, and it is, I suppose, no use discussing its cause, or where the responsibility lies; but I should like to say to you that I wish you and Dorothy every happiness and the best of luck. At one time I thought it probable, and then it seemed to have become remote again. In some

> ways I think you are both very brave, not entirely in a worldly sense, but bravery is always the best wisdom.
>
> There is no more to be said; but I hope that the *vita nuova* will strengthen your work, (or play if you like). I don't think my first feeling toward you, which was one of affection, has changed in essentials; and whatever accidental vicissitudes it may have passed through, to its apparent damage, I have always had for your poetry a very great admiration.
>
> yours always
>
> Fred

A generous act has rescued many a sinking friendship, and it did so on this occasion. Within days the two men were exchanging pleasantries, and Manning was talking about an article he wished to write on Pound — provisionally entitled "The Irrational Element in Poetry" — as well as asking his friend to look at a poem he had left at the Fowlers'. He also suggested that the two of them, together with Richard Aldington, should start up a new magazine to be called the *Hellenist.* Despite thinking it might be "an excellent counter blast" to Wyndham Lewis's proposed anti-establishment journal (*Blast*), Pound was not interested, just as three years earlier he had been indifferent to Manning's suggestion that they undertake a "joint translation" of *The Divine Comedy*. What kind of hell they would have made for themselves if either partnership had taken life needs no conjecture. As Manning wrote in 1915, when Pound was trying to enlist *his* support (and capital) in taking over the *Academy* so as to turn it into an international journal of letters, "We shall rage against each other like bears."

Though Manning's face is not among those of the poets who gathered to honour Wilfrid Blunt, it does appear in his friend Max Beerbohm's gallery of caricatures. Drawn in 1913, but not shown publicly until 1923 when it appeared in a controversial exhibition and then in a book (*Things New and Old*), the sketch portrays Manning seated in a chair, his face a meeting of points and sharp angles dominated by his vivid eyes. On each knee, with the aid of an outstretched arm, he is balancing a small figure, one a pope, the other a Prussian soldier. The two figures are apparently in conversation, with Manning both watching and guiding their discourse. Manning termed the sketch "My own final and complete apotheosis". He recognised that Beerbohm had caught the essence of his art, which was to give speech to those who had already spoken. "Your caricature of me", Manning later told the artist, was "the wisest and wittiest" critique of *Scenes and Portraits*. It was a just compliment even though it ignored Beerbohm's lapse in thinking the book contained a dialogue between two such characters. Or was it a lapse? Did Beerbohm deliberately put the Prussian on Manning's knee because in 1913 it seemed a pope had more reason to be talking with a soldier than with a savant?

When the war broke out, Manning was at Daisy Meadow. To Eva Sumner, who had not seen him in over a year, he was the same old Fred, "teasing me as always", yet looking so well that she thought to note the impression in her diary. Several other friends were at the Fowler house that week but the party had not the same carefree air as in summers past.

> August 17 Had a short walk with Fred. It is horrible not to get any news from over the channel.

The war was literally just over the horizon; futher south in Kent the rumble of the guns was sometimes heard. Whose they were would have been hard to say. The war that had been long expected, and yet had seemed impossible, had finally arrived.

More than a year would pass before Manning went into uniform, and nearly two before he set foot in France as a soldier. He did not immediately volunteer for service because (according to Galton) he imagined he would fail the medical examination;* perhaps, too, like many others he thought that hostilities would be over by the year's end. And so he continued to scratch away at his romance and to write poetry. The only marked change in his literary routine involved the *Spectator*. After August 1914 he did not publish a review in its pages for 11 months, apparently as a result of Strachey's decision to cut costs by using in-house writers as reviewers.* There were no such sudden breaks in life at Edenham. Men enlisted and marched away, but the fields were still ploughed, the pub was still crowded, and Mr Binns, the agent for the Ancaster estates, was still keeping a sharp eye on pounds and pence. Except now he served a new lord, for the first Earl of Ancaster had died in 1910, leaving "the little kingdom over which he ruled" in the hands of his eldest son. But if the pattern of life was largely the same, what men talked and read and worried about was not. The war occupied a corner of people's consciousness hitherto unused and probably no man in the village was more obsessed with it than the vicar.

Now for the second time in Galton's life German armies were invading his beloved France. Still remembering the "desolation" he had seen as a youth in villages along the Seine, he had no difficulty in 1914 accepting the atrocity stories blowing back from this invasion. The "innate bestiality" of the Germans promised nothing less. He followed avidly the war's progress, asking Houtin early on for French newspapers so that he might obtain a fuller view. And he did what lay in his power as the vicar of a distant English parish to defend civilisation against the barbarians. He preached the cause, gave lectures on the progress of the fighting, and removed from the church a standing brass eagle that was too suggestive of the Hohenzollerns. He also did what he could to assist a family of Belgian refugees that was settled in Edenham in December of 1914.* But it was Galton's outspoken loathing for anything teutonic — including Goethe, who wrote only "platitudes" and was "at bottom a savage, like all his countrymen" — that left its mark: one villager told me that when the war broke out Galton deliberately destroyed his dachshund, Hans. In fact, the dog lived until the autumn of 1915, and if it was destroyed (it died at the age of 15) it was an act of mercy. In all my interviews I did not hear a better example of how memory converts what did happen to what ought to have happened.

Soon Edenham was mourning its losses. The plaque on the north wall of St Michael's lists 13 killed in the course of the war, a small figure until one recalls the size of the parish, or multiplies 13 by the thousands of parishes across the land. One of the first to be killed was the brother of the Earl of Ancaster. He was an officer aboard the cruiser *Monmouth* when it, together with the *Good Hope*, was sunk off the coast of Chile in the Battle of Coronel on 1 November 1914. There were no survivors from either ship. The general public, as yet unfamiliar with such carnage, was stunned, and so was Manning, who had at least a passing acquaintance with all the Ancasters. He dashed off a poem that was never published, and that reads as if it were never finished:

> Lordlier laurels crown you than victory,
> Whom your own valour crowns with invincible
> Pride; and the starless night of ocean
> Sacredly hearses. Ye whom earth held not...

The bravery of the English sailors, who had not fled from an engagement they could not win, obviously touched him. Two years earlier, the sinking of the *Titanic* had also preoccupied him: "I really couldn't get much more done for thinking of the *Titanic*." Every report had to be read, not for explanations of how the disaster had occurred nor for the "hysterical and vain" outcries about future "precautions", but for details of the passengers, who had "behaved so splendidly and died under such horrible conditions." What he read impressed him "enormously, and I have come to consider bravery as a kind of saintliness." This conclusion fitted well with his congratulatory salvo to Pound on his impending marriage: "bravery is always the best wisdom."

Perhaps stung by the *Monmouth* and *Good Hope* episode, Manning was soon trying to find his place in the war. To his friends he spoke of wanting "to do something useful". What that would be he did not know, nor did it matter. Like millions of others his "military ambition" involved a view of himself as a patriot ready to defend King and Country against enemies "who have become degenerate without ever having become civilized". But enough clues exist to indicate that he also saw the war as an opportunity to test himself, and quite possibly as a means of escape. Despite occasional poems and reviews his career was now a litter of projects he could not finish; and however much he defended a rustic existence, its conditions left him unfulfilled. When finally he was accepted into a regiment, and went to Shrewsbury in October 1915 to don a uniform, he was not unhappy to be leaving one life behind and entering another. Probably he was very eager, which is only to say that he sensed himself beginning an adventure. Unfortunately, like his trip to Paris two years before, this adventure would also fall short of expectation — not only because that is often the way of adventures, but because of the adventurer himself.

War

CHAPTER FIVE

Manning was in the army for almost 28 months, and for much of that time he was in disgrace. In June 1916 he was thrown out of an officers' training unit for drunkenness, in August 1917 he was court-martialled for drunkenness, and several months later he barely escaped being court-martialled again for the same offence. He was finally allowed to resign his commission and leave the army when it became clear to his superiors that nothing was to be gained by keeping him. *The Middle Parts of Fortune* does not mention these troubles. Except for an occasional flashback to his training as a recruit, it is occupied with his experiences in France.

None of this was known to me when I started my search, or for some time thereafter. I assumed that Manning's military career had been honourable because there was no reason to believe otherwise. His wartime letters to Rothenstein, though indicating some difficulties in Ireland, had not left a different impression. They were not, it turned out, meant to. How much about his life in the army Manning revealed to friends I do not know, but the impression I have is that it was little. No one I spoke to in England or Australia knew that he had been in serious trouble; he apparently hid his difficulties, as for years he hid his drinking problem. Had I not followed a hunch I would not have discovered those difficulties myself.

In the summer of 1977 I checked the Public Record Office in London for material on the Shropshire Light Infantry Regiment. In particular, I wanted to know why Manning had not completed the officer training course which his letters to Rothenstein revealed he had begun in the spring of 1916. The holdings on the regiment at the Record Office did not, however, include the

1914–18 War, and I was advised to write to the Army Records Centre in Hayes, Middlesex. A good omen, I thought, was their address: Bourne Avenue. When I wrote I asked about the unfinished training course, and also inquired if Manning's entire army record — assuming it existed — might be made available to me. In response I was told that the "general practice" was not to make disclosures unless the person concerned had given his consent. However, "in view of the special circumstances", I was provided with the precise dates of his service, first with the Shropshire Regiment, and later with the Royal Irish. Wanting more, I wrote back inquiring whether Manning's records could be released if permission were given by his niece. This request met a bureaucratic wall: "I am to inform you that it is contrary to the practice of the Department to allow access to documents of members or ex-members of Her Majesty's Forces." A friend then put me in touch with Brian Bond, Director of War Studies at King's College, London, in the hope that he might have some idea as to how to gain access. An exchange of letters with Bond led to the same wall: "I've just been on the phone to the War Office and discovered that service records are closed for *one hundred years* no matter who the enquirer is or the subject of the enquiry. No exceptions!" One other possibility I tried was the Regimental Museum of the Shropshires, thinking it might have some company records, possibly even photographs. It did, but nothing with any trace of Manning who, the curator surmised, "appears to have been a man who would pass by without drawing attention to himself." I then let the matter drop for a time, hoping that other inquiries and perhaps as yet undiscovered letters might turn up information about Manning's war years. After all, serendipity had struck before.

By the summer of 1979 these hopes had just about evaporated. I decided therefore to jump up the chain of command, knowing from my own experience in the army that rules are more easily bent by those with real power. And so I wrote to the Right Honourable Francis Pym, Minister of Defence, pleading that to do justice to Manning I needed to learn as much as I could about his military service. Sir Francis never answered my letter and perhaps never saw it. But someone did. After several weeks I received from the Records Centre a letter stating that "authority has been obtained for you to have access to the personal records of the late Lieut. F. Manning." Once more I had that sense of triumph — one part relief, one part pleasure, and one part conceit — that arises from solving the seemingly insoluble. Luckily, a good friend of mine was in London, and as my "representative", he was allowed to "peruse the files". The pages of notes he sent back disclosed that for all his dreams, Manning had been, not surprisingly, ill-suited to military life. My friend's notes were necessarily abbreviated, so that when I returned to England in 1981 one of my first stops was at Hayes, Middlesex.

The Records Centre is a series of long low buildings surrounded by a fence. I entered through a gate where after being checked by a guard I was met by a clerk who escorted me to the appropriate building. There I was welcomed by the Executive Officer of the Archives, who led me to a small bare room where on a table already lay Manning's file. Up to this point, I had sat in many comfortable houses and libraries gathering the evidence of Manning's life. This dreary cell was an appropriate place for examining possibly its most dismal chapter. On opening the folder one of the first items to catch my attention was a pencilled note someone had scribbled during the period of my laying siege to the Centre: "Mr Marwil is becoming rather persistent."

I spent six hours with the file, sifting through official forms, personal letters, and numerous messages up and down the chain of command. Among this welter were some biographical titbits. These included clues as to his whereabouts — from them I learned of the stay at Calverton; details of his physical condition — he was 5 ft 8 in and weighed 127 lb when he entered the army and had already had pneumonia once in his life; and a fib to ease his passage in the service — he claimed to belong to the Church of England. But it was of his troubles that the file spoke most fully, telling a story few men would have wanted known.

> I joined the King's Shropshire, the finest marching regiment in the British Army, at the beginning of October. I did not think I had sufficient experience of men to apply for a commission.

So Manning, now Private 19022, wrote to Will Rothenstein in November 1915 when the two men resumed their acquaintance after 15 years. What the proud new recruit did not bother to explain — perhaps because Rothenstein, addressed still by his surname, was not yet a good friend — was how he had been trying for some time to win a commission so as to fulfil his "military ambition". He had applied in December 1914 to the Royal Flying Corps because he "like[d] flying". Rejected, perhaps because of his less than optimal vision,* he then contemplated (and presumably tried for) a commission in several other units: the Artists' Rifles, the Inns of Court Regiment, and the Naval Brigade. In seeking officer status Manning was doing what someone of his background would be expected to do. Whether he was turned down for reasons of health or because, in fact, he had no "experience of men" is unclear. Perhaps it was a combination of the two. How he finally came to select the Shropshires in which to enlist as a private I also do not know, nor do I know if he approached any other units. But since the doctors "all passed him as sound", he must have been an acceptable risk, at least by the standards prevailing 14 months into the war.

After joining the regiment Manning was sent for training to Pembroke Dock in South Wales. There, attached to a reserve battalion, he learned how to soldier, going through endless marching drills, shooting a musketry course, and enduring fatigue duties that soldiers at least as far back as Caesar's legions have grumbled about. His own complaints fixed on the primitive conditions of the camp: three planks and some straw for a bed, dirt everywhere and in everything and, on one occasion, no water for three days because of frost. What discomforted him the most, however, was the incessant "babel" and crowded conditions of life in the camp. Only at night, sitting up in bed after lights out, smoking a cigarette, the hut silent except for the breathing and turnings of men asleep, could he find the quiet to compose a few lines of verse or to feel himself alone with his "own thoughts". Occasionally he secured a more extended privacy in the home of the local vicar:

> Saturday and Sunday afternoons I can escape into its quiet and civil life for a few hours, and remember that I am a civilized man. It is not that I want to escape from the men, because I have honestly come to love them, with all their faults and defects, which they carry bravely enough as being their own concern. But I do find it necessary to escape into a silence that is not of sleep. It is like a bath of quiet, one can almost feel its coolness rippling upon the flesh.

Within six weeks "the very hard life" of an enlisted man together with the praise and urging of his commanding officer and the battalion adjutant had persuaded Manning to apply for a commission: "Just the few extras an officer gets, hot water, food on a dish, and quiet, will be very welcome." Years later, while admitting that he had had a "bad time" as a recruit and was "*not* cheerful", he would look back at the experience as one that "woke up my powers of resistance".

The "love" Manning voiced for the men around him at Pembroke Dock was based rather more on curiosity than affection. He lived and trained with the men, but he watched them as a stranger might:

> The greater part of the camp are now recovering from a three days saturnalia, which culminated last night in something like a gladiatorial show. When I first came here I told everyone that I was a teetotaller, simply as a measure of self-protection; because this life is so rough and hard, that it is easy to find an excuse for drinking, simply as a way of escape from the pressing and

> imperious necessities of it. I am heartily glad I did. No one bothers me to drink with them, and both the NCOs and men seem to like me, because I can go out with them and let them go as they please, without either joining in their orgiastic rites, or seeming an outsider to them. That is only one of the things which makes me glad I came. These men are like children. When drunk their acquired character is all dissolved away, and they are simply traversed by their emotion. A mixture of discipline and drunkenness is funny enough: it exemplifies Bergson's theory of the comic, the disparity between the ideal and the reality: but perhaps the addition of piety to the other two brings it too close to tears. The orderly sergeants were both drunk, one of them put his fist thro' a pane of glass, cut an artery, and came in covered with bright blood. We stopped the bleeding, and in return for this kindness he threatened to lock up our corporal who came in two minutes late, excusable enough on Xmas Day. Then the corporal went mad and wanted to fight him. I was the first person to interfere, and then with some more stalwart men held our corporal until the "orderly sergeant" got away. There were other lesser fights and squabbles, but the sober section of us didn't care so long as our corporal, who is really a splendid fellow, didn't get into trouble and lose his stripes. Mid-night brought quietness. Well, this training develops the brute in us, but at the same time there is a curious inward reaction from the brute: just as the middle ages brought forth the ideal of Galahad as a reaction from the reality of their life. These people have the primitive passions, and broad simplicity of an earlier age: "We be sinful men" they say, and don't know how close that spirit is to the true heart of religion.

The writer of this letter sounds like a cultured traveller eager to understand a rude people in whose tongue he is not yet fluent. Years later, after the success of *Her Privates We*, Rothenstein asked for permission to publish the letter (along with several others) in his memoirs. Manning, uncomfortable with its "priggish tone" — the "naive egotism. . .was washed out of me, very rapidly" — told his friend that he "should prefer" that he did not use it. Rothenstein nevertheless printed it, noting in his text that the letter conveyed the "first impressions" of military life by a man with "fastidious tastes and habits". And so it did, and so, truly, did Manning shed his "naive egotism", or at least most of it. But the habit of disengagement from his fellows was not so easily broken, and lucky for us that it was not. The war novel would not be the book it is if its author had completely merged with, in Rothenstein's words, all the other "Tommies in the trenches".

Manning had expected to receive his commission shortly after Christmas of 1915 and then to be transferred to a service company to await assignment to a fighting battalion. This did not happen; instead, he was sent in the middle of April 1916 to an Officers Cadet Battalion at Oxford to train for his commission. "So many incompetent and undesirable people got their commissions through the old OTC system, or simply through personal influence, that a new and very rigorous course has been devised to weed out the unfit." This letter to Rothenstein, dated 7 May 1916, went on to chat about "youths in flannels" having been displaced by "young men in khaki" ruled over by sergeants "with greater authority than that of dons". His next letter to Rothenstein, written in September 1916, came from the Somme where he was still Private 19022.

A 3 in × 5 in card in Manning's file explains why he went to war as a private:

> 13.6.1916 Bringing alcoholic liquor into college,
> contrary to Battn. Order 12. Drunk.
> Admonished. Returned to unit 14.6.16.

"Returned to unit" meant that he was sent back to Pembroke Dock without finishing the course. He had been found unfit.

Behaviour that might have been overlooked in a recruit was unacceptable in a soldier training to be an officer. The incident occurred well along in the "very rigorous" course, which suggests that the pressure and fatigue might have got the better of him. But the record is uninformative about the circumstances, noting only that the "common room boy Fitzbrant" had been a witness. In trouble, Manning apparently reached out for help. "I was in Oxford about a fortnight ago," Galton wrote to Houtin on June 24, "to see Fred who was quartered there then. He was getting on well, and is in splendid health. He has now gone back to Wales, and I expect will go to the front soon." There was little Galton could do except what he did so well in this letter: conceal as much as possible. Houtin was not to know of the failure, and certainly not its cause. By avoiding mention of the reason for Manning being in Oxford, Galton was practising the sort of discretion that falls just short of lying. It was neither the first nor the last time that he helped to conceal his protégé's shame. It was, though, probably the only time in his life that he had dreaded a visit to Oxford.

For Manning it must have been a very painful experience. He had failed in his hopes and publicly embarrassed himself. How he explained the episode to friends who, unlike Houtin, knew that he had gone to Oxford to become an officer can only be guessed at. Did he minimise the infraction, insinuate another cause — sickness — for not finishing the course, or simply allow silence to gather over his failure? Rothenstein, at least, may have surmised that there had been a problem. After May, Manning seems not to have written to him again until September, and then made no mention of the incident. His next letter (2 October 1916), which shifts from "My dear Rothenstein" to "My dear Will", begins with an expression of gratitude: "Your letter touched me more than I can say, and that Max [Beerbohm] should think well of me is only natural, for I have always loved him: I am only proud to have your good opinion and his — I can't tell you — but it was, as tho' you had patted me on the back." No reason is given for the thanks, and possibly it has nothing to do with the unfortunate episode. But then again it may. Rothenstein, a compassionate and energetic man, with multitudinous connections, could have been expected to ask around after receiving a letter from a private who was supposed to be a lieutenant. Having solved the mystery, he would then have sat down and written the kind of supportive note that turned acquaintances into friends.

Manning lingered at Pembroke Dock for two months before being sent to the front in the second week of August 1916. To see him off Eva Fowler came up from Daisy Meadow with her niece.

> August 11 Went to Paddington at 3.30 and met Fred. Then we went to Waterloo and had until 7.30 with him. It was good to see him.

The outbound soldier's feelings were presumably those of any soldier: anxiety and excitement, overlaid by the wish to calm his friends and himself. But Manning was not any soldier. He had just passed his 34th birthday, and if lacking much experience of life, he was armed with a set of attitudes and values that would enable him to see the war whole. Twenty years spent reading and reflecting on the classics with a sceptical tutor whose heroes included Caesar and Marlborough had not been without their impact. Manning knew already that war was "in the nature of things", that it was man-created, man-suffered, and would endure as long as man. He could (like H. G. Wells's Mr Britling) acknowledge himself as a writer to be merely "a footnote to reality", with "no trick of command over men", but the culture he had imbibed had not left him an innocent. The experience of battle might very well be instructive, but it could not disillusion him, either about war itself or its reasons. For a long time he had imagined "slaying Germans to dung the earth of France", but he sensed before he crossed the Channel that in the maelstrom there would be more important struggles. And I suspect, though without any evidence except the tone of the letters and poems written in France, that he found the prospect of death less frightening than did the average soldier. Perhaps it was his philosophical temperament, perhaps the sickly man's awareness of vulnerability, perhaps his by now often expressed commitment to the moral role of bravery. Whatever the case, he went off to war quite possibly already thinking what he was to say later to console Rothenstein when he was called up: "It is good that a man should throw dice with God once in his life." Far from trying to jolly Rothenstein into accepting danger, Manning is asking him to see the value of the experience. "If I could think that you would ever go into the line I should be more reconciled to the prospect, in spite, or because of its hazards."

He was sent, as part of the 7th battalion, "straight to the hottest part of the line" (Guillemont), and later saw hard fighting in the Serre sector. Attached in October to the signal section of the battalion, his primary duty was as a relay runner between the trenches and brigade. From 12 midnight until 6 in the morning he was on call to carry messages, often along roads that were being shelled. "We are supposed to go in pairs, but so far I have always gone alone." Though he sometimes felt fear "walking beside me like a live thing", along with it was mingled an "indifference which is not pious enough to be termed resignation". The sights and sounds he encountered on those dark journeys quickly became letters and poems, the latter depending as much as ever on classical allusions, but freer in form and feeling.

Transport

The moon swims in milkiness,
The road glimmers curving down into the wooded valley
And with a clashing and creaking of tackle and axles
The train of limbers passes me, and the mules
Splash me with mud, thrusting me from the road into puddles,
Straining at the tackle with a bitter patience,
Passing me...
And into a patch of moonlight,

With beautiful curved necks and manes,
Heads reined back, and nostrils dilated,
Impatient of restraint,
Pass two gray stallions,
Such as Oenetia bred;
Beautiful as the horses of Hippolytus
Carven on some antique frieze.
And my heart rejoices seeing their strength in play,
The mere animal life of them,
Lusting,
As a thing passionate and proud.
Then again the limbers and grotesque mules.

The only surviving letters I could find from the Somme are those to Rothenstein, scrawled for the most part at odd moments, the writing sometimes smudging into a parody of his usually neat script. They try to evoke the scenes and sounds of war: Rothenstein should be there to paint "these Shropshire lads" — victims in a world Housman had not conceived of — "as they come in from the trenches, weary, plastered with grey clay, in their steel helmets that are like chinese hats and the colour of verdigris". Or he should be there to hear the "music" of the various guns, "full of overtones blending into each other", sounds that Debussy or Walter Rummel (a composer friend of Manning and Pound) would have known how to use.* Or to pity four men, accompanied by a shellshocked dog, as they huddle around a brazier in a dugout, trying to cook dinner over a fire of damp wood while smoking cigarettes, "yours in this case". Rothenstein was impressed by these letters, which gave him the "most poignant" account of what life was like at the "mysterious front". But in describing to his friend the "realities" of war, "the dirt, misery, and madness", Manning was also searching for its lessons. "I can't sort out and analyse my experiences yet — they're too immediate — tedium, and terror, then a kind of intoxication — one can only put the bare heads — we really deal not with the experience itself but with the traces of the experience.'' Even in war Manning maintained his habit of detachment, in part because all men became ''more or less indifferent'' to the horror, became ''spectators'' even as they were participants. But Manning sought to distinguish himself from his companions, whom he continually praised (and perhaps sometimes envied) for their capacity to endure.

> I think the heroism of these men is in proportion to their humiliations; the severest form of monastic discipline is a less surrender. For myself I can, with an effort, I admit, escape from my immediate surroundings into mine own mind; but they are almost entirely physical creatures, to whom actuality is everything: that they can suffer as they do and yet respond to every call made upon them is to me, in some measure, a vindication of humanity.

The tribute in that statement overwhelms any note of condescension. At the same time the affection and respect owed something to his often expressed view that simple people have a special capacity for heroism because their lives are ''alternately a conflict with the blind forces of nature and an acquiescence in them''. Manning not only allowed his attitudes to influence his reading of experience, but also to shape the experience itself. War found men acting as he expected, but it also found them less foreign. While never relinquishing his awareness of himself as an intellectual, an outsider, he merged with his comrades more thoroughly than he had at Pembroke Dock. On the Somme there was no vicarage to escape to, only the fellowship of the other men. Comradeship was a very special discovery for so private a man, and no account of the war is as eloquent in rendering its nuances as the one he would later write.

Of a piece with his letters to Rothenstein are the poems he wrote while on the Somme. In them, he later told an interviewer, he could record feelings which in a letter might not have passed the censor.* And when he came to write *The Middle Parts of Fortune,* these poems would be used to refresh his memory. Several dramatise his discovery of a larger identity: the "I" contemplating its condition has given way to a "We" enduring horrific events.

Grotesque

These are the damned circles Dante trod,
Terrible in hopelessness,
But even skulls have their humour,
An eyeless and sardonic mockery:
And we,
Sitting with streaming eyes in the acrid smoke,
That murks our foul, damp billet,
Chant bitterly, with raucous voices
As a choir of frogs
In hideous irony, our patriotic songs.

These lines might have easily been wrapped around the self, the observant "I" sharing and at the same time detached. But the bitterest ironies of the poem, those below its literary reference, were common food. To have even implied a unique recognition would have amounted to a kind of betrayal. Other poems he wrote during these months acknowledge aloneness as primary; each man is engaged in a private struggle and must bear his own thoughts:

αὐτάρκεια **[Self-sufficiency]**

I am alone: even ranked with multitudes:
And they alone, each man.
So are we free.
For some few friends of me, some earth of mine,
Some shrines, some dreams I dream, some hopes that emerge
From the rude stone of life vaguely, and tend
Toward form in me: the progeny of dreams
I father; even this England which is mine
Whereof no man has seen the loveliness
As with mine eyes: and even too, my God
Whom none have known as I: for these I fight,
For mine own self, that thus in giving self

Prodigally, as a mere breath in the air,
I may possess myself, and spend me so
Mingling with earth, and dreams, and God: and being
In them the master of all these in me,
Perfected thus.
            Fight for your own dreams, you.

Every poet of war since Homer has sung of this duality, for every soldier has felt it. The feeling of collectivity, eventually extending to the enemy, can comfortably coexist with a frightening sense of isolation. Death is near and takes a man by himself. Manning was deeply touched by this duality, for he had gone to war with a highly developed sense of his own separateness as well as a longing to immerse himself in the world of men and experience. The theme and tone of *The Middle Parts of Fortune* are anticipated in a poem such as ''Relieved''.

We are weary and silent,
There is only the rhythm of marching feet;
Tho' we move tranced, we keep it
As clock-work toys.

But each man is alone in this multitude;
We know not the world in which we move,
Seeing not the dawn, earth pale and shadowy,
Level lands of tenuous grays and greens;
For our eye-balls have been seared with fire.

Only we have our secret thoughts,
Our sense floats out from us, delicately apprehensive,
To the very fringes of our being,
Where light drowns.

For Manning to title one of the poems αὐτάρκεια was in keeping with all his literary inclinations. An English title could have been found, but it would have lacked the precision and hardness of the Greek, the suggestion — starkly toned — of things as they must be. Our sense of fitness extends to the other poems that employ classical and literary allusions, including the summons to Dante.

Experience — or as Eva Fowler put it, "the realism of what he is going through" — has forced these poems into being, and they bear easily and persuasively the symbols that habitually focused his imagination. They also demonstrate the truth of what he had argued in his *Spectator* columns: that a poet must draw on his own experiences and emotions if he is to write effectively. Perhaps Manning would have claimed that his earlier lyrics had sprung from emotions no less real than those aroused by war. However, the onslaught of feelings and perceptions rising out of life in the trenches obviously vitalised his muse. The sheer quantity of verse he produced — most of his nineteen war poems were written in five months — was unparalleled for him. Dramatic, life-wrenching experiences can produce bad literature, but they can also generate exact and eloquent documents, in prose and poetry alike, from people who have never before written a line, as well as from writers who have previously searched in vain for a distinct, commanding voice.

Manning is not classed among the "war poets". A few of his war poems appeared in anthologies published during and immediately after the war, but later they slipped from notice, perhaps because they are more reflective and less outraged than some of the more celebrated poetry from the trenches. Perhaps, too, they simply were lost in the welter of poems and reminiscences that the war generated. Manning's contribution was small, occupying only a third of his volume of poems, entitled *Eidola,* which was published in April of 1917.

Its genesis had been unexpected. Since the relative failure of *Poems*, Manning had sold his work to magazines, while hinting that he might never again publish a collection of poetry. But as poems rushed to his mind in France, he had a change of heart, quite possibly influenced by the public's appetite for war literature, and perhaps even by the experience of Laurence Binyon, who had become a popular poet overnight with the publication of "For the Fallen". Once the decision was made to publish, he tried to maximise the book's chances of success. He asked Murray to publish it for Christmas, the highpoint of the publishing year, and to keep its price low. Neither request could be met, but otherwise Murray, "sorry" that he had not been more successful with Manning's previous books, did what he could to assist this one's chances. On C. E. Lawrence's advice, the war poems appeared together at the front of the book: "They are better attuned with these days than the Sapphic ecstasies that Manning also pens." The poet was also urged to scrap the title *Eidola* and choose instead one that would "call to readers (& purchasers)". Manning, though, stuck with his choice; it conveyed his sense of the uniqueness of the "material" from which literature, distinguished from the other arts, is composed. His firmness was supported by Galton, who brushed aside objections by declaring that "if people don't understand it, it is their disgrace." (Lawrence's rejoinder was that Galton "must walk in a rarer air than ordinary mortals breathe.") Not to be defeated, Murray had printed on the book's dustcover a countervailing message for those who did not know that the title translated as "visions" and that it came from Aeschylus. "It is six years since Mr Manning last published a book of poems, and seven since he won a triumph through his masterly volume of prose, *Scenes and Portraits*; but his work had [*sic*] made a deep impression on the best minds. In this new volume of verse the old world of classical authority and scholarship and the new passing world of havoc are brought together."

The "old world" poems in *Eidola* retain the smooth, wistful qualities of his earlier work, but a few have more spirit. Manning is still the silent watcher, standing guard at the well of classical inspiration, but he is now more likely to mock the world than to describe his soul's trembling, and to draw from tradition what suits his scepticism:

The Image Seller

I would bring them again unto you,
The gods with broad and placid brows;
And for you have I wrought their images
Of carven ivory and gold;

That your lips may be shaped to praise them,
And your praises be laughter and all delights of the body,
Dancing and exultation, a dance of torches
In scarlet sandals, with burnished targes:
A dance of boys by the wine-press
Naked, with must-stained purple thighs:
Of young girls by the river in saffron vesture
Dancing to smitten strings and reed flutes.
Praise then mine images: Helios; Artemis,
With a leash of straining hounds: and the Foam-born.
Turning from love to sleep, drowsy and smiling,
With the fluttering of doves and dreams about her
And softer than silk, Hephaistos' golden net.
Lo, Bacchus and his painted beasts!
Praise ye mine images!
A dryad whom clinging ivy holds while laughs
The swarthy centaur pursuing; and a troop
Of small Pans delicate and deformed.
Yet your lips praise not,
Crying: We too would be deathless as these are,
We, the hunted! But dance and adore them,
Praise my sweet grave gods of the blue, and the earth-born!
Praise their strong grace and swiftness!
For in these gods mine hands have wrought,
In these alone are ye deathless.

That poem, written in 1914, can be read as a companion piece to Pound's "The Return", which Manning greatly admired. It is a far more interesting effort than almost anything in his earlier collections, which he had come to dismiss as "mainly childish things". Poets frequently deny their early work, often with good reason. Manning was certainly justified in thinking that he wrote better poetry as he matured, for his early work often sounds like the product of someone who "knows the rules and writes beautiful language", but who has not "the art of writing poetry which is vitally interesting". Thus Pound remarked, speaking generally, in *The Spirit of Romance* (1910). To him

Manning had continued to owe a debt. As Pound moved out of his imagist phase to work in free verse, so too had Manning experimented. Indeed, without the stimulus of Pound's work and criticism Manning might have written less verse. It may be coincidence only, but after Pound moved to Paris in December 1920 Manning seems to have published just one further poem. He unquestionably attempted more, and may actually have published more — there are probably haystacks I did not even see — but as a poet his career was effectively finished. Friction between personalities can be a marvellous goad to activity, especially to a writer who was used to, and would increasingly depend upon, outside inspiration.

As was Manning's practice, several of the poems in *Eidola* were dedicated to friends. One went to the vicar at Pembroke Dock who had kindly given him the run of his home; another to Miss Una Taylor, one of the two literary daughters of a minor Victorian writer, Sir Henry Taylor;* and a third to Jelly d'Aranyi, the Hungarian born violinist who had been living in England since the outbreak of the war. This last dedication deserves amplification.

Today the name Jelly d'Aranyi (1893–1966) carries little of the magic it had when she was in her prime, giving concerts on her own or with her sister Adile, or playing duets with Myra Hess. Audiences loved her playing, and composers, seemingly charmed as much by her personality as by her artistry, wrote works specifically for her. Manning, too, was enamoured with the "adorable Jelly". He made a point of attending her concerts when he was in London, and became quite friendly both with her and with her sister. The poem dedicated to Jelly, "Paroles sans Musique", is one of his duller efforts in *Eidola*. But a better poem in that collection also acknowledges his affection for the beguiling musician.

To Saï

You chase the blue butterflies,
The shining dew is shaken by your feet,

That are white in the young grasses;
Swift, you hesitate, poised;
And they elude you; fluttering
In the windless gold.

Sàï is small,
But a little child,
With little sorrows;
Yet her tears shine with laughter,
Her face comes and goes between the wet leaves,
As a face in sleep
Comes and goes between green shadows,
As moving lights hide and shine in the marshes.

I shall not look at her,
Lest she should hide from mine eyes
In the shadow.
I bring her pale honey in a comb, apples
Sweet and smelling; and leave them beside me;
Then comes she softly.
There is a bee in the willow-weed,
From flower to flower it climbs, and I watch it
Till the honey and apples are eaten.
Sàï is quite close to me; now she has gone
She has forgotten me.

Sàï is small,
But a little child.

Sàï (pronounced shy) was a pet name given to Jelly as a young girl by her family. I learned this from her biographer, Joseph Macleod, to whom I wrote in the hope that he had come across traces of Manning in the course of his own research. He hadn't, except for the autographed original of "To Sàï", dated 13 August 1915, when both poet and violinist, according to Eva Sumner's diary, were staying at Daisy Meadow. I was pleased to be able to date the poem — it may well be the last he wrote before entering the army — but I was more pleased by some comments Macleod included in his letter. They represented his interpretation of the poem, written for a book on poetic thought which he never published, and I was struck by how his comments about a poet of whom he was essentially ignorant paralleled my own reading of Manning. It was comforting to have a concurring opinion.

> Thought and form are loose, and the child is seen from the outside with a tender understanding as for a young animal. But there are hints that it is not just sentimental description...And when this poem was written, she had ceased being a child prodigy and was beginning, in the difficult position of an enemy alien in a major war, to make a name as one of the finest violinists of her time...She was 22. So this is not a sketch of a small girl but of a grown woman...The poet himself intrudes, lying on a rug on the lawn, if you like. In his description of the butterfly- or bee-like girl there is a suppressed yearning, which hovers on the edge of self-pity and settles on a wistful self-comfort. Human nearness (sex) and human remoteness (unrequited interest) have seldom indicated so richly chromatic a colour-scheme in a water-colour sketch...
>
> Now, anyone who knew Jelly d'Aranyi would agree that to her last days she had a childlike simplicity, very far from *simplesse,* and often an endearing childlike behaviour, very far from coyness. The poem explains one thing by pleasant description and quite another by leaving out the main fact.

The diffident, yearning figure, desiring from afar with gestures too indefinite to be understood; this was certainly an aspect of Manning I had come to know. There is also in the poem, as in the man, a muted cry of neglect — "She has forgotten me." Six months before this poem was written its author was complaining to Eva Sumner that he was "always thinking of friends" who were "never thinking" of him: "I know half a dozen people who will love me with the utmost devotion for five minutes and then forget that I exist for weeks." As a writer whose work appealed to a limited audience Manning could tolerate, even relish, a lack of notice. But in his personal life, where he carefully cultivated his privacy, yet readily depended on others for assistance and concern, a lack of attention could be distressing. Something of the child's egotism — captured so well in "To Sài" — never left him.

The praise for *Eidola,* particularly for the war poems, was far greater than it had been for his two earlier books of verse. The most enthusiastic applause came from Richard Aldington, writing in *The Dial*. Already a great admirer of Manning's prose, he found in the war lyrics a poetry "stern and true yet beautiful", and announced that he was ready to give a "whoop of joy that so delicate a scholar and so sincere a poet has been converted to *vers libre*". It was a conversion with only a modest reward. Though *Eidola* sold better than *Brunhild* or *Poems,* and in America, where the publisher Dutton served as distributor, sold better than any of his books except, later, *Her Privates We,* it could not escape drowning in the general flood of war poetry. Had Manning chosen to publish the war novel under his own name these poems might possibly have received a second look. But this was not to be. The records of John Murray show that from the publication of the novel in 1930 to the death of its author five years later there was not a single order for *Eidola,* leading the publisher, when settling accounts with Manning's executors, to state that for purposes of probate the volume had "no value". From 1937, when a new impression of *Her Privates We* was printed, a few copies of *Eidola* were sold each year, but Murray's file on the book ends on a depressing note: "wasted 8/5/41". The demands of a new war required that it be pulped.

On Christmas day 1916 Manning, now a lance corporal, arrived in London on leave. He had applied for a commission in November and was awaiting orders to go to an Officers Cadet Battalion. It was in this application that he had altered his age and his religion. He also stated that he had "now outgrown the asthma" which had afflicted him as a youth. This too was untrue: while there were periods when he was free from attacks, the disorder never left him. He gave as character references

Galton and the Earl of Ancaster, and offered the journalist Charles Whibley, whom he had known for several years, as someone who could "certify to my educational attainments". Whibley did so, signing himself "Honorary Fellow of Jesus College, Cambridge". Included in Manning's application was an affidavit from his mother agreeing to the false birth date and stating (wrongly) that "although my son was born in Australia he has been living in England for the past 18 years". Perhaps in Nora Manning's mind he never really had returned to Sydney after his first leaving. Her address, according to the affidavit, was 7 Park Place, London. She had recently come to England with her daughters, presumably to be near not only Fred but Jack and Charlie, who were themselves now in uniform and bound for Aldershot and further training before going to France.

Though Manning was happy to have another chance at a commission, for the moment all he wanted to do was rest, "never having had time since I went out to know how tired I was". He also was eager to see *Eidola* through the press. In the weeks before Christmas, Eva Fowler had served as his "literary godmother", handling the multifarious chores of publication with patience and tact. Her desk was littered with correspondence: from Galton, who had originally sent her the poems to be typed and forwarded to Murray, and who evidently had to be consulted on important decisions; from the people at Murray, who needed to have authorial decisions made about text and design; from magazine editors, who had to give reprint permission for poems they had originally published; and from Manning himself, who every once in a while sent one or two more freshly minted poems together with instructions and suggestions. "If he keeps sending," she wrote to C. E. Lawrence on 28 November, "we'll never get the book out by Xmas unless you can work marvels." Obviously Lawrence couldn't, and no less obviously Eva gave a small sigh of relief as well as exclamations of great joy when the poet himself showed up at Gilbert Street on the day after Christmas.

Apart from fatigue, a normal response to months in the line,

Manning had come through the experience remarkably well. The closest he had been to injury was when he was knocked over by the concussion of a shell that had rocked a dugout he was in,* and he had been sick only once — a bout of flu just before his leave. Galton thought he looked "better and stronger than I have ever known him". His spirits also were good; the months in France had, indeed, been liberating. "I found that I felt most free in precisely those conditions when freedom seems to the normal mind least possible — an extraordinary feeling of self-reliance and self-assertion." This was written to Rothenstein, who did not need the paradox explained. To Harriet Monroe, the editor of *Poetry,* he would later make the same point, though more impersonally: "I do not envy the men who escaped the experience, and I know most of the ideals which moved us 'private soldiers' to be illusion and '*pâturage du vent*' before I joined. That is really our reward, not to have gained anything: but to have achieved freedom for ourselves in our own will." That last sentence draws the basic lesson of the war as he thought about it over the years, and *The Middle Parts of Fortune* would try to establish its truth in fictive form. He was certainly not alone in viewing the experience as a testing of the will, but the test had had a great and special importance for him. Manning seems to have come away from the trenches with a confidence about himself that he had never known before. To suggest that war may have a temporary tonic effect will possibly disturb, but many men have found it so, even some who, unlike Fred Manning, did not go willingly to battle.

This buoyancy of spirit carried him through officer training, which he took at Whittington Barracks, Lichfield. Except for a touch of bronchitis on his mid-course leave, during which he stayed with the Fowlers, he encountered no problems and passed third from the top in his class.* On 30 May 1917 he received a temporary commission as a second lieutenant in the Royal Irish Regiment. His ties with the King's Shropshire Regiment, however, were not broken, for when *Eidola* came out he had copies sent to two of his former officers, and to the battalion chaplain. While waiting for orders he spent several weeks with his family and friends. Much of the time he was with his mother, but there were frequent visits to the Fowlers. One evening Eva arranged a poetry reading, where Yeats and Binyon also read. During this interlude Will Rothenstein did a pencil portrait of Manning in uniform, one that the subject found "too pure and fine a thing to be myself, and yet subtilly [*sic*] revealing what I wish I were, and what in moments of supreme vanity I imagine I have become. Well, I think every man should be judged by the best of him; and that is what you have done for me."

I could not locate this portrait; it may well no longer exist. But a similar pencil sketch done by Rothenstein some time later explains Manning's enthusiasm.* Strength, determination, and sensitivity are written on the profile, and the suggestion of firmness is enhanced by the lines of the uniform jacket. A photograph of Manning in uniform, taken some time after he had become an officer, also invites respect. The wideset mouth beneath the brim of his hat nicely conveys resoluteness, giving the lie to character assessments that trust too much to physiognomy. Another photograph of him in uniform, taken perhaps while he was on leave or later when he was in Ireland, shows him in a less idealised posture. He is standing on a road with a walking stick in his hand, gazing at his mother beside him. She faces the camera directly, and is heavily shrouded in widow's weeds against the cold. Behind the pair looms a tree, barren of foliage, its branches outlined against the sky like gigantic ganglia. There is a marked feeling of desolation in the scene — except for the attentive angle of the son's head.

Early in July 1917 Manning joined the 3rd battalion of the Royal Irish Regiment stationed at Templemore, near Dublin.* It was apparently the first time he had been to Ireland, a place hitherto of no importance to him except as the birthplace of writers like Swift, Shaw, Synge and Yeats. His own roots in Ireland he seems never to have discussed; they had even less significance for him than his Australian ones. But what he saw in the summer of 1917 intrigued and amused him, and in a lengthy

Manning as lieutenant in the Royal Irish Regiment, 1917
(Eleanor Manning)

letter obviously crafted to charm its recipient, Rothenstein, he described the life about him:

> Some day soon I shall send you a poem about Ireland. I feel the country intensely, every acre has a kind of forlorn glamour about it, and one comes to believe again, with an equal tolerance, in the old gods, and the

saints; and in the loves of Deirdre and Naisi, and the preachings of Patrick. Close by Templemore Barracks is a park full of great trees, and wild undergrowth; the paths and drives obliterated by encroaching vines and brambles. It surrounds an ugly house, castellated, which dates from the Mid-Victorian era, and is fortunately empty. But the park itself is enchanted, and I am sure that all the creatures of Irish legend inhabit there. In any case there is always the holiness and patience of the trees, and I can escape into it from the companionship of my brother officers, only half a dozen of whom are good fellows, while all of them are stupid. Then there are the shawled women, driving their asses along the roads, with their pleasant brogue, and friendly greeting; the unkempt, half-savage children one meets with turning off the high road into some lonely boreen; the characters too of a small market town, my dear old Doctor, who is as mischievous as a school-boy, and Father O'Neill, who breeds horses, and is a mighty hunter before the Lord; and the bank-manager, prim, with precise old-maidenly ways. It's a world I have never known, so completely detached from "the great world", and so perfect in itself. Everyone does what is right in his own eyes: except as regards those twin curses of humanity, religion and politics. They ride bicycles, even motor bicycles, on the foot-path, and without motor or driver licenses; they exceed the speed-limit; they ignore the food-regulations; they keep unlicensed dogs, they distil illicit whiskey, and only a soldier fails to get a drink after hours. I could fill the page with their complete ignoring of law. Their politeness consists in saying that nothing matters; their politics, in saying that everything matters. Their thought abides not on any thing, but they have a genius for surrendering themselves, physically, to the stress of an overmastering passion, to the wave of a momentary and fluid emotion, and can shut themselves, like children, within a world of their own imagining,

> divinely improvident as regards the world of our somewhat[?] futile action. A disorganized and unsystematic Utopia: I don't believe they're real people, who inhabit it.

The promised poem never appeared, though Manning would later pen some "indecent lines" (now lost) on Clongowes School and send them through Pound to the school's most famous alumnus, James Joyce. There would be very few more letters written during his succeeding months in Ireland, for already he was in trouble.

The story begins on 10 July, within days of his joining his new unit, when he was found to be drunk. The circumstances are not disclosed in the official records, but a comment in a letter — "I have broken all the rules of the mess" — suggests a more public spectacle than the episode at Oxford the preceding year. He was placed under arrest, and on 6 August came before a general court martial at Cork. He pleaded not guilty, but the court found against him, and on 8 August he was sentenced to be "severely reprimanded". Following standard procedures the case was then reviewed by the commander-in-chief of the forces in Ireland and the sentence confirmed. No other details of the incident are available. When he reported to Rothenstein on 21 July that he was "liable to be tried by court martial", his tone was one of indifference: "I rather like being under arrest, as it spares me the company of my brother officers at mess. . . Nothing, I think, will happen; I am only to be 'strafed' in canting phrase; then I shall be told how vastly I have improved under the treatment." His prediction proved only half right.

A few days after the reprimand, Manning reported sick to the doctor at Templemore, complaining that he felt he would lose his balance, "especially in the middle of a large open space like the parade square". The doctor seems to have thought that he might be experiencing delayed effects of shell shock, and had him sent to the Military Hospital at Fermoy to be examined by a Medical Board. Their report, dated 24 August, stated that

Manning was suffering from the symptoms of "neurasthenia" accompanied by "nervous depression and insomnia". Their negative answer to the question, "Was the disability contracted under circumstances over which he had no control?" indicates that they did not believe that they were dealing simply with a case of shell shock. A month's rest before returning to "light duty" was ordered, and it was determined that he would not be fit for "home service" for two months, or "general service" (meaning combat duty) for three. He then spent a week in "a very decent room" at the Fermoy hospital, attended by doctors and nurses who were "pleasant" to him. The rest and care apparently had excellent results for on 31 August he was back "at duty" at Templemore, though still under some medical restrictions, and assuring Rothenstein — who had previously been told of a quarrel with his colonel — that there had been nothing "disciplinary" about the Medical Board's evaluation. He also mentioned that had he not been in the hospital, "I should probably have had to go overseas next Tuesday." When asking C. E. Lawrence at Murray for copies of *Eidola* to be forwarded to him, he expressed this possibility more dramatically. "I. . . may be fired overseas at any moment." To Rothenstein he was putting the best face he could on the situation; to Lawrence he was dissimulating. And by 17 August he had not written to Galton "for weeks", or at least that was what Galton was telling Houtin.

His condition deteriorated. Still suffering from insomnia and "nervous exhaustion", he had, in his own words, "recourse to stimulants". Alcohol compounded his difficulties and early in October 1917 he was hospitalised in Cork for delirium tremens. On 9 October he went before a "confidential" Medical Board which determined that there were no longer any symptoms of his latest problem. Crossed out in their report was another diagnosis, "delusional insanity". More details about his condition in this period would be helpful, but the impression left by the official record is clear enough.

Once he was released from the hospital (11 October) and

assigned again to light duty, Manning, probably with some official encouragement, decided to salvage what honour he could. On 22 October he formally requested that he be "allowed to resign my commission on the grounds of ill health. Owing to nervousness and constant insomnia I feel that I am unable to carry out competently my duties as an officer." This request was forwarded and recommended for approval by the acting commanding officer of the battalion, Major E. F. Milner, a career soldier and veteran of the western front. Before there was a response, however, the petitioner aggravated his troubles. On 29 October, Milner reported to Cork that Manning "has again become unfit to perform his military duties through the effects of drink." He had been absent from mess on 27 October and the next morning reported himself "unwell". At noon the medical officer reported to the adjutant: "I have seen 2nd Lieut. Manning. This officer is in a stupor, quite unfit for any duty evidently the result of a drinking bout." Manning was confined to his quarters and Milner, obviously hoping to save his subordinate from further embarrassment while allowing the army its due, attached two carefully worded conclusions to his report:

> 2nd Lieut. Manning has submitted his resignation and if this is to be accepted I cannot see that any useful purpose will be served by again trying this officer.
> 2nd Lieut. Manning is a gentleman but apparently has no strength of will and is quite unsuitable as an officer.

With this episode Manning's military career collapsed. The only question remaining was how he was to return to civilian life. Would he be permitted to resign without disgrace, or would there be a second court martial, a penalty harsher than a reprimand, and possible ignominy? The higher echelons in Ireland were prepared to accept his resignation, but the War Office in London hesitated. They wanted to know why Manning had not *already* been court-martialled again for the early October incident that had landed him in the hospital. The answer, that he could have explained this second episode as an extension of the first, did not sit easily with those who examined the case only as a file of papers. But it was one that Manning was prepared to argue. This is clear from a formal statement, dated 22 December, that he submitted while questions and answers volleyed back and forth between the War Office in London, Headquarters of the forces in Ireland at Parkgate, Dublin, and the battalion at Templemore:

> For some time previous to the 29th of October I had been suffering from continual insomnia and nervous exhaustion. I was in an extremely weak condition of health generally, and in those circumstances had recourse to stimulants. I think that my condition subsequently was in a considerable measure the result of these circumstances.

This argument could, of course, have also been employed to account for all that had happened after August, not just the early October incident. Skilfully handled it might have saved Manning at a court martial. Further pause was gained by a technical point: there was only one witness, the medical officer, to the latest offence. This too, the authorities felt, could pose a problem in court. Finally, the Army Council in London was prepared to be swayed by Major Milner's observations: what "useful purpose" would be served by another court martial?

Pragmatism prevailed. In January 1918 the War Office decided that Manning's service could be "dispensed with", and so notified officials in Ireland. A new letter from Manning requesting resignation was filed on 29 January, and took effect on 28 February. On 27 February the fact was duly announced in the *London Gazette* for all the world to see. What the world did not see, however, was the official understanding that he had been allowed to resign because of "ill health brought on by intemperance".

If Manning's correspondence with Rothenstein is a reflection of the way in which he informed friends of his resignation, then he was less than forthcoming or candid. After August of 1917 there are only single letters in November and December, neither of which mentions his problems except to note an attack of "lumbago", and to sneer at his brother officers, "who have neither an intelligent idea nor coherent speech". Later in the same letter he complains of being "tired of listening to schoolboy chatter about loose women, from the lips of grown men." His next letter is not until July 1918 when he informs Rothenstein that he has resigned. In this letter he offers as his reasons "disorganized nerves" and conflicts with the colonel of the regiment; spreads more camouflage by noting that he has been made an "hon. member of the mess" and that the new adjutant suggests "I should try to rejoin"; and offers the obligatory apology for his long silence: "I have meant to write to you for the past couple of months." Probably no more than a handful of people — if that many — ever learned the full story of why "I was not a conspicuous success in the R. I."

The official record tells one story, the letters to Rothenstein another. Naturally, neither fully explains what Manning went through in the months after he joined the regiment. Was the cause of his loss of control delayed shell shock, the "hard" time he had at the very beginning with the colonel, the boredom and contempt he increasingly felt for the "imbecilities" of his brother officers, or the demands made on him as a parade-ground and now commissioned soldier? It may have been of all these, and more besides. What is clear is that, having fallen foul of authority in July, he could not recover his balance. The more he drank, the more anxious he became; the more anxious he became, the more he drank. And so he was perceived as a misfit, as "a nice gentlemanly young fellow, but weak in character". The judgement was neither unkind nor unfair; from a Commanding Officer's point of view, it was sufficient.

What this judgement omitted was the record of Private 19022, the private who had been on the Somme. He survived as the subject of Manning's talk and memories, the soldier of whom he was proud.

The story of Manning's resignation is not complete without a comment from a letter I received in January of 1979. "My father, as was possible in those days, pulled strings & was instrumental in getting him released from the army on medical grounds & he came to stay at Belfield where my mother by her influence made him pull himself together & cease drinking." The author of that sentence died before I could question her, even before she could answer my follow-up letter. Her name was Sybil Gowthorpe, nee Lynch, and the pity was that I had not found her earlier.

After his resignation, and before he left Ireland, Manning's letters had been addressed from Belfield, Stillorgan Road, Dublin. A little checking revealed that this had been the residence of Sir John Patrick Lynch (1853–1920), an eminent solicitor of the day and one time (1905–06) president of the Incorporated Law Society of Ireland. Various biographical dictionaries also told me about an American-born wife, Frieda Ottman, and three daughters, but I could find nothing to connect the family with Manning. So I wrote to the Law Society asking for information about the elder Lynch and any living descendants. In reply I was sent the contemporary *Irish Law Times* obituary notice of Sir John, and the promising news that the firm he had founded was still in existence. No word, however, about descendants. I then wrote to the law firm and was informed that Sir John's daughter Sybil was still alive and lived at Poulton Glebe, Poulton, Cirencester. It was an address to be savoured, as was the letter that eventually came from it:

> I met Fred Manning in 1918 towards the end of the war when he received a commission in my husband's regiment, the Royal Irish Regiment, stationed in Dublin. It could not have been a worse choice for a man of his type. He started drinking, got himself into trouble & was confined to barracks. My husband

> thought Fred Manning more than just a misfit & asked their Colonel, who knew my father, if he might take him out to Belfield if he made himself responsible for his safe return to barracks.
>
> Fred was a man "sans age" & this was the beginning of a close friendship with my father, his senior by many years, my mother, who was his contemporary in age & myself, which lasted until his death in 1935.

I now had the bond between Manning and the Lynch family. (Sybil's husband, Roy Gowthorpe, had been an officer in the Royal Irish, and gets a favourable mention in the standard history of the regiment.) Exactly how Sir John had used his influence was beyond recovery, though it is easy to imagine discreet inquiries and veiled hints of a vigorously contested court martial helping officials in Dublin to see how profitless it would be to pursue Manning. (Under British military law, the accused may bring into court a solicitor or barrister of his choice.) I also had the promise of several letters from Manning to various members of the Lynch family and, most important of all, the expectation of a continuing correspondence with a woman who remembered a great deal. But Sybil Gowthorpe's letter had mentioned poor health, and before she could write again or annotate the letters she was having copied for me, she died. With her went the details of a crucial period in Manning's life. Hints of it are contained, though, in the copied letters, which eventually were sent to me. "You and Polly [Barry]," he wrote to Sybil's mother Frieda in February 1930, while basking in the fame of the war book, "helped me such a lot towards the close of what was my part of the war. Whatever was good in me, was pretty well obscured, but you both could forgive a lot, and that is sometimes a kind of genius."

Belfield itself had been part of the cure. Today it forms the campus of University College and is well within the city of Dublin, but in 1918 it was a rural estate of almost 80 acres, dominated by a splendid Georgian mansion. At the back of the property were farm buildings where a small herd of Jersey cows was kept to supply the house. (Manning's love for fresh milk was easily catered to.) There was also a poultry maid, three gardeners, a chauffeur, and several odd-job boys — and that was only the outside staff. Within the house was a cook, a butler, and an army of maids, all carefully trained and supervised to keep life comfortable for the Lynch family and their frequent houseguests who — as was then the custom — sometimes stayed for weeks and months at a time, becoming veritable members of the family. Most of this I learned from Mrs Patricia Hope, a cousin of Mrs Gowthorpe, to whom I had been referred after the latter's death. "Puddy" Hope had often visited Belfield as a young girl during the twenties and, though too young to have personal memories of Fred Manning or Sir John, she recalled the life at Belfield with the passionate nostalgia of one remembering a lost paradise.*

It was obviously the ideal environment for someone in as rattled a condition as Manning was in the spring of 1918. At Belfield he could rest, read, and be attended to by a covey of solicitous women. Besides Frieda Lynch and her daughters there was Polly Barry, a longtime friend and semi-permanent guest of the family who, it had been rumoured, might have been romantically involved with Manning. But since she was at least ten years his senior, I suspect that she simply filled the familiar, though important, role of providing all those gestures of concern and affection that he depended on when things were not going well. The Polly Barry I heard about seemed eminently suited for the role: "kind", "widely read", and "very witty", she was a natural companion for the recuperating writer. She liked to listen to good talk — she had employed Sean O'Casey as a workman, before he gained fame, primarily to hear him talk* — and she could be expected to laugh at the nonsense poems Manning took to composing when he was ill. (It was at this time that he wrote the "indecent lines" on Clongowes School, the alma mater of his host as well as of James Joyce.) Toward the end of his stay at Belfield, Manning's mother and sisters crossed over from England to see him. They found, among other things, that he had acquired a nickname, "Tony", given to him by Frieda Lynch. Every member of the Lynch family sported a nickname and, as if to symbolise his rebirth, Fred was given one too.

As his strength and spirits returned, Manning took advantage of the world beyond Belfield, meeting, for example, the writers Æ (George Russell) and Stephen Gwynne, to whom Rothenstein had provided introductions. According to Victor Woolmer, Manning also became "friendly" with the Countess Markiewicz, the fiery Sinn Fein leader who was the first woman elected to the British parliament. None of her several biographers supply evidence for this friendship (which conceivably derived from one of Manning's later visits), nor do the selection of her letters that are in print. Still, I cannot imagine why (or how) Woolmer would have invented the connection. And there are clear signs that Irish politics — like the Irish themselves — began to exercise a fascination for Manning.

He had arrived in Ireland a Unionist; he left convinced that the old union was dead. "The war which tested us as individuals, or as parties, tested the Union also and proved by the inexorable logic of facts that it had no reality." Such is the drift of "An Unionist's *Apologia*", a closely reasoned article that was published in the *Nation* in March of 1919. Like subsequent letters he sent on the same topic to *The Times* and the *Spectator*,* it asks readers to look beyond their prejudices and even their principles — "no principles are immutable, and least of all those governing political practice," spoke the author of *Scenes and Portraits* — and to recognise that "the apparent unity" of Great Britain and Ireland is "an unreal and dangerous fiction". Some other form of governance had to be worked out, one that would not necessarily exclude England, but one which gave the Irish responsibility for themselves.

> The Irish have no public spirit, no civic sense, because they have no power and no responsibility. They need

> that return upon themselves which complete autonomy would give them, that experience which is only to be gained by a continuous reference of ideals to realities, of aims to achievements, that tolerance which comes only by realizing in one's conscience the flaw in the material which thwarts entirely, or at least deforms, so often, the images of our desire.

Wise words, not to mention prophetic, and if they were rather more philosophical than the average political editorial, perhaps that was what the issue needed. Certainly that was the perspective Manning brought to political questions, past as well as present. Ever the anti-sentimentalist and anti-idealist, he had no sympathy for policies and politicians who ignored fundamental realities, whether the realities were (as in Ireland) the need for a people to make its own mistakes, or (as with the League of Nations) the "fallacy" of nations being equal. "A true equilibrium is brought about by every nation developing its utmost strengths: weakness leads only to dissolution and chaos." Logic, history, and a sceptical temper would produce such a view in any sane man, Manning would have argued, or as he has Bagoas say in *Scenes and Portraits,* "My outlook upon things is historical and therefore necessarily pessimistic." Machiavelli, though, had served as the more complete spokesman for Manning's outlook.* The smiling Florentine knew that in politics, as in religion, the important questions have to do with timeless conduct rather than "principles", theological or political.

Had Sybil Gowthorpe lived longer many questions about Manning's stay in Ireland, and subsequent years as well, would have been answered. With time only for one letter she had given me much, but had also withheld much, apparently waiting to see what sort of person I was. I gathered this from talking to her family and friends when I went to Cirencester in September of 1981. Listening to them it seemed that I had lost the chance of meeting a very interesting woman, not merely a good source, and I could see for myself from her house at Poulton Glebe, which she had taken a hand in designing, that Sybil Gowthorpe had been a woman of sense and taste. In addition, I learned from her granddaughter that Manning's letters had been preserved long after other correspondences were destroyed. Evidently they had been treasured, and, it was guessed, saved in the hope that one day someone would want to see them.

After two days in Cirencester I left the West Country one evening, bound for Oxford. As I drove along the nearly deserted road I thought about a copy of a letter addressed to Manning at Belfield that I had seen in the Army Records Centre. Dated 22 October 1918, it informed him that his application for "reappointment" to a commission could not be considered until he had re-enlisted and had "been recommended by your Commanding Officer after service in the field". Apparently he had followed the suggestion of the adjutant about trying to "rejoin" the Royal Irish and had at least made inquiries. The application itself is not in the file, but a comment in a letter to Rothenstein offers at least one motive. "It will always," he wrote two days before the Armistice, "be a regret to me that I wasn't in at the finish." That was easily said to Rothenstein, and it was true as far as it went. It also inspired the question of how he would have ended *The Middle Parts of Fortune* if his own war had finished differently. Would he have killed Bourne if after the Somme his own career as an officer had not been itself a kind of death?

Starting Over

CHAPTER SIX

Manning returned to England in early October of 1918, "just missing" being aboard the *Leinster* when it was sunk by German torpedoes in the Irish Sea. Instead of returning to Edenham he stayed for several months in London with his mother and sisters, who were living in a flat in Carlisle Place, near Westminster Cathedral. No surviving letter describes what he did on Armistice morning, but if his distaste for crowds kept him from the delirium of the streets — Ezra Pound that day was atop a bus, "his hair on end, smacking the front with his stick and shouting to the other people packed on the tops of other buses" — he at least must have heard the bells and maroons welcoming the end of war. And though Manning worried about a "dangerous" peace — "so many cupidities and explosive passions have been loosened on earth, and victory is a heady wine" — he had already begun to pick up the pieces of his old life. He was back in touch with friends and accepting offers to write, eager to be about the "business of clearing one's head", and young enough still to believe his best efforts lay in the future, not the past.

Pound, now London editor of the *Little Review,* asked him to write an article for an issue to be devoted largely to the work of Remy de Gourmont, the French philosopher and critic. Manning obliged with a short essay questioning Gourmont's emphasis on sex as "the unique source from which our aesthetic sense derives its being", while characterising the Frenchman's style and thought as "essentially feminine. ., unscrupulous, contradictory, full of those provocations and slight perversities, even the childish malice that a woman will use toward men". This was too much for Pound, a longtime champion of Gourmont.* He asked Manning to make some changes, and when his friend declined, he appended a footnote to the piece. ''The article seems to me a typical expression of one holding ideas and affected by ideas in exactly the manner de Gourmont never was by them affected.'' Pound concluded the note by printing Manning's response to his strictures, giving him, in effect, the last word. The argument showed that their friendship was in good working order.

Forty years later Pound came across the article and, having read it again, told Richard Aldington that it was a ''remarkably close bit of crit'' — which indeed it is. Though Manning had worried that ''three years of life as an automaton'' had dulled his critical faculties and style, the essay is a little gem. It also reveals the author himself. ''Just as Nietzsche, a neurasthenic, worshipped the idea of force and power, so M. de Gourmont with a passive and reflective nature, with a woman's critical faculty and instinct for detail, her unconscious immorality, practises the cult of the male.''

Pound also asked Manning to write a story for a quarterly he was planning to start.* Neither project, however, was to be realised: Pound did not get the backing he needed and Manning fell desperately ill. It began as an attack of the dread influenza of the day and developed into double pneumonia. He spent several weeks in a nursing home in Devonshire Street, and ''just missed'' dying. ''For two nights I was so much over the border, that the remainder of the way had no terrors for me.'' When he was strong enough to leave London he went to Mundesley Sanatorium on the Norfolk coast as a ''precautionary measure''. Now a rehabilitation hospital, the sanitorium was designed for the open-air treatment of tuberculosis.

For some time I wondered whether Manning had been consumptive himself. There was no talk of it in his letters, but his past and future lung problems — asthma, chronic bronchitis, emphysema — encouraged the possibility, as did the claim of

Richard Aldington, that he "certainly had it [TB] during or after the War". "During" was out of the question; "after" might be settled by an inquiry to the hospital. Thus I sent off a letter, on the *very* long shot that medical records had survived 60 years.

> 12th September, 1979
>
> Dear Mr Marwil
>
> I was very interested to receive your letter but unfortunately it came about two years too late. For many years our old case notes were kept in a storeroom here but two years ago because of fire risk we were asked to destroy them...

Death had removed Sybil Gowthorpe and J. G. Fairfax; now caution had swept away records that probably would have disclosed more than his immediate medical problems. Timing is all, and not just in politics and love. Had someone gone in search of Manning only a few years earlier, the number of mysteries about his life would have been noticeably fewer.

In 1981 I went to Mundesley. I wanted to see the hospital and take some photographs; I also wanted to examine an "old register" of patients that the director, upon receipt of my letter expressing a desire to visit, told me his secretary had recently discovered. (By now I had formulated a law of research: send a letter of inquiry and people will try to remember what they have; announce your coming and they will have a look around; arrive on their doorstep and you are apt to be given something of value.) The trip also gave me a chance for a little sightseeing around the Norfolk coast. In my pursuit of Manning I had long since decided to take whatever pleasures the trail afforded.

The register, while silent on Manning's actual condition, was nevertheless informative. It listed the precise dates of his stay (1 April–21 June 1919) and revealed that three physicians — an unusually large number — had looked after his case. One of them, Sir James Kingston Fowler (no relation to Alfred), was then a leading figure in the study and treatment of lung disorders. Manning, I was not surprised to learn, had had access to the best medical attention available. Whose decision it was that he should go to Mundesley the record does not say — Fowler was then associated with a sanitorium in Sussex and had no formal connection with Mundesley — but the length of his stay corroborates Manning's speaking of it as a "precautionary measure". This does not, however, rule out the possibility that he may also have been under observation for tuberculosis. In 1919 chest X-rays for diagnosing the disease were "untrustworthy", so that to eliminate the possibility patients were watched for "some weeks".

Writing on 18 May 1919, Manning attributed the length of his illness and recuperation to the war: "Even those who have survived their experiences in France must have spent a large part of their reserve energy, and a sudden call upon it finds them bankrupt." There is much truth in what he says, but the general observation cannot allay my suspicion that a long convalescence was not an uncomfortable state of being for him. Even in good health he enjoyed his ease, and when illness (or anxiety) struck he adopted a strategy of passive resistance. "Get well soon", he wrote to Laurence Binyon many years later, "but don't hasten out of the convalescent stage; and even when you have emerged from that, take things quietly. People talk a lot of nonsense about will: it is better to let the will sleep a little, and then happens a kind of imaginative reconstruction of the mind which makes for health." A wise patience is contained in that prescription, which he gave to other friends as well,* but its acquiescence should also be heard in the context of his chronic valetudinarianism and indolence.

Manning returned to Edenham in July 1919, and slipped back into the routine of the vicarage as easily as if he had been away for the afternoon instead of almost four years. The house more than ever resembled a gallery lodged within a library. Books were "overflowing into all the rooms" and much of the Piranesi collection, now virtually complete, hung about the walls. In the vicar's study, just over his armchair, was an old coloured print of Voltaire wearing a coat with a fur collar to go with the bust given him by Houtin years before. Galton himself was in his sixty-seventh year, troubled more than ever by the cold, satisfied to re-read his favourite authors, pleased that "Latin civilization" had triumphed over German barbarism, but furious at the terms of the armistice and the naivety of the idea of a League of Nations. "The whole world seems to have gone mad." Travelling had become so "disagreeable" in the past few years that he had seldom left Edenham, and he seems to have stopped writing as well. His last significant literary undertaking had been in 1915: a translation of "Guerre et Religion", a pamphlet by the French scholar and friend of Houtin, Alfred Loisy, to which Galton had added a 15-page prologue. But as he gradually withdrew into himself, he did not shirk his correspondence. If anything, his letters became more voluminous, long jeremiads saved from tediousness by their bilious ironies: "The world is arranged so stupidly that it must have been made by twilight, instead of in the light which the authors of Genesis boast about." One of his letters (presumably to Olivia Shakespear) came to the attention of Pound who took some paragraphs from it to construct a brief article, "Thoughts from a Country Vicarage". It was not the first time Pound had made use of Galton, nor the first time he had quoted him anonymously in his work.* He respected "Old Galton" for his learning, and most of all for his prose. One can see why: in tone, pith, bite, and candour it was a style that met Pound's standards as well as being a style agreeably similar to his own.* Galton, though, judged Pound's prose efforts "detestable".

During his long convalescence in the spring of 1919 Manning was told by his doctors "to stop all regular work and write idly". He followed orders and as a result had to give up an "interesting" task: prior to coming down with pneumonia he had been "asked" by Sir George Arthur to help write the official biography of Lord Kitchener. Manning had accepted the offer and had already done "most of the preliminary work" on the period 1911–14 that he had been assigned when he fell sick. Arthur, pressed for time, became impatient. "Sir George is or seems annoyed, as tho' sickness were a deliberate naughtiness on my part." It wasn't; though one would like to know Arthur's side of the story. The papers concerning the project at the Public Record Office make no mention of Manning — evidence that "preliminary" did not extend very far into the actual work?

Another project arrived almost immediately. He was "invited" to write the official biography of Sir William White who, as Manning explained to Rothenstein, had "designed practically the whole navy before the coming of the dreadnought". White did not have the glamour of Kitchener (though his life might have some parallels with that of Lawrence Hargrave), and the "technical side" was likely to be dull, but the pay was good and Lady White promised to be a kindly patron.* She, unlike Sir George, was willing to wait for Manning's health to improve before expecting him to start work. And so he accepted the invitation, probably shortly before he asked Murray on 25 June to send Lady White a copy of *Scenes and Portraits.*

It was an unlikely commission, as if Ezra Pound had agreed to write the biography of Henry Ford. So it seems today, and so it seemed to friends like Eva Fowler in 1919.* Manning excused his decision by saying that those who had approached him to write the book (apparently Lady White and John Murray) were "very pressing, and also because I wanted to make some money", presumably in order to pay the medical expenses of the past several months. He was still receiving an income from home, and would continue to do so until his death, but it was not large enough to cover a sizeable debt. (His father's passing in 1915 had not really improved his finances, for while all the children had been generously provided for, none of the bequests became operative until their mother's death.)* A dozen articles and poems could not have paid what Lady White was offering, and he could also anticipate royalties from Murray, who was to publish the book. Indeed, if he could finish the book in 12 to 18 months, which seems to be what he had in mind, he might tabulate the loss of time from more satisfying work as a sound investment.

But while money was an incentive, as he himself indicates, it was not the overriding reason for his finally consenting to undertake the work. What arguments "they" pressed on him — aside from the willingness to wait until his health had stabilised — he does not say. Whatever they were, they met with little resistance. For when Manning returned from Ireland — where his pen had gone dry — he was eager to write. Waiting for him was "The Gilded Coach", which he told Rothenstein in November 1918 he planned to take up "as soon as possible", but a manuscript that had gathered dust for four years and stymied his imagination for ten was not easily faced. And so he wrote the essay on Gourmont because "he was asked to do it", and began work on the Kitchener biography because he was "asked". When he was "invited" to the repast of drawings, blue books and statistics which the life of White promised, he accepted because he did not know what else to do.

Many articles and books, of course, are born in minds other than those of their authors. The ancients well understood that the muse was to assist in the *process* of creation. But the evidence of Manning's career points to a regular willingness (amounting to reliance) to let others set him projects — and to keep him at them. As early as 1908, while finishing *Scenes and Portraits*, he is asking Fairfax: "What am I to do now? Please suggest something. Shall I write a novel, or some critical essays?" And as late as 1930 he would acknowledge in the dedication his debt to the publisher who "asked" him to write *The Middle Parts of Fortune* and then kidnapped him to ensure its completion:

To Peter Davies
Who made me write it

During many of those years Galton had been a steady source of ideas, and a more or less efficient prod; the White biography was apparently no exception. Galton was not only a staunch admirer of British seafarers and an addict of biography,* but a friend of White. For I discovered while searching the volumes of the *Spectator* that under his pseudonym "Oùtis" Galton had written a long encomiastic letter about the architect after his death in 1913.* It is a letter revealing extensive knowledge of the man as well as of his work, so that even without precise details of how the commission came to be offered to Manning it is easy to detect in the process the hand of Galton. Once that hand was stilled, its importance in providing Manning with a sense of direction became manifest. Rudderless, he drifts, waiting to be asked before he writes, his spasms of activity separated by periods of illness and idleness. Sometimes the two are impossible to distinguish. Richard Aldington may have been in error about his having TB, but he came closer to the mark when he judged that his one-time friend and collaborator needed "the urging of a stronger personality to make him write".

From an asthmatic child too frail (or thought to be so) to fend for himself, encouraged to expect someone else to define and set limits to his activity, and cautioned to conserve his energies lest he undermine his health, Manning developed into an adult ready to let others look after him and into a writer as uncertain of what to do with his talent as he had been (and remained) uncertain of what to do with his body. When others do not provide impetus, he naturally gravitates to a condition of rest, which some people disparage as indolence and which he describes as idleness. Had there been no steady allowance, no cushion, perhaps he would have written more. And had there been less illness — especially after the war — perhaps he would have been able to write more. But the fact remains that from beginning to end he was inclined to wait on others to nudge him across that hard ground from inspiration to effort. A literary career of 30 years adding up to so little in terms of quantity and so much in terms of unfinished and/or ill-suited projects demonstrates how often he did not make it. Illness, alcohol, fastidiousness — "he spent as much energy in rewriting and destroying what he had rewritten, as would suffice to account for a number of ordinary books'' wrote Eliot — they all played a role. But so too did the habit of dependency, formed long before his literary ambition, long before he could help himself.

The work on White quickly proved unsympathetic. When Manning was not ''chained'' to his desk he was out interviewing shipbuilders, engineers, and armament makers, the last a class of people, he told Pound, who ''stink of money and blood''. Interviews with them made him think of the ''ploughboy'' soldier, the archetypal innocent, lying dead in France so that profits might be made for the ''accursed stockholders''. Pound did not need to be instructed about

Profiteers drinking blood sweetened with sh-t,
[*Canto 14*]

though he may have recalled his friend's diatribes — as he did the stories of Taffy Fowler — when he was composing the *Cantos.*

By the end of 1919 Manning had written the first section of the biography, a portrait of White's childhood, and the White family had been impressed. ''Goya painting grandees must have experienced a similar gratitude.'' Praise normally lifts hope, so that while the book was already becoming a ''nightmare'' — the image he had used in describing progress on ''The Gilded Coach'' — Manning thought he saw in White's life a ''moral tale'' out of which ''a few ironical values'' might be culled.

Relief from his labours was found in translating the Homeric Hymns and in reading ''endless memoirs'' of the seventeenth century so that he might ''recapture the atmosphere of my romance''. The old manuscript beckoned as the new became an act of drudgery. Escape was also to be had in reviewing. Ties, ''though more casual than ever'', were re-established with the *Spectator,* and T. E. Welby, a critic of very conservative political and literary tastes, asked him to write once a fortnight for a weekly he was organising. As things turned out, the *Piccadilly*

Review collapsed after a few issues, only giving Manning time to contribute one article, "The Poetry of Mr Binyon", which took as its immediate text Binyon's volume of war poems, *The Four Years*.

In writing about a poet to whose work his own had often been compared, Manning could at moments almost be writing about himself. Their lives touched at many points, and so too did the disciplined, classical temper of their minds. "There is no striving after effect," he writes of Binyon's verse, "no torment of appreciation, no intoxication of the senses." Confessing "a personal interest" in Binyon's war poetry, Manning finds in it what he believed to be (and what is) in his own, "the clear vision of a disciplined mind face to face with reality, untroubled by anger or fear, only blessed with the pity that is the last fruit of wisdom, and the sweetness which comes from strength." There is scant projection in all this; there did not need to be. But when, later in the review, "frankness...the first duty of the critic" forces him to concede that much of Binyon's poetry ultimately misses its mark, it is not just the voice of the critic we are hearing: "Every man has a right to be judged by what he has achieved, and not by what he may have failed to achieve, or by achievements at which he never aimed." It is a just principle, one that he would find other occasions for enunciating. And it is a principle that often gave me pause as his biographer. I was arguing his significance by its logic, yet the story that frankness obliged me to tell might make it appear otherwise.

Friends also helped to break the tedium of his work on White. Occasionally he went to London, and in November of 1919 Olivia Shakespear visited Edenham, as much no doubt to see "Matt-Matt" (her, and Yeats's, nickname for Galton) as to see Fred. If memoirs and photographs are to be believed, she was still, in her mid-fifties, a dazzling woman. But the people Manning saw most regularly were village people, among them now the Woolmer family, who had settled in Edenham during the war in a cottage not far from the vicarage. Manning seems quickly to have developed a special fondness for the family. He would often walk down to their cottage for a chat and a glass of fresh milk, and in the evening Vic Woolmer, who had served with the West Yorks regiment in the war, would come up to the vicarage and tap at Manning's study window to see if he wanted to play a game of chess or simply talk. When Vic told me these things he always referred to "Mr Manning", evidence that the friendship was conducted within the proprieties of age — Vic was 16 years Manning's junior — and no doubt of class as well. Yet Manning was no snob, and he obviously saw that Vic and Chick Woolmer were smart, well-spoken lads. There was enough to talk about even if boundaries were set, and even if Manning was "rather secretive in many ways". I also got from Vic a fine example of Manning's sharp tongue. A bone left in a mince pie became stuck in his teeth, and the anguished housekeeper hoped that he would not think that it had been left there due to "carelessness" on her part: "Well, damn it," he retorted, "did you do it on purpose?"

By the end of 1919 Manning was complaining of having "bags of work" to do and, as a result of another attack of influenza, not a great deal of energy. In January he was taking a "rest hour" in bed every day, and sounding very sour about the "incompetence" in the world. Neither his health nor his spirits improved much in the next several months. There was nothing specifically wrong with him; he just felt "ill and tired", and talked of returning to Mundesley in the summer as "a precautionary measure". By then, he wrote to Rothenstein in March, the White book will be finished — little more than a year after it was begun. This was a dream, an understandable desire to be quits with the disagreeable. Although a swift writer once he had his subject in focus, he had too much to digest to expect to complete a biography within so short a time. (In August 1920 he would still be "interviewing shipowners".) In the same letter to Rothenstein he also talked of finishing "The Gilded Coach" after the Mundesley visit, and after that writing another series of "studies" along the lines of *Scenes and Portraits*: "I have it in skeleton." More dreams. A writer's next book is often written in his mind while he struggles with his current albatross. Another dream featured a more dramatic escape: "I see Feisal is coming to England: if he wants a secretary to take back with him, I shall apply for the job." This dream of serving the hero of Arab independence was projected in the context of Manning's distaste for the "new England", in which he saw "neither honour nor sense". But his despondency over politics — "I think this is a good age to be dead in" — stemmed as much from his own personal situation as it did from external events. He was unhappy with what he was doing, and so was ripe for the "interior nihilism" he told Pound he was cultivating.

His mood seems to have seeped into a review he wrote for the *Spectator* on *Some Winchester Letters of Lionel Johnson.* It is a harsh and unforgiving piece, quite out of keeping with the principle of judging a man by his best which he had invoked on Binyon's behalf. Johnson is criticised for his lifelong "intellectual dishonesty" and his obsessive determination to escape from reality into religion and literature. The letters under review are dismissed as "dull", and his criticism as "not sure"; nothing is said of his poetry. It sounds almost as if the reviewer has a grievance against his subject, though all that is known of their personal relations is that there was an exchange of letters during Manning's first stay in England.* Did Manning fear that after a "golden prime" — Galton's judgment on Johnson's early years — he, like Johnson, had been wasting his talent? And was his silence on Johnson's most notorious means of escape, alcohol, a product of his own embarrassment? These questions are not meant to be rhetorical, nor should they be charged as unfair. Certainly Manning's strictures on Johnson were come by sincerely, and frankness *is* the "first duty of the critic", but they may also have served to exorcise a spectre that his own unhappy letters do not speak of. To live with Galton, after all, was to live with the memory and remains of Johnson, whose papers still resided in the vicarage waiting for Galton to write a memoir of him. And to live as well, perhaps, with the periodic suspicion of being silently compared with Johnson.

More engaging products of Manning's pen, as well as more overtly revealing of his attitudes, were three untitled fables he published in the spring of 1920.* Neatly turned, when summarised they lose the charm of their cadence but not their point or the evidence of their inspiration. The first portrays God, at the "hour of judgment", summoning all things that have ever existed to be brought before him and then deciding who (and what) shall be "cast into the abyss". All are spared until mankind is judged, and only a single man is "found worthy" of the abyss.

> And God looked at the abyss and at the soul before him, and God spoke: I shall not cast even you into the abyss lest you be lonely there.

In the second fable we meet "a man of the city of Ur called Shaman", who after many years of looking for God goes to the priests of Bel for help. "Confounded" themselves, they take Shaman to the head priest, "who dwelt apart on the highest tower looking at the stars", and asked him where God could be found.

> And the old priest lifted up his head, and spake unto Shaman saying: When you have found God by what signs will you know him?
>
> And Shaman was dumb.

The war had not altered Manning's view that God was a quest, "an adventure which perhaps ends in a discovery". A bleaker view of that quest is contained in a sketch he wrote at this time to accompany a drawing by Rothenstein of Dean Inge: God is the "eternal silence" who reveals himself to none, and is reached only by complete negation. Nevertheless, on those occasions in Ireland when he had gone to mass with the Lynch family, he may have found more in the spectacle than the "order and measure of a fine art". He may, as the first of his three fables suggests, have also sensed the merciful God, the God who had thought to create Eve lest Adam "be alone".

The last of the fables is brief enough to quote in full, transparent enough to need no gloss.

> When Anulallat was a young man, his mind was given up wholly to wisdom, and as he considered astrology the finest of all the branches of science he became a servant of the priests of Bel, and abode with them. For many years he abode with them, and passed through all the orders of the hierarchy until he became head-priest, and he had all the knowledge of the priests.
>
> And being come to the age of eighty years, a great loneliness came upon him, and his life seemed to have been but a day, or the hour of a day.
>
> "It is not knowledge that men should strive after, but love," he said. "I shall go down into the city and find a woman who will love me."
>
> So he left the high places of the temple and went down into the streets of the city; and a woman passed him, a young woman, very beautiful, and richly attired; and her feet hastened like the feet of one who hasteneth after a great joy; and he laid hands upon her beseeching her that she would teach him love.
>
> But she put him aside, saying: "What have the old to do with love? I am looking for my lover, a young man in his first strength. Get thee away!"
>
> And she left him; her feet hastening like the feet of one who hasteneth after a great joy.

The fables had been commissioned for the magazine *Coterie* by a member of its editorial committee, Richard Aldington, a young writer who had long been an admirer of *Scenes and Portraits.* Like Pound, he was generally unimpressed with Manning's poetry, having confined his praise of *Eidola* to admiring the truth of the war poems. (A truth, he told Lawrence Durrell 40 years later, that was worth more than the war poems of such "chairborne warriors of the knife-and-fork brigade as Auden and Spender.") To Aldington, Manning was "most significant, most poetic in his prose, which is philosophy expressed by a poet''. This lofty praise sets the tone of a two-page sketch, ''On Frederick [*sic*] Manning'', that Aldington included with the fables. That such an introduction was necessary, though, illustrates how small was the circle of readers who knew Manning's work. ''Remembered'' might be a more precise term, as eleven years had elapsed since the publication of *Scenes and Portraits*. Poetry that sold modestly and reviews published anonymously had not enlarged a reputation small to begin with. Aldington's sketch was basically a condensed version of an article he had written in 1914, ''The Prose of Frederic Manning'', which argued that Manning, along with Ford Madox Ford and T. Sturge Moore, was the only writer who might have a claim to be the successor of Ruskin and Pater, and so determine ''the literary taste of the next 20 years''. It was a bold prophecy for a 22-year-old writer to make, but one for which there was cause and already a kind of tradition. By 1920 there were other claimants, as Aldington knew, but he still retained a great respect for Manning's critical values, enough to show him his own (prose) work, and enough to ask him in the autumn of 1920 to contribute an essay on prose poetry to Harold Monro's periodical, the *Chapbook,* the following spring. Aldington, an enthusiastic advocate of a genre more recognised in France than in England, hoped to stir up some interest in prose poetry. In addition to pieces by Manning (''a fine prose poet'') and himself, he also solicited a contribution from T. S. Eliot even though he was known to be ''rather against prose poetry''. But it was light, not sparks, that the eager organiser wanted. Or as he put it in a letter to Monro: ''Eliot and Manning are really profound, their intelligence is consistently at play.''

At almost the same time Pound, who was looking for publishable manuscripts in his new role as London correspondent for the *Dial,* sent 100 pages of ''The Gilded Coach'' to the magazine's editor, Scofield Thayer, in New York. It was all he had seen of the presumably somewhat revised 1913 version, and thinking it ''great stuff'', hoped to arrange for serialisation. Manning, who described himself as ''damned hard up'', was overjoyed at the prospect. Letters discussing terms went back and forth between Edenham and London, with Pound simultaneously trying to use Manning's connections to obtain other contributors who might be expected to "ginger up" the recently reorganised magazine. Manning's hopes slumped, however, when Thayer informed Pound that, though he too had fallen "for Manning", the "rule" of the *Dial* was not to accept anything for publication "until we have seen the complete product". And so the troublesome question: "Has Manning finished the novel?"

The answer, of course, was no. Manning told Pound in October 1920 that it was "practically complete in extent but not in detail", and assured him that he could "keep it going" if it were accepted. He expected the manuscript of the White biography to be finished in December, so that starting in January he would be able to give the novel his full attention. Pound rejected as "bloody rot" the *Dial*'s rule and pursued the negotiations while urging Manning to send him more of the manuscript. Little, if any of it, seems ever to have been forwarded. Manning had one more chapter, a description of an "Epicurean supper party", almost complete. The rest, as he had told Pound even before Thayer balked, needed "rearrangement and perhaps some revision", and even then there were apparently parts as yet unwritten. Indeed, it looks very much as if Manning had a far from finished manuscript, and that, like most authors in his position, he was minimising the extent of the work left to be done. But it was also a manuscript on which he had not worked in a concentrated way for years.* His reading of memoirs of the seventeenth century had rejuvenated his interest in the book — "I don't want to write anything but the Romance", he told Pound as they waited to hear from New York — but if Thayer had accepted it and started printing it in January, the task facing Manning would have been substantial. Would he have been able to complete the novel? Luckily for him and the *Dial* the gamble was never taken, since an unforeseen event was about to cast him into one of the darkest stretches of his life.

13 January 1921 [Letter to Rothenstein]:

> Poor Galton has been seriously ill and I had to take him up to a nursing home for an immediate operation last Saturday. He will probably have another in a few weeks time, so perhaps I shall close the house here, as he is unlikely to be back for ten weeks. I settled everything in $\frac{3}{4}$ of an hour, and borrowed Lord Ancaster's car for him (to carry us to Essendine.) It was a miracle I got him there.

14 January 1921 [Letter to Houtin]:

> His cousin, Father Galton S. J. of Farm Street, has been with him. Our friend was charmed by his visit, but he thinks to save his soul by his own efforts, without troubling anyone. He sees clearly, always.

15 January 1921 [Letter to Rothenstein]:

> Galton seems to be improving. I left him in bed, like a great baby, with all his toys beside him on a small table: his most cherished books, a small ivory foot-rule, which he has had since he was twelve; and two or three small pebbles picked up in various parts of the world. All small, all toys, and all possessing those magical virtues which children give to their belongings.
>
> Vraiment, les hommes forts sont des petits enfants. I felt an hundred years old.

27 January 1921 [Letter to Houtin]:

> Yes: it was an operation for the removal of the prostate: it took place yesterday, and Mr Galton stood it well. The conditions are all favourable, tho' the process of recovery is always slow.

4 February 1921 [Letter to Rothenstein]:

> Mr Galton recovered on Monday, and I came home. I thought if I left him he would regain confidence more quickly. Poor old man, he has had a very bad time.

24 February 1921 [Letter from Eva Fowler to Albert Houtin]:

> Our dear Arthur Galton left us Sunday morning. Fred was with him; his end was like everything in his life: calm and full of dignity. . . Cremation took place here yesterday morning, and in the afternoon Fred and the sister of Arthur Galton left with the ashes for Edenham where he will be buried today. . . We don't know yet what Fred will do. His life will be very upset and changed, but for the moment he remains at Edenham. Mrs Fox remains with him for several days; afterwards Mrs Shakespear will go and on the eleventh I go. We don't want to leave him alone these first weeks, which will be very hard for him.

2 March 1921 [Letter to Houtin]:

> I feel as though a part of my own mind were dead. We were so closely bound together, in our affections, in our ideals and beliefs, spiritually and intellectually, that now I cannot realize his absence.
>
> Each of us was, in a sense, an extension of the other's conscience and thought: we could see with each other's eyes, and feel with each other's hands. I think that his fondness for my little book [*Scenes and Portraits*] came from the fact that I had made explicit many of the beliefs and desires he held implicitly. His mind was clear, firm and decided to the end. There was no doubt, no anxiety, no hesitation. I feel that it was not a life being ended, but a life being completed. He was full of courage for himself, and of tenderness for me. It was our separation that was bitter.

These last scenes show Galton to be worthy of the classical virtues he had long espoused. Death found him at once patient and indifferent: Marcus Aurelius had not done better. His ashes, housed in a small oaken casket, were placed beneath a tombstone close to the church by Manning. He, Galton's sister (Mrs Fox), and the Earl of Ancaster were the chief mourners. The vicar of Bourne led the service, and Galton's favourite hymn, "Lead kindly light", was sung.* On 7 March *The Times* published a modest obituary written by Laurence Binyon, and three weeks later the *Spectator* printed a short letter about Galton by another of his old friends, Alfred Fawkes. Manning thought of eventually writing "une petite mémoire" but, as the years passed, the "difficulties" of what he came to call a "biography" mounted — the correspondence had "gaps"; there were too few "records" of the years in the Catholic Church — and it was never done. A pity; had he acted on his impulse he might have painted his finest portrait.

Sixty years after Galton's death I toured St Michael's church for a second time. On this occasion I climbed into the belltower behind the sturdy frame of Bill Holmes, whose father had been parish clerk and bellringer for many years and who himself now rang the bells. Born in 1912, his memories of Manning and Galton were understandably few, but he had many stories from his father and a fine memory for what he had seen himself. Our ascent into the tower had been inspired by a bequest in Galton's will.* With a few notable exceptions — the Piranesi collection to the Countess of Ancaster, an edition of Voltaire to Olivia Shakespear — virtually everything had gone to Manning: books, prints, furniture, and personal effects "of every description", as well as "all my property in money". A hundred pounds, though, was singled out for the church wardens "to complete their peal of eight bells". The bequest was not honoured, according to Bill Holmes, because one of Galton's sisters disputed the terms of the will, which led to the money in the estate being largely swallowed up in legal expenses. Manning's letters indicate problems with probate but are too thin on the matter to offer a clear picture. He himself finally realised £200–£300, some of it from the seven tons of Galton's books that went to London for auction. Bill Holmes was quite insistent about the weight; presumably it gave the vicar added stature as a scholar in his eyes. Several pounds of that mighty lode, in the form of C. G. Heyne's eight-volume edition of the *Iliad* with a Latin commentary, eventually found its way to the library where I read the works of Galton and Manning and hunted for evidence of their lives.

While up in the tower I was shown the old facing of the church clock, dating from 1695. Some museum would no doubt pay handsomely for it, but it seems more appropriate that it should stay propped in a corner of the church it had served. On one wall was a more ordinary clock with roman numerals, a present given by Galton to the men who had rung the bells in his time. Bill Holmes was also eager to explain bellringing to me, and so for 15 minutes, not far from where Lord Peter Wimsey had solved the case of the Nine Tailors, I let myself be instructed in the various changes and the degree of their difficulty.

Downstairs Holmes took me for a walk around the village during which we made several stops: at the schoolhouse where a class of children of mixed ages were learning their lessons much as their grandparents had; at the Five Bells where the interior was very different from the days when cottage tenants had toasted the first Earl at the half-yearly rent suppers; and at a house where three ducks in the front yard furiously honked at our arrival and set off in turn the gabbling of dozens of turkeys in the backyard. The house belongs now to Mrs Stubley, but in 1921 it was lived in by the Kirby family with whom Manning went to lodge after Galton's death and where he stayed for about 20 months before moving to Surrey in January 1923. Thanks to Bill Holmes I was able to find and talk to one of the Kirby children, who recalled Manning quite well.

Nellie (Kirby) Bates was 17 when Manning came to live in her parents' home, and like all my other respondents whose memories of him derived from their youth, Nellie cherished a fond image of the man. It was not because she still had the necklace he had brought back from Rome for her in 1922, nor because of the whalebone hairbrush he brought her another time, nor because he had arranged at a store in Bourne for her to be

Manning standing in front of the Kirby home, c. *1921*
(Eleanor Manning)

given a half pound of chocolates any time she asked — though such gifts were doubtless magical to a child when affluence was less common — it was because of the simple niceness of the man. With his precise understanding and sympathy for the young, Manning easily won them to him. His manner and intentions were unlike Galton's; he did not wish to advise and assist as much as he hoped to befriend. He got on well with all of the Kirbys and at least once after leaving Edenham came back to visit Mrs Kirby. However, one episode, reported to me in a subsequent letter from Nellie, intimated how troubled he was during this period:

> My cousin who was brought up in our home at Edenham called on me yesterday evening. Before telling him that you had called to see me I asked if he remembered Mr Manning. He said that he had never forgotten Manning asking for my father to go into his room when he [Manning] had been drinking. He didn't know what he wanted but said my mother was very worried as she had seen the gun under the table and

> wondered what he was going to do. After that he said there was some very straight talking about drink being smuggled into the house.

Suicide? Unlikely for the Manning I thought I knew. He had a pistol — Vic Woolmer had told me that — but this story suggests more fright and imagination in Mrs Kirby than dire purpose in her lodger. And yet the possibility of suicide was not in itself ridiculous, for Galton's death was not the only shock Manning was to receive in what he later called "a terrible year".

In the midst of the upheaval in his life Manning was able to finish his brief contribution to the *Chapbook*'s symposium on prose poetry — not in time for Eliot and Aldington to take note of it in their essays, as they were able to do with each other's essays, and not in a form smooth enough to please its author, but at least he was willing to let it be published. "My head refused to work, and I could only give a bare indication of the way in which the problem might be solved." Manning seems the odd man out in the symposium in another way as well. Instead of rambling through several literatures to discover instances of, and arguments for, the prose poem — the strategy of the others — he looks exclusively to the Greeks, to a literature that had done "everything which it is possible to do and make with language", and which had "completed itself". Manning took for granted that what the Greeks practised, other cultures did (or might do). With the assistance of Plato and Aristotle — poetry was an imitation of life, not of "a measure of verse" — Manning confidently argues that the prose poem is not a contradiction in terms. Prose and poetry may be defined by their separate rhythms, but since poetry is "continually tending towards the form of prose" it profits us little to force distinctions between them. It was the argument of someone less preoccupied with the issue of whether the prose poem deserved status as a formal genre than with the development of the phenomenon itself. As a consequence Manning's essay is more learned than the others. "Dull and dusty", criticised Harold Monro, who predicted that "the ordinary reader will skip most of him". Perhaps, but the question of how many "ordinary" readers bothered with the *Chapbook* at all requires answering first. For all its choppy and unpolished brevity, Manning's article was finished in its logic and deserved Aldington's compliment that it was "very instructive".

Just as he was getting his bearings, having settled in with the Kirbys and having begun to write again, Manning took another blow. On 3 July Eva Fowler suddenly died of heart failure. "She was, after Arthur Galton, the person to whom I owed most in England: they were in a sense, the two poles of my consciousness." And of much more. There were still other friends to draw close to for "warmth and company", but the loss of Eva Fowler so soon after Galton's death seemed almost to empty his life of meaning. "All the interests of 20 years" were now closed, and he began to think of leaving England and settling in France. "There is little to keep me in England now, and I am of those who have no country." But for the moment there was only Eva to be thought of. He undoubtedly went to London for the funeral, his mind, as he sat in Holy Souls Chapel of Westminster Cathedral, recalling images of "the most loyal and generous friend a man could have". Then the long ride out to Kensal Green with Taffy Fowler and the others, with everyone feeling the shock of having suddenly to say goodbye to someone who by all rights should still have been alive. The weather that July was very hot; it would have been a fine time to have been at Daisy Meadow.

Instead Manning spent it at Edenham, trying to finish the biography of White. Had he not felt himself under an obligation to both Lady White and John Murray he would have quit the book. The events of the last six months, he wrote in early August, had so "disoriented" him that he found it difficult "to concentrate my mind on a single subject for very long". That confession was made to Aldington, and was followed by an entreaty: "With someone else working with me, I think the book could be finished in about six weeks. I wish you would come and help." He offered Aldington £50 to help him revise some of the earlier chapters and to write some of the later. There was another lure as well: "I have all the letters and papers of Lionel Johnson in my possession, and I could easily get permission to publish them. We might go shares in the book and make a scoop as there is a boom in L. J." These were the papers that Galton had been given years before by Johnson's sister, Isabella, on the understanding that he would write a "memoir", and as late as 1919 he still was thinking he would do it. Manning also did his case no harm when he alluded to the recent death of Aldington's father: "Do let us hunt as a couple for a few months, it will do us both good." He cautioned, however, that the "business" would have to be "confidential though I would acknowledge your revisions and assistance in general terms". Aldington quickly accepted.

Manning had had evidence other than Aldington's respect to be confident that he would agree to help him. The younger man had demonstrated his generous nature two months earlier when Manning, knowing of Aldington's links to several literary periodicals, had asked if he might get him "some books to review". To Aldington, the request had suggested a man in financial difficulty, and so besides doing what he could to arrange for the reviewing, he had straightaway offered Manning some cash. Obviously embarrassed, Manning gracefully declined the offer, explaining that he had "a small private income" and had only been looking for "some pocket money". Now in August the tables were turned: Aldington needed pocket money himself for a proposed trip to Italy. Having accepted Manning's offer, he went to Edenham to look at the material and to work out the details of the partnership.

What began as a friendly collaboration serving the interests of both men ended in a nasty dispute. Long after Manning's death Aldington told a friend what had happened:

> Manning became impossible through dipsomania, but my break with him was due to intense irritation with

> him. He had taken money to do a book on Sir William White. . . .and partly from drunkenness and partly TEL [T. E. Lawrence] indolence couldn't finish it. He begged me to do it, and needing the money for a trip to Italy I unwisely consented. After I had done the work and he had sent it in he did not pay and left letters unanswered. Under legal suasion Manning eventually coughed up.

Six years later, in the article on Manning commissioned by *Australian Letters*, an Australian literary journal, he gave a sanitised version:

> . . . the book gave Manning endless trouble, for he was a creature of whim and impulse in his writing, and he was paralysed by a mere literary task. At his request I tried to help him out, but I fear not very successfully.

The two accounts are easily reconciled, for in trying to interest Australians in one of their own, Aldington would have defeated his (and the magazine's) purpose by scratching an old wound. The facts as he presented them are nonetheless true: he did write some chapters, which Manning told him he "altered. . .a good deal", and Manning was very delinquent in paying the £50 they had agreed upon. What caused the delay is unclear, for there is a break in Manning's letters to him between November 1921 when he talks of Aldington's going on with his allotted chapters, and January 1923 when Manning, addressing him no longer as "My dear Richard" but as "Dear Aldington", apologises for the long delay in sending him money. "I am selling some property either this week or next, and when the sale is completed I shall send you some of the money pending a settlement with Lady White." Aldington underlined most of this passage and wrote in the margin: "Nothing was sent." What "legal suasion" was actually employed — a casual threat of legal action, a formal letter sent by a solicitor, a suit filed? — I do not know. And the files at John Murray, the publisher of the biography, are of no help. They lack any trace of the book. "It is really most strange that there should be nothing about this book anywhere in the archives. We have no records at all about it...It is all very mysterious." The people at Murray knew of one other case, involving an author sued for plagiarism, where all the letters concerning the book were missing, "obviously all kept out of sight in JM's care with other legal matters, and never seen again!". Had this instance been as embarrassing? And what did Manning's comment, "pending settlement with Lady White", refer to? Did he owe her money — for excessive expenses, or for exceeding the time of the contract? And did she ever learn of Aldington's role in the making of the book? The answers may lie in Lady White's papers, which I had no luck in tracing. But even without them the collaboration has the force of symbol: of the unhappy history of the biography itself, and of the career of its principal author.

Sometime in the autumn of 1921 Rothenstein did what was to be the last of his drawings of his friend. The face is fleshier and there is a noticeable melancholy in the expression. The drawing was shown at the Cotswold Galleries in Frith Street, London, along with several others the artist planned to publish in "a kind of Liber Juniorum, with a few middle-aged gentlemen who can still expect to be cast for youthful roles". The book appeared in 1923, but without the Manning sketch, which did not appear until 1939, when Rothenstein published *Since Fifty*, the last volume of his autobiography. Unfortunately, neither the reproduction nor the original in the National Portrait Gallery comes to life. Like the earlier drawings of the young poet and the vigorous soldier, this one of the burdened friend is mainly surface.

But if Rothenstein still could not render a convincing image of Manning, the two men had nurtured their friendship since the war. They exchanged letters frequently and the Rothenstein home in Airlie Gardens became a stopping place for Manning when he was in London. There he befriended as well the young Rothensteins, and with each he would correspond separately.

John and William were both invited to visit him, and when the former — at the age of 25 — was considering conversion to Catholicism he chose to discuss his doubts about the move with "the most sceptical Catholic I knew". It was their sister Rachel, though, who gained special attention from Manning, primarily because of a long illness. Manning sent letters and gifts to "my dear Rachel", as well as soothing reassurances to her father: "I feel sure that Leysin will be the best thing for her..." Rachel's memory of him 50 years later intimates that in his deep sympathy for her he may have disclosed more of himself than he thought. "I always enjoyed seeing him, listening to him talking to my father, and feel there was some sort of affinity between us." Still, the Rothensteins were allowed only so far into his life; they, too, seldom breached those "reticences about himself" that Aldington noticed. Manning's letters and conversation could be affectionate, witty, and candid, but he was loath to give details of himself; and when he mentions feelings like loneliness he expects understanding rather than invites discussion. Perhaps this insistent privacy ("I wish we could meet and talk more frequently, though perhaps I talk better with a pen, and am most eloquent in my silences while they are unobserved") contributed to Rothenstein's failure to produce a vital image. However that may be, the artist accepted his friend's reserve, and Manning's visits and letters, with their ripe talk of art and literature, were occasions to be savoured.

On one of those occasions Manning surprised his host. The date of this scene is early 1922, the other principal actor, T. E. Lawrence.

> Now Lawrence was reticent about his Arab Campaign. People tried all manner of ways to get him to talk of his adventures, but in vain; yet before Manning Lawrence was ready to open out, for once to spread his peacock's tail, and again and again he began, to be interrupted each time by Manning, who broke in, to my amusement, to talk of himself!

Lawrence's volubility on this occasion of their first meeting may be explained by his long-standing admiration for *Scenes and Portraits,* which he first read at Oxford. What triggered Manning to talk, or what he actually talked about, is not reported. But at a guess it would have included his own experience of battle. It was the one part of himself he had shared freely with Rothenstein in his letters, and Lawrence, though a stranger to Manning, was someone whose temper and exploits indicated that he too understood why "bravery is the best wisdom". Following their introduction Manning invited Lawrence to Edenham, "if ever you feel like a quiet not to say lonely weekend". Lawrence could not make it, but asked if he might read the manuscript of the romance. "Soon", Manning promised, whispering a hope to himself, perhaps, as well as answering the request. Shortly thereafter Lawrence was off on another of his adventures, and eight years would pass before these two secretive men talked to each other again.

If Lawrence had made it to Edenham in the spring of 1922 he would have found his host "not evolving a proper rhythm of prose, but still digesting official reports, and translating the Jargon of Admiralty documents into a reasonable, if pedestrian, speech". It was now nearly three years since he had begun the White biography, and he was no longer predicting when he would be finished. He simply tells friends that he is "revising", and announces to the Kirbys that when he is finished "we will have a bottle of champagne". Slowing his progress is illness. A month of flu in late 1921 is followed by lethargy and depression: "I have resisted several temptations to go away, as I do not feel particularly festive, or very well." In January 1922 comes another attack of flu, with three weeks confinement in bed. Finally, in June, worn down by "anxieties and overwork", he is ordered by his doctor to take "a complete rest" and goes to the west coast of England. When he returns home in July he begins thinking of moving into a flat in London at the end of September: "I find Edenham too lonely now." However, thoughts of moving temporarily subside when his brother Will and his family arrive in England, followed a week later by his mother and two of his sisters. The White book is still unfinished but for a time Manning will be too busy to be lonely. And always on the horizon looms "The Gilded Coach", an assurance to himself and others that he will not always be a "reporter". Versailles, he dreams, will be a good place to finish the romance.*

In November of 1922 Manning was in Rome and found the city he had first seen through the eyes of Galton as beguiling as ever. With his family he saw the Pope, and on his own talked with secretaries and cardinals. Papal Rome was "amusing", and possibly even useful to the author of "The Gilded Coach", but it was the Rome of museums and fine prospects that Manning cherished — "I wish I might go there this winter", he had written in 1908, "and haunt the lovely Borghese gardens, or look from the Pincio toward a long line of terebinths which cut the sky behind the Vatican." After 1922 he returned often, and at moments thought of settling there. On this visit he was once again supplied with letters of introduction from Rothenstein to people the artist felt his friend might enjoy. He had lunch one day with Eugenie Strong, the Assistant Director of the British School, and on another occasion met Geoffrey Scott, the author of *Portrait of Zelide,* who subsequently reported back to Rothenstein how impressed he was by Manning's "fine perceptions". The respect was mutual, and Manning thanked Rothenstein in one of those graceful phrases that came so effortlessly to him when he talked of friendship: "Thank you so much my dear Will, for your kindness in introducing me to them both. You presided over our discourse, and were present with us, and therefore will know how we praised you."

On the way home Manning stopped in Paris for a few days, and saw Albert Houtin for the first time since his abbreviated visit to Paris in 1913. Theirs was a rendezvous presided over by the memory of Galton, and from it their friendship ripened. Over the years Manning had written sporadically to Houtin, usually in late December to wish him a happy New Year "and the best gifts of the best gods''. But Galton's illness and death had prompted a series of letters, and after this meeting Houtin, until his death in 1926, became a regular correspondent. With his strong views and challenging scepticism, he filled a vacuum in Manning's life. To him Manning wrote easily about his work and his thoughts, engaging by letter in the kind of conversation that once had been within a few steps. ''It is I who should thank you for your friendship, your encouragement, and your example: neither time, nor distance, nor silence has affected them. To put it in a few words you mean much to me; and I think of you most days.'' This tribute was paid to Houtin a few months before his death. The only other place where Manning used ''example'' in the same sense was in the prologue to *Scenes and Portraits,* where he acknowledged his debt to Galton.

Paris was also the occasion for a rendezvous with the ''Ezras'', whom he had not seen since they had left England at the end of 1920. Amongst talk of old friends and current projects Manning doubtless explained more fully his appreciation of *Hugh Selwyn Mauberley*, an inscribed copy of which Pound had given him soon after its appearance.* If one reads *Mauberley* as Pound's farewell to ''a botched civilisation'', then one can readily understand how Manning, himself a ''stylist'' who lived ''unpaid, uncelebrated'', had heard the poem echoing his own postwar complaints. It was during this visit, and apparently through Pound, that Manning met James Joyce, ''very Irish, very realist in the practical way that Irishmen are, and very egotistic''. The letter to Dorothy Pound (13 December 1922) in which these remarks are made is the last I came across between Manning and either of the Pounds. Probably there were later notes, and perhaps a meeting or two; but no longer pulled by the common literary centre of London, their orbits were rarely to cross. Whatever either wanted to know about the other, or pass on, could be done through Olivia. In that letter to Dorothy, though, was a special message for her husband: ''No, Ezra it was not the most excellent chop.'' A difference over a meal; how typical of their relations! After Manning's death Pound had several opportunities to judge his "first licherary" companion. In print he once placed him, along with Henry Newbolt, the "backwash" of Lionel Johnson, and "the Quarterlies", in the "arthritic milieu that held control of the respected British critical circles" before World War I. And in his letters he could be equally dismissive. "The HELL of a lot that needs doing," he told Aldington when the latter asked for information for his article, "MORE than retrospective peonies on graves of DEEP-arted aussies or others." And yet the letters continue to recommend *Scenes and Portraits*, regard its author among the finest English prose writers of the period 1890–1920, recall his words and wit as if he and they really mattered, and acknowledge the war novel: "Fred, remerged [*sic*] in Privates We/and then rather faded." Had the two men never met, the shape of their careers would scarcely be different. But they did meet, their lives and ambitions for a time intertwined, and for all their mockery of one another they never lost respect.

On a rainy August morning in 1977 I visited Buckstone Farm near Chobham in Surrey, the Tudor timber-framed house to which Manning moved shortly after returning from Paris. Edenham had become too lonely, and so he bought a home near the river Bourne, not far from where Matthew Arnold had lived the last 15 years of his life. Simple coincidence, almost unavoidable in a country as small as England, placed him near reminders of Galton and Lincolnshire; always very conscious of the "character and personality" of a house, Manning was no doubt drawn to Buckstone by its Shakespearean resonances and its proximity to London friends.

I came unannounced, having no idea who the current owner was but hoping to meet with typical English hospitality. After parking my car just inside the gate, I sprinted to the house, shielding myself against the rain. I knocked several times before a young woman, looking to be in her middle twenties, opened the door to the blare of hard rock music. I explained who I was and asked if I might have a look inside the house. Even as I talked,

Buckstone Farm, c. *1923* (Patricia Hope)

however, I could see that I had made a serious mistake. The woman said that she was only occupying the house while the owner was away, and that in the circumstances she could not let me in. Her distrust was apparent, and I could not really fault it. How else would you receive a foreigner who comes to your door in the middle of a driving rainstorm asking admittance because someone you have never heard of lived there more than 50 years ago?

And so I had to content myself with taking photographs of the house from the outside. The following July in Australia Chick Woolmer described the interior for me as it had been in the 1920s. Then — for the house is much enlarged now — there had been eight rooms, four up and four down connected by two staircases, and even by the standards of the day, Chick felt the accommodations were somewhat primitive. There was no floor covering in the kitchen, no inside toilet, and all water was supplied by pump. When Manning wanted to bathe, Chick would have to carry buckets of heated water upstairs to a tin bath tub placed in the bedroom for the occasion. Little was done while Manning lived there to improve conditions. There was never adequate furniture, and many months went by before the "hideous" blue doors and window frames were painted. There was, however, a telephone.

Besides Chick's word pictures of Buckstone, several photographs of the house in the period of Manning's occupancy survive in Lynch family albums. Sybil Gowthorpe and Polly Barry visited there in 1925 and brought back a number of quite good snapshots, including three of Manning himself. In one he is standing in a field dressed in a three-piece suit, his left hand resting on his hip, his right hanging by his side and holding the habitual cigarette. He is looking to his right with a vaguely annoyed look on his face, while behind him two cows are working their way along the grass, unaware that in their midst is a selfstyled "Epicuri de grege porcum". The second photo offers a new mood. It is of an open window of the house, where on the sill looking out stands the bust of Voltaire, cherished by Galton and now an important keepsake for Manning. Standing just behind the bust is Manning, his head seeming to rest on Voltaire's, and with a smile stretched across his face in apparent imitation of the grin on the bust. The moment is pure play, and so not lacking in seriousness. The last photograph catches Manning in yet another mood. He is seated, his legs crossed, gazing at a fire in a small grate that sits in a large fireplace. Taken from the side, the photo does not reveal an expression, but setting and posture bespeak meditation.

Manning's life at Buckstone Farm was hardly different from his life at Edenham. He left the running of the house to a succession of housekeepers, and spent much of the time by himself. Visitors, aside from his family, were few and infrequent: a neighbour in for cards or chess, a London friend down for a weekend. However, with one of his neighbours, Henry Serpell, an elderly and quite wealthy biscuit manufacturer, he seems to have struck up a friendship, taking him, for example, to a show of Rothenstein's work and enjoying Serpell's ability to "still look at things with a child's unsophisticated candour''. For lengthy periods Manning was sick, or convalescing. During the spring of 1923 he was in bed for three months — he does not say what the trouble was — nursed by his mother, ''tho' if age were in question I should be nursing her'', and the next year found him down with influenza, which left him feeling ''poisoned and lethargic''. This was followed by an emergency appendicectomy which kept him in a nursing home for five weeks. Owing to his asthma and bronchitis he was not a ''good subject for the knife'', and his recovery was slowed by fits of coughing that made it difficult for the wound to heal. ''The trouble,'' he told Houtin, ''evidently had existed for some time, and may account for my ill health, lassitude, and inability to work usefully during the past six months.''

But if he did not write much in the two years he was at Buckstone — a 20-page critical essay and four reviews ranging in length from 600 to 4000 words — he did finally clear his desk of the White biography. The book, essentially completed before he moved to Surrey, came out in September of 1923 and was favourably reviewed, especially in the technical journals: ''Naval architects throughout the world will be grateful to Mr Manning for having undertaken and accomplished a task which might easily have daunted a less gifted writer.'' It was to be the last book he published with John Murray, and of the five it almost certainly sold the best. A month before publication about 1000 copies had already been ordered,* and after the book went into the shops — in America under the Dutton imprint — sales continued briskly. Were purchasers drawn by the biographer's reputation? Manning would have laughed at the question. Even some of the reviewers wrote as if they had never heard of him and had cribbed his identity from the title page information, ''author of *The Vigil of Brunhild, Scenes and Portraits,* etc.'' By 1923 these were mere titles, the works of a writer, as one friendly critic noted, ''whose name never appears in the literary gossip of the day''. (A year later *The Times* altered his nationality when referencing a review he had just published: ''M. Frederic

Manning discusses..." The mistake amused him: "They have made me completely French.")

Manning did not imagine that *The Life of Sir William White* would enhance his literary reputation. Only people who found "shipbuilding an interesting subject", he thought, would ever pick it up. He did not, therefore, follow his usual practice of giving copies to friends, and the *Life* is the only one of his books absent from the collection in Eleanor Manning's home. Though satisfied with its workmanship and with what its sponsor had paid him, the book had been an odious chore.

The biography is less a portrait of White than a history of the Royal Navy, and its structure merely conforms to the chronology of the naval architect's well-documented accomplishments. Each chapter, like a watertight compartment, encompasses a particular incident or situation, and within most chapters there are large chunks of material quoted from White's papers. Something of the flavour of the biography can be derived from successive chapter titles: Dockyard Reform (1886); The Naval Defence Act (1888); The Naval Defence Act (1888–89); The Second Class Battleships (1889–90), etc.

Of course a dozen other biographers might have chosen the same structure, and since the book was commissioned to be a record of professional achievements, its structure could be defended as appropriate. Moreover, it was a book written for money, and Manning had long ago lost any pleasure he had in writing it. Still, the reader is entitled to wonder why a more imaginative framework was not found; to wonder how a poet could be satisfied with a book of segments in which the whole is only an accumulation of the parts — parts envisioned to be so separate that they could, in fact, be easily shipped out to a collaborator.* What interest or skill Manning had in narrative structure was, it seems, exhausted within the smaller forms.

Some of the chapters necessarily read like technical reports, with numerous pages — too numerous for some critics — devoted to quoting great chunks of memoranda and correspondence. Reading these extracts numbs the mind after a while, and induces the suspicion that the author has shirked the necessary duty of digestion. Annoyance, however, is quickly transformed into pleasure when the dutiful "reporter" changes back to the poet and philosopher, and when Sir William, who "never rid himself of that shyness which is common to all sensitive men", is made to step out of his privacy. Try reading aloud, for example, the description of the Grand Review held at Spithead in 1897 to honour Queen Victoria's Diamond Jublilee:

> The spectacle was superb: the sea brightened under a forest of masts gay with innumerable points of colour, and one looked down apparently endless avenues of ships in diminishing perspective, massive in the foreground and melting away into the distance as delicate silhouettes suspended vaguely in a golden and humid air. They were things of beauty and mystery, until the guns spoke, revealing their true use and nature. The festivities in London had been an act of homage to the person of the Queen, but the Review off Spithead was the consecration by an imperial people of the principle of sea-power.

Or enjoy one of the "ironical values" that had been promised to Rothenstein:

> Great armament firms have no national or political prejudices; they are concerned not with the ulterior objects of war, but with the immediate means by which victory may be secured; and the value of such abstract ideas as justice or liberty they leave for the discussion of idle and metaphysical minds; or employ the terms as convenient euphemisms, by which the real objects of statesmen may be cloaked and the warlike energies of a people directed. White was not unwilling to play the part of *honnête courtier,* by pointing out the growth of the Japanese Navy to his Chinese clients, or of the Chinese to their indomitable rivals. In doing so he was always careful to insist upon the confidential nature of

> his designs, and the daily progress of our scientific knowledge. By such means he was able to increase the profits of the great Company which employed him; to extend and perfect the resources of what is perhaps the most important of our national industries; and to kindle in the hearts of two Asiatic peoples the flames of an enlightened and sacred patriotism.

Then there is the scene of White leaving his office for the last time, having resigned after an error in his design overturned the new Royal yacht:

> When it came to his last day in the office, which was January the 31st, a Friday, he sat for some time alone, collecting himself, as it were. Then he opened the door of the adjoining office, and said to his chief assistants, "I am going now. Good-bye to you all!" No one rose from his seat, no one came forward to shake his hands; it may be, possibly, because they were taken by surprise and embarrassed. He turned and walked down the stairs alone. As he passed his messenger he said, "This is good-bye," and the man came forward at once and said: "May I shake your hand, Sir William, and say how sorry I am you are so ill as to be obliged to leave us!"
>
> And so he passed on finally from the scene of his labours and triumphs and fall. Could one find a better application of the Tacitean phrase: *cesserunt prima postremis*? His successes, which had set the stamp of his character upon the navies of the world, were extinguished by his failure, if it were his, with a mere pretty, white, and gilded toy; and men who had learned everything they knew from him, forgot the man who had been their teacher.

The hand of the moralist almost squeezes the life out of that passage. How much better it would be without Tacitus — but it survives, and is quietly moving. Also worthy of note are several descriptions of White's mother ("One seldom finds so much domestic wisdom and so just a sense of proportion joined with tender and lovable qualities''), and the assessment of White's ''perfect understanding'' with his children: ''His own quick responsive nature would enter equally well into their freakish mischief, to an extent that was sometimes indecorous, though always effective. He could sympathise, too, in their obscure troubles and perplexities. Even with the inexplicable and native Adam, appearing in every child, he was reluctant to expostulate.'' By virtue of these and other moments we never lose sight of subject or author in the long voyage through this ''dull technical book''.

Neither dull nor technical was ''Critic and Aesthetic'', an essay by Manning that appeared in the *Quarterly Review* of July 1924. It is the longest piece of criticism Manning ever published, and while writing it he thought it might eventually grow into a book. The 20 pages that were printed bear out his sense of its potential. The article has a general focus — what is the artist doing when he creates — but Manning has so much ground over which to lead the reader, and so many points of interest at which to pause, that by the end of the piece the reader may justifiably feel as if he has travelled too far too quickly. Still, it is one of those journeys that one does not regret.

In many respects the article is a working out of themes and positions stated in earlier pieces. It extends the attack on Remy de Gourmont and the aesthetic school of criticism that goes back to Pater and, ultimately, according to Manning, to the *homo mensura* philosophy of Protagoras; it enjoins the reader to study again his Plato and Aristotle if he would grasp firmly the fundamentals of critical discourse; it examines how and why we must distinguish between the world of art and its concern for ''value'' and the world of science and its concern for ''fact''; and it describes with wonderful clarity the process by which the artist (or poet) isolates and rationalises an experience to produce a work of art.

> The point of view from which an artist considers his sitter, or the object he seeks to represent, is a critical

> point of view: it is rather like the point of view from which a doctor considers a patient, as a case awaiting diagnosis. Any beautiful or cultivated woman sitting to a portrait-painter is already, without any intervention on the part of the painter himself, a consummate and perfect work of art: she presents him gratuitously with the ideal synthesis which she has composed out of the elements of her own character, and she is her own medium of expression. She is unconcerned by his examination, for her whole training in life has fitted her admirably to provoke curiosity while remaining apparently indifferent to it; and, as the artist examines his patient, while concerned, it would seem, with no more than the point of his pencil, or the colours on his palette, he resolves that carefully composed synthesis into its component parts: just as a doctor asks a number of questions the purport of which it is difficult for the patient to understand, so the painter interrogates the elaborate simplicity of the ideal character which she has built up from the material of her subjective consciousness. It is dissolved under his analysis. He sees her as a type only: *virgo, mulier, mater, meretrix, musa;* and still sharpening his pencil he proceeds to eviscerate the type. He confronts eventually an abstraction of qualities and a more or less irrelevant fact. It is at this point, where the critical faculty has exhausted itself, or its object, that the creative faculty begins to assemble a new synthesis. The two processes of course may proceed *pari passu,* but the measure of an artist's originality is the measure in which his critical faculty has dissolved the objective synthesis presented to him in reality.

Along the way Manning takes aim again at Gourmont's preoccupation with sex as the source of our idea of beauty, and in so doing produces some keen practical criticism.

> The function of art being to create with reflexion, and love being a spontaneous and irreflective action, whose

> effects are natural and necessary, not as art's are, contingent and at the will of the artist, it would seem that, while love may be the subject-matter of art, it is not the source from which art derives: it is simply one of the many forms taken by the desire to assimilate what is desirable. Even as the subject-matter of art it has no peculiar excellence. Turn from the Attic to the Elizabethan stage, and set "Romeo and Juliet" beside "Antony and Cleopatra". The former, dealing with love to the exclusion of all other desires, is pathetic; the latter, dealing with love as the pretext or means of ambition, has the true profundity and extension of tragedy, expressing perfectly, in the spectacle of an ambition cloaked in the guise of love, shattered by an ambition to which love is alien, its finer retributive function. Set "Othello", the greatest of Shakespeare's love tragedies, beside "Macbeth" and only the diabolic genius of Iago saves it from being infinitely less. Set it beside "King Lear" and attempt to measure, not the difference in greatness, but the difference between the pathetic and the sublime.

This is the classical temper writing extremely well, so well, in fact, that the editor of *Quarterly Review* asked Manning to write another article on the same subject.* Provisionally entitled "The Moral Consequence of Value", it was apparently intended to discuss religious values in art. But there is no evidence that Manning did anything more than contemplate the subject.

Several months before "Critic and Aesthetic" appeared in the *Quarterly Review* Manning sent his proof copy to T. S. Eliot for comment. By then the two men were corresponding about the possibilities of Manning writing for the *Criterion.* His first contribution, a review of Houtin's biography of Charles Loyson, *Le Père Hyacinthe,* was written less to please Eliot or himself than to assist his old friend. "My only object in writing is to be of some service to you by attempting to interest others in what has interested me." Loyson (1827–1912) had been a priest who, after breaking his formal ties with the church and subsequently marrying, had led a reclusive life of great spiritual purity. To his death he always thought of himself as a Catholic. Manning's essay focuses on the central issue of such a life, the "religious impulse", and examines how personal faith, which he elsewhere describes as an "arbitrary act of the mind", makes its way in the world of fact and rational argument.

> The tragedy of faith is in its attempt to penetrate and inform the world. Churches, rites, creeds, dogmas, are no more than the deposit left by the action of faith on fact, the vestiges of attempts to reconcile forces opposed and incompatible. Every church may, in this special sense, be termed a *depositum fidei.* Launched upon the world as the expression of individual and personal values, faith is absorbed by the society enveloping it, and translated into the terms of moral, social, and political fact. A Church, in so far as it has a worldly and temporal object, represents the compromise which society makes with God.

There, spelled out, was one of the implicit themes of *Scenes and Portraits.*

Of the seven additional reviews* that Manning did for Eliot between 1924 and 1927 two centred on books by Houtin, and the rest (Greek civilisation, a translation of Catullus, Newman, J. G. Frazer, Prosper Mérimée) spoke to longstanding concerns, reflecting the historical sensitivity and conservative aesthetic so apparent in all of his work. "What Professor Toynbee has done is this: he has fastened upon a generalisation, 'Hellas', and injected into it his own value and his own truth, or what he accepts as equivalents for truth and value. This subjective method, a characteristic defect in Professor Gilbert Murray, Mr Zimmern and Mr Livingstone, becomes in Professor Toynbee almost a vice. They each present us with an ideal Hellas in which there is no time."

Eliot liked what he wrote and wanted more,* including, on

occasion, translations of other materials. For his part, Manning, though disagreeing with some of Eliot's "rather reactionary" opinions on political and social questions as well as some of his "revolutionary" literary opinions, certainly shared the view that criticism ought to derive from a set of principles and seek to educate taste. His available letters to Eliot confirm, however, the impression left by Eliot's obituary of him: intellectual concerns alone established and sustained the terms of their relationship. They referred to common friends like Pound and Charles Whibley, gave each other copies of their writings,* and offered reports of their illnesses, but Manning addressed Eliot as a fellow writer rather than as a friend, signing himself always with his full name.

While at Buckstone Farm, Manning also had another round with "The Gilded Coach". In November of 1923 Houtin sent his friend a biography of Louis XIV. "It recalls me to my duty; but alas! I have done nothing to it as yet, as I have had to turn to other things." Six weeks later, however, Manning reported that the romance "is again unfolding itself; and I shall hope to finish it by the summer." But attached to the prediction was a telling caveat: "In any matter the will, mighty as it is creatively, is still dependent on the imagination." In the circumstances this remark encourages the suspicion that a sense of embarrassment more than a creative desire had driven him back to his "duty". Friends and publishers were always asking about the book, and such queries, especially now that the biography of White was finished, caused twinges of guilt. But if the novel was a responsibility he could not escape, it seems also to have been a crutch he was reluctant to throw away. As long as there was a manuscript to be finished, something he could periodically work on, show to friends for encouragement, or even try to sell, he need not face the possibility that it was dead, that years of effort and expectation had been wasted, and that he would have to find some other creative project. And so the various strategies to keep the patient alive: a trip to Paris, a long soak in seventeenth-century memoirs, a sojourn at Versailles, and in September 1923 an offer

Manning at Buckstone Farm, c. *1923*
(Patricia Hope)

to Eliot: "I wonder whether you would care to publish my Romance in instalments. It might induce me to finish it." Already aware that Manning's fastidiousness and ill-health prevented his being a punctual contributor, Eliot had reason to avoid such a commitment. Besides, Eliot decided to stay with the *Criterion* rather than start the new quarterly he had been formulating and in which Manning had presumably envisioned the "Coach" running. Contemporaries felt that Manning's great mistake as a writer was the White biography, and during that ordeal he promised that he would stray no more. But the biography, while a waste of his talents, was finished; "The Gilded Coach" was not, and Manning could never bring himself to cut his losses. Too much effort had been invested in it; too much of his artistic identity seemed to depend on it. The book was both a cause and a symptom of his troubles as a writer.

In October 1924 his sister Beatrix died suddenly in Paris after a brief illness. Manning spoke of the loss to his mother and himself as "immeasurable", suggesting a close affection between brother and sister that no one in the family can now recall. The importance of Beatrix to her mother is clearer: she managed Nora's expeditions between Australia and England and the Continent, and was instrumental in looking after Edith. Dot, by this time, went her own way, sometimes accompanying her mother and sisters, sometimes not. With Beatrix' death, mother and son would have further cause to draw closer together.

Arrangements were made to take the body back to Sydney, and on 28 November 1924 Manning, together with his mother and his two surviving sisters, sailed from Marseilles for Australia. He could hardly have thought of himself as going home. It had been half his lifetime since he had been in Sydney, and he had not missed it. Indeed, if he had been asked in the winter of 1924 to designate his home, he might have paused. Edenham now belonged to the past, and Buckstone Farm, his "toy" as he called it, was beginning to seem like a mistake. At times he contemplated leaving England altogether. He may have wished home to be France or Italy, favourite haunts of those "who have no country", as he was now wont to speak of himself, but they were as yet visionary prospects, no more holding his emotional allegiance than Australia. In short, the journey to Sydney came at a time when he had renewed feelings of rootlessness, and these, as well as the immediate sadness and desire to assist, may have urged him to go.

Fame

CHAPTER SEVEN

A single haunting image, recorded by the journalist/poet Leon Gellert, is all that I could find of Manning's stay in Sydney in 1925. Though not written down until almost a quarter of a century later, it has the quality of something freshly seen rather than manufactured by memory and opinion:

> ...when the door opened and a pair of large dark penetrating eyes surveyed me disinterestedly or, perhaps, a trifle disgustedly, I recognized, from published photographs, the keen visage of the author of "Scenes and Portraits".
>
> By a piece of phenomenal luck I was able to extract from my scantily equipped bookshelf a first edition of his "Poems", a circumstance which the poet, not altogether lacking in human susceptibilities, observed without any visible symptoms of displeasure. He asked if he might inscribe a few lines on the fly-leaf, and, before any opposition could be raised, very slowly and painstakingly, like a mediaeval scrivener, wrote out a neat quatrain which he had composed at sea on his way from England.
>
> He attached no signature, nor did I ask him to do so, thinking, with vanity, that he might mistake me for an autograph hunter. Then, suddenly remembering an appointment, he asked to be excused. We left my office together and I walked with him to the end of the street, noticing how fragile he was and how sudden and uneasy were his movements. He betrayed all the indications of a man who had barely recovered from a severe illness. We parted at the corner and, I remember, as I looked back

> to watch the frail figure cross Pitt Street with its one-way traffic, how long and arduous his progress seemed, and how apprehensively he looked to right and left as he moved. That was the last I saw of Frederick [*sic*] Manning.

So vulnerable a figure naturally felt threatened by the busy streets of Sydney, and after an absence of 20 years the city must have seemed strange to him. Friends of his youth, seen now as they verged on middle age, were doubtless even more foreign. Did he, though, even bother to hunt them up? Or, for that matter, did he go by the houses he had lived in as a boy, or take a trip into the Blue Mountains? If not I would be surprised, for while he scorned sentimentality and thought of himself as having no roots, the force of memory is imperious. One place he would have gone to was South Head cemetery, to bury poor Beatrix and to see for the first time the grave of his father. What else he might have done is beyond speculation, and he did not linger in Australia for very long. By April he and his brother Charlie were on their way to England together.

After landing in May, Manning made a short visit to Dublin and planned another for Paris, but illness once more short-circuited his plans. It was another bout of influenza, this time complicated by what he rather mysteriously termed a "troublesome" heart: "It is nothing," he assured Houtin, "beyond a temporary functional weakness." A month of "lying on a chair in my garden" cured both problems. Work, once he felt better, consisted of a penetrating article for the *Criterion* on Cardinal Newman, written as a response to an earlier essay by the French critic, Ramon Fernandez. Manning chastised Fernandez for bending Newman's thought to fit twentieth-century ideas and for misunderstanding the man himself.

> He is conscious of God in him; he is conscious also of himself as an instrument of God; and because he does not remain a contemplative, but turns to "the foolishness of preaching", is he the less a mystic? His is

> not, in Milton's phrase, a fugitive and cloistered virtue; if he is to touch and move the world he must find some common measure with other minds. How else is he to act upon his age?

Newman held a powerful appeal for Manning. He admired the "ease and precision" of his style, recognised (and shared) the debt to eighteenth-century rationalism and searched in himself for that faith, that real assent, which had been the basis of Newman's actions. If the writings of Renan spoke more forcefully to his intellect and imagination, the figure of Newman seems to have touched him more deeply. "Once we have known the influence of Newman," his article began, "we do not escape from it easily. It renews itself in us."

Otherwise Manning seems to have been doing no writing, justifying the reputation he knew that he had gained among some of his friends as being "the idlest of men". What his garden had not been able to cure was what had driven him from Edenham: "I seem to grow more alone every day of my life. True, I lunch and dine with my neighbours from time to time, but I doubt whether they exist." The levity may soften the sense of isolation, but by the time he made this comment Manning had decided to sell Buckstone Farm, and had almost made up his mind to go and live in Rome for a couple of years. "I want to go to the sun," he told John Murray in October 1925, "but all the same in six months time I shall be homesick for English lawns and roses in June." For the remainder of his life he was to be a wanderer, worried about his health and uncertain of where (and with whom) he belonged.

The new year found him back at Belfield rather than in Rome, waiting for his mother to arrive from Australia in March "before deciding on what to do next". He spent almost three months in Ireland, during which time he renewed his acquaintance with Æ and Yeats. The latter gave him first night tickets for Sean O'Casey's new work, *The Plough and the Stars.* A play that soon infuriated many — a riot broke out in the Abbey Theatre three nights later when the audience vented its displeasure at seeing Dubliners who were less than heroic during the Easter rising — overwhelmed Manning. Writing to Eliot a week later he spoke of the play as an "extraordinary tour de force" and "the central fact of my experience here". Precisely what he admired in the play he does not say, but O'Casey's willingness to have his characters not only behave as some Dubliners actually did, but talk as they actually talked — "that old bitch", "lousy bastard" — presumably left an impression on a writer whose own works depended on dialogue. The visit also included dental surgery in which he had 13 teeth extracted. This left him "exhausted" and cut short yet another try at the romance. He did, however, publish in Æ's weekly, *The Irish Statesman,* what seems to be the last of his poems to appear in print.

Animae Suae

You are too brief and wild
With the shy ways
Of an inconstant child:
Keeping your grace,
As stars their light,
Tho' drowned in greater day's
To illumine night,
Which is their dancing place.

And when I sleep you wake
To leap and sing
With lost Gods, in a brake
Of vine and thorn:
The ashen grass
They turn to blossoming;
And secret pass
Or ever day be born.

This song of the soul as child, inhabiting a world of "lost Gods", is not a memorable poem, but it finely represents Manning's art, his instincts, and his irony. He also tried to place in the *Irish Statesman* a review of Houtin's latest book, *Un Prêtre*

Symboliste: Marcel Hébert, a biography of another French cleric who had taken off the cassock, but Æ feared to publish lest it stir up "religious controversy". Rewritten to include notice of the first volume of Houtin's autobiography, the article was subsequently published in the *Criterion.*

Ready as he was to spread notice of Houtin's books, Manning was far more concerned in early 1926 with his friend's deteriorating health. "I hope you are better, and are well cared for by your doctor. If I were near you I should not trouble you with encouraging words; but I should help to nurse you." The depth of his affection for Houtin can be measured in this offer, one that I found him making to no one else. But Houtin was only one of many friends whose illnesses generated a concern far more encompassing than the sympathy customarily bestowed on the sickness of friends. Manning was experienced in illness; it seemed to him to be the condition of his existence. And he was always ready both to furnish advice on how the patient was to meet the struggle and to offer words of caring noteworthy for their tenderness. Indeed, all those who were unmistakably vulnerable — the sick, the aged, the young — occupied a special place in his affections, and the solicitude with which he spoke to them or of them was, like his cynicism, influenced by the frustration he felt with his own fragility.

In March his mother and sisters arrived in England, and Manning returned to London to be with them. For several weeks the family resided in the Garland Hotel in Pall Mall, and then, on the day the General Strike began (4 May 1926), they moved into a flat in Mount Street, Mayfair, where they lived, waited on by two servants, until October. This appears to have been much the lengthiest period Manning ever spent in London, a city he had years ago determined he could not tolerate for very long. On this occasion he took advantage of the many pleasures London offered as well as the opportunity to see friends on a regular basis. There were numerous luncheons and teas, recitals and concerts, excursions to the Chelsea Flower Show and the British Museum to see some new Chinese paintings, and one evening an obligatory appearance at a poetry reading by Lord Dunsany: "I prefer music." He also made several visits to parliament, where James Fairfax now sat as the Conservative member from Norwich, and listened to the debates during the national crisis. He found the spectacle impressive but frustrating: "Why has no one the courage to rise up in the House and say: we are not bound to the employers, and we are not bound to labour, both are well organized, and can fight their own battles. We as a govt. represent the whole body of consumers, who are not organized at all, unless they are organized in us." Ever an advocate of firm leadership, he had little patience for purposeless authority and little respect for leaders who had only "that courage for dreams, which is less than the courage for realities". One afternoon he could have been seen pouring at a tea party given by Fairfax's wife on the terrace of the House of Commons, a duty that much amused him: "I had one of my rare moments of 'social success'." Twice he left the city, once in April for two weeks to visit the elderly Miss Ida Taylor, now living alone in the New Forest after the death of her sister Una, and once in late June for a weekend at the home of Charles Whibley. All of this matters little, except for one fact: during the entire seven-months period there is no mention of ill-health. The weather was often "deplorable", his privacy was contained within a "rather small" bedroom, and by July the city was "very tiring and difficult to work in". Yet he was well.

And working. "You would not believe from this," he says in a letter to Sybil Gowthorpe teeming with social news, "that I have done any work, but as a matter of fact I have got thro' enough to surprise myself." We should believe it, for we have seen enough of his life to question whether he might have been happier, more productive, and even healthier had he lived among friends and occasions. Alone in the country, his work was all that he had to do. There was really nothing else to give form and freshness to his daily existence, and so it was easy to slip into lethargy and loneliness, and to fall victim to physical complaints, real and imagined. Had he not lived such an isolated life perhaps he would have written (and finished) more than he did. Illness and alcohol would likely still have taken a toll, however, for there was a systemic brittleness to the man, but in the demanding presence of life in motion he might have done better.

The particular work that Manning was engaged in during his stay in London was the writing of an introductory essay for a new edition of Walter Charleton's *Epicurus's Morals* — newly titled *Epicurus His Morals* — a seventeenth-century translation that is roughly one part Epicurus (or those reporting his doctrines) and three parts Charleton (or those influencing his ideas). It was a congenial task for one so imbued with the Epicurean tradition as Manning, and years of reading for the romance had given him a scholar's knowledge of the revival of Epicureanism in sceptical thought of the seventeenth century. Five years before, while writing a short piece on St Evremond, he had thought of writing "later" an "imaginary letter, or dialogue" giving Gassendi's opinion of Descartes. The essay he wrote on this occasion was a capable piece of work that compressed a great deal of knowledge and careful analysis into a small structure, while still allowing space for some ruffling insights ("...the most curious thing in memory is its timelessness, the illusion, if it be one, of our own eternal existence") and a few mood-easing ironies (Charles II is described as a king who "could discern and appreciate genius as well as beauty, and selected a bishop with an even finer judgment than he brought to the choice of a mistress"). Reviewers of the book applauded the essay, as did John Murray, though his old publisher-friend — who had not given up hope that Manning might yet finish the romance — admitted finding it "sometimes rather difficult to follow all the intricacies of πράληψις and κατάληψις". Aside from providing biographical information on both Epicurus and Charleton, Manning's closely argued pages stripped away the misunderstandings that had grown up around the "philosopher of the garden" to provide an outline of a doctrine strongly sympathetic to his own mind:

> He had no interest in making man a moral being, that was the concern of the Stoics: to him morality was the order arising from the conflict of rival egoisms equally valid. His doctrine of free-will is a necessary implication of that which makes the feelings (πάθη) a criterion of truth, a means by which choice and aversion are determined, for where there is an element of choice there is an element of freedom...In that unending procession of images which throngs the consciousness of man, there is one alone which is invariably present, which is repeated with so much rapidity as to seem constant and continuous, and that is the image of oneself. It is because this fundamental self-consciousness pervades the whole system of Epicurus that he is reproached with egoism by those who forget, or ignore, the words, Know thyself; and the *Cogito, ergo sum,* of Descartes. In self-consciousness we have the clear and evident proof of our existence, and the guarantee of our freedom; but our existence is not distinct from other existences, nor from the whole of existence; and our freedom is not distinct either, though we are none the less free because we obey the law of our own nature, which is the universal law finding in the consciousness of man perhaps its highest if still imperfect expression. Our freedom is in direct proportion to the degree of consciousness possessed by us...

Condensed to a sentence later on in the text, "To the Epicurean ...αὔταρκεια, a perfect self-mastery, was the condition of any free activity of the mind, of all right choice", the thought reminds us of the war poem by the same name (αὔταρκεια). Stretched by retrospection, it will pervade the war novel that he was soon to write.

In Eleanor Manning's home I found an inscribed copy of *Epicurus His Morals*: "To my dearest mother, the first completed copy of this book." Compared to earlier inscriptions the hand is rather shrunken, but obviously not the feeling. As the reader has perhaps already speculated, the presence of Nora Manning that summer in London no doubt contributed to her son's sense of well-being.

The *Epicurus,* like most of Manning's books, is not readily found today. Anyone lucky enough to come across one of the 750 copies that were printed will find it a most handsome volume, for this was no ordinary reprint of an older work. Printed on pure rag paper with large borders framing type similar to that used in the seventeenth century, it sold as a deluxe edition for 15 shillings a copy. Nor was the publisher, Peter Davies, an ordinary figure in London publishing. He had only just established his firm, and at the age of 29 had thus far led the sort of life from which movie scripts are written.* And the connection between Davies and Manning was to be no ordinary relationship between publisher and author.

In another incarnation Peter Davies is actually a very familiar figure to readers, for as Peter Llewellyn Davies — to give him his full name — he and his four brothers served, each in their turn, as inspiration and model for J. M. Barrie's Peter Pan, the boy who never grew up. Barrie was an intimate friend of the boys and their parents, and when the boys' father died in 1906 Barrie, childless himself, assumed financial responsibility for the family; after their mother died in 1910 he became the boys' guardian. Thereafter he watched over them as if they were his own flesh, absorbing the disappointments and tragedies that come to boys who must grow up. George, the eldest, was killed in France in 1915; Michael, the second youngest, was drowned while a student at Oxford in 1921; and Peter, fresh from Eton where he had been endlessly teased about his fictional self, went off to fight on the Somme for two months before being sent home suffering from eczema and shell shock. He recovered and went on to win the Military Cross, but the war left scars on a personality already bruised by the Barrie association:

> What's in a name? My God, what isn't? If that perennially juvenile lead, if that boy so fatally committed to an arrestation of his development, had only been

> dubbed George, or Jack, or Michael, or Nicholas, what miseries would have been spared me.

After his army years Davies was at loose ends for some time before going to Edinburgh to learn the publishing business. Subsequently he worked for a time for Hodder & Stoughton in London, and then in 1926 established his own firm in Henrietta Street. His 1927 catalogue shows that fine editions were an early mainstay of the firm. *Epicurus,* published in late 1926, was one of his first books. His invitation to Manning, asking him to name his own terms, shows the respect in which the young publisher already held the man he would cajole into writing a classic.

But admiration does not guarantee access: "I am sorry to say," Davies replied to a scholar's inquiry in 1939, "that, although I knew him exceedingly well during the last few years of his life, I am deplorably ignorant with regard to the facts of his career." It is a familiar pattern: Manning would share his thoughts and wit, and even some of his moods, but the details of his life were kept back. Still, friendships thrive without such "facts", and Davies' letters record a great affection for Manning. "It is quite extraordinary," he wrote to Harry Manning on the third anniversary of Fred's death, "how often I find myself missing Fred. He was an extraordinarily good friend to me, and apart from that, his brain was so much better than anyone else's that it was of the greatest value to learn his opinion of any current problem." Davies had met Manning a few years after the war and this encomium suggests that he was impressed, like many others, by the power of Manning's conversation. On the basis of his writings, listeners expected to hear a man of taste and culture. What they experienced, though, was a mind formidably rich and acute, able both to recall what it had read with astonishing detail and to analyse a problem with an engaging subtlety. The boy who had amazed adults with his reading and sophistication had grown into an adult whose insights impressed many of his peers. Manning's best dialogues may have been those he had with friends.

By 1977 Peter Davies was long dead, having thrown himself under a moving train in the Sloane Square underground 17 years earlier. No one currently connected with the firm had known Manning, and even Nico Davies, Peter's youngest brother, who had worked in the firm in the 1930s and had met Manning on a few occasions, could not offer much help. "I can't at all say that I 'knew' Manning, alas." Nor did there seem to be hope of finding the kind of records that Murray held. German bombs had decimated the Davies archives during World War II. Still, a visit to the office was obligatory, if only to meet Joan Waldegrave. She had gone to work for Peter Davies in 1950, and if anyone could help me, I was informed, it would be her.

Joan Waldegrave proved to be one of the more fascinating people I encountered in my search for Manning. Her age, concealed partly by cosmetics but more by her charm and spirit, was a mystery. She knew the publishing business very well, and handled my inquisitiveness with a skill I had to admire even while suspecting that she was holding back one or two things. An assistant was sent to fetch what evidence there was of Manning in the files, and he came back with the contract for the war book and a copy of Davies' 1939 letter about Manning. These were helpful, and so too was listening to Joan Waldegrave talk of an author she had never laid eyes on. For around Manning's name was a nimbus, placed there, of course, by her former boss. The same halo was in evidence when I chatted with the publisher's son, Ruthven, in his London home. He had not been born when the book was published, but his father's respect for Manning was imprinted on his mind. As I learned more about Peter Davies from the people I spoke to, and later from Andrew Birkin's *J. M. Barrie and the Lost Boys*, the book written about him and his brothers, I sensed that his worshipful respect for Manning was based on something other than his friend's "brain": Manning's novel had explained to him his own war experience.

Davies had come out of the war broken in health and spirit, yet proud of his service, and for the remainder of his life he seems to have been alternately fascinated and horrified by his memory of battle. *The Middle Parts of Fortune* speaks to that not uncommon ambivalence with rare insight and understanding. As a result it not only could re-enact for Davies his feelings while on the Somme but could serve as a text by which to comprehend his subsequent feelings. Hemingway said he reread Manning's book every year "to understand how things really were so that I will never lie to myself nor to anyone else about them". How often, I wondered, did Davies read what in 1955 he said was one of the "two best books" he ever published? The other was a reprint of *Scenes and Portraits.*

When *Epicurus* came out, Manning was on his way to Ireland, "to pay", as he whimsically and somewhat mysteriously told Rothenstein, "my long deferred visit to the Irish Rebels". He had been hoping since the spring to visit the Lynches again, "but I have really to chain myself to the table to write the Epicurus." What for other writers would be a casual metaphor is for Manning a familiar statement about his difficulties in sustaining a piece of work. Rothenstein would ultimately decide that he did not finish the romance because "he dallied and delayed".

This visit to Ireland was not a happy one. Once more Belfield became a place in which to convalesce. Sybil Gowthorpe tells the story.

> In due course the [Mannings] came over to Ireland & were staying in Bray near Dublin & Lady Manning invited my mother & me to lunch. We found Fred in a deplorable state & after consultation with his mother, we brought him back to Belfield with us. This was . . . the beginning of another period of rehabilitation under my mother's wing, after which there was no further drink problem to the end of his life.

The conclusion may be more wishful than factual. His isolated existence and personal reticence had always made it difficult for friends to be sure of what he was doing, and once he left Buckstone Farm in 1925 there were undoubtedly periods when

Manning with his mother and sister Edith at the Grand Hotel, Rome, 1931 (Eleanor Manning)

friends did not even know his whereabouts. He was gone from England much of the time, or so it seems — tracing his movements is no less troublesome today — and used the Australian Bank of Commerce in London as a mailing address. At the same time his correspondence becomes patchy. Except for a series of letters in 1931, even the dialogue with Rothenstein has long breaks. And when he went to Australia in November 1932 he seems to have put out of mind his friends back in England. Letters were probably written, but few. If he stopped writing to Rothenstein, an old and comfortable friend, and to Lawrence, a new and cherished friend, then he presumably was not writing to very many people. To be certain, therefore, about something he found as embarrassing as his drinking binges is not possible.

Once he left an established residence his movements are often linked to those of his mother. When she is in England, they are apt to be together, in London or visiting friends in the country; when she is in Italy or Austria he is there, or planning to go there. In May of 1927 he thinks of returning to Australia "with my mother'', and in 1932, when he actually makes his last trip, it seems to have been partly for his mother's sake. Their emotional attachment, always very strong, was now charged with new dependencies: the mother caring for a son whose life has become a succession of illnesses; the son watching out for a mother growing old and burdened with a daughter (Edith) who is now an outright alcoholic. There is a photograph taken of the three of them in Rome in 1931. On the back is written ''Coffee after lunch at Grand Hotel. Mother in shadow.'' Nora Manning, clothed entirely in black, sits a little away from the others. Her son, dressed in a three-piece suit with a handkerchief in his breast pocket, looks rather uneasily into the camera, a cigarette in his right hand, a coffee pot resting on the table in front of him. Next to him is Edith, the upper part of her face cast in shadow by a helmet-style hat. Her passport picture at this time suggests the toll of her disease. They appear a very ordinary group of travellers, and had you stopped to chat with them for a few minutes they undoubtedly would have given you no reason to think otherwise.

During a visit to Rome in 1927 Manning had occasion to act as cicerone to a friend of his brother Harry. A description of his efforts, written eight years later when the friend sent a letter of condolence to Harry on hearing of Fred's death, offers a vivid portrait of the manners of a private man.

> On my arrival a letter was put into my hand in which he wrote he was down with influenza, and in fact he was in bed during all but the last days of my visit. Notwithstanding this — I saw a great deal of him, for I used to go to his room every morning to hear of the plan for the day which he had sketched out for me. His knowledge of the contents of the galleries, etc. in Rome was truly marvellous, & was willingly put at my disposal, as he seemed to take a genuine interest in making my stay in the ''Eternal City'', which he loved, as profitable to me as was possible. The evenings I used to spend in his room in talking over all things in heaven

> & earth. He insisted that I must pay my respects to the Pope, and procured an invitation for me through a friend in the British Legation to the Vatican.
>
> On one day only was he well enough to go out with me, when he took me to see some newly discovered Etruscan relics in which he took the deepest interest. Next morning I left for Florence where I had been staying with my daughter. From there I wrote to him, but received no reply. Nor did he communicate with me when he afterwards came to England. It seemed very strange after our close friendship, as I thought, in Rome, but so it was.

One place where Manning went without his mother was to Lincolnshire, at first for short visits, later for stays of several months. What brought him back to the area is not difficult to surmise. Having no permanent home in England he gravitated toward the familiar. Edenham had once been home, the only one he willingly acknowledged; everywhere else he felt himself a visitor. "I wish I had roots," he told Sybil Gowthorpe in 1928, "and you could plant me at Belfield for a few months." When he returned to Lincolnshire he did not take lodgings at Edenham but in Bourne, at The Bull, a small family and commercial hotel run by Frederick Scott and his partner H. G. Penfold, known to everyone as "Pen" and the subject of one of Manning's extant pencil sketches. Today The Bull does not offer accommodation, and the pub is entered through a door in a wall where once was a passageway for cars, and before that, horses. An advertising postcard from the 1920s shows the hotel with its two proprietors standing in front of it. Alongside the picture are listed the various services offered: "Parties catered for"; "Luncheons, Teas"; "Motor Garage". While not an elegant establishment, The Bull had more to offer Manning than a private home in Edenham. And it was to be in his sitting room on the second floor, as close to associations that mattered as he was distant from the trenches, that he would write his memories of the Somme.

The Bull Hotel, Bourne, in the 1920s
(author's collection)

The earliest mention of them I found was in a letter of May 1927 to John Murray: "Mr Peter Davies...has asked me to write him some actual experiences of the war in the form of a short story or rather a short novel. He offers me very attractive terms." Davies, foreseeing the eventual popularity of books about the war, had apparently been suggesting the project off and on since the early 1920s.* Now that he was a publisher, he was prepared to make a serious offer. Manning was tempted. Still wishing — but still unable — to finish the "long-neglected Romance", he viewed the proposed memoir "of an actual experience" as less demanding than "a piece of really creative or imaginative writing". It would, he felt, "keep me in the vein for writing". But he was uncertain about accepting the offer, feeling an obligation to finish the romance first, and so "only attempted two or three rough sketches of detached incidents" before the reception of *All Quiet on the Western Front* confirmed Davies' prophecy. Then, stroked once more by his publisher, who had read the sketches, Manning began to write, and quickly fell into the rhythm writers hope for: "It was wilful and spontaneous, and took its own way. It came so hurriedly that some things were forgotten."

But the process was not all speed and flow. Manning would send Davies chapters of the work, and the publisher, presumably familiar at least with the history of "The Gilded Coach", became uneasy. Smart publisher that he was, Davies knew that the season for books about World War I would not last indefinitely, and that an author "obstinately averse from finishing what he had begun" could cost himself the chance of success. Accordingly, Davies is reported to have "lured" his friend to London and to have "shut him up in his flat" for several weeks to write, "not allowing him out, and keeping his friends from him." Manning later told friends essentially the same story. "Peter took it from me sheet by sheet, and cast it into adamantine type. But for him I might have rewritten it. What an escape." No word of the abduction, only relief at having been rescued from shackling habits. Under unique pressure to get on with the book, he did just that. Kidnapping was not a tactic of the house of Murray; had they employed it they might have been able to issue "The Gilded Coach". On this occasion the tactic eased the birth of a masterpiece.

Manning later told T. E. Lawrence that "even during the war I thought of writing it". It had likely been a passing thought, for during or after the war he nowhere speaks of it, and was perhaps content with the war poems as an expression of his feelings. Besides, no publisher had come to him asking for such a book. If, after the armistice, one had, Manning might still have hesitated. "The Gilded Coach" then appeared the more natural and suitable project, and subsequently White's life had preoccupied his attention. Moreover, his military record after the Somme — and after *Eidola* — was sufficiently embarrassing to give a sensitive man pause before picking up his pen. The Kitchener biography may have been as close as he was willing to go in 1919 to writing anything further about the war; indeed, one could speculate that in contributing to the biography of the field-marshal he hoped to exorcise the guilt he felt about the dismal denouement of his own military career.

Ten years later a lingering embarrassment conceivably entered into the decision to conceal his identity under the pseudonym "Private 19022". (The limited, unexpurgated edition lacked even the *nom de plume*.) But I suspect — unfortunately there are no letters explaining his motive — that in signing himself as an anonymous private he wished to testify to the authenticity of what he had written and to pay the sincerest tribute he could to his comrades. It was not Frederic Manning the professional writer who had told their story, but one of them. And given the trance-like process of writing — Clio had come at first bidding — in a very real sense Private 19022, the Frederic Manning of 1916, *had* written the book, ably assisted by his comrades: "In recording the conversations of the men I seemed at times to hear the voices of ghosts." Writers often experience the sensation of characters coming alive and telling their own story; Manning had sensed this at moments when working on "The Gilded Coach". The voices of former comrades, however, who had marched alongside him might well have humbled the pride of authorship.

While the decision to use a pseudonym was no doubt Manning's — "I really want to remain unknown", he told Sybil Gowthorpe a month after the book came out, when the identity of Private 19022 had become a guessing game — Peter Davies probably had few objections. He certainly knew how to take advantage of the disguise. His pre-publication advertisements announced a war book of "unique interest and significance, written by a distinguished man of letters who served as a private soldier". Substitute Frederic Manning for "distinguished man of letters" and the message sagged. A little known writer had much to gain by becoming a mystery. And soon after the book came out, T. E. Lawrence unwittingly did both author and publisher a great favour. Thinking he recognised the book's author, he rang up Peter Davies and without identifying himself offered his opinion:

UNKNOWN VOICE: I want to congratulate you as strongly as possible on "Her Privates We". It's magnificent, a book in a thousand. You've published a masterpiece. But tell me this: How did you get..........to write it?

SELF: Thank you very much, and I'm delighted to hear you like it, but —

VOICE: Like it! It's not a question of like! The book's a classic! And it is by..........isn't it?

SELF: The author of "Her Privates We" prefers to be known only as Private 19022. I've said so to dozens of literary detectives, and I've said so on the jacket of the book. So how can I answer the question? Besides, I don't even know who I'm speaking to.

VOICE: Oh, Shaw's my name, you probably won't know who I am, but I once wrote a book myself, called "Revolt in the Desert".

SELF: (*An ejaculation, indication of impressed astonishment*)

VOICE: But about Private 19022. You see, I've read "..........." at least 50 times; that's a masterpiece, too, and the man who wrote it is the only man who could possibly have written "Her Privates We". I'm right, of course?

SELF: (*After a pregnant pause*) You know, I'm not supposed... When he went abroad, I promised him... He can't have foreseen this, though...Oh well, here goes; You, Sir, and your method of attack combined, are too much for me, and must surely justify my surrender in the eyes of Private 19022. Yes, of course, you're right. Only do please keep the secret, or I'm lost.

VOICE: I won't tell a soul, though it's bound to come out before long. Meanwhile, will you let him know how enormously I admire and love his book? If people don't run to it in thousands, it'll be because they don't care to see themselves in a glass, magnificently...I can't say half of what I feel about it on the telephone. Look here, I'll write to

> you now, and you can pass on my letter, or the substance of it, to him...*

The dialogue comes from a pamphlet ("Colonel Lawrence and others on *Her Privates We* by Private 19022") that the shrewd publisher distributed to bookstores. As Manning wryly noted, Davies was "an adept" at publicity.

The book Lawrence claimed to have read "at least fifty times" was, of course, *Scenes and Portraits*. While he was no doubt exaggerating, only someone who had reread the earlier book often (and recently) would have seen that the preface to the war book was "pure *Scenes and Portraits*". Twenty years is a long time to keep in mind the specific texture of a style unless it is noticeably idiosyncratic, and in subject and design the novel was as far removed from *Scenes and Portraits* as had been *The Life of Sir William White*. Aldington, who knew Manning's prose and values about as well as anyone, having looked at his work as both critic and collaborator, was unable to identify the author of *Her Privates We* when he reviewed it — though years later he would claim to have been "practically certain" it was Manning. On the other hand, if the two books are read successively, their subtle pursuit of moral and philosophical issues, their expertly crafted dialogues, their ironies, their abiding compassion for man's effort to penetrate or simply to make peace with the mysteries of existence — all these suggest their common authorship. "Life was a hazard enveloped in a mystery," thought Bourne, and that idea controls the sketches of the creator's youth.

Indeed, the Fred Manning of 1929, though older, sicklier, and more reserved than his 1909 self, had not changed his intellectual and aesthetic values. He still treasured and practised the critical virtues of "tact" and "sanity", he still deplored the sentimental and subjective in literature, and he still distrusted "modern" tastes. Proust was mocked for his "interminable 'subjectif epic'", Freud he quickly came to distrust ("I shall not trouble very much with psychoanalysis"), and there is no evidence that his meeting with Joyce prompted him to read *Ulysses*. A man of fastidious culture and tastes, a writer imbued to a fault with the restraint, the discipline, and the scholarship cherished by the classical tradition, he seemed to some of his friends almost a throwback to Pater and Arnold.* Had he not been, he would have written a less important book about the war. For the values that made him suspicious of certain modernist tendencies, enabled him to take his experiences on the Somme — which were "only that of the average" — and find in them meanings above the merely personal. He had read too much, thought too much, and stood apart too much to make his work an act of confession or a cry of horror and disillusionment. He was too much the artist and too much the philosopher to write solipsistically of war. Edmund Blunden spoke truly when in the preface for a new edition of the novel (1964) he wrote that if Manning had not been "a master of many classics I doubt if he could have written such a modern classic". Galton would have said the same.

The writing of the book came "hurriedly" because it was "a record of experience on the Somme and Ancre fronts, with an interval behind the lines, during the latter half of the year 1916; and the events described in it actually happened." It was, as that prefatory note implies, an act of memory rather than imagination, and fluency, therefore, was not surprising. Of course the author selected and embellished as it served his purpose, and exercised the technical prerogatives of fiction, but the story of Bourne and his fellow "Westshires" follows precisely the passage of the 7th battalion of the Shropshires while Manning was with them. Peter Davies, on checking various "scenes, times, and names of trenches", expressed amazement at the accuracy of his friend's memory. Now Manning had an excellent memory, and he had also his war poems — one originally intended to clue his friends as to his whereabouts — to remind him of scenes, events, and impressions. He had not kept a war diary, however, and in reconstructing the complicated peregrinations of 13 years before he very likely had help from the same *History of the King's Shropshire Light Infantry in the Great*

War (1925) that Davies presumably consulted in checking his recollections. In keeping to the actual movements of the 7th battalion Manning had most of the shape he wanted for the novel. So closely, indeed, was he following memory — his own or recorded — that the reader is apt to sense that the narrative is only a pronoun away from being a diary. And sometimes not even that. Describing how Bourne shifted to a mare (whom he named Rosinante) the responsibility for pulling a gun cart, the narrator observes: "She bore no malice, the old lady, as though she knew *we* [my italics] had a pretty thin time." Enmeshed in memory or fatigue, Manning has momentarily switched from a third to a first person narrator. The characters, too, were drawn from life, and then disguised — by a change in name or rank or fate, possibly even a transfer of a personality from one battalion or regiment to another — allowing the author to say that they were "fictitious". But veterans of the Shropshires, once apprised that the Westshires were themselves, claimed to recognise several of their old comrades — predictably, since "ghosts" are commonly more visible to those alerted to their presence.* Often the necromancer, Manning was at the top of his form when summoning former companions, and by not troubling to invent a cast of characters to inhabit real memories he avoided risks that he was all too familiar with.

Some critics have imagined a carefully developed plot in the book, but it was precisely the need *not* to have to invent which enticed Manning to take up his pen: "Actual experience[s] would not entail the same amount of work as a piece of really creative or imaginative writing would." To say that *The Middle Parts of Fortune* is more memoir than novel does not diminish its power or authenticity, nor does it compromise those parts that are invention, principally the wonderful talk of its characters. Instead, that knowledge allows us to appreciate what its author was able to do with great skill and ease — the book was written in six months — and what he was not. And we can understand how its author was subsequently tempted to mould other prose fictions from his life, to stretch the ambition of his art.

Bourne, the book's central character, is obviously Manning himself. He did not even bother to alter his face:

> His impassive face was thrust forward, and the beaky nose between the feverishly bright eyes, the salient cheek-bones above the drawn cheeks, the thin-lipped mouth, set, but too sensitive not to have a hint of weakness in it, and the obstinate jaw, had a curiously still alertness in its expression.

Bourne's habits, tastes, humour — they are all Manning's: his small handwriting, his preference for short hair, his love of horses, his fondness for Horace, his constant smoking and periodic prodigious drinking, his "delicate sensibility", his "sardonic" and "ironical" intelligence, and his occasional whip-sharp sarcasm. He is also a soldier who thinks he would have preferred the "solitary and, up to a point, inconspicuous" career of a sniper, and a man who has "the faculty of withdrawing right into himself, his consciousness shrinking into its inmost recesses, contracting to a mere point, while the bodily part of him followed its ordinary train of habit". Bourne's character almost perfectly reflects his creator; his fate, however, shatters our sense of a mirror image. What there is of a plot in the novel involves Bourne's gradual and grudging relinquishment of his desire to remain an enlisted man, which differs from Manning's pre-Somme efforts to leave the ranks. And the novel is brought to a close with the killing of Bourne on a raid, just before he is to go back to England for officer training. These changes served both conscience and art; simple ego may have had rather more to do with the decision to portray Bourne as being able to outdrink any of his companions, and with no discernible effect.

By depending on real events and real people Manning left himself free to write the kind of book he wanted to write and the kind of book he knew how to write. He sought to record the emotional responses and intellectual strategies by which soldiers endured what by all accounts should have been unendurable.

Preparing for an attack the men are led through a rehearsal in a mock-up area. "What they really needed," the narrator tells us, "was a map of the strange country through which their minds would travel on that day." *The Middle Parts of Fortune* was intended to be such a map, a book about an experiential challenge in which the moral and the psychic parts were more pressing than the physical. The novel form, however attenuated, gave Manning a flexibility of viewpoint and the opportunities for dramatic focus; it also gave him privacy. If readers' traditional expectations of the novel were disappointed, if they did not, for example, feel themselves caught up in a riveting plot, or if they had difficulty caring for characters without faces or pasts — "I have drawn no portraits" — they might read another book. Though he was reaching for a larger audience than ever before, Manning still wrote for readers accustomed to thinking.

Formally, the narrator controls the story. Distant, precise, ironic when it suits his purpose, the voice is Manning's. But Bourne is also Manning, and so as often happens in highly autobiographical narrative, it is sometimes hard to distinguish between the voices. Not that it much matters, for we quickly learn to listen to what is being said rather than to worry about who is saying it. Bourne attracts our attention less for what he is or does than for how he sees. He remains as distant from us as he feels himself to be from his comrades. If he has not quite the omniscient capacity of the narrator, who once or twice coughs and suggests that Bourne's view of the matter at hand may be "limited", he nevertheless has the same values and concerns. To both, the war is a stage on which the players come and go largely according to chance. But until an exit cue — whether back to "Blighty" with a good wound, or to a numbered grave far from home — a man had the responsibility for writing his own script. He might be trained and treated as an "automaton" by the army "machine", but he retained a consciousness of himself as an individual, and retained as well, therefore, a freedom of choice. At one point Bourne concludes that as a "moral effort" the war was "magnificent". He is not talking of politics and causes but of ordinary men, each of whom will ultimately fight for himself, having his own reasons and relying on himself.

The heart of the book, however, is not in the battle scenes, finely drawn though they are. Like any serious book about war *The Middle Parts of Fortune* recognises that most of a soldier's time is spent out of battle. And so the novel focuses on Bourne and his companions during the days and nights when they are marching, training, grousing, and staving off yesterday or tomorrow with food, drink, and laughter. They are a mixed lot, and have few illusions about each other or themselves. Brave, lazy, belligerent, cunning, and tender, they draw all the closer to each other for knowing that when they go over the top they will be alone. Manning does not idealise them, but as once their comrade and now their chronicler he sees them as he had always been inclined to see ordinary rural people: "Bourne sometimes wondered how far a battalion recruited mainly from London, or from one of the provincial cities, differed from his own, the men of which came from farms, and, in a lesser measure, from mining villages of no great importance. The simplicity of their outlook on life gave them a certain dignity, because it was free from irrelevances." These are men, like the tactful and intelligent Sergeant Tozer or the pathetic, complaining Weeper Smart, who will stand up to what they must, and the overwhelming number will not "break". That is a running concern of everyone in the book, officers and privates alike: will they be able to "stick it", and for how long? Bourne, too, ponders the questions, but with powers his comrades do not possess:

> Power is measured by the amount of resistance which it overcomes, and, in the last resort, the moral power of men was greater than any purely material force, which could be brought to bear on it. It took the chance of death, as one of the chances it was bound to take; though, paradoxically enough, the function of our moral

> nature consists solely in the assertion of one's own individual will against anything which may be opposed to it, and death, therefore, would imply its extinction in the particular and individual case. The true inwardness of tragedy lies in the fact that its failure is only apparent, and as in the case of the martyr also, the moral conscience of man has made its own deliberate choice, and asserted the freedom of its being.

This, the classical view of the matter, was in keeping with the view that war was "part of the natural order of things".

Though Bourne imagines the men to be "a little less reflective and less reasonable than he himself", Manning gives them speech that is ripe, incisive, and wise. They may not know books but they know their own thoughts and so talk with the special eloquence such knowledge gives. They speak in a dialect meant to be reminiscent of the West Country, their home ground, and they are profane because their characters and predicament insist that they be.

> "We're fightin' for all we've bloody got," said Madeley, bluntly.
>
> "An' that's sweet fuck all," said Weeper Smart. "A tell thee, that all a want to do is to save me own bloody skin. An' the first thing a do, when a go into t' line, is to find out where t' bloody dressing-stations are; an' if a can get a nice blighty, chaps, when once me face is turned towards home, I'm laughing. You won't see me bloody arse for dust. A'm not proud. A tell thee straight. Them as thinks different can 'ave all the bloody war they want, and me own share of it, too."
>
> "Well, what the 'ell did you come out for?" asked Madeley.
>
> Weeper lifted up a large, spade-like hand with the solemnity of one making an affirmation.
>
> "That's where th'ast got me beat, lad," he admitted. "When a saw all them as didn't know any better'n we

did joinin' up, an' a went walkin' out wi' me girl on Sundays, as usual, a just felt ashamed. An' a put it away, an' a put it away, until in th' end it got me down. A knew what it'd be, but it got the better o' me', an' then, like a bloody fool, a went an' joined up too. A were ashamed to be seen walkin' in the streets, a were. But a tell thee, now, that if a were once out o' these togs an' in civvies again, a wouldn't mind all the shame in the world; no, not if I 'ad to slink through all the back streets, an' didn' dare put me nose in t'Old Vaults again. A've no pride left in me now, chaps, an' that's the plain truth a'm tellin'. Let them as made the war come an' fight it, that's what a say.''

''That's what I say, too,'' said Glazier, a man of about Madeley's age, with an air of challenge. Short, stocky, and ruddy like Madeley, he was of coarser grain, with an air of brutality that the other lacked: the kind of man who, when he comes to grips, kills, and grunts with pleasure in killing. ''Why should us'ns fight an' be killed for all them bloody slackers at 'ome? It ain't right. No matter what they say, it ain't right. We're doin' our duty, an' they ain't, an' they're coinin' money while we get ten bloody frong a week. They don't care a fuck about us. Once we're in the army, they've got us by the balls. Talk about discipline! They don't try disciplinin' any o' them fuckin' civvies, do they? We want to put some o' them bloody politicians in the front line, an' see 'em shelled to shit. That'd buck their ideas up.''

''I'm not fightin' for a lot o' bloody civvies,'' said Madeley, reasonably. ''I'm fightin' for myself an' me own folk. It's all bloody fine sayin' let them as made the war fight it. 'twere Germany made the war.''

''A tell thee,'' said Weeper, positively, ''there are thousands o' poor buggers, over there in German lines, as don' know, no more'n we do ourselves, what it's all about.''

''Then what do the silly fuckers come an' fight for?''

> asked Madeley, indignantly. "Why didn' they stay 't 'ome? Tha'lt be sayin' next that the Frenchies sent 'em an invite."

Almost every novel of the war has an exchange of this sort. But the explicit language of this and other colloquies conveys the frustration of real soldiers, not book soldiers; and in 1930 the gap between the two was considerable. Of course, in the edition of the novel (*Her Privates We*) that was then reviewed and read by most people the choicer barrack epithets were perfumed before they hit the page — "bugger" became "beggar", "fucking" transmuted into "bloody" — but that was a compromise only with the censor. With the precedent of O'Casey perhaps in mind, Manning wrote the dialogue as he had heard soldiers speak, just as in *Scenes and Portraits* he had constructed the conversation of saints, popes, and philosophers from what he had read them to say. In both efforts he caught the tone and the spirit as well as the substance of the talk, which is why his dialogues are generally captivating. If his soldiers occasionally sound more self-consciously philosophical than might be expected from country privates, that only reveals an admirer of Synge working "faithfully" as an artist to let the opinions of the anonymous ranks — "often mere surmise and ill-informed but real and true for them" — be heard.

Bourne's speech, properly accented and seldom spiced with obscenities, marks him out from the other privates, as do many of his other habits and tastes. He is not a typical private and was not meant to be. Fluent in French, he is useful as an intermediary for both officers and privates alike, and he manages to cadge many small comforts for himself as well. Once, however, his knowledge leads to a scene out of Euripides by way of Molière. Asked by a young girl to help her compose a response in English to a love letter written by another English soldier, Bourne loses control:

> "Je t'aime, chéri! Je t'aime éperdument! Je n'aime que toi;" she almost chanted it; and suddenly his arm was

> round her shoulder, and his mouth was shut fast down there behind her ear, where the hair swept upwards from the firm white neck. She collapsed astonishingly under his touch; neither towards him nor away from him; she seemed to go to nothing in her chair. She pushed him away with her right hand, firmly, quickly. He shifted, shifting his chair away, too, and then put up a hand to his brow. He was sweating lightly. The other hand went into his pocket. He stood up, feeling criminal, and looked at her.
>
> "Vous m'aimez?" There was a kind of rage in his suffocated voice, and she turned her face to him, looking at him with eyes in which was neither anger nor fear, but only the surprise of recognition. It was as though she had not known him before, but now she remembered. He sat again, turned sideways towards her; and put his hands over her hands lying clasped in front of her on the table. They remained still, impassive.
>
> "Vous m'aimez? C'est vrai?"

Did this actually happen to Manning? If not, it might well have, for it is in perfect harmony with the pent-up eroticism found in many of his poems, and which the flippant comments in his letters poignantly intimate. Bourne, says the narrator, "always treated women with a little air of ceremony, whatever kind of women they might be". One can understand why. Diffidence and inexperience create artificial modes of address. In this instance, acting as an amanuensis and mildly attracted to the girl, he hears himself called through words meant for another. Or were they? Was she also calling to him? And why did so private a man bother relating this incident? The answer to both questions is in what he says when he goes back later to say goodbye to the girl:

> And they said good-bye, with that slight air of formality which Madame's presence imposed on them, their eyes searching through it to try and read each other's thought, and each warding off the other. Madame

> might have her suspicions, but she evidently could restrain an unprofitable curiosity; and part of their secret was even a secret to themselves. In all action a man seeks to realize himself, and the act once complete, it is no longer a part of him, it escapes from his control and has an independent objective existence. It is the fruit of his marriage to a moment, but it is not the divine moment itself, nor even the meaning which the moment held for him, for that too has flown feather-footed down the wind. Bourne had a positive hatred of the excuse that "it does not matter" being given as a reason for any action: if something does not matter, why do it? It does matter. It matters enormously, but not necessarily to others, and the reasons why it matters to you are probably inexplicable even to yourself. One need not confuse them with the consequences which one has to shoulder as a result, and one cannot shift the burden with a whimper for sympathy.

Their brief, confusing encounter had mattered too much to be left out, for it symbolised the elusiveness and uncertainty of human contact that Manning was so sensitive to.

Bourne's relations with his two "chums", Shem and Martlow, are less ambiguous. Shem, the Jew with eyes "like the fish-pools of Heshbon", is the typical comrade. Like Bourne he is a champion scrounger and when necessary an artful liar; he is also a "tough, sturdy and generous" companion, a dependable man for any occasion. Yet after being wounded and sent back to the hospital, he dissolves rapidly into a "vague memory". Comradeship grew out of common necessity, and apart from that necessity Bourne and his friends have nothing in common. Martlow, however, is not so easily forgotten. He is important enough for Bourne to tell us his Christian name (Charlie), and we are shown scenes from his childhood. Not yet 17, "little Martlow" is to Bourne "the kid", a foul-mouthed, worldly-wise, yet vulnerable youth, whose "precocity" Bourne finds sometimes disconcerting and to whose "impudence" he always succumbs. And it is to Martlow alone that Bourne will unbend when explaining his decision to become an officer: "He was a reticent and undemonstrative man, but after a few more steps through the silent shadows he put his arm around Martlow's neck, his hand resting on his shoulder. 'I don't want it. I have got to go,' he said." Just how deeply attached Bourne is to the boy becomes apparent when Martlow is shot.

> Bourne flung himself down beside him, and, putting his arms round his body, lifted him, calling him.
>
> "Kid! You're all right, kid?" he cried eagerly.
>
> He was all right. As Bourne lifted the limp body, the boy's hat came off, showing half the back of his skull shattered where the bullet had come through it; and a little blood welled out on to Bourne's sleeve and the knee of his trousers. He was all right; and Bourne let him settle to earth again, lifting himself up almost indifferently, unable to realize what had happened, filled with a kind of tenderness that ached in him, and yet extraordinarily still, extraordinarily cold. He had to hurry, or he would be alone in the fog. Again he heard some rifle-fire, some bombing, and, stooping, he ran towards the sound, and was by Minton's side again, when three men ran towards them, holding their hands up and screaming; and he lifted his rifle to his shoulder and fired; and the ache in him became a consuming hate that filled him with exultant cruelty, and he fired again, and again. The last man was closest to him, but as drunk and staggering with terror. He had scarcely fallen, when Bourne came up to him and saw that his head was shattered, as he turned it over with his boot. Minton looked at him with a curious anxiety, and saw Bourne's teeth clenched and bared, the lips snarling back from them in exultation.
>
> "Come on. Get into it." Minton cried in his anxiety.
>
> And Bourne struggled forward again, panting, and muttering in a suffocated voice.

> "Kill the buggers! Kill the bloody fucking swine! Kill them!"

Grief as rage; it is Achilles and myriad others who have slaughtered so that they might revenge a loved one.

Afterwards, Bourne cannot dispel Martlow's image from his mind; he thinks he will "always see those puckered brows, and feel the weight of him". Of course, it is really Manning who could not forget the "freakish schoolboy, jealously obstinate in all resentments, but full of generous impulses, distrusting the whole world, and yet open and impressionable when one had gained his confidence". And he had, it seems, already memorialised him in his poem "The Face". Did Charlie Martlow really exist, or was he a type, a composite of all the young innocents that Manning saw die? We need not find an answer to realise how necessary it was for Manning to create him.

Bourne's own death quickly follows. Despite being "down for a commission" — which should exempt him from hazardous assignments — he is pressed by his commanding officer to go along with a raiding party that was to have been drawn only from volunteers. He is shot while returning, at the very moment when "a sense of triumph and escape thrill in him", and dies in the arms of Weeper Smart.

> Weeper turned his head over his shoulder, listened, stopped, and went back. He found Bourne trying to lift himself; and Bourne spoke, gasping, suffocating.
>
> "Go on. I'm scuppered."
>
> "A'll not leave thee," said Weeper.
>
> He stooped and lifted the other in his huge, ungainly arms, carrying him as tenderly as though he were a child. Bourne struggled wearily to speak, and the blood, filling his mouth, prevented him. Sometimes his head fell on Weeper's shoulder. At last, barely articulate, a few words came.
>
> "I'm finished. Le' me in peace, for God's sake. You can't. . ."

> "A'll not leave thee," said Weeper in an infuriate rage.
>
> He felt Bourne stretch himself in a convulsive shudder, and relax, becoming suddenly heavier in his arms. He struggled on, stumbling over the shell-ploughed ground through that fantastic mist, which moved like an army of wraiths, hurrying away from him. Then he stopped, and, taking the body by the waist with his left arm, flung it over his shoulder, steadying it with his right. He could see their wire now, and presently he was challenged, and replied. He found the way through the wire, and staggered into the trench with his burden. Then he turned down the short stretch of Delaunay to Monk Trench, and came on the rest of the party outside A Company's dug-out.
>
> "A've brought 'im back," he cried desperately, and collapsed with the body on the duck-boards.

The image of Bourne being carried back to the Westshires's trench may remind readers of the scene in *All Quiet on the Western Front* where Paul Baumer carries his beloved Katczinski on his back to an aid-station, only to discover that his friend is dead.* But Manning is not imitating that scene, for while affection motivates both characters, Weeper's act risks his own death. His, therefore, is one of those "moral" efforts by which the war could become "magnificent" in Manning's eyes.

When Bourne's body is brought back, Sergeant Tozer comments that it was "hard luck" that he was killed so close to safety. We know that it was another man's will that is responsible for "hard luck", but Manning does not mean to leave us angry. Nor are we left to lament his hero's death. Manning had to kill off Bourne to provide the book with a proper sense of closure, and he does it so as to remind us that death is less the crucial issue than the "affirmation" of one's will in the face of death. Bourne's last thoughts on the matter are those we would expect from a sceptical Catholic Epicurean of uncertain will:

> Anyway, he argued, probably none of our actions are

> quite voluntary; if compulsion is not explicit, it is perhaps always implied; and then he found himself wondering whether the determination [to go on the raid] which became stronger and stronger in him, was not after all his real self, which only needed the pressure of circumstances to elicit it.

The book's last scene is carefully wrought, its essence acknowledging the strategy of a life as well as the theme of its art.

> . . . the sergeant-major looked at the dead body propped against the side of the trench. He would have to have it moved; it wasn't a pleasant sight, and he bared his teeth in the pitiful repulsion with which it filled him. Bourne was sitting: his head back, his face plastered with mud, and blood drying thickly about his mouth and chin, while the glazed eyes stared up at the moon. Tozer moved away, with a quiet acceptance of the fact. It was finished. He was sorry about Bourne, he thought, more sorry than he could say. He was a queer chap, he said to himself, as he felt for the dug-out steps. There was a bit of a mystery about him; but then, when you come to think of it, there's a bit of a mystery about all of us. He pushed aside the blanket screening the entrance, and in the murky light he saw all the men lift their faces, and look at him with patient, almost animal eyes.
>
> Then they all bowed over their own thoughts again, listening to the shells bumping heavily outside, as Fritz began to send a lot of stuff over in retaliation for the raid. They sat there silently; each man keeping his own secret.

It is the men nursing their own doom, rather than Bourne, who linger in our memory — as they did in Hemingway's, who has a strikingly similar image in *For Whom the Bell Tolls.** And that is the way Manning wanted it. "I thought the majority of war books libelled them and I tried to praise them in the only possible way, by a sincere record which would show how their splendid qualities lifted them above all defects, even of their own nature." That does not keep us, however, from realising that they are fortune's privates, that like Rosencrantz and Guildenstern they play in a drama not of their own devising, never knowing when death will sweep the stage of them.

Manning found his title and chapter headings in Shakespeare. He wanted perspective, and the companions of Pistol, like the privates of 1916, had understood what it meant to cling to life and each other with all the strength they had. But even without the Shakespearean references the reader knows that these Westshires, this "fuckin' fine mob" as they call themselves, are men for all seasons, that they, like their fathers and sons, can survive whatever the "blind forces of nature" hurl at them, including war, and in doing so will ennoble themselves. At least that is how Bourne, who knew that he really was not one of them, was prepared to see his companions. E. M. Forster labelled the book a "love story" as much as a war story. While the same could be said of many other books of war, beginning with the *Iliad,* of none does it seem quite so true as it does of *The Middle Parts of Fortune.*

To invoke the *Iliad* will seem a preposterous claim, until one disengages *The Middle Parts of Fortune* from the other novels of the trenches and appraises its full ambition. Intending to write a memoir of the war, Manning in fact achieved more because it was not in his nature to be a simple memoirist. It is a book about a group of men in a particular war, but it is also a book about the phenomenon of war in general, and, finally, a book that quietly addresses even more fundamental matters. What else would we expect from such a mind reflecting on its own experiences? And because Bourne and the narrator keep glancing at the larger issues, *The Middle Parts of Fortune* must be read as one would read the book it resembles in so many ways, *Scenes and Portraits* — except now the central issue is man's being, his potential for enduring pressure and thereby, perhaps, becoming "most intensely himself", rather than God's being and how man has gone about defining it. (Manning knew that issues which philosophers would join were by soldiers severed — once they had been in battle.) The central issue of the later book, however, does not allow for definitive answers any more than it stimulates easy ironies, and so Manning leaves us finally with a sense of mystery about ourselves. The book ends with each man clutching his "secret" in the "murky light" of a dugout, as unable to solve it for himself as he would be willing to share it with others. "Tout homme à s'expliquer se diminue. On se doit son propre secret." The privacy of each man is inevitable and essential; it is also absolute. Sorrow, not anger or pride, permeates Manning's view of our aloneness. Neither the Catholic nor the Epicurean ultimately feels himself an alien in a wasteland. And though both as shy young poet and sickly middle-aged novelist Manning explored a theme of other writers, his own experience perhaps earned him a special right to it. He also deserves to have his finest book read and applauded as more than just an authentic account of war. In 1930 a young American critic who had barely grasped the larger focus recognised why others had not: "It is a fine book and it is a pity that its restraint is too likely to hide its meaning." Lionel Trilling went on to become an authority on Matthew Arnold.

When the book in its expurgated form appeared in January of 1930,* it was an instant success with critics and readers alike. Impression after impression was snapped up by a public still ravenous for graphic descriptions of an experience now comfortably remote for some, and still dangerously close for others. What almost everyone agreed upon was that *Her Privates We* was the first book to tell the truth from the common soldier's point of view. There were, of course, doubters,* an occasional reviewer, or an ex-soldier writing to a periodical to question the accuracy of certain details or to complain that Bourne was scarcely your everyday private. But in the booming praise the book received,* these voices were overwhelmed, and they had no effect on sales. By April 1930 over 15,000 copies had sold* — roughly three times the total sales of all of Manning's previous five books — and within weeks of publication negotiations for German and Swedish editions had begun. Manning greeted success with appropriate philosophic calm: "I am not puffed." But there must have been an inward gladdening at the reception and, as he banked the substantial royalties, he may have reconsidered his opinion that "the work we live by doesn't live; and the work that lives, we can't live by." A large audience had welcomed a book easily written; its subject had made all the difference.

Or almost all, for the book got the help popular books do. The *Sunday Referee*, for example, offered copies as a prize one week in their crossword puzzle competition, while Selfridge's devoted one of its largest windows to displaying the book accompanied by a sign quoting the opinion of "Colonel Lawrence" and with a drawing of a soldier reading the book.* Beneath the drawing ran a caption, "Who is the author of this book?" The mystery spurred interest, and we have already seen how Peter Davies took advantage of the name of T. E. Lawrence. Now disguised as T. E. Shaw, Lawrence accepted the use of his image in a good cause:

> Peter Davies is trying to use my dregs of reputation as one more lever in the sales. Do not let that worry you. Adventitious sales and adventitious advertisements are very soon forgotten: the cash will remain with you, and your book be famous for as long as the war is cared for — and perhaps longer.

Other levers kept offering themselves to Davies' ready hand. When a critic remarked that the only "adverse" reviews had been written by women, Davies quickly issued an advertisement entitled "*Her Privates We* and Women". Meanwhile, standard advertisements were kept running in the book sections of newspapers and magazines, celebrating the achievement of that mysterious author, Private 19022. Manning had always felt that John Murray was insufficiently aggressive in promoting his books, but with Peter Davies his complaint was the reverse; he confessed to being "a little terrified of the publicity".

While the book was becoming a bestseller its author was out of the country. "Private 19022," laughed the *Daily Mirror,* "has fled to Italy rather than face the praise of his friends." If he was fleeing from anybody it was certainly not his friends. Many were given copies and he admitted to being "greedy enough" for their praise. His only hesitation involved a matter of propriety: "You, and Polly," he wrote to Frieda Lynch (now Mrs Frank Bernard), "and my mother are the only three women to whom I have given it — and Mother is not to read it, except in the expurgated edition." Even that version distressed Nora Manning, but it was not the coarseness of its language that made her put it down. She found the book "beautiful but too terribly sad. So she is very proud of it now but doesn't want to read it."

In Sydney a copy dedicated to his mother does not survive, but there is one with Edith's signature on it. Below her signature is written "Semmering January 23rd 1930", and below that her brother has signed himself "Private 19022", as he signed the copies of close friends and mere acquaintances alike.* The insistence on his *nom de plume* — long after his identity as the author was common knowledge — was not entirely whimsical. As long as he acted as if the book were the work of Private 19022, it asked to be judged as the testimony of a serving soldier. Once the name Frederic Manning appeared on its cover, it became a book by an experienced if not familiar author. When he originally determined on anonymity, Manning cannot have expected to escape detection; some part of him may not have even wanted to. But even after his authorship was disclosed he very much wanted his book to be read for itself alone, and for the reader to end up remembering the soldiers more than the author.

Lawrence's appetite for the war book was as unslakable as it had been for *Scenes and Portraits.* Within six weeks of its publication he had read *Her Privates We* twice and *The Middle Parts of Fortune* once, "and am now deliberately leaving them alone for a while before reading them again". His phone call to

Peter Davies also served to put him back in touch with Manning after eight years of silence. "I had your address a couple of years ago from Cherry-Garrard of Lammer: but somehow I did not write." Either man — each hesitant, private, self-absorbed — could have written that line; in fact, it was Manning. Once more the two men discovered how easily they could talk together, and over the next several months they often exchanged letters and on one or two occasions met in London. What they talked about most in their letters was writing, their own and each other's, with Lawrence casting himself in the role of apprentice. In his eyes Manning had now written a second great book, one more than Lawrence confessed to be his own "ambition", and two more than he felt he had accomplished. Even Manning's praise for *Seven Pillars of Wisdom,* welcome though it was, could not lift Lawrence from his knees: "That would have been a pleasant letter to get for the tallest author alive: and therefore many times pleasanter for me, who think myself no great shakes at writing, from one whose writing I so vainly admire." He preferred, and not without cause, to see Manning as his master.

In Eleanor Manning's home I found a letter written by James Fairfax in December 1936, thanking Harry Manning for copies of Lawrence's letters to his brother.

> It is perfectly clear that there existed an extraordinarily close mental affinity between Fred and Lawrence, based a good deal, I read it, on the fact that they balanced and complemented one another in a manner deeply satisfying to each — Fred primarily an intellectual, but debarred from more active life by poor health: Lawrence primarily a man of action, but whose battles were fought first on an intellectual plane.
>
> Another thing emerges: Lawrence had the generous admiration of the fighting man for the man of letters when he is a master of his medium. You remember how General Wolfe said he would rather have written Gray's "Elegy" than captured Quebec. Lawrence knew that in "Scenes and Portraits" Fred had achieved a classic and a

> masterpiece beside which his own fighting and writing were tentative and spasmodic. Also, in "Her Privates We" Fred had got inside the mind of the fighting man with the intuition of a great writer: he was the more complete and rounded personality. Lawrence continued at odds with the world and himself, and his bungled exit from the stage confirms that impression.

As far as he goes, Fairfax is right. Manning saw in Lawrence the embodiment of what he sometimes yearned to be and what for a few months of his life he had been: an active man, even a fighting man. But in his letters to Lawrence — which Fairfax could not then have seen — Manning is decidedly more interested in Lawrence the recorder of himself than in Lawrence the man of action. "I did not want an historical record; I was completely satisfied to follow the action of a mind reflecting its past experience and still a little tremulous and excited by it." That, he told Lawrence, had been his reaction to *The Revolt in the Desert,* the abridged edition of *Seven Pillars of Wisdom.* His response to the full book, which he read "practically without intermission" when Lawrence sent him a copy in April of 1930, exhibits the same fascination. "To me your book, however I may criticize it, is a great action: it has the reality of action. I do not mean of the action it describes, but the action it is. I found it profoundly interesting because it leaves me asking myself and you and life so many questions."

Millions were dazzled by Lawrence the hero, and so, slightly, was Manning; but Lawrence the warrior poet, the man who had gone down into himself to find his "magnificent book", who could examine his ambivalences as bravely as he could describe the struggles of his will, was a more seriously engaging figure. The immediate sympathy Manning had felt for him, evidenced by the sudden rush of talk about himself that had so amused Rothenstein, denotes minds touching, and shared sensibilities. Interests greater than war drew them together:

> You took me right back to Genesis and Job. When you

> describe the action of the nomad on the town-dwellers I see that Jahveh was the desert in all its naked heat moving up to consume the baalim of settled communities, who had exchanged the rigorous asceticism imposed on them by the desert life, for a sensual indulgence which the previous starving had only enhanced. Job, of course, was an Arab, and his present day progeny stand in the same relation to Allah as he stood in relation to Jahveh, so passionately asserting his own individuality against that engulphing one-ness. How far "the eternal illusion" as I might call it, took hold of your own mind, I can guess, and yet in all your overt acts you are only harnessing its power to serve some temporal and even momentary ends, in which you do not altogether believe, at least not with the spirit of worship which you feel towards the power it was your business to subjugate and canalise. That's the whole moral problem: one not very different in kind from that confronting Paul on his road to Damascus. As I read your book, and it is a riddle, that is the conflict which subsists at least implicitly under the material action of the book. Or is it some bent in my own mind which forces me to consider you *sub specie aeternitatis*?

That, a portion of Manning's response to *Seven Pillars,* is excellent criticism of a book about which much silliness has been written. It is, moreover, that special criticism in which one feels the writer momentarily assuming control over the author he is discussing and saying with passion what he has found in the book to be important for himself. After reading *Seven Pillars* Manning would have better understood why Lawrence had read *Scenes and Portraits* "fifty times". And had their fates been otherwise, had Manning outlived Lawrence, I can imagine him at least contemplating a portrait of his friend, perhaps in a scene with the "smooth" and "ironical" Feisal, the two of them sitting cross-legged under a sky of stars and conversing of the one God and his many prophets.

Instead Manning would dedicate to Lawrence the sketch he wrote in the summer of 1930 for a new and expanded edition of *Scenes and Portraits.* It was a gesture of personal affection for the book's most faithful friend. The opportunity for making it arose out of a disagreement with John Murray (the fifth) — who had succeeded to his father's job in 1928 — over whether a new edition of the book "in a more modern and agreeable form" ought to be published. Murray was reluctant because he and Manning could not agree on the need for one. Manning had originally broached the idea through his friend Stanley Dunn, who was then an editor at Murray. Dunn made some inquiries and reported back that it was generally felt a new edition would not be "profitable". At that point, early in March 1930, Manning approached Murray directly. The publisher, with 100 copies still in hand from the reprint of 20 years before, and the plates long since destroyed, was less than eager. "You will realize that to ask a publisher to bring out a new edition before the current one is exhausted is rather an unusual proceeding, and from the business point of view somewhat wasteful. Am I to take it that you are willing to buy up the remainder of the existing edition and so clear the way for the new one?" Manning acknowledged that Murray was within his "rights" to hold back on a new edition until the old was sold out, but he questioned the "wisdom and justice" of Murray's reluctance. A brief and more or less gentlemanly quarrel ensued between author and publisher, and ended with Manning buying up the remaining copies as well as the rights to the book itself. Had Manning been willing to "disclose" his authorship of *Her Privates We*, Murray sounds as if he would have been willing to chance a new edition — both men had counted the sales of the war book. But Private 19022 was not ready to remove his veil, and it seemed unnecessary as well. "The newspapers have already announced that I am the author. . . and I have been twice interviewed on the matter; so that, even without an explicit admission on my part, the fact is generally known."

After conferring with Dunn but before consulting Murray, Manning had spoken to Peter Davies "merely in a tentative way" about Davies taking over the book. What understanding they had reached is impossible to determine, but Davies must have indicated he would be all too happy to have his imprint on *Scenes and Portraits* if the opportunity arose. Certainly the assumption that Davies could be depended on would explain Manning's rather arbitrary negotiating style with Murray. He sounds in his letters a little too willing to have matters reach deadlock, and when Murray eventually indicated that he would be willing to consider a new edition if some "new matter" were introduced into the book, Manning simply ignored his offer. The fact that after coming to terms with Davies he began making revisions and added a new sketch — and that the subsequent advertising for the new edition identified him as the author of *Her Privates We* — enhances the suspicion that he was only going through the motions when corresponding with Murray. Of course, he may have been persuaded of the wisdom of both disclosure and "new matter" only after he signed on with Davies, but the evidence available suggests that he was not unhappy to have *Scenes* in the hands of the more aggressive publisher.

Murray remained all tact and balm. He genuinely did not want to lose Manning, especially after the success of the novel. His concern had less to do with the immediate loss of sales than it had with the possible permanent loss of an author who seemed finally to have found a popular voice: "I hope. . . that it may still only be a temporary separation and not a 'divorce', and that we may some day have the pleasure of bringing out another book by you." Though Manning shared no such dream, he acknowledged feeling "rather melancholy" when the last accounts for *Scenes* were settled. The book had now (1930) reached its majority, and while its future seemed bright there was a natural twinge of regret at seeing it leave its old home.

The revisions that Manning made in the book consisted almost entirely of changing individual words and transposing phrases. Only in the last pages of "At the House of Euripides" was there a substantial modification of the text. Also the preface was wisely dropped and replaced with a more easily ignored sentence (in Greek) from Plato's *Parmenides*. Readers could now step directly into the most charming of the pieces, "The King of Uruk", without having to wade through a tangle of argument and explanation listening to a "young man", Manning told Arnold Bennett, "parading his authorities".

The new sketch, "Apologia Dei", is a monologue addressed to Satan, imagined here not in Milton's phrase as an angel "hurled headlong flaming from th' ethereal sky", but as one who has chosen "voluntary exile with mortal dust". Manning's God is simply a declarative voice, formless, remote, almost indifferent, a fair copy of the Platonic One, or of the Divine Being of Epicurus. His terms and references are Judaeo–Christian but his essence and tone are classical. From his vantage point in eternity, which is not as most men think "simply endless time", but "indivisible", lacking alike the characteristics of time or space, God justifies himself by describing man as profoundly ignorant of both the conditions of his existence and the nature of the Eternal Mind. Man incessantly seeks God, or as the voice claims, "wishes to become a God". The process is full of error and confusion, not to mention false allegations about God, but it is not without interest: "Sometimes I have pity for the gods of man, and at all times patience; since in even the most inhuman and revolting of his gods is his own strange nature manifest." Aside from its newness, there was a nice logic in the addition of this sketch to the book; for by examining the book's principal theme from the standpoint of God himself, and thereby offering a new perspective from which to judge the other pieces, a more obvious sense of conclusion was achieved. As the reader might suspect, the "Apologia", which Rothenstein termed "the metaphysical addition", is by far the most abstract and least engaging of the sketches. It was also "difficult" for Manning to write. "The child I am fathering on you," he told Lawrence, "has gone to the printer, and I shall say no more about it than that it was conceived in sorrow, and brought forth in pain; you will have to decide for yourself whether you own to the brat or not.''

The ''sorrow'' may well have been for ''poor Charles Whibley'', as Manning spoke of his long-time friend who had died on 4 March. They had known each other since at least 1912, and though of different temperaments they shared common tastes. Galton had praised Whibley for his ''scholarship'', his ''sturdy Toryism'', and his ''familiar acquaintance with the Greek and Roman classics'', which explains why Manning recommended to Pound that Whibley should be asked to contribute to their projected magazines, and why Manning used him as a reference when applying for a commission in the army. What Galton's praise did not include was mention of Whibley's exuberant self, which friends like Manning and Eliot treasured. ''He was distinct, and in his way unique.'' The respect had been mutual. A few years before, Whibley had asked Manning to write an introduction for a new edition of Savile's famous translation of Tacitus, while hinting at an invitation to give a public lecture at Cambridge. The introduction was never written, the lecture never even seriously considered. ''I don't fancy myself in the character of the preacher.'' His unwillingness, which was based also on the fear that he might ''funk'' the occasion, is reminiscent of his refusal to take the chair, years before, at Pound's lecture on Guido Cavalcanti. But if he was too shy to speak in public, around those with whom he felt comfortable (''I like or dislike people, spontaneously and as Falstaff has it on instinct. I may invent reasons for my likes and dislikes later'') he talked easily and well. ''I was very glad to see you yesterday, & look forward to another talk with you next week.'' So Whibley, in the only note I found between these good friends. I searched for Whibley's papers in the hope of discovering something of their discourse, but the trail vanished with his widow who went off to Australia and married a blind man.*

Work on the new edition of *Scenes* took up the spring and summer of 1930, during which time Manning mostly lived in

London, staying either at a hotel or at 26 Gilbert Street with Taffy Fowler. Except for further dental troubles, his health seems to have withstood the strains of the city and periods of "close and unpleasant weather". He saw few people aside from his mother, his sister Edith, and Peter Davies, who now held him on a looser rein. One day Eliot came to see him for a half hour to tell him how much he had liked *Her Privates We* and to ask him to do "some political writing" for Faber & Faber. Manning turned the offer aside for "some future time"; he was too busy at the moment and had plans to go abroad in October. He rejected outright Eliot's other request that he translate an unidentified war book: "I do not know German well enough." As it turned out, his trip was delayed as the work on *Scenes and Portraits* was not finished until October, and then to a sort of fanfare. "As I put the last words to the 'Apologia Dei' yesterday they fired a royal salute in the Park. Wasn't it nice of them?" Heard from my study decades later, those shots sound like the knell to a career.

When *Scenes and Portraits* was reborn in December of 1930 publicity focused on its being by the author of *Her Privates We*.* How else to sell 2000 ordinary and 250 special and signed copies of a book that few readers of the war book had ever heard of?* Davies even had the ordinary edition bound in the same cloth as the ordinary edition of *Privates*. He did not mean to deceive potential buyers as to its contents — one advertisement specifically warned that "the earlier book is not a war book" — but he naturally wanted to encourage a hope of common quality and interest. The ordinary edition had "satisfactory" sales; the special edition was less successful. A guinea is a lot to pay for the signature of an author who has only just been recognised. One of these copies went to an old friend and, as if to confirm how much this new edition was a child of the war book, Manning erred when signing it for a second time in January 1931.

Olivia Shakespear
Jan. 1930
from Frederic Manning

There is nothing strange, let alone deliberate, about this alteration of the calendar; we all misdate our lives in January. I found this copy in Eleanor Manning's home. Tucked away next to the title page of "At the House of Euripides", the sketch Manning had dedicated to Olivia, was a newspaper clipping announcing a BBC broadcast of the story. Arranged and produced for a series called "Imaginary Conversations", it was aired on 15 June 1947.* Earlier that year "Jesters of the Lord" was produced in the same series, and five years later a new production of this sketch was done. That it received a second production only proves the obvious: a clash between a saint and a pope has more drama than a Socratic dialogue. I found another copy of the signed edition in Sydney. This one had also been signed a second time, but without a mistake:

To his dearest Mother
from Fred Xmas 1930.

Reprints of books, even when they are revised and enlarged, seldom gain much press attention, and this was the case with *Scenes and Portraits*. The *Times Literary Supplement* was content to send its readers to the library: "First published in 1909 and reviewed in our columns on 27 May of that year." Those critics who did review the book, though, echoed their predecessors. "*Scenes and Portraits* should be regarded as one of the lovely and thoughtful pieces of modern literature." And reviewers other than E. M. Forster urged readers to compare *Scenes* with *Her Privates We*, though not always for the best of reasons. "It is a portrait of the writer. Those who enjoyed Mr Manning's war book, will find him here revealing himself more fully than he did in the drama of the war." Naturally some reviewers felt compelled to decide which was the better book, and the earlier one usually took the prize. In the spring of 1931 Scribner's put out an American edition,* and practised even more thoroughly the strategy of Peter Davies. For example, stamped prominently beneath Manning's name on the board cover was the phrase, "author of Her Privates We". The war book, however, had never caught on in America the way it had in England, and Scribner's, it seems, had no more luck with *Scenes* than had Putnam 20 years earlier.* And perhaps of little help to a publication in 1931 were reviews that commenced their praise by declaring the book to be "thin juice" or "beyond reach of the crowd" and "wholly innocent of vulgar appeal".

Meanwhile, Manning was in Rome, staying at the Grand Hotel with his mother. From there he responded to the congratulations of friends and critics. The doubts he had had about the new monologue — and he seems to have had one or two about its difficulty* — evaporated in the glow of praise. He was especially "pleased" by E. M. Forster's review and asked Lawrence, who was a friend of Forster, to tell him as much. "I have always liked his work, his point of view and way of writing. He has individuality. I should like to tell him so myself, but it would seem immodest." There speaks again the diffidence that was so much a part of his character — no less so after he had gained a certain celebrity status. And his dependence on intermediaries did not slacken either. "I heard the other day that you [Rothenstein] sent Arnold Bennett *Scenes and Portraits.* That is so like you. You make friends for people who can't make them for themselves." Manning knew his worth as a writer, and was not backward in measuring his mind or his wit against an adversary in talk or print; but a hesitancy, a sense that he lacked what others had or might expect of him, stayed with him. "I feel that it needs the movement and exaggeration of a restaurant to distract the attention of my guests from the dullness of my company." Rothenstein, to whom those words were written when a lunch was being arranged, recognised something more than humour in such a comment and so should we.

When Manning returned from Italy he returned to Bourne and settled in at The Bull "to write my romance". Once more, and not for the last time, he would try to breathe life into a corpse. It did not work. Neither writing in the place where the war book had come so effortlessly, nor knowing Davies's "insatiable appetite for another book" could move his pen. Nor could residing in London, where he took a small service flat for a couple of months in the spring. Had the return to *Scenes and Portraits* induced him to think that this time he would find the needed inspiration? Possibly, for the early book had carried him back in time, and back also into the imaginative mode. Severely hampering this attempt at the romance, as it had many others, was illness. He came down with a nasty cold in London, which prevented his attending Eliot's memorial lecture on Whibley, and which later developed into the flu. Did his persistence in going back to this most frustrating of enterprises ("I want to get it done for the purely selfish reason that I wish to be delivered of it") help to undermine his health? Again, that is possible. In any event his symptoms were becoming more menacing. He mentions frequent attacks of bronchitis, followed by periods of "lassitude", and it is possible that he was now suffering from emphysema. In July he went to St Moritz for seven weeks: "The air here has already done me so much good that I feel rather an impostor. I have just come in from a two-mile walk, mostly uphill; and when I left England almost eight days ago, I could not walk a hundred yards on the flat, without feeling breathless." Once back in England, however, ensconced again at The Bull to wrestle with the intractable romance, the cure lapsed. By the end of 1931 he was both frustrated and apologetic over his failure to accomplish "any satisfactory work". But there was no help for it: "I have not been really well for the whole of the past year, and one of the most marked features of my infirmity is the lassitude which succeeds to an attack."

His health was not to improve. For over a month in the spring of 1932 he was in a London nursing home with double pneumonia, and at one point he "nearly died". At the end of May he returned to Bourne to complete his recovery. He seems to have done no work, but germinating in his mind was the novel about village life. Once Edenham had inspired only pastoral idylls; now it would be described as it really was. Once a concern for "style and form" had shaped Manning's art; now, as he told Lawrence, "I am more absorbed in the difficult language of facts, which by its own nature achieves both spontaneously." Writing *The Middle Parts of Fortune* had been a liberating act; reading it had been a disquieting experience. Yet if that novel had shocked people, what he had in mind now would disturb them even more, for everyone accepted war as a shocking business, but the English village (Hardy and others notwithstanding) was a national treasure. The assault on it would have to wait, however, for in the autumn he had a "relapse", and as soon as he was on his feet his doctor encouraged him to go to Australia. There he would find at least a more amenable climate.

And so at the age of 50 he once more took ship for Sydney, hoping to improve his health. The sea voyage alone would be beneficial. But I suspect he had reached the point where death had become plausibly imminent. As a realist — and a gambling man — he must have sensed that his lungs would not last another ten years, probably not even five, if the last 18 months gave a sound reading of how ravaged they were. Still, there might be time for one more book, especially one fetched out of personal experience. And if not, well, as Lawrence had told him, *Scenes* and *Privates* were enough to have made it all worthwhile. The second book had been long in coming, but it had made up for his failure to finish the romance and had wonderfully extended his reputation. Indeed, he was going to Australia with the kind of acclaim that almost 30 years earlier he had left there to achieve.

Denouement

CHAPTER EIGHT

When Manning arrived in Sydney on 30 December 1932, a photographer from the *Sydney Morning Herald* took his picture. The face is gaunt, almost in pain; the boyish look is wrinkling into old age. The eyes, however, retain their piercing gaze. Along with the picture in the next day's edition was a story spun from the kind of interview famous writers often have to withstand.* What war book did you like? How did you write your own? And so on. Those appear, anyway, to have been the questions, for the story carried only the answers, indirectly quoted. Eight years before, Manning's arrival in Sydney had not been noticed. Now he was "one of the finest literary stylists of the day", and author of a book that had stirred "a great deal of controversy". He also happened to be the brother of the Attorney-General of New South Wales — a fact duly noted in the caption to the photograph — as well as the son of a former Lord Mayor, which made him familiar despite his long residence in England. And so another question was put to him: what were his favourite books about Australia? He named only *The Fortunes of Richard Mahony,* the recently completed and much praised trilogy by Henry Handel Richardson, the pseudonym of another expatriate.

Three months later Nettie Palmer, in her role as crusader for Australian literature, took up the inevitable conundrum of whether, and in what sense, Manning could be labelled an Australian writer. If he were accepted, the article suggested, he would be "in the front rank" of "our prose writers of this century", alongside Joseph Furphy. A half century later Manning might still be there, but then and now the decision has been that "we cannot call him an Australian writer". It is a just

Manning on his return to Sydney in 1932
(author's collection)

view of the matter, and was certainly shared by Manning himself. Yet there is a moment in the war novel when Bourne, enraged at having been turned away from a canteen wrongly restricted to officers, draws upon his creator's roots. "You want a few thousand Australians in the British Army...They would put wind up some of these bloody details who think they own the earth."

Once past the reporters Manning slipped from view. For the next 16 months he was only marginally more visible than he was during his previous visit home. He stayed, it seems, with various members of his family, seeing his eldest brother Will and his wife Lucy more than anyone else.* He was also ill for a time, which may account for the length of his stay. Shadowy though his movements and activities are, his view of this visit — confided in a letter to Harry once he was back in England — is sadly clear: "I think my visit to Australia one of the most distressing things that ever happened to me; but if I was any help to Mother I am sorry I left her there; though I don't think I could have gone on without a breakdown. I am glad anyway I could help her for a time, even if it amounted to no more than giving her company and sympathy." What precisely was "distressing" is not discussed, but it is not difficult to imagine the strains of dealing with an ageing mother and a deteriorating sister. Attached to his mother as he was, he could not ignore family problems and, being none too well himself, he paid a heavy price for his sympathy and love.

He also alludes to some "bright spots" in his visit, which presumably included the time spent with Harry and his family. Besides family and Fred's career the talk between the two brothers would have focused on politics, especially now that Harry was Attorney-General. In the Manning home I found partial drafts of a speech and a letter (or article) that Manning drew up for his brother.* Whether either was used or even finished, and whether there were others as well, I do not know, but Harry must have been pleased to have to hand a pen so gifted in composing speeches. Of course, a speech writer who shares his subject's views will not necessarily share also his cast of mind. From what I learned of him I could not imagine Harry saying the following: "Ultimately all the problems which the apparently arbitrary forms of law have been designed to meet are involved in the individual man's relations with his fellow men, or with the social system enveloping him: they are problems of conduct, of right action, that is to say they are moral problems."

Of literary work during this visit there are only hints, like the story mentioned to me by Bill and Dora Manning of Fred tearing up a piece of work he deemed not "good enough". Another hint comes from Manning himself in a letter to Harry written after his return to England: "I am not working on the play." Whether this play was begun in Austràlia or merely contemplated is a mystery, as is its subject and how far he got with it. But among the papers at the Mitchell Library is a five-page discussion/outline — intended for an unidentifiable collaborator — about how *The Westcotes* (1901), a novel by Sir Arthur Quiller-Couch, could be converted for the stage. Does this prospectus belong to the play mentioned to Harry, or does it represent some earlier effort? Neither the talk nor the handwriting tempt even a guess. Its existence, nevertheless, is not surprising.

A reader of Manning's works will quickly sense their author's potential as a dramatist. *Brunhild* and *Scenes* could easily be staged — two sketches of the latter, the reader will recall, were played as radio dramas — and entire chapters of *The Middle Parts of Fortune* ask to be performed before an audience. If, in short, Manning had not yet tried his hand at playwriting, except for the prewar verse dramas on classical themes and an even earlier four-page effort ("The Critic") in the youthful copybook, it was not because he lacked the skills. Nor was it due to a lack of exposure to the theatre. In his youth he had gone to the theatre, seeing among the moderns Shaw and presumably Ibsen, and his reaction to *The Plough and the Stars* in 1926 reveals a man powerfully stimulated. Indeed, it is imaginable that the experience in Dublin inspired thoughts of playwriting.

But a talent and an interest may not be sufficient to prompt (or sustain) an effort, especially in a writer nurtured to be the heir of Arnold and Pater, and dependent on the will of others for direction. Galton certainly would not have encouraged such an effort. He had sparse interest and less taste in drama, once telling Binyon that "most" of Shakespeare was "not good to act". Nor, we may assume, was it (or much else) good to see, which may help explain why during their years together at Edenham the London entertainments Manning describes as attending are concerts and recitals. Even after Galton's death, however, it is unlikely that Manning would suddenly have turned to playwriting. Leaving aside the obligation to finish the White biography and the obsession with "The Gilded Coach", the very isolation in which he continued and preferred to live would in itself, I suspect, have discouraged his writing for the stage. Of all the literary forms, drama most depends on a certain absorption in society; it is a genre of the city, rather than of the "hermitage". And finally there is the character of Manning's art, an art that was perhaps a little too restrained and inward to try to appeal to stage audiences. "Unfortunately," he realised while revising *Scenes and Portraits*, "I am perhaps too much of a philosopher to be an artist, and too much of an artist to be a philosopher." Yet it is understandable how a writer so skilled at dialogue and character, and who could examine ideas easily and clearly, might be tempted periodically to try his hand at a conventional play — particularly when he heard critics pronounce "Mr Manning has the genius of a dramatist", as one of the reviewers of the new edition of *Scenes* had exclaimed. It is unlikely that a reviewer's comment set him to the task, but it seems clear that after the success of *Her Privates We* Manning was taking a more flexible view of what he might write. Unfortunately it was too late.

Besides the Quiller-Couch proposal, however, there does exist another fragment of Manning the playwright, though perhaps it is really more of Manning the parodist, since it is a burlesque of Shakespeare. The scene is an inn, situated on the road to heaven. Several ghosts are enjoying their ale, waiting for a coach to take them to their destination, when they hear that "a man in the flesh" is on the doorstep. The ghosts quickly take up a position behind the hostess, Mistress Ursula, and watch timidly as, into the room, a little worn from "carrying this great parcel of guts up the very hill of eternity", strides Sir John Falstaff:

> Page (*fearfully*): Good Sir John, prithee Sir John! Let us not tarry here. I am all in a sweat o' fear! 't is not true inn! It hath no reality! 't will be full o' ghosts.
>
> Falstaff: Ghosts! You piece of goose-flesh. What is a ghost? A nobody! (*Sensation among ghosts*) An' you are afraid of a pack o' nobodies, then you are an intolerable coward. If this inn be not a real inn, then for to-night I must e'en make shift with mine imagination, for I can carry this monstrous bulk of me no further. I have sweated so prodigiously the whole length of the Milky Way, that 't will be called the Greasy Way hence forward, and those who follow me will find it a slide of butter.
>
> Here we rest. Reality! What is this riddling reality? Hath it ever stood us in good stead? Hath

> it clothed us, or fed us; hath it found us a warm bed, or kept us in wine? I have never met with a piece of reality that had not a sour, sharp, cold, needy, hungry look to it.

It is fine parody, evoking the Bard and yet serving Manning's wit; had he taken more seriously his gift for mimicry he could well have developed into a master. Falstaff continues:

> A man hath wits for no other purpose than to circumvent it. I will have none of your reality. What am I? What are you? Why, yesterday we were but the creations of one man's dreaming mind. Had you a mother? Nay, nor I. Like Ixion he begat us on the cloud of his desire. We are chimeras. While he lived, we passed from one man's body to another's, so that it took on our semblances, our habits, our humours, our desires. We were live nimble spirits informing for a time their grosser clay. But when he died, from whose brain we had sprung, as it were full-armed, like Minerva from the head of Jove, his soul had so dispersed itself through all these phantasms of his begetting, that we must needs go to Heaven in his stead. I know now where the rest of him may be. 't is against all sound theology and Christian belief that a man's soul can be in more than one place at any one time; but I doubt whether theology hath ever had such a case as ours before it. I care not; there's no man can say I ever took the risks of Fortune but in good part. I would care less, if Fate had left us mere spirit; but 't was a sorry trick that even as he put off mortality, we should put it on. 't was as a second birth whereby we have achieved a separate existence; and now we cannot change our nature an' we would. We are immortally mortal!

The clues for dating this concoction, which breaks off after 13 pages, are thinner even than Falstaff's memory of Justice

Shallow. When working on the war book, Manning would seem to have reread *Henry IV*, while in a letter of July 1934, he uses the Falstaffian epithet, "this coster-monger age". Together they can only be read as saying Shakespeare was on his mind, scarcely enough on which to rest a case, but enough to hazard a guess that he may have worked on the exercise while he was in Australia.

He left Sydney for England on 11 April 1934, two days after making out a will. His departure drew no reporters and it was just as well, for he might have singed a few ears if asked about his impressions of his homeland. "I shall leave Australia with very few regrets: it has nothing to recommend it except its climate, and the skies, which are an effect of the climate." As for Sydney, it had become "quite spoilt except for the water". Had his stay been less unhappy perhaps he might have been more charitable. At least, though, his health had improved. Except for his chronic asthma, he felt much better and looked forward to doing some work again. Where that might be had not been decided. The Bull had changed hands, and so he was not sure that he would go back to Bourne. "You might let me know," he wrote to Gladys Gelsthorpe, the daughter of The Bull's former owner Frederick Scott, "what the Bull is like, now, in case I should want to go down later — you know the sort of thing, what the people are like? And whether I could get the same rooms? I don't suppose you and Jack want a boarder." He wanted to resume his place in familiar surroundings, but it seemed as if there might have been disturbing changes.

Settlement of the problem was delayed. He had a "succession of colds" on the voyage home, and a fog in the Channel "brought on" an acute attack of bronchitis "which went", he told Harry, "pretty close to pneumonia". Once again his body had betrayed him. "I don't know why my illness comes so suddenly. I expect this climate will always be troublesome for me." He spent a month in a nursing home in Hampstead and then was "promptly" sent away from London by his doctor. He went to stay for a short time at the cottage of one of Eva

Fowler's sisters, and then after two nights back in London so that he could see his doctor, he took lodgings with a retired valet and his wife at their home in Milton, just north of Cambridge. The couple treated him well, but it was "a dreadful old house", he reported to Olivia Shakespear, lacking a bathroom, with the sitting room a foot below the level of the ground, the bedroom "a kind of garret", and a "pervading smell of damp". He soon made arrangements with Gladys Gelsthorpe to board with her and her husband, and after a stay with some friends he went to Bourne on 14 July, eight days short of his 52nd birthday. Fewer than eight months later he would be dead.

Mrs Gelsthorpe was in her 70th year when I talked to her in 1977. Her husband Jack was dead, and she no longer lived in "Gleneden", the house where Manning had boarded with them. In chronological order, she was the first person I interviewed who had actually known Manning, and in my innocence I hoped that having been his landlady she would be able to recall all sorts of interesting details. But I soon discovered that Manning had kept pretty much to himself. He had been given the front rooms, up and down, which were the largest in the house, and had been allowed to have guests. Lawrence was invited to visit but delayed his call until it was too late. Occasionally other friends would stop by — Carl Holmes, his rich American friend, drove over from The Node one day in his "magnificent Rolls" — but for the most part Manning was alone. He seldom went out, and when he chose to enter the Gelsthorpe family circle it was usually for a game of cards. Familiar with her boarder from his days at The Bull, Gladys Gelsthorpe adjusted to his tastes and habits as best she could. He was a finicky eater, and could be demanding at times, wanting things done "straight away", and she recalled having to get rid of the family cat when he took up his rooms. She knew that he had been a "heavy drinker", but she never saw him drunk. To her and her husband he was always "Mr Manning", someone they liked and respected, but someone who offered little of himself. At least not to them. On their little boy's first birthday he was given a rocking horse by the boarder.

In the midst of our conversation Mrs Gelsthorpe went out to fetch what few traces of Manning she had retained. Among them was the letter he had sent her inquiring about The Bull, his drawing of "Pen", her father's partner at The Bull, drafts of two opinions Manning intended for *The Times,* and some sheets of calculations about race horses — the last written out in as fine a hand as any of his literary manuscripts. In themselves none of these things were of value, and except for the letter there was nothing of significant value to a biographer. But to Gladys Gelsthorpe these random sheets had been important. When sorting through Manning's possessions after his death she had thought nothing of burning some letters from Arnold Bennett.

Later the same day I walked over to "Gleneden". It is a modest brick and stucco structure, with a slate roof. Only its name would distinguish it from a million other English homes. After his experience in Milton, though, Manning had been glad to have "modern and comfortable and hygienic" quarters. I stood in front of the house for a few minutes, took a couple of photographs, and left. For reasons not clear to me, I had no desire to go up to the door and seek entry. Perhaps I had not yet developed the boldness that later made such attempts so easy, perhaps the sheer architectural dullness of the place — it was the least interesting of all the homes he had dwelled in — dampened my curiosity. Perhaps, too, it was knowing that he had lived at "Gleneden" so short a time and that it had been the last stop in a nomadic existence. Whatever the reason(s), I walked away.

It was soon after settling in at Bourne that Manning wrote to his brother Harry that he was putting aside the play he had begun in Sydney, "as a book seems the more immediately profitable". There is no mention of the novel about village life. Had he attempted it while in Australia, and given it up? If so, I could understand why. Fashioning a novel from an environment that he knew intimately but which did not naturally organise itself into a narrative would have required more inventive effort than the war book, quite possibly more than he could muster. It might well have seemed easier to go another fall with the romance, for that, indeed, was the "book" he took up now. At least one friend cringed when he heard what Manning was doing: "Peter Davies wrote to me that you were still consumed with a longing to write that old book, which has so often refused to come to you. I beg of you, don't." Lawrence's plea, written in November 1934, need not have been made. In July Manning had been "getting on quite well" with the manuscript — another of Gladys Gelsthorpe's scraps was a paragraph not included in the typescript of "The Gilded Coach" — but by September he was down on the mat. "I have not been able to write with any inventive ease, or with any satisfaction to myself."

Lawrence's plea had also been based on reports he had been getting of Manning's health. He knew from Davies that Manning had been sick while in Australia, and the wording of the invitation Lawrence received in July from Manning to come to Bourne could only have intensified his concern: "If you come to visit me here, I shall give you my Heal bed, and dispose myself on the sofa, as most nights I have to sleep sitting up." It was an offer of hospitality any friend might hesitate to accept. However, in the course of the autumn Manning's health stabilised. No new problems developed, and he was well enough to go to London once or twice. There he saw his mother and Edith, who had arrived from Sydney in October. Edith was much improved: "One can't of course feel that she is altogether reliable; but there is no comparison between her behaviour now, and in Sydney." As a result, his mother was "much happier". But these changes did not diminish the responsibility that he had felt growing on him over the last few years. In September 1931, when Britain had gone off the gold standard, he had wired his mother and Edith in Rome advising them to come to London directly instead of going on to Budapest: "I thought it might be very troublesome among suspicious and excitable foreigners to get money, and to keep track of the fluctuations in the exchange." Three years later he felt it his duty to be "within call if wanted".

The aged mother, the alcoholic daughter, the ailing son: what love and what frustration — and even what anger — they must have felt; and what subterfuges their anxieties about each other (and about themselves) must have led them to practise.

Manning hoped to go abroad in January 1935. According to Gladys Gelsthorpe, his doctor had told him that another English winter might very well kill him. But by 1934 his income was worth considerably less than it had been a decade before, thanks to the depreciation of the pound, and he had long since spent or given away the early rush of royalties from *Her Privates We*.* As it was, he had had to borrow money from his brother Will to pay off debts incurred as a result of his illness in June. As long as he lived in Bourne and did not go often to London his income was sufficient, but to winter in the Austrian Alps or in Rome was now beyond his means. The only European country he could afford, Spain, fell short of his tastes: "Food, hotels, and practically everything are so hopeless that nothing is to be gained by going there." Australia was an alternative he preferred not to consider. If his health fell apart, he told Will, he would return there; otherwise, it was too far, "while I should hate to go back and leave Mother here".

His last letter to Lawrence, then with the RAF in Bridlington in Yorkshire, is dated 21 December 1934 and carries the usual season's greetings. He praised Lawrence's new translation of the *Odyssey* and informed him that from 3 January he would be in London for five or six days. He planned to stay at his familiar *pied à terre,* 26 Gilbert Street, even though Alfred Fowler was no longer there. He had died of pneumonia on a golfing trip in Scotland during the time Manning had been in Australia. The house was now occupied by the family of Fowler's nephew, Paul Hasson, who were to be away but who had told Manning he could use the house as his own. "Not that I shall use it as mine, but I shall be alone there." Lawrence did not go to London, so that Manning had the house and a quarter of a century's memories to himself. Unless, that is, he did not go himself. For his next surviving letter, addressed to his sister Dot on 4

February, finds him in the Butterfield Hospital in Bourne, recovering from an attack of flu. "The doctor would not let me go back to Gleneden today, and I think he was right, al tho' normal again I am rather the worse for wear." When he did go back to the Gelsthorpes, an oxygen tank went with him.

Dr J. A. Galletly joined his father in practice in Bourne in 1928, and in the same year he met Manning for the first time. He recalls visiting Manning in his rooms at The Bull and being shown pages of the manuscript of the war book. But it was not until Manning returned to Bourne in July of 1934 that Dr Galletly began treating him as a patient.

I had learned of Dr Galletly from Richard Cody, and wrote him a letter before going to England in 1977. His response did not promise much information but it did suggest a willing and interesting man. "I shall be delighted to see you whilst you are in Bourne this summer...My own Telephone Number is Bourne ___. It is ex-directory as the first thing I did when I retired was to become ex-directory!" Lunch with Dr Galletly validated my expectations. His memories of Manning were as a patient: he recalled his build, his tapered fingers, his emphysema and chronic asthma. Of the man or the author he had little to say. But when he came to talk of the last service he rendered, there crept into his voice something other than professional calm. Manning had not been long back at "Gleneden" from his stay in the hospital when he fell ill with pneumonia. Thinking his patient would get better care in London, Dr Galletly arranged to take him by taxi to the nursing home in Hampstead where Manning had been in June. The journey proved to be "hair-raising", for pneumonia on top of asthma and emphysema made breathing very difficult, and at many moments it seemed as if Manning would die in the midst of the trip. Listening to this story I could easily understand the horror felt by the young doctor, and why this particular memory had etched itself on his brain. A man gasping for breath is a sight not easily forgotten, especially if it goes on for two to three hours. But Manning survived the trip, and Dr Galletly returned to Bourne. By a morbid irony Manning's last surviving letter, dated 15 February, informed Dot that a sister of Eva Fowler was "taking my furniture out of Harrods" to give to a friend for use in a new home.

After lunch the doctor and I walked around his large garden, where in between soliloquies on plants and soils he gave me anecdotes closer to my purpose. He remembered, for instance, the day Ezra Pound's son, Omar, had suddenly appeared in his garden asking questions about Manning, and then almost as suddenly gone away. It seemed that my source was well known, and had been frequently interviewed. Had he in the repeated telling of his tale shaped and burnished it? I hoped not, and the more I thought about it later, the less likely it seemed. Knowing what I did of Manning's health, Galletly's report of that journey to London was altogether believable.

Manning died on the morning of 22 February 1935. Stanley Dunn, of John Murray, always cool and efficient in difficult moments, made the necessary phone calls and sent the obligatory telegrams. Only one went to Bourne, and that was to Mrs Scott, Gladys Gelsthorpe's mother.* "Manning died this morning inform doctor." Mrs Gelsthorpe later packed up her boarder's clothes and papers and sent them to Dunn who, as she told me, never bothered to thank her. Peter Davies, after hearing the news from Dunn, immediately wrote a note to the sorrowing mother who was still in England: "I am so dreadfully sorry for you. If there is anything in the world I can do to help, please let me know, and accept my deepest, most heartfelt sympathy." Davies did not speak of his own grief in administering to a greater; he would have known that a favourite child had been lost. Lawrence heard about it while on his way to pay Manning a call. He had just received his discharge from the RAF and was biking south from Bridlington when he got the news. It filled him with sadness, he told Davies, and a certain anger.

> Strange to think how Manning, sick, poor, fastidious, worked like a slave for year after year. . . on stringing words together to shape his ideas and reasonings. That's what being a born writer means, I suppose. And to-day it is all over and nobody ever heard of him. If he had been famous in his day he would have liked it, I think; liked it deprecatingly. As for fame-after-death, it's a thing to spit at; the only minds worth winning are the warm ones about us. . . How I wish, for my sake, that he hadn't slipped away in this fashion; but how like him.

Error and hyperbole slip into that eulogy but do not spoil its essence. Lawrence declined, however, to make a public statement about the man he admired, a silence which annoyed Rothenstein and hurt Manning's mother.* Had they seen this letter to Davies they might have been less upset — and possibly fathomed the reasons for his silence.

The world did not learn of Manning's death for several days, and then it took little notice. Despite the surge of fame for *Her Privates We,* his name meant nothing to the average man, and not much more to the educated reader. Had it not been for Rothenstein, *The Times* would have overlooked his passing, while the Sydney papers managed only a couple of brief paragraphs.* His few admirers in America did not learn of his death for months. "If the death of Frederic Manning was commented on at the time," wrote novelist and critic Christoper Morley in May, "I missed it." Harriet Monroe was to be similarly surprised: "News does not always reach us — somehow we failed to hear of the death last winter of. . . Frederic Manning." Truly he had passed away in the "fashion" in which he had lived.

A requiem mass was held on 26 February at the Farm Street Church in Mayfair, the church which his mother regularly attended when she was in London. The service apparently provided a mystical experience for Rothenstein: after the mass had been sung he sensed something "happening" at the altar.

Many copies of the service book used at the mass are still in the Manning home in Sydney, and I also found there a note thanking Nora for her "very generous" contribution to the church. "I shall not forget to say mass for your dear son on 26 March (the month's mind of his requiem) and on 22 July; and shall pray that God who sends you the cross may send you the strength to bear it." Burial was at St Mary's, one grave away from where the Fowlers lay, a site more fitting than the cemetery at Edenham. Missing from the funeral because of illness was Fairfax, but he was not too ill to compose his elegy, "my own private memorial".

A few weeks after Manning's burial his mother and sister sailed back to Sydney. Nora would not go again to England, and before her death in 1940 she was to lose two more of her children, Edith in 1936 and Will a year later:

> The dead leaves fluttered round her, and she sate
> There by the well-side filmed with silver frost,
> Like some old woman, stricken in her fate,
> With no more heart to wail what she hath lost:
> And silence grew about her, as though grief
> Stilled the rude winds, and every withered leaf.

The poet son had always envisioned his mother as a model for Demeter.

The probate of his will showed Manning to have £257 12s 7d at his death, which was not sufficient to settle his debts. Money was sent "ungrudgingly" from Australia, as William Roscoe, the solicitor who handled the estate, remembered the matter. He was 92 when I talked to him on a warm Sunday afternoon at his daughter's home in Dorset. It had taken me some time to locate the dirge-sounding address (Youngs Farm, Organford, near Poole) and the man I found waiting for me was every day of 92. Still, Roscoe was alert, and his memory as intact as one could reasonably hope. He had met Manning only once, in the late twenties or early thirties, and recalled him as looking younger than his years but not at all strong. Their meeting had occurred in the offices of Shakespear & Parkyn, which Roscoe had joined after the death in 1923 of Henry Hope Shakespear, Olivia's husband. While talking to me of how he had acted as the attorney for Eleanor and Bill Manning, their uncle's executors, Roscoe kept rummaging through a thick sheaf of papers he held in his hands, trying to find facts or references that might be helpful. The pages were yellow and many were quite tattered; once they had been part of a neat file, but now they looked as if they belonged in a wastebin. Those papers, however, were obviously very important to Roscoe, and he was reluctant to let me touch them. Was it the lawyer's caution, or the old man's fear of letting out of his hands powerful instruments for inducing memories? Whatever the reason, it prevailed. But Roscoe wanted to be helpful, and a month later he sent me a letter saying that he had "looked again" into his papers and discovered that in 1969, during negotiations over the film rights of *Her Privates We,* he had been asked about its copyright status. Rights to the novel were later purchased, but the film has not yet been made. It is an all too familiar story.

After a man's property has been dispersed and his soul prayed for, there is still the question of how he will be judged. In 1935 it looked as if *Her Privates We* might secure Manning the "spacious and comfortable niche in our literature" that Lawrence felt he deserved. A second "classic", this one hailed by a large audience, seemed capital enough for lasting fame. But obscurity soon closed in and endures, despite the respectful attention given the 1977 unexpurgated edition of the novel. Perhaps if critics had realised that the novel was more than a "war book", or if Bourne and his chums had been transferred to the screen, or if the various late efforts to publish the unfinished romance had been successful — Eliot read it in 1954 and found it "quite delightful", but Faber & Faber did not offer to publish it — Manning would be better known. Still, a writer's fame is largely, and properly, of his own making, and Manning's career had been too thin, too hidden, and too muddled by false starts and lost opportunities to hold the recognition won by early and late books.

Had he lived longer there might have been another book, but it is doubtful. The strength was not there, perhaps not even the will. For the pattern of his career suggests that he lacked the vital compulsion of which major careers are built and artistic anxieties overcome. Or if he had it, then it was intermittent. To be sure, he did not think of himself as an amateur let alone a dilettante, and no one who knew him ever intimated as much. But did he possess a sustaining ambition to create? Was his art the controlling force of his consciousness? These questions would not be asked of Pound or Eliot, writers who respected Manning and viewed him as an equal, as a companion in the tireless struggle for excellence. That these questions should be asked of a writer who talked so often and so perceptively about the role of the will may seem odd. But Manning would not be the first who wrote eloquently of what he missed in himself, nor would he be the first to discover that the muse is seldom generous to those not wholly devoted to her. Illness, alcohol, indolence, fastidiousness — each could explain his modest output. Together they appear more than sufficient. And yet in Manning's case they do not quite persuade. He wanted to be a writer, and surely worked at his trade, but missing from the evidence of his life is the driving will to achievement.

Any niche, therefore, that Manning occupies in English (or Australian) letters will be small; it is fair to say that he did not expect otherwise. He never exaggerated either the extent or the appeal of his accomplishment; indeed, he often acted and spoke as if fame mattered not at all. It did, of course. But in his last hours he perhaps thought less of how future generations might honour his work than he did of the Paradise of the Disillusioned, the resting place for Epicureans, that awaited him. There he would be among friends, never again to be lonely.

Epilogue

In writing the finish to Manning's life, I was writing also the finish to an extraordinary experience in my own. And I felt more than the usual sadness common to writers when they say goodbye to a book that has absorbed them for a number of years. Manning had taken me on a splendid journey, the more splendid because I had never been sure of what I would find or whom. The cost in terms of time and money had been greater than I had anticipated, but that is the way of adventures. I had no complaints.

Manning, I suspected, would have. Even less than authors noted for their hostility to biographers — Auden and Eliot come to mind — would he have wanted anyone to invade his privacy, so that quite apart from my judgement of his accomplishments he would have thought my purpose misconceived, even presumptuous. But Manning's own accomplishments surely argue for why the shape and texture of literary lives need to be assessed. By whom and in what form no writer should expect to dictate. Manning had got me, as unlikely a candidate in some respects as he himself had been for Sir William White. I had the advantage, however, of enjoying my task.

Just how much became clear when I returned to England in June of 1985 to look at Manning's letters to T. S. Eliot. By then my attention was turned to other projects and I had little time or funds to fly off to England. Yet as soon as I sat down with the letters in a dusty back room of Faber & Faber my annoyance passed, and I felt a surge of recognition and pleasure. Here once more was the script and the man I had come to know so well.

I was surprised by how the simple act of reading the letters moved me. What I felt may have been prompted by the excitement of finally having a chance to see them. But I suspect that something more fundamental was at work, something other biographers who have had to piece together obscure, unwritten lives, have felt: our creations necessarily have a special familiarity, even a kinship with us, for they are wholly of our making rather than retouched versions. As such they stay with us long after they have left our desks. Frederic Manning might have objected to my search for him, but he would have understood its consequences.

Notes

Sources for quotations are arranged by page number and key words. An asterisk designates a source for an unquoted statement. Interviews are not cited in the notes; the text should make clear the comments and information derived from them.

Manning's letters to James Griffyth Fairfax — with the exception of those held by his daughter, Benita Fairfax Biso — are in the National Library of Australia, Canberra, and so I do not cite a location in each note. I have followed the same practice with Manning's letters to Richard Aldington (Harry Ransom Humanities Research Center, University of Texas), with his letters to T. S. Eliot (possession of Mrs Valerie Eliot), with Galton's letters to Laurence Binyon (possession of Nicolete Gray), with Manning's, Galton's, and Eva Fowler's letters to Albert Houtin (Bibliothèque Nationale, Paris), and with Manning's letters to William Rothenstein (Houghton Library, Harvard University). Those letters to Rothenstein that can be found in his autobiography are so referenced, though readers should be warned that the printed versions are not always complete or accurate. Unless otherwise noted, all letters to and from Ezra Pound are in the Beinecke Rare Book and Manuscript Library, Yale University.

Manning's works frequently cited have been abbreviated.

Vigil	*THE VIGIL OF BRUNHILD*
Scenes	*SCENES AND PORTRAITS*
White	*THE LIFE OF SIR WILLIAM WHITE*
Middle Parts	*THE MIDDLE PARTS OF FORTUNE*

Other works frequently cited have also been abbreviated.

Herald	*SYDNEY MORNING HERALD*
Telegraph	*SYDNEY DAILY TELEGRAPH*
Memories	*MEN AND MEMORIES, RECOLLECTIONS OF WILLIAM ROTHENSTEIN* (London, 1931–32), 2 Vols.
Ezra and Dorothy	*EZRA POUND AND DOROTHY SHAKESPEAR, THEIR LETTERS: 1909–1914*, edited by Omar Pound and A. Walton Litz (New York, 1984).
Letters to TEL	*LETTERS TO T. E. LAWRENCE,* edited by A. W. Lawrence (London, 1962).

The following initials have been used in place of full names:

RA Richard Aldington
TSE T. S. Eliot
JGF James Griffyth Fairfax
AG Arthur Galton
AH Albert Houtin
TEL T. E. Lawrence
FM Frederic Manning
EP Ezra Pound
WR William Rothenstein

Introduction

ix "a record": *Her Privates We*, Prefatory Note.
ix "already distinguished": The phrase appeared on the book jacket.
x "full of horrors": *Evening Standard*, 23 January 1930. Reprinted in *Arnold Bennett: The Evening Standard Years*, ed. Andrew Mylett (London, 1974), 341.
x "fled": *Daily Mirror*, 26 February 1930.
x "without ambition": *Criterion*, 14 (April 1935), 436
xi "at least fifty times": "Colonel Lawrence and others on 'Her Privates We'", pamphlet issued by Peter Davies Ltd., 1930.
xi "early and valued" and ff.: *Criterion*, 14. 436.
xi "remembered in literature": *The Sketch*, 21 July 1909, 52.
xi "I am sending you": FM/Henry Newbolt, 9 November 1909.
xii "First licherary": EP/RA, 3 October 1958.

xiii *informative article: L. T. Hergenhan, "A Neglected Australian Writer", *Quadrant*, 6 (Spring 1962), 5–18.

xvi "I am delighted": Eleanor Manning/author, 18 January 1977.

xvi "recovering": Donald Davie, "Ezra among the Edwardians", *Paideuma*, 5 (Spring 1976), 3. Reprinted in Davie's *Trying to Explain* (Ann Arbor, 1979).

Chapter 1

1 "I guess": Ivor Woolmer/author, 17 May 1978.

3 "In Memoriam": James Griffyth Fairfax, *The Fifth Element* (London, 1937).

3 "Birthday Ode": James Griffyth Fairfax, *Poems* (London, 1908). The other published poems dedicated to Manning are "Roucoulement" and "Epistle to F.M.", both printed in James Griffyth Fairfax, *The Troubled Pool* (London, 1911).

6 "One day": *Memories*, 2. 26.

6 *years later: FM/JGF, 11 September 1911.

8 "His dignity": *The Arrow*, 20 January 1906, 1.

8 "a period": 4 February 1895, Sydney City Council Letter Books. See also the lengthy editorial praise given to Manning in the *Telegraph*, 15 March 1895. There his gamble to float a loan in the London money market on behalf of the city council during the crisis and his efforts to improve Moore Street, thereby "establishing the important principle of 'betterment'", were singled out for special praise. When the voters finally ended his aldermanic career in December 1900, he chose in his concession speech to highlight the Queen Victoria Markets, now the Queen Victoria Building, as "a monument of his municipal labors" and one that he was "proud of". *Telegraph*, 8 December 1900. The William Manning building in the Sydney market area was named after William Patrick.

10 *Lord Jersey: Lord Ripon/W. E. Gladstone, 18 December

1893, British Library, Add. Mss. 44,287, f. 179. Rosebery was Prime Minister when the knighthood was bestowed.

10 "the fact": *The Arrow*, 1.

10 "absentee capital": *Bulletin*, 29 July 1893, 8.

10 *New South Wales: *Checklist of Royal Commissions, Select Committees of Parliament, and Boards of Inquiry, Part IV New South Wales 1855–1960*, ed. D. H. Borchardt (Bondoora, 1975), 163–64, 169.

10 "intimately associated": W. P. Manning/Edmund Barton, 26 September 1903, National Library, Canberra.

10 *meetings: Manning chaired the meeting "of gentlemen favorable to federation" that was held on 22 June 1893, and 10 days later he chaired the first "public" meeting that had grown out of Edmund Barton's initiative. At the latter meeting, which was cut short by disorder, Manning was designated to be the first president of the League. *Telegraph*, 21, 23 June, 4 July 1893.

10 *Papal Chamberlain: The document making him "Camerieri d'Onore di Spada e Cappa Sopranumerarii" is date 25 September 1903, and is now in the possession of Bill Manning. For W. P. Manning's services to the church see "The Catholic Mayor of Sydney", *Freeman's Journal*, 15 December 1894, 16. When Leo XIII died in 1903, W. P. Manning was among those who met to arrange the requiem mass to be held in Sydney. *Herald*, 29 July 1903.

10 "My father": FM/JGF, 1 November 1908.

11 *probity: In October 1898 a question was raised about overdue rates being written off on property for which Manning was the agent. *Herald*, 14, 15, 20 October, 30 November 1898.

11 "He had little sorrow": FM/Ryllis Hacon, 17 May 1915.

11 "very just man": FM/WR, 29 April 1932.

12 "kindly": *Bulletin*, 30 May 1891, 8; 16 March 1895, 8.

12 "still very nervous": *ibid*. 10 December 1892, 8.

12 "Lady Manning": *Herald*, 30 July 1940.

14 "Another point": FM/William Manning, 18 December 1934.

15 "one of the outstanding": *Herald*, 17 May 1957.

18 **Herald*: See especially 7 May, 3 September 1913.

20 "like a Rossetti": *Memories*, 1. 198, 200. Amaryllis' Christian name was Edith. On the friendship between Conder and the Hacons see also John Rothenstein, *Life and Death of Conder* (London, 1938), 141–42.

21 "home": Stella Bowen, who was born in Adelaide in 1893 and would later marry Ford Madox Ford, notes in her autobiography that England was "home" even to people who had never been there "and whose fathers had never been". A "real English accent" was prized, and English customs followed to a fault. "At Christmas, which came at midsummer with the temperature at — perhaps — 100° in the shade, we sat down at mid-day to turkey and flaming plum pudding, having sent each other cards depicting robins in the snow". *Drawn from Life* (Maidstone, 1974), 12–13.

23 "everyone since the flood": EP/Isabel Pound, 11 October 1909.

23 *death: "An Elegy in Memory of My Grandmother, Isabella Galton". D. M. S. Watson Library, University College, London.

23 "rector of": Arthur Galton, "Why I entered, and Why I Left, the Roman Catholic Church", *National Review*, 35 (May 1900), 483.

24 "practically banished": Arthur Galton, "Why I Left the Roman Catholic Church", *National Review*, 35 (June 1900), 582.

24 "But that": *ibid*. 590–91.

24 "the case": "Mark Pattison" in Arthur Galton, *Urbana Scripta. Studies of Five Living Poets; and Other Essays* (London, 1885), 192. Cited hereafter as *Urbana*. See also A. G., "Francis Newman", *Telegraph*, 9 October 1897.

25 "passion" and ff.: Arthur Galton, *Church and State in France 1300–1907* (London, 1907), viii.

25 "a king of words": Arthur Galton, "Assisi", *Hobby Horse* (July 1886), 104. The poem "Matthew Arnold: April 15, 1888" appeared in the *Hobby Horse* (April 1889) and was, like the elegy to his grandmother, privately printed as well. See *The Collected Poems of Lionel Johnson*, edited by Ian Fletcher, 2nd rev. ed. (New York, 1982), 339.

25 "The fifteenth of April": Arthur Galton, *Two Essays Upon Matthew Arnold* (London, 1897), 61. See also 122. Cited hereafter as *Two Essays*. These essays originally appeared in the *Hobby Horse*.

25 *1885: In 1894 Galton privately printed *Studies of Five Living Poets*, which was comprised of the first five essays in *Urbana*.

25 "the natural home": AG/W. E. Gladstone, 26 October 1892. British Library, Add. Mss. 44,516, f. 204.

25 *pretensions: For his role in the magazine see Ian Fletcher, "Decadence and the Little Magazines", in *Decadence and the 1890s* (London, 1979).

26 "strong, too strong": *Two Essays*, 114.

26 "Thyrsis": *ibid*. 105. Galton later sent him some "Oxford fritillaries consecrated to 'Thyrsis'". *ibid*. 112.

26 "a very dear friend": AG/Laurence Binyon, 9 January 1889. In Eleanor Manning's home I found a brief note from Pater to Galton dated 14 March 1887.

26 "better and more interesting": *Telegraph*, 2 August 1894. The obituary was headlined, "A Sketch by one who knew him".

27 "I like": AG/Laurence Binyon, 1 June 1890.

27 *preparing: Lionel Johnson/AG, 4 September 1890. See also 19, 20 September. Galton was ready to express his gratitude by dedicating the volume to Johnson but no dedication appeared.

27 *correspondence: Basil Gray/author, 28 August 1979.

27 "To Arthur Galton": Arthur Patrick, *Lionel Johnson (1867–1902) poète et critique* (Paris, 1939), 36. The poems dedicated to Galton were "Oxford", "Romans", and "Laleham", the last a tribute to Arnold. A fourth poem,

"On the Memorial Verses upon Matthew Arnold Written by his Friend. . . Arthur Galton", would seem to open up endless possibilities for commemorative verse. The two friends were also very active in the New College Essay Society. See the Minute Books of the society, nos 3560 and 3561. New College Archives.

28 "transient feelings": *Two Essays*, 80.

28 "Really, Dickens": AG/Laurence Binyon, 17 August 1890.

28 "scholarly punctuation": *The Annals of Tacitus. The Reign of Tiberius,. . . translated by Thomas Gordon*, edited by Arthur Galton (London, 1890), xxv.

28 "which added" and ff.: *ibid*. xxvii.

28 "smartness" and ff.: *Urbana*, 4.

28 "Among its defects": review of *Nicholas Ferrar*, edited by Canon Carter, published in the *Academy*, 15 April 1893, 318.

28 "evil age": AG/Laurence Binyon, 1 February 1890.

28 *France: *Urbana*, 227. A later friend spoke of him as "ne vit que dans le dix-hutième siècle". Eva Fowler/AH, 26 October 1912.

29 "tempted": This is the term Galton used when mentioning his decision in 1902. AG/Edmund Gosse, 14 December 1902. Brotherton Library, Leeds.

29 *sentences: AG/W. E. Gladstone, 12 November 1888. British Library Add. Mss 45,405, ff. 116–17.

29 *Wilde: AG/Sir Samuel Way, 12 September 1894. State Library of South Australia. For Symonds' view of Galton see *The Letters of John Addington Symonds*, edited by Herbert M. Schueller and R. Peters (Detroit, 1969), 3, 275. Wilde's view, at least of the edition of Tacitus — "a charming little book" — can be found in a letter to Galton of October 1890. *More Letters of Oscar Wilde*, edited by Rupert Hart-Davis (New York, 1985), 91.

Chapter 2

31 "Retrospect": Article found in Eleanor Manning's home.

31 "playing again": *Middle Parts*, 8.

31 "on July the 22": FM/Harriet Monroe, 18 May 1913. Regenstein Library.

32 *1897: I owe this information Mr K. M. Saxby, the school librarian and archivist.

32 "left Australia": *John O'London's Weekly*, 22 March 1930, 964.

32 *dictionary: *Fred John's Annual*.

34 "thundering air": FM/JGF, 10 August 1907.

34 "The doctors": AG/AH, 22 December 1915.

34 "pallid and unwholesome": Mark Twain, *Following the Equator* (New York, 1899), 1. 134.

34 "with delight": *John O'London's Weekly*, 964.

35 *see and meet: Twain gave three lectures in Sydney in September 1895. The evening before the first one he spoke at the Athenaeum Club in Castlereagh street — a rendezvous of writers, artists, musicians, and even some professional men, and where famous visitors to Sydney often were invited. For the club and its members, which owed their building to Lord Rosebery, see Charles Bertie "Old Castlereagh Street", *Royal Australian Historical Society*, 22 (1937), 45–47. Galton was a member of the club, and so too was W. P. Manning, who is listed as having been present on the evening Twain spoke. *Telegraph*, 19 September 1895. For the Sarah Bernhardt reception, *Bulletin*, 16 May 1891, 9.

35 *Greek: Sybil Gowthorpe/author, 11 January 1979.

35 "Arnold": "Military Art" and "Marlborough" were subsequently published. The lecture on Arnold was summarised in the *Herald*, 4 May 1894. See also the *Telegraph* of 17 February 1896, for a review of G. W. E. Russell's 1895 edition of Arnold's letters.

35 "a quiet corner": *Telegraph*, 6 January 1894. For a poem and cartoon on the incident see the *Bulletin*, 13 January, 10, 12.

35 *replaced: C. B. Mackerras, "Dibbs versus Duff", *Royal*

Australian Historical Society, 56 (1970), 296–314, AG/W. E. Gladstone 27 July 1896. British Library Add. Mss 44,523, f. 165; AG/Samuel Way, 24 July 1894. State Library of South Australia. In the letter to Way, Galton wrote that he thought his uncle might be "a little jealous,. . . of my popularity".

35 "petty distractions": AG/Henry Parkes, 29 January 1894. Mitchell Library.

35 "the compilation": *Telegraph*, 8 August 1894. For more on the background of this project see R. M. Crawford, *A Bit of a Rebel* (Sydney, 1975), 119–23.

36 *Adelaide: The story is told in Galton's letters to Samuel Way.

36 "He was": AG/John Murray, 29 July 1907. Murray Archive.

36 "I had a certain": AG/Samuel Way, 24 November 1894. State Library of South Australia.

36 "I have trained": AG/Henry Parkes, 19 February 1895. Mitchell Library.

36 "a lover": Walter Pater, "Style", in *Appreciations* (London, 1889), 12.

37 "What we require": Arthur Galton, "Some Modern Literature", *Cosmos*, September 1894, 28. This is a revised version of an article ("An Examination; of Certain Schools and Tendencies, in Contemporary Literature", that Galton originally published in the *Hobby Horse* in July 1889. "Austerity" as a literary virtue is praised often in his letters and writings.

37 "a writer condescends": *English Prose from Maundeville to Thackeray*, edited by Arthur Galton (London, 1888), xiv.

37 "great style": *Two Essays*, 46.

37 "especially to people": *Herald*, 21 July 1894. Some of Galton's enthusiasm for Milton may have rubbed off on the senior Manning, for Sir William singled out Milton

to quote at the banquet given in his honour in March 1895. *Telegraph*, 15 March 1895. Two years before, at the dinner given for the Earl of Jersey and his wife before their departure from Sydney, W. P. Manning had gone to Tennyson for inspiration. *Telegraph*, 28 February 1893.

37 *ode: FM/JGF, 9 June 1907.

37 "apostolical succession": The phrase comes from an essay of a good friend of Galton's, Alfred Fawkes, whose own religious pilgrimage closely resembled that of Galton. *Studies in Modernism* (London, 1913), 148. For Manning's early skepticism, see Houtin's comments, written (it seems) in 1920, when he was preparing his autobiography. Houtin Papers, nouvelles acquistions françaises, 15,722, f. 477.

38 "first city": *Herald*, 19 January 1898. These hopes were expressed in a speech given to the annual meeting of the Sydney Philharmonic Society. W. P. Manning's stewardship of that society was much praised when he had to step down from the presidency a few months before his death. *Herald*, 29 January 1915.

38 "Nunc scio": AG/Laurence Binyon, 17 February 1896. The line is from Vergil (*Eclogues*, VIII. 43), whose works Galton had lately read in their entirety.

38 *return: I owe this information to Mr K. M. Saxby.

40 *gene pool: See his letters to Gladstone, particularly one of 27 July 1896. British Library, Add. Mss 44,523, ff. 160–71. See also a letter to Samuel Way, 18 December 1894, State Library of South Australia, and Galton's later article, "Government House", *National Review*, 36 (December 1900), 537–44.

40 "I have used": Testimonial in Mitchell Library, along with supporting letter dated 28 September 1897.

40 *friends: AG/Edmund Barton, 4 May 1915. National Library, Canberra.

40 "Waiting, reading": AG/W. E. Gladstone, 14 March 1897. British Library, Add. Mss 44,525, f. 124.

41 "one of the silliest": *Freeman's Journal*, 29 January 1898, 19. Reviewers for secular papers were not as scathing, though hardly enthusiastic for so slight a volume. See *Telegraph*,, 25 December 1897; *Academy*, 1 January 1898, 10; *The Saturday Review*, 18 December 1897, 719.

41 **Life*: *Telegraph*, 12 April 1896. On April 19 the *Telegraph* printed a lengthy criticism of Galton's review signed "A Catholic". It was perhaps the same "Catholic" who later responded to Galton's review of Froude's *Council of Trent. Telegraph*, 30 May, 6 June 1896. Galton also had his prose taken to task when he reviewed W. H. Hutton's *Sir Thomas More. Telegraph*, 18, 25 July 1896.

41 "pet aversion": AG/W. E. Gladstone, 16 August 1897. British Library, Add. Mss 44,526, f. 57. See also the letters to Gladstone of April 19 and July 27, 1896. The campaign against Galton apparently stopped when a friend of his became the editor, and promptly started asking him for material.

41 "neither Hume": AG/W. E. Gladstone, 27 July 1896. British Library, Add Mss 44,523, f. 161. Galton was shaving the truth pretty closely, however, since he allowed the *Telegraph* to print (25 July 1896) Gladstone's letter of praise to him about the review of Purcell: "Among many reviews, I think yours is one of the ablest".

42 "not of his Excellency": *Telegraph*, 16 March 1895. Galton was by this time already writing book reviews for the *Telegraph*.

42 "No better English": *An Emigrant's Home Letters*, edited by Annie T. Sykes (London, 1897), ix. These were letters written by Parkes after first coming to Australia a half century before.

49 "passion for perfection": *Criterion*, 14. 436.

51 *would be: Extensive quotations from the letters are printed in L. T. Hergenhan, "Two Expatriates: Some Correspondence from Frederic Manning to James Griffyth

Fairfax'', *Southerly*, 39 (March 1979), 59–95.

51 *book of his: In an early letter to Fairfax (2 June 1907) Manning speaks of sending him ''two of my stories, written four years ago''. These may have formed part of the ''book''.

52 ''doing nothing definite'': FM/WR, 29 April 1932. For Manning's return see *Herald*, 22 September 1900.

52 ''read Bergerac'': FM/JGF, 29 June 1908. For Galton and Berenson see Ernest Samuels, *Bernard Berenson: The Making of a Connoisseur* (Cambridge, Massachusetts, 1979), 61, 319.

52 ''with my head'' and ff.: ''Why I Left'', 589.

52 ''our last classic'': ''Assisi'', 107.

52 ''one of Nature's'': *ibid*. 98.

52 ''close mingling'' and ff.: Arthur Galton, ''Perugia'', *MacMillan Magazine*, 55 (March, 1887), 366. See also Arthur Galton, ''Ecclesiastical Architecture'', in *Companion to English History*, edited by Francis Pierrepont Barnard (Oxford, 1902), 5.

53 ''no man'' and ff.: FM/JGF, 17 November 1908.

53 ''Undeserved neglect'' and ff.: FM/TEL, 4 January 1932. *Letters to TEL*, 144.

53 ''drawn so many poets'': *Memoirs*, 2.26.

55 *mid 1920s: *Portrait Drawings of William Rothenstein, 1889–1925*, edited by John Rothenstein (London, 1926), 18.

55 ''studied under'': Manning file, Army Records Centre.

55 ''people much older'' and ff.: FM/JGF, 9 May 1908.

55 ''spoilt'': FM/WR, 14 November 1915.

55 ''many a deserved whipping'': FM/WR, 29 April 1932.

55 ''Ill-health'': Manning file, Army Records Centre.

55 ''just'': FM/WR, 29 April 1932.

56 ''Xmas Camp'': I found a copy of a brief skit referring to this trip in Eleanor Manning's home. It was apparently written (by E. M. Mitchell) when Manning was back in Sydney in 1933–34.

56 *visit: Writing to Harriet Monroe in 1915, Ezra Pound reported that Manning thought Tahitians "a very beautiful people". If Manning had been in Tahiti, it would almost certainly have been while on a voyage to or from the West coast of North America. *The Selected Letters of Ezra Pound*, edited by D. D. Paige (New York, 1950), 66.

56 "early years": C. Kaeppel, "Frederic Manning, Soldier, Scholar, Artist", *Australian Quarterly*, (June 1935), 48.

57 *Mannings: For a time in 1873–74 Hargrave worked in the foundry of P. N. Russell & Company, where W. P. Manning might still have been employed. From 1884–93 Hargrave lived at 40 Roslyn Gardens, Rushcutters Bay, which was close to the Manning home at 29 Upper William Street. Finally, as mayor of Sydney it would seem that W. P. Manning would have had occasions to meet Hargrave, at least formally. Since Hargrave died in 1915, his familiarity with Fred Manning must date from before 1904. On the other hand, Hargrave's biographer, W. Hudson Shaw, has found no hard evidence connecting him with Manning, W. Hudson Shaw/author, 11 August 1977.

57 "stirred up": Dorothy Shakespear/EP, *Ezra and Dorothy*, 296.

57 "I like flying": FM/AH, 28 December 1914.

58 "constant reading": FM/JGF, 9 June 1907.

58 "romantic subjectivity": FM/JGF, 11 April 1912.

58 "chaotic enthusiasm": FM/JGF, 27 October 1911.

58 "romantic": *Criterion*, 6 (November 1927), 449.

58 "used the English" and ff.: FM/JGF, 9 June 1907.

58 "seem a mother": FM/TEL, 12 January 1931. *Letters to TEL*, 140.

60 "essentials to civilization" and ff.: *Telegraph*, 3 November 1900.

61 "no taste" and ff.: AG/John Murray, 29 July 1907. Murray Archive.

61 "the Patron Poet": Victor Daley in his poem, "The Australian Bachelor's Soliloquy".

61 *Cosmos: This was the article, "Some Modern Literature", that had appeared in *Cosmos* in September 1894. In reviewing the article the *Telegraph* admitted that some readers would find it "bookish and pedantic, but that will be chiefly because of unacquaintance with the old school of grace and dignified literary statement, whose influence is so strong upon him [Galton]". *Telegraph*, 8 September 1894.

61 *England: On October 22, two days before Manning sailed for Italy on the *Orotava*, Henry Lawson published a piece in the *Bulletin* urging would-be authors who wanted to do "good work" to go to London. *Australians Abroad*, edited by Charles Higham and Michael Wilding (Melbourne, 1967), 81.

Chapter 3

66 "Cast thy bread": *Grantham Journal*, 8 October 1904.

67 *adherents: In 1902 Galton was "commissioned" by leaders of a group of disheartened secular clergy to write an article expressing their frustration with Rome and their intention to "set up a bishop of their own". Given his own views, formidable pen, and many links to Catholic clergy, it is not surprising that Galton should have been asked (and accepted) such a request. The leader of the movement was Father Richard O'Halloran, founder and builder of a church in Mattock Lane, Ealing. Galton's article, "The Incompatibles", appeared in the *Fortnightly Review* of 1 September 1902. The London *Daily Chronicle* published in advance a summary of the article and there followed a flock of letters supporting and challenging the reality of such a "revolt" against Rome. The *Fortnightly* itself carried a long "reply" to Galton and his "Rejoinder" in their 1 October issue. Galton sent a circular letter to papers in Sydney announcing the article.

For the reaction see the *Telegraph*, 1, 9 October 1902. For more on the episode see also G. K. A. Bell, *Randall Davidson* (Oxford, 1938), 404–5.

68 *Jowett lecturer: *The Times*, 15 January 1903. It is possible that Galton did not complete the lectures. The *Times* noticed only the first two, and contrary to custom they were not published.

68 *Johnson: *Athenaeum*, 13 December 1902, 797.

69 *sort: FM/AH, 1 November 1908.

69 "Forever calm": Lucretius, *De Rerum Natura*, vi. 648–52, Rolfe Humphries translation, (Bloomington, 1968).

69 *speech: "When I first came to Lincolnshire, thirty years ago, there were old country folk who still pronounced 'meat' and 'beast' as words of two syllables 'mëat' and 'bëast'. An old lady, so old that her father was an ensign at the Battle of Waterloo, told me once that in her salad days, ladies spoke of 'dimonds' and 'vilest'." This information is contained in a draft of a letter to the *Times* which has no date, but which was written sometime during Manning's last months.

70 "essay": Arthur Galton, *The Claracter and Times of Thomas Cromwell* (Birmingham, 1887), vi.

70 *odour: John Michael Hardwicke, *A Literary Gazetteer of the British Isles* (Newton Abbot, 1973), 106. There is no evidence to place Kingsley in Edenham during the time he was writing the book. Hereward's association with the area, however, is a well attested fact.

72 "Through my windows": "The Crystal Dreamer", *Poems.*

72 *drawings: Eva Sumner/author, 15 May 1979.

74 "most attractive" and ff.: FM/JGF, 19 April 1909.

74 "I'm not a gregarious": FM/JGF, 10 April 1909.

74 "this hermitage": FM/JGF, 26 June 1907.

74 "the centre": W. B. Yeats/Dorothy Wellesley, 8 October 1938. *Letters of William Butler Yeats*, edited by Allan Wade (New York, 1955), 916. For more on their relationship see John Harwood, "Olivia Shakespear and

W. B. Yeats", *Yeats Annual*, No. 4, edited by Warwick Gould (London, 1986).

74 *belovedest aunt": FM/Dorothy Shakespear, 6 March 1914.

75 *respect: In a letter of 22 December 1910, he notes she "will like at least one phrase in my article on Swift". In late 1918 he sent her a copy of an article on Remy de Gourmont, asking her opinion as to whether he had lost either his critical faculties or his style during the war. This letter is addressed to "My dear Aunt". Beinecke.

75 "friends": FM/JGF, 6 December 1907.

75 "My dear Dorothy": Mitchell Library.

76 "peace offering": FM/Dorothy Shakespear, 17 July 1905. Mitchell Library. By her own admission Dorothy read poetry "only with great difficulty. I never did much care for it". Hugh Kenner, "D. P. Remembered", *Paideuma*, 2 (Winter 1973), 486.

76 "entertaining": Hergenhan, "Expatriates", 93.

76 "I have known you": FM/Dorothy Shakespear, 6 March 1914. Mitchell Library.

76 "The principal hope": *Oxford Magazine*, 21 October 1909, 28.

76 "After reading": *Times Literary Supplement*, 23 June 1910, 224.

76 "I must": St Loe Strachey/FM, 18 December 1911. UCLA Library.

76 *rules: Henry Newbolt/FM, 29 November 1911. Mitchell Library.

77 "compliment" and ff.: FM/Henry Newbolt, 30 November 1911. Beinecke.

77 "As Mr. Manning": *Spectator*, 15 October 1910, 608. For further references to *Scenes*, see also *Spectator*, 6 November 1909, 743; 4 November 1911, 711.

77 "Perhaps if Mr Galton": FM/JGF, 30 June 1907.

77 "I want you": AG/John Murray, 29 July 1907. Murray Archive.

78 "first duty" and ff.: Newbolt Report, 3 August 1907. Murray Archive.
78 "great promise" and ff.: AG/John Murray, 29 July 1907.
78 *revealed: "Bal Masque", 19 May 1906, 686; "The Secret", 16 June 1906, 814. Neither would be reprinted.
78 "a picture of life": TEL/E. M. Forster, 27 September 1927, *Letters of T. E. Lawrence*, edited by David Garnett (New York, 1939), 536.
81 "I ceased": *Westminster Gazette*, 18 November 1905, 4.
82 "The Sacrament of Death": UCLA Library.
83 "His reserve": *Criterion*, 6 (November 1927), 455. For criticism of Strachey, *Spectator*, 16 March 1912, 445.
83 "the symmetrical": *The Outlook*, 25 November 1905, 735.
83 *church: For the debate see *The Times*, 9, 10, 15, 19 January 1907.
84 "My dear Dot": Mitchell Library.
84 "I have been living": FM/JGF, 23 December 1907.
84 "maladies" and ff.: FM/JGF, 13 February 1908.
85 "Though I lay claim": *Vigil*, 62. A few years later Manning's sister Dot would write in one of her articles that "history is certainly prophecy turned inside out".
85 "essentially" and ff.: *ibid*. iv.
85 "Ye, who": *ibid*. 6–7.
86 "An empire": *ibid*. 55.
86 "But answer": *ibid*. 12–13
86 "And Galswintha's page": *ibid*. 11.
87 "Complex psychology": *ibid*. iv.
87 "strange mixture": G. W. Kitchin, *A History of France*, 3rd rev. ed. (Oxford, 1892–99), 1. 89.
87 "a figure in a void": FM/JGF, 26 June 1907.
88 "interesting and often beautiful" and ff.: Newbolt Report, 3 August 1907.
88 "find a public" and ff.: AG/John Murray, 29 July 1907. Murray Archive.
88 "echoes": Newbolt Report, 3 August 1907.
88 "moderate demand": FM/A. H. Hallam Murray, 8

December 1907. Murray Archive.

88 "doggerel anecdotes": Newbolt Report, 3 August 1907.

88 "give the book away": John Murray/AG, 6 December 1907. Murray Archive. The firm's advertisements tried to capitalise on Brunhild's unfamiliarity, a shrewder tactic than trying to capitalise on Manning's. See *Spectator*, 14 December 1907, 1030.

89 "We had intended": AG/John Murray, 9 December 1907. Murray Archive.

89 "sleepy owls" and ff.: Mrs Cara David/John Murray, 21 January 1908. Murray Archive.

90 *in hand: Manning apparently learned this from his sister Dot. FM/JGF, 30 October 1908.

91 *1907: Manning was a rapid writer and it is altogether possible that he composed the *Vigil* in a few months. The earliest mention of it in his existing correspondence is 30 May 1907, and subsequent references do not suggest that it was drafted years before and then picked up again.

91 "of those needless": *Bulletin*, 6 February 1908, The Red Page.

91 "Arnoldesque": *Isis*, 8 February 1908, 205.

91 "virility": *Cambridge Review*, 30 April 1908, 336. See also *The Scotsman*, 12 December 1907, 3; *The Nation*, 1 August 1908, 646.

91 "dramatic force": *Times Literary Supplement*, 23 January 1908, 27.

91 "tranquillity" and ff.: *Isis*, 8 February 1908, 205. Another review of the poem in the same issue was distinctly less appreciative.

91 *Fowler: FM/JGF, 15 June 1907. Letter in possession of Mrs Benita Biso. By the spring of 1908 the two were in correspondence, and would seem to have met first when Mrs Fowler invited Manning to visit when he came to London in July. FM/JGF, 23, 26 May 1908.

91 "most loyal": FM/AH, 10 July 1921.

93 *Hawaii: Ralph Kuykendall, *The Hawaiian Kingdom* (Honolulu, 1967), 3, 267–68, 603, 617; Jacob Adler, *Claus Spreckels* (Honolulu, 1966), 123, 138, 162, 174; obituary of Neumann, *Pacific Commercial Advertiser*, 2 July 1901. Neumann also defended Queen Liliuokalani at her trial in 1895.

93 *Kent: Several of Eva Fowler's letters to Yeats discussing automatic writing are to be found in *Letters to W. B. Yeats*, edited by Richard J. Finneran, George Mills Harper, and William M. Murphy (New York, 1977). See also George Mills Harper, *W. B. Yeats and W. F. Horton: The Record of an Occult Friendship* (London, 1980), 34.

93 "most fascinating": FM/JGF, 15 October 1908.

93 "Willie": Lord Gorell, *One Man...Many Parts* (London, 1956), 118.

93 "grimy": Eva Sumner/author, 15 May 1979.

94 *ordered: The story is told in detail — with long quotations from some of the letters — in Michael R. Lane, *The Story of the Steam Plough Works: Fowlers of Leeds* (London, 1980), 231-32.

94 "delicate sensibility": FM/AH, 10 July 1921.

94 "Tell Mrs Fowler": FM/JGF, 29 December 1908.

94 "I was most": Eva Sumner/author, 1 May 1979.

95 "I hope": Eva Sumner/author, 15 May 1979.

96 *Manning: Siggy Don (1896–1943) was the son of Marie Don Sargant, a long time friend of Manning. Unfortunately, no family papers seem to have survived. D. E. Don/author, 9 October 1980.

99 "seeking for a classical": FM/JGF, 9 February 1909.

99 "My day": FM/JGF, 9 March 1908.

100 *day: FM/JGF, 10 August 1908.

100 "The text": FM/JGF, 26 September 1908.

100 "this stupid body" and ff.: FM/JGF, 10 April 1909.

101 "I shall be": FM/JGF, 10 August 1908.

101 "The art of letter-writing": FM/JGF, 10 June 1907.

101 "A desire": "Hylas." This poem, apparently never published, is among the Manning papers in the Mitchell Library.

101 "the garden full of daffodils": FM/JGF, 10 April 1909.

101 "the garden full of nightingales" and ff.: FM/JGF, 9 June 1907.

102 *know: .The Gascoignes did not know, according to Lady Sandys. Neither did John Rothenstein, though he does not know what his father knew. Eva Sumner knew of the problem "only by hearsay". Eva Sumner/author, 1 August 1979.

103 "monastère": Eva Fowler/AH, 10 April [1913?].

103 "Theseus followed": "Theseus and Hippolyta", *Poems*.

104 "Ce n'est pas": FM/AH, 14 April 1913.

104 "Women never": "The Crock of Gold", *Spectator*, 15 March 1913, 454.

104 "mystery": *Middle Parts*, 108.

104 "always treated" and ff.: *ibid*. 107.

104 "desperate adventure" and ff.: FM/WR, 9 October 1918.

104 "I'm an unlucky man": FM/Sybil Gowthorpe, 6 July 1926.

105 *bond: Jeffrey Meyers has asserted that Manning was a homosexual. *Homosexuality and Modern Literature, 1890–1930* (London, 1977), 121; *The Wounded Spirit: A Study of Seven Pillars of Wisdom* (London, 1973), 123. His only evidence for the assertion is Manning's friendship with Lawrence. Telephone conversation with Meyers, 1977.

106 "whole folios": Lionel Johnson/Campbell Dodgson, 15 April 1889, in Raymond Roseliep, "Some Letters of Lionel Johnson", unpublished Ph.D. dissertation, Notre Dame University (1953), 82.

106 "little *apologia*": AG/AH, 13 July 1907.

106 "un homme": Albert Houtin, *Mon Expérience I. Une Vie de Prêtre*, Nouvelle édition, revue et augmentée (Paris, 1928), 410.

106 ''incomplete form'': FM/AH, 6 December 1907.

106 *him: FM/AH, 2, 16 June 1908.

107 *Pater: ''Manning n'est pas un poète ignorant. Il a prouvè dans un livre publié depuis [*Brunhild*] une vaste erudition philosophique et historique. Peut-être seron-t-il un autre Walter Pater, et même, plus encore, s'il veut travailler''. Houtin Papers, nouvelles acquisitions françaises, 15,722, f. 477.

107 ''interesting'': Newbolt Report, 3 August 1907.

107 ''undoubtedly a new force'': Newbolt Report, 27 October 1908. Murray Archive.

107 ''Caviar'': *The Methodist Recorder*, 15 July 1909.

107 ''though under ordinary circumstances'': John Murray/ FM, 17 January 1910. Murray Archive.

107 ''exceptional'' and ff.: Memorandum of C. E. Lawrence/ John Murray, 16 January 1910. Murray Archive.

108 ''many paradises'': *Scenes*, 242–43.

108 ''perhaps...the most'': *London Daily Telegraph*, 16 December 1930.

108 ''quote from memory'': Ezra Pound, ''A List of Books'', *The Little Review*, 4 (March 1918), 55.

108 ''When Merodach'': *Scenes*, 1–2.

109 ''in a way'': *ibid*. 95.

109 ''There are in reality'': *ibid*. ix.

110 *affection: ''He is the one saint in the calendar that I honestly admire, almost worship''. FM/JGF, 7 September 1908.

110 ''trust something'': FM/JGF, 19 April 1909.

110 ''He ceased'': *Scenes*, 136–37.

111 ''Adam broke'': *ibid*. 17–18

112 ''I deny'': *ibid*. 43.

112 ''principal influence'' and ff.: *ibid*. x.

113 ''pour des lecteurs'': Ernest Renan, *Dialogues Philosophiques*, in *Oeuvres Completes*, edited by Henriette Psichari (Paris, 1947–1961), 1. 552.

113 ''I do not think'': *Scenes*, xi.

113 "desirable": FM/C. E. Lawrence, 14 January 1909. Murray Archive. He was thinking of *Imaginary Portraits* and *The Renaissance*.

113 *imitation: More than one critic heard echoes of "The Procurator of Judea" in Manning's "The friend of Paul".

113 "his example": *Scenes*, xii.

114 "God speaks": Arthur Galton, "The New Theology of the City Temple", *Independent Review*, 12 (March 1907), 291.

114 "Is not that awful": C. Huntington/C. E. Lawrence, 6 December 1910. Murray Archive.

114 "This book was placed": *Sydney Stock and Station Journal*, 9 July 1909. See also *Booklover* (Melbourne), 6 August 1909, 90.

114 "obscure": *The Outlook*, 29 May 1909, 2.

114 "too abundant": *Daily Chronicle*, 24 June 1909.

114 "a little too literary": *Daily Express*. Date not determinable.

114 "twenty-five years out of date": *Morning Post*, 3 June 1909.

115 "competent reviewers" and ff.: AG/AH, 23 July 1909.

115 "Since Mr Arnold": *Edinburgh Review*, 210 (October 1909), 442.

115 "My aim": FM/C. E. Lawrence, 29 October 1909. Murray Archive.

115 "dwindling class": Newbolt Report, 29 October 1908. Murray Archive.

116 "rather good" and ff.: FM/JGF, 4 August 1909.

116 *spirit and ff.: FM/JGF, 9 February, 10 April, 30 May 1909.

116 "I am very disappointed" and ff.: FM/JGF, 30 May 1909.

116 "condensed": *The Outlook*, 29 May 1909, 2.

117 "an ecclesiastic" and ff.: FM/AH, 1 November 1908.

117 "I met his father": Fairfax Papers, Item 233, National Library, Canberra. In early 1908 Manning had sent Fairfax's review of Vigil "out to my people in Sydney, to

show them how very noble you were''. FM/JGF, 13 February 1908.

Chapter 4

118 ''Tomorrow'': EP/Isabel Pound, 11 October 1909. The ''book'' then in progress was to become *The Spirit of Romance* (1910).

119 ''Be sped'': Ezra Pound, ''Canzon: The Yearly Slain''.

119 *Pound: For Pound's own awareness of this see Donald Hall, *Remembering Poets* (New York, 1978), 232.

119 ''half-savage'' and ff.: ''Hugh Selwyn Mauberley''.

119 ''quite much'': EP/Isabel Pound, 21 January 1909.

119 ''I feel sure'': *Book News Monthly*, 27 (April 1909), 621.

119 ''quite beautiful'': EP/Ford Madox Ford, November 1909.

119 *Pound/Ford: The Story of a Literary Relationship*, edited by Brita Lindberg-Seyersted (New York, 1982), 6.

119 ''a stupendous work'': EP/Isabel Pound, 15 March 1909.

119 ''realy writes'': EP/Isabel Pound, 1 February 1909.

119 ''as much as I do'' and ff.: FM/JGF, 9 February 1909.

120 ''we are the generation'' and ff.: EP/Isabel Pound, 22 March 1910.

120 ''best criticism'': EP/Harriet Monroe, 22 October 1913. Paige, *Selected Letters*, 13.

120 *poems: *A Lume Spento and other Early Poems* (New York, 1965). ''Chocolate Creams'' was presumably intended as a parody of ''Picadilly'', which first appeared in *Personae* (1909). Louis Martz, writing in the introduction to Pound's *Collected Early Poems* (New York, 1976), heard only an echo of ''Picadilly'' in the phrase, but the fact that Pound placed quotation marks around the phrase would seem to indicate that he knew he was not quoting himself. In 1913 Pound praised the ''Ballad'' and ''Chocolate Creams'' as ''Things of Lasting Delight''. EP/Harriet Monroe, April/May 1913. Regenstein Library.

120 "most matters": EP/Isabel Pound, 22 March 1910.

120 "reality": FM/Dorothy and Ezra Pound, 28 December 1920. Letter in possession of Omar Pound.

121 "conceit": A frequent refrain in Manning's comments about Pound. For example, when Pound was preparing to go back to America for a visit in 1910, Manning penned the following to Fairfax: "Poor devil, I am sorry for him, and I do like some of his work, but his conceit is beyond endurance sometimes; and I'm so tired of having Milton's fair fame to defend every time I see him, and to amuse myself at P's expense generally, that I am rather glad he is going." FM/JGF, 14 June 1910.

121 "He [Pound] is not": *Ezra and Dorothy*, 9. This comment was originally contained in a letter to Olivia Shakespear. It quickly passed to her daughter and Pound himself — who never forgot it. See *Bridge between Worlds: Ezra Pound Letters to John Theobald*, edited by Donald Pearce and Herbert Schneidau (Redding Connecticut, 1984), 85; *Pound/Lewis*, edited by Timothy Materer (New York, 1985), 280.

121 "It seemed": Mary de Rachewiltz, *Discretions* (London, 1971), 46.

121 "In fact": EP/Isabel Pound, 22 March 1910.

121 "I am moving": FM/JGF, 5 October 1909.

122 "The mere fact": "The Gilded Coach", 55. Mitchell Library.

123 "The script": Tom McCormack/author, 31 October 1977.

124 "Quand on étudiera": Houtin Papers, n.a.f. 15722, f. 477.

124 "shock": *Herald*, 31 December 1932.

125 "I sent": FM/JGF, 17 November 1908.

127 "His tone": *Spectator*, 18 December 1909, 1056.

127 "Half a dozen": FM/JGF, 26 April 1911.

127 "very anxious" and ff.: FM/JGF, 12 May 1911.

127 "worthwhile": FM/JGF, 26 April 1911.

127 "afford": FM/JGF, 16 June 1911.

128 "In *Tess*": *Spectator*, 7 September 1912, 336.

129 "a critic": *Spectator*, 28 September 1912, 454.

129 "I have just": FM/JGF, 11 September 1911.

129 "his more envenomed": EP/Iris Barry, 13 July 1916, Paige, *Selected Letters*, 85.

129 "As we have said": *Spectator*, 4 July 1914, 19.

130 "as a single": *Spectator*, 4 April 1914, 567.

130 "representation": *Spectator*, 30 March 1912, 514.

130 "is never": *Spectator*, 7 December 1912, 931.

130 "drawn from": *Spectator*, 21 December 1912, 1064.

130 "inspiration" and ff.: *Spectator*, 24 July 1915, 114–15.

130 "true poet" and ff.: *Spectator*, 4 July 1914, 19.

130 "rooted": *Spectator*, 8 July 1911, 70.

130 "consistently": *Spectator*, 13 April 1912, 587.

131 "accidental" and ff.: *Spectator*, 29 October 1910, 694.

131 "He makes me feel": FM/Henry Newbolt, 29 September 1910. Beinecke.

131 "superficiality": *Spectator*, 29 October 1910, 695.

131 *Belloc: It was over the church in France. *Spectator*, 12, 26 August, 2, 9 September 1911. Galton's original piece was published over his pseudonym (Oūtis) as was the mixed review he had given Belloc's *Marie Antoinette* in the issue of 11 December 1909. The later squabble carries no memories of the earlier review.

132 "King Demos": *Spectator*, 19 November 1910, 828.

132 "Rome": *Spectator*, 25 September 1909, 450.

132 "incubating" and ff.: AG/John Murray, 9 December 1907. Murray Archive.

132 "delighted" and ff.: FM/JGF, 5 October 1909.

132 "a profound criticism": *Spectator*, 2 July 1910, 22.

133 "a Tory" and ff.: FM/EP, 13 January 1912; FM/WR, 14 October 1931.

133 "cant" and ff.: FM/EP, 13 January 1912.

133 "really hate[d]": FM/JGF, 22 October 1912.

133 "sentimentality": FM/C. E. Lawrence, 14 June 1910. Murray Archive. This was in reference to Theodore Roosevelt's Guildhall speech of 31 May 1910, where the

former president cautioned his listeners about the "unwise sentimentality" of those who objected to Britain's "civilizing" policy in Egypt. Manning congratulated Roosevelt as "half a God-send" on the matter. He also noted that Roosevelt was "intensely interested in *Scenes and Portraits*. Flattering unction." How he came by this knowledge, and exactly what it meant, is unclear, but two days after the Guildhall speech Roosevelt was a guest at a dinner held by St Loe Strachey. For the Guildhall speech see *Theodore Roosevelt's Speeches in Europe* (New York, n.d.), 74, 79; *The Times*, 1 June 1910. For the Strachey dinner, *The Times*, 3 June 1910.

133 "which has": FM/EP, 13 January 1912.

133 "the laws which govern": *Scenes*, 249.

133 "revered only" and ff.: "The Gilded Coach", 49.

133 "as elsewhere" and ff.: "Greek Genius and Greek Democracy", *Edinburgh Review*, 217 (April 1913), 351. That this is Manning's work is evident from its argument and style. He also refers to it in a letter to C. E. Lawrence of 12 December 1912. Murray Archive. The essay can be read as part of the longstanding debate in British intellectual circles over how Athens should be valued as a parallel for contemporary British politics and culture. On the debate see Frank M. Turner, *The Greek Heritage in Victorian Britain* (New Haven, 1981), chap. 5.

134 "if the miners" and ff.: FM/Aubrey Herbert, 6 March 1912.

134 "a profoundly democratic": Introduction by Peter Davies to 1943 edition of *Her Privates We*.

134 "revive the circulation": FM/John Murray, 16 January 1910. Murray Archive.

134 "I do not think": FM/C. E. Lawrence, 7 July 1910. Murray Archive.

134 "It is far too early": C. E. Lawrence/FM, 8 July 1910. Murray Archive.

135 "truly golden": C. E. Lawrence/FM, 22 July 1910. Murray Archive.
135 "...this volume": *The Daily Chronicle*, 22 July 1910.
136 "You really are": FM/JGF, 10 April 1910.
136 "swords rust": *Poems*, 68.
136 "what are": *ibid*. 44.
138 "kingly spoil": *ibid*. 50.
138 "I have": *ibid*. 66–67.
138 "fickle sea": *ibid*. 47.
139 "visions of myself": FM/JGF, 22 October 1912.
139 "the informing spirit": FM/John Murray, 27 April 1910. Murray Archive.
141 "Tout homme": Henri de Régnier, "Monsieur D'Amercouer", in *La Canne de Jaspe* (Paris, 1897).
141 "modernists" and ff.: Richard Cody, *Newsletter of the Friends of the Amherst College Library* (Fall 1977), unpaginated.
142 "Next May": FM/EP, 30 August 1910.
142 "slowly": FM/JGF, 16 June 1911.
142 "I have": FM/JGF, 18 June 1912.
142 "Some of the first": FM/Henry Newbolt, 26 December 1912. Beinecke.
142 "wise": FM/AH, 27 March 1913.
142 "sedulously" and ff.: FM/EP, 26 May 1913.
142 **Smart Set*: The editor, Willard Huntington Wright, called on Pound in London in the spring of 1913. Noel Stock, *The Life of Ezra Pound*, expanded edition (New York, 1982), 140. On 1 June Manning wrote to Pound saying that if Wright "likes" what he has read he [Manning] will send more of the manuscript to him.
143 "I feel": FM/Henry Newbolt, 2 November 1909. Beinecke.
143 "without quiet": FM/JGF, 26 April 1911.
144 "symposiarch": The title given to a *Spectator* column Manning wrote on Thomas Love Peacock.
144 "The historical basis": FM/JGF, 14 November 1911.

144 "I aint a realist": FM/JGF, 18 June 1912.

145 "Sometimes I wonder": FM/John Murray, 5 May 1927. Murray Archive.

145 "It would" and ff.: EP/Harriet Monroe, 17 March 1913.

145 "a long semi-dramatic": FM/Harriet Monroe, 11 December 1912. Regenstein.

145 "only poem": FM/Henry Newbolt, 10 March 1912. Beinecke.

145 "seriously concerned": Ezra Pound, "Prologomena", *The Poetry Review*, 2 (February 1912), 76.

145 "experiment": FM/Henry Newbolt, 10 March 1912.

146 "being improper": Dorothy Shakespear/EP, 14 March 1913. *Ezra and Dorothy*, 191. The punch that Pound threw at Strachey in "Salvation the Second" (*The New Freewoman*, 15 August 1913) probably owes some of its spite to this occasion.

146 "art has no morality": FM/JGF, 15 June 1907. Letter in possession of Mrs Biso.

147 "mischievous and unjust" and ff.: *Spectator*, 3 February 1912, 187. Manning's respect for Strachey, circumscribed though it was, is captured in a letter he wrote in 1910. "Strachey is not a smug! You would be more just if you called him a fanatic; but fanaticism is one of the principles of progress. I admire him. I admire the way he consults expert advice in matters which he does not understand. I admire the way he takes a side not because he thinks it the only right one, but because he thinks it the least wrong and the most practical. I admire the way he runs the *Spectator*, so that it has a prestige equal to, if not greater than *The Times*. I admire his conscience". FM/Ralph Straus, 4 October 1910. Northwestern University Library. Manning's distaste for prudery extended to the visual arts as well. In the same letter he defends Norman Lindsay's "obscenities, which I have known and admired for many years" in the "classic pages of the *Bulletin*".

147 "respected": EP/Harriet Monroe, 17 March 1913.

Regenstein.

148 "Have I the presence?": FM/EP, 21 February 1912. This was the first of three lectures on medieval poetry that Pound gave in Lord Glenconner's home. For a copy of the invitation see *Ezra and Dorothy*, 89.

148 "one man": This phrase occurs in a lecture, "Psychology and the Troubadours", Pound gave at the Kensington Town Hall and then printed in *Quest* (October 1912). It is reprinted in all the editions of *The Spirit of Romance* starting in 1932. Donald Gallup, *A Bibliography of Ezra Pound* (Oxford, 1963), 201. Manning is not named in the published version, but there can be little doubt that he is the person Pound had in mind. For the quote, *The Spirit of Romance* (London, 1952), 92; for the lecture, Stock, *Life*, 113.

148 "Villainous" and ff.: FM/JGF, 21 April 1912. Like Galton, he seems to have been prone to finding miracle cures. In September 1911 he is taking sour milk, sent from London, as a "panacea". FM/JGF, 11 September 1911.

148 "I enjoyed": FM/Aubrey Herbert, 11 August 1912. Manning returned to Pixton in December.

149 "frugal et austère": FM/AH, 14 October 1912.

149 "idleness and philosophy": FM/RA, 23 June 1921.

149 "un petit enfant" and ff.: FM/AH, 13 March 1913.

150 *allowance: In 1910 he earned £39 12s and in 1911 £50 6s. The ledger breaks off after a few entries in 1912. But an estimate can still be made on the basis that for almost all his reviews in *Spectator* he was paid £3, and that, on average, he received the same amount for a poem. Thus in 1912 he earned at least £54; in 1913 at least £30, and in 1914 at least £18. These figures do not take into account what his book earnings were, or what he earned from any journalism I have been unable to find. He was probably well paid for the essay he published in the *Edinburgh Review* in April of 1913.

150 "Poems for": FM/JGF, 22 October 1912.

150 *Daisy Meadow: "Eva and Taffy Fowler were definitely the most important people in Fred Manning's life." Eva Sumner/ author, 15 May 1979.

151 "through the post": FM/JGF, 26 February 1914. On the lunch see Elizabeth Longford, *A Pilgrimage of Passion: The Life of Wilfrid Scawen Blunt* (London 1979), 393–98. Manning did send a short note of regret to Blunt about his not coming, but offered no explanation. FM/Wilfrid Blunt, 24 January 1914, Blunt Papers, West Sussex Record Office, Chichester. On Pound's 84th birthday (1969), Cyril Connolly asked him about a recent assertion that Manning had, indeed, attended the famous lunch: "Pound shook his head indignantly." Cyril Connolly, *The Evening Colonnade* (London, 1973), 270.

151 "I have been cranky": FM/EP, [?] March 1914.

151 "My dear Pound": In possession of Omar Pound.

152 "The Irrational": FM/EP, 12 March 1914.

152 "an excellent": EP/Dorothy Shakespear, 25 March 1914. *Ezra and Dorothy*, 337.

152 "joint translation": FM/EP, 24 September 1911. In possession of Omar Pound.

152 "We shall rage": FM/EP, 27 May 1915.

153 "My own final": FM/Max Beerbohm, 30 May 1923. Merton College, Oxford.

153 "Your caricature": FM/Max Beerbohm, 11 July 1930. Merton College.

153 "teasing me": Diary of Eva Sumner, 9 August 1914.

153 *examination: AG/AH, 24 September 1914.

154 *as reviewers: AG/AH, 7 May 1915; C. A. Seaton (Librarian of *Spectator*)/author, 1 April 1980.

154 "the little kingdom": *Grantham Journal*, 31 December 1910.

154 "desolation" and ff.: AG/AH, 11 August 1914.

154 *1914: *Grantham Journal*, 5 December 1914. A house was provided by the Earl of Ancaster.

154 "platitudes" and ff.: AG/AH, 7 May 1915.

155 "Lordlier": "The Monmouth and Good Hope", UCLA Library.
155 "I really" and ff.: FM/JGF, 21 April 1912.
156 "to do something": FM/AH, 28 December 1914.
156 "military ambition": FM/EP, 27 May 1915.
156 "who have become": FM/AH, 28 December 1914.

Chapter 5

158 "general practice" and ff.: J. W. Stevens/author, 16 December 1977.
158 "I am to inform": J. W. Stevens/author, 11 January 1978.
158 "I've just been": Brian Bond/author, 2 March 1978.
158 "appears to have been": M. E. Jones/author, 15 February 1978.
159 "authority" and ff.: Mrs Joan Chapman/author, 2 October 1979.
160 "I joined": FM/WR, 14 November 1915.
160 *vision: On the Snellen test he was 6/9(20/30) and 6/18(20/70). His history of asthma would also have diminished his chances.
160 "all passed him": AG/AH, 22 December 1915.
161 "babel" and ff.: FM/WR, 24 January 1916.
161 "the very hard" and ff.: FM/WR, 14 November 1915.
161 "bad time" and ff.: FM/TEL, 26 March 1930, *Letters to TEL*, 132. Manning's emphasis.
161 "The greater part": FM/WR, 26 December 1915. *Men and Memories*, 2. 293–94.
163 "priggish tone" and ff.: FM/WR, 19 July 1931.
163 "first impressions" and ff.: *Men and Memories*, 2. 293.
164 "very rigorous": FM/WR, 7 May 1916.
165 "Went to Paddington": Diary of Eva Sumner, 11 August 1916.
165 "in the nature of things": FM/WR, 10 November 1916. *Men and Memories*, 2. 297–98.
165 "a footnote" and ff.: H. G. Wells, *Mr. Britling Sees it*

Through (London, 1916), 233.

165 "slaying Germans": FM/EP, 29 May 1915.

166 "It is good" and ff.: FM/WR, 1 July 1918.

166 "straight to": FM/WR, Mid-September, 1916. *Men and Memories*, 2. 295.

166 "We are supposed" and ff.: FM/WR, 31 October 1916. *Men and Memories*, 2. 296.

167 "these Shropshire lads" and ff.: FM/WR, Mid-September, 1916. *Men and Memories*, 2. 295.

167 *to use: Manning had apparently stayed with Rummel for a few days while he was in Paris in March of 1913. In April of that year he had a copy of *Scenes* sent to him. Murray Archive.

167 "yours": FM/WR, 31 October 1916. *Men and Memories*, 2. 296.

167 "most poignant" and ff.: *Men and Memories*, 2. 293.

167 "realities" and ff.: FM/WR, 31 October 1916. *Men and Memories*, 2. 296.

167 "I can't sort out": FM/WR, Mid-September, 1916. *Men and Memories*, 2. 295.

168 "more or less indifferent" and ff.: FM/WR, 31 October 1916. *Men and Memories*, 2. 296.

168 "I think the heroism": FM/WR, 10 November 1916. *Men and Memories*, 2. 298.

168 "alternately a conflict": *Spectator*, 1 April 1911, 482. See also *Scenes*, passim.

168 *censor: *Herald*, 31 December 1932. He also on one occasion let his friends know where he was located: "Bois de Mametz: August 16". Published originally in *Quest*, December 1916, when reprinted in *Eidola* the date was removed from the title. Manning joked about his subterfuge when interviewed in 1932: "The censor apparently said, 'Only a poor fool writing poetry', and let his works go through untouched." *Telegraph*, 31 December 1932.

171 "the realism": Eva Fowler/C. E. Lawrence, 11 November

1916. Murray Archive.

172 "sorry": John Murray/Eva Fowler, 9 November 1916. Murray Archive.

172 "They are better attuned": C. E. Lawrence Report, early November 1916. Murray Archive.

172 "call to readers": C. E. Lawrence/Eva Fowler, 22 November 1916. Murray Archive.

172 "material": "Where literature differs from the other fine arts is simply in its material, which is not inert or inarticulate as the material of other arts; it is a material which, even before the artist touches it, is composed of εἴδωλα *Spectator*, 30 March 1912, 514.

172 "if people": Eva Fowler/C. E. Lawrence, 21 November 1916. Murray Archive.

172 "must walk": C. E. Lawrence/Eva Fowler, 22 November 1916. Murray Archive.

173 "mainly childish things": FM/WR, 26 December 1915. Left out of published version of the letter.

174 *Sir Henry Taylor: While at Oxford in the spring of 1916 Manning had acted as a go-between in arranging for the daughters' bequest of Sir Henry's papers to the Bodleian. Una Taylor/Bodleian Librarian, 13 May 1916. Bodleian Library. In Ida Taylor's will Manning was left a bequest of £50.

174 "adorable Jelly": FM/WR, 16 March 1920.

176 "Thought and form": Joseph Macleod/author, early July, 1979. For more on Jelly and her sister his book should be consulted. *The Sisters d'Aranyi* (London, 1969).

177 "stern and true" and ff.: *The Dial*, 17 May 1917, 427.

177 "no value": Letter to Shakespear and Parkyn, 9 March 1935. Murray Archive.

177 "now outgrown" and ff.: Military File.

178 "never having": FM/WR, 2 January 1917.

178 "literary godmother": C. E. Lawrence/FM, 27 December 1916. Murray Archive.

179 *he was in: FM/WR, 31 August 1917.

179 "better and stronger": AG/AH, 6 February 1917.

179 "I found that": FM/WR, 7 January 1918.

179 "I do not envy": FM/Harriet Monroe, 18 May 1919. Regenstein.

179 *in his class: Eva Sumner's diary, 2 June 1917.

180 "too pure": FM/WR, 21 July 1917.

180 *enthusiasm: The first pencil portrait was done in June 1917, and was inscribed "to my dear Fred". When John Rothenstein made up an iconography of his father's portrait drawings this particular one was listed as being in the possession of Manning. The later pencil portrait is in the Mitchell Library and the date assigned to it is "1918". This is a little odd, for while Manning in a letter of 9 November 1918 refers to what ostensibly was a fresh drawing of himself, it also appears that he had not yet seen Rothenstein since returning from Ireland. So when was the *second* drawing done — and was it done from life or the previous drawing? Another oddity is that it is hard to imagine Manning allowing himself to be drawn in uniform in 1918 since he had ceased being a soldier in February. Finally, the 1918 sketch, despite its heroic tone, is not a good likeness — further evidence, perhaps, that it was not done from life.

180 *Dublin: The third battalion was used to feed men to units at the various battle fronts, but during the Easter Uprising (1916) the battalion had played a significant role in putting down the rebels. Stannus Geoghegan, *The Campaigns and History of the Royal Irish Regiment* (Edinburgh, 1927), 2. 102–104.

181 "Some day soon": FM/WR, 25 August 1917.

183 "indecent lines": EP/James Joyce, 17 July 1918. *Pound/Joyce Letters of Ezra Pound to James Joyce*, edited by Forrest Read (New York, 1967), 144.

183 "I have broken": FM/WR, 21 July 1917.

183 "severely reprimanded": Military File.

183 "especially in": FM/WR, 31 August 1917.

184 "neurasthenia" and ff.: Military File.
184 "a very decent room" and ff.: FM/WR, 31 August 1917.
184 "I...may be fired": FM/C. E. Lawrence, 29 August 1917. Murray Archive.
184 "for weeks": In subsequent letters to Houtin (7 November 1917; 5 January, 8 June 1918), Galton merely reports that Manning is still in Ireland.
184 "nervous exhaustion" and ff.: Military File.
186 "ill health": Memo datd 20 February 1918.
187 "lumbago": FM/WR, 6 December 1917.
187 "who have" and ff.: FM/WR 12 November 1917.
187 "disorganized nerves" and ff.: FM/WR, 1 July 1918.
187 "a nice gentlemanly": Military File.
188 "My father" and ff.: Sybil Gowthorpe/author, 11 January 1979.
189 "You and Polly": FM/"Dick" (Frieda Lynch, then remarried to Frank Bernard), 1 February 1930.
190 *paradise: Mrs Patricia Hope/author, 29 September 1979.
190 "kind" and ff.: Sybil Gowthorpe/author, 11 January 1979.
190 *talk: This story is contained in the rough draft of the letter Mrs Gowthorpe sent to me. I was shown this draft when I visited Cirencester.
191 **Spectator*: *The Times*, 7 May 1919; *Spectator*, 4 October 1919, 437.
192 "fallacy" and ff.: FM/WR, 14 October 1931.
192 "My outlook": *Scenes*, 17.
192 *outlook: For more evidence of Manning's respect for Machiavelli see *Spectator*, 19 October 1912, 601.
193 "It will always": FM/WR, 9 November 1918.

Chapter 6

194 "just missing": FM/WR, 9 November 1918.
194 "his hair": Stella Bowen, *Drawn From Life*, 60.
194 "dangerous" and ff.: FM/WR, 9 November 1918.
194 "the unique source" and ff.: "M. de Gourmont and the

Problem of Beauty'', *Little Review* 5. (February/March 1919), 22.

194 ''essentially feminine'': *ibid*. 25.

195 *champion of Gourmont: Between 1912 and 1922 Pound devoted ''more pages of enthusiastic appreciation and translation to Gourmont than to any other single contemporary''. Richard Sieburth, *Instigations: Ezra Pound and Remy de Gourmont* (Cambridge, Massachusetts, 1978), 1.

195 ''remarkably close'': EP/RA, 5 June 1959.

195 ''three years'': FM/Olivia Shakespear. Addressed to ''My Aunt'', this undated letter was written presumably in late 1918. Beinecke.

195 ''Just as Nietzsche'': *Little Review*, 25–26.

195 *start: EP/Isabel Pound, 23 January 1919.

195 ''just missed'' and ff.: FM/WR, 22 March 1919. It was serious enough for one of his brothers to be called back from France.

196 ''certainly had it'': Richard Aldington, ''An Introduction to Frederic Manning'', *Australian Letters*, 2 (June 1959), 2. In the draft of this article — now at the Southern Illinois University Library — Aldington wrote, ''I distinctly remember him telling me [circa 1920] of the long treatment he had had in a sanatorium''.

196 ''old register'': Dr J Burrows/author, 19 August 1981.

197 ''precautionary'': FM/WR, 22 March 1919.

197 ''untrustworthy'' and ff.: Dr George Day/author, 2 November 1981. Dr Day, now retired, was a partner in the hospital when it was still a sanatorium.

197 ''Even those'': FM/Harriet Monroe, 18 May 1919. Regenstein.

197 ''Get well soon'': FM/Laurence Binyon, 28 March 1932.

197 *well: FM/WR, 9 October 1925; FM/Arnold Bennett, 12 February 1931. La Fayette Butler Collection of Arnold Bennett, Pennsylvania State University Libraries.

197 "overflowing": AG/AH, 7 November 1917. See also 24 July 1919.
198 "Latin Civilization": AG/AH, 29 December 1918.
198 "The whole world": AG/AH, 24 July 1919.
198 "Guerre et Religion": Galton had approached Loisy to do the translation. Alfred Loisy, *Memoires pour servir a l'histoire religieuse de notre temps* (Paris, 1930–31), 3. 311. Loisy's final comment on Galton is worth recording: "Il avait un certain gout pour les études austeres, car il s'appliquait à la lecture des Actes des Apôtres lorsque la mort le surprit." *ibid*. 3. 406.
198 "The world is arranged": AG/AH, 7 March 1916.
198 "Thoughts": *Little Review*, 4 (January 1918). While the paragraphs are attributed only to a "vicar of a country parish", their style is clearly Galton's.
198 *work: Pound quotes from *Urbana* in an essay on Landor, which can be found in *Selected Prose 1909–1965*. Neither book nor author are identified however, and Pound takes exception to Galton's views. In 1915 he very likely depended on Galton for insights into Lionel Johnson when preparing his introduction for *The Poetical Works of Lionel Johnson* (London, 1915).
198 *own: "I value his opinion of prose as much as anyone's." EP/Isabel Pound, 31 August 1917. Years later Pound named Galton (and Manning) among those who should be included in a book on "serious English prose from 1890 to 1920". EP/RA, 5 June 1959.
198 "detestable": AG/Olivia Shakespear, 30 April 1920. Possession of Omar Pound. His view of Pound's poetry was mixed. While he thought it had "no construction" and that its vocabulary was "sometimes mean and incorrect", he acknowledged that it did "convey a sense of power which can only be explained as genius".
198 "to stop all" and ff.: FM/WR, 22 March 1919.
199 "invited" and ff.: FM/WR, 29 July 1919.

199 *patron: FM/WR, 29 July 1919. The only hint of the financial terms appears in a letter where Manning says he has "another £100 to come from Lady White, £50 on completion of the book and £50 when ready for the press". FM/RA, 8 August 1921.

199 *1919: Eva Fowler/AH, 2 March 1921.

199 "very pressing": FM/WR, 29 July 1919.

199 *death: By the terms of the will Fred and his sisters were each to receive £5000 in trust, the income from which would be paid to them by the trustees (Will and Harry). The other sons were to receive £3000 clear.

200 "as soon as possible": FM/WR, 9 November 1918.

200 "What am I": FM/JGF, 17 November 1908.

200 "asked": FM/John Murray, 5 May 1927. Murray Archive.

201 *biography: "I like any life; however badly it be done, and however stupid the person: I should like nothing better, than to have someone's life given me to do." AG/Laurence Binyon, 5 October 1890. More than a third of the books Galton reviewed for *Spectator* were biographies.

201 *1913: *Spectator*, 15 March 1913, 441. The biography itself mentions that a "close friend" of White was Douglas Galton, Arthur's uncle. Moreover, all his life Galton had been interested in naval matters, and during the war he had looked to the navy to save England.

201 "the urging": This comes from the draft version of the 1959 article. In the published piece Aldington softened his view to "Manning depended greatly on others in life, and Galton's death left him at a loose end". Aldington, "An Introduction", 26.

201 "he spent": *Criterion*, 14 April 1935, 436.

202 "chained": FM/WR, 12 August 1919.

202 "stink of money" and ff.: FM/EP, 11 November 1919.

202 "Goya painting": FM/WR, 24 December 1919.

202 "nightmare": FM/EP, 11 November 1919.

202 "moral tale" and ff.: FM/WR, 24 December 1919.

202 "endless memoirs": FM/WR, 12 August 1919.

202 "though more casual": FM/EP, 29 January 1920.

203 "There is no striving" and ff.: the *Piccadilly Review*, 23 October 1919, 7.

203 "Matt-Matt": Wade, *Letters of Yeats*, 679.

204 "rather secretive" and ff.: Victor Woolmer/author, spring 1978.

204 "bags of work": FM/EP, 11 November 1919.

204 "rest hour" and ff.: FM/EP, 29 January 1920.

204 "ill and tired" and ff.: FM/EP, 15 February 1920.

204 "interviewing shipowners": FM/EP, 7 August 1920.

204 "studies" and ff.: FM/WR, 16 March 1920. As far back as 1909 he had thought of doing another book of sketches one day, with "one on Shakespeare". FM/C. E. Lawrence, 15 November 1909. Murray Archive.

205 "I see Feisal" and ff.: FM/WR, 3 August 1920.

205 "I think this is": FM/EP, 15 February 1920. (Wrongly dated in Beinecke.)

205 "interior nihilism": FM/EP, 18 September 1920.

205 "intellectual dishonesty" and ff.: *Spectator*, 10 January 1920, 51.

205 *England: Hergenhan suggests this, based on a letter of Manning's in his possession which I have not seen. It seems plausible that Galton would have introduced the two. Hergenhan, "Two Expatriates", 94.

205 "golden prime": AG/Edmund Gosse, 14 December 1902. Brotherton Library, Leeds.

206 *1920: "Three Fables", *Coterie* (Easter 1920), 17–19.

206 "an adventure": FM/WR, 10 November 1916. *Men and Memories*, 2. 297.

206 "eternal silence": "The Dean of St. Paul's", in William Rothenstein, *Twenty-four Portraits* (London, 1920), unpaginated.

206 "order and measure": FM/AH, 29 May 1924. Sybil Gowthorpe had written that he "often came to mass with us".

207 "chairborne warriors": *Literary Lifeline: The Richard Aldington–Lawrence Durrell Correspondence*, edited by Ian MacNiven and Harry T. Moore (New York, 1981), 110.

207 "most significant": Richard Aldington, "On Frederick [sic] Manning", *Coterie* (Easter 1920), 15–16.

208 "the literary taste": "The Prose of Frederic Manning", *The Egoist*, 1 October 1914, 375.

208 "a fine prose poet" and ff.: RA/Harold Monro, 24 October 1921. UCLA Library.

208 "great stuff": EP/Homer Pound (father), 1 September 1920. See also EP/TEL, August 1920. Paige, *Selected Letters*, 155.

208 "damned hard up": FM/EP, 22 July 1920.

209 "ginger up": EP/TEL, 20 April 1920. Paige, *Selected Letters*, 152.

209 "for Manning" and ff.: Scofield Thayer/EP, 18 September 1920. Beinecke.

209 "practically complete" and ff.: FM/EP, 10 October 1920.

209 "bloody rot": EP/FM, 9 October 1920. UCLA Library.

209 "Epicurean supper": FM/EP, 10 October 1920.

209 "rearrangement": FM/EP, 24 August 1920.

209 *years: He had not been working on it while writing White's life. FM/WR, 16 March 1920. It seems that the *Dial* relented somewhat in their terms later on, and were ready to make a decision based on having in hand three quarters of the manuscript. FM/EP, 19 November 1920.

209 "I don't want": FM/EP, 28 August 1920.

212 *sung: *Grantham Journal*, 5 March 1921.

212 "une petite mémoire": FM/AH, 25 June 1921.

212 "difficulties" and ff.: FM/AH, 7 January 1926.

212 *Galton's will: The will was signed 26 July 1916.

214 "My cousin": Nellie Bates/author, 16 September 1981.

215 "a terrible year": FM/AH, 29 December 1921.

215 "My head": FM/Harold Monro, 5 June 1921. UCLA Library.

215 "everything which it" and ff.: "Poetry in Prose",

Chapbook (April 1921), 11.

215 "Dull and dusty" and ff.: Harold Monro/RA, 4 April 1921. UCLA Library.

216 "very instructive": RA/Harold Monro, 7 April 1921. UCLA Library.

216 "She was": FM/AH, 10 July 1921.

216 "warmth and company" and ff.: FM/WR, 15 August 1921.

216 "There is little": FM/AH, 12 August 1921.

216 "disoriented" and ff.: FM/RA, 8 August 1921.

217 "memoir": AG/Edmund Gosse, 14 December 1902. Brotherton Library, Leeds. See also *Letters of Louise Imogen Guiney*, edited by Grace Guiney and Agnes Repplier (New York, 1926), 2. 205, 255.

217 "Do let us" and ff.: FM/RA, 8 August 1921.

217 "some books": FM/RA, 18 June 1921.

217 "a small private" and ff.: FM/RA, 23 June 1921.

217 "Manning became": *A Passionate Prodigality: Letters to Alan Bird from Richard Aldington 1949–1962*, edited by Miriam J. Benkovitz (New York, 1975), 96.

218 "...the book gave": Aldington, "An Introduction", 27. In the draft of the article Aldington makes no mention of his role in what he there calls a "hack biography".

218 "altered" and ff.: FM/RA, 16 January 1923.

219 "It is really": Virginia Murray/author, 3 June 1981.

219 "obviously all kept": Virginia Murray/author, 25 June 1981.

219 "a kind of": *Max and Will*, edited by Mary Lago and Karl Beckson (Cambridge, Massachusetts, 1975), 115.

220 "the most sceptical": John Rothenstein, *Summer's Ease* (London, 1965), 124.

220 "my dear Rachel" and ff.: FM/WR, 5 July 1924.

220 "I always enjoyed": Rachel Ward/author, 25 July 1977.

220 "reticences about himself": Aldington, "An Introduction", 26.

220 "I wish we": FM/WR, 18 September 1924.

221 "Now Lawrence": *Man and Memories*, 2, 367.

221 "if ever you feel": FM/TEL, 7 March 1922. *Letters to TEL*, 127.

221 "Soon" and ff.: FM/TEL, 31 March 1922. *ibid*. 128.

221 "not evolving": FM/TEL, 31 March 1922, *Letters to TEL*, 127.

221 "revising" and ff.: FM/WR, 9 January 1922.

221 "I have resisted": FM/WR, 22 December 1921.

221 "anxieties" and ff.: FM/AH, 21 July 1922.

222 *the romance FM/AH, 29 December 1921.

222 "amusing": FM/AH, 8 December 1922.

222 "I wish I": FM/JGF, 17 November 1908.

222 "fine perceptions": Geoffrey Scott/WR, undated. Houghton.

222 "Thank you": FM/WR, 26 November 1922.

223 "It is I": FM/AH, 7 January 1926.

223 *appearance: For the gift, FM/EP, 14 August 1920; for Manning's comments on the poem, FM/EP, 18 September 1920. What Pound inscribed is a mystery, for I have not been able to find this copy.

223 "very Irish": FM/Dorothy Pound, 13 December 1922. Possession of Omar Pound.

224 "first licherary" and ff.: EP/RA, 3 October 1958.

224 "backwash" and ff.: Ezra Pound, "Ford Madox (Hueffer) Ford: Obit", *The Nineteenth Century and After*, 126 (August 1939), 179.

224 "The HELL" and ff.: EP/RA, 3 October 1958.

224 "character and personality". FM/WR, 3 October 1916. *Men and Memories*, 2. 297. Arnold lived at Pains Hill Cottage, Cobham, about 8½ miles from Chobham.

226 "Epicuri": FM/WR, 18 September 1924.

226 "still look": FM/WR, 9 October 1924. As a result of the outing, Serpell asked Manning for an introduction to Rothenstein, which he quickly gave. "I do not know whether he wants a drawing or a painting. Be kind to

him, for my sake and because he is a very kindly man.'' FM/WR, 19 October 1924.

227 ''tho' if age'': FM/AH, 8 August 1923.

227 ''poisoned'': FM/WR, 4 April 1924.

227 ''good subject'': FM/TSE, 20 June 1924.

227 ''The trouble'': FM/AH, 21 June 1924.

227 ''Naval architects'': *Shipbuilding and Shipping Record*, 25 October 1923, 523. The book was reviewed also in many of the standard English and American journals, e.g., *The Times*, *Spectator*, *New Statesman*, *Nation and Athenaeum*, *Saturday Review*, etc.

227 *been ordered: FM/AH, 8 August 1923.

227 ''whose name'': T. E. Welby, ''Mr. Frederic Manning'', *Life and Letters*, 1 (November 1923), 29.

228 ''They have made me'': FM/AH, 25 July 1924.

228 ''shipbuilding'': FM/AH, 28 December 1923.

228 *collaborator: One admiring critic has felt the same lack of narrative flow in the war novel. William H. Pritchard, ''Telling Stories'', *Hudson Review*, 31 (Autumn 1978), 525.

229 ''never rid himself'': *White*, 60.

229 ''The spectacle'': *ibid*. 369.

229 ''Great armament'': *ibid*. 161.

230 ''When it came'': *ibid*. 444.

230 ''One seldom finds'': *ibid*. 54.

231 ''perfect understanding'' and ff.: *ibid*. 221–22.

231 ''dull technical book'': FM/AH, 28 December 1923.

231 ''The point of view'': ''Critic and Aesthetic'', *Quarterly Review*, 242 (July 1924), 141–42.

232 ''The function of art'': *ibid*. 138.

233 *subject: FM/AH, 8 February 1924.

233 ''My only object'': FM/AH, 6 February 1924.

234 ''religious impulse'': ''Le Père Hyacinthe'', *Criterion* 2 (July 1924), 462.

234 ''arbitrary act of'': ''A French Criticism of Newman'',

Criterion, 4 (January 1926), 22.

234 "The tragedy of faith": "Le Père Hyacinthe", 465.

234 *seven additional reviews: The index to the *Criterion* mistakenly assigns to Manning several other pieces which were signed "F. M.". These belong to Fanny Marlow.

234 "What Professor Toynbee": *Criterion*, 3 (October 1924), 136.

234 *wanted more: FM/AH, 4 February 1924.

235 "rather reactionary" and ff.: FM/AH, 11 May 1924.

235 *their writings: In 1926 Manning had Peter Davies send Eliot a copy of *Epicurus, his Morals*, hoping that Eliot would review it himself in the *Criterion* or elsewhere. The book was reviewed in *Criterion* but not by Eliot. In 1931 Eliot sent copies of *Ash Wednesday* and *Thoughts After Lambeth* to Manning.

235 "It recalls me": FM/AH, 11 November 1923.

235 "is again unfolding": FM/AH, 28 December 1923.

236 "I wonder": FM/TSE, 14 September 1925. For the new magazine, see Peter Ackroyd, *T. S. Eliot* (New York, 1984), 153.

237 "immeasurable": FM/WR, 19 October 1924.

237 "toy": FM/WR and Alice Rotlenstein, 10 October 1924.

237 "who have no country": FM/AH, 12 August 1921.

Chapter 7

238 "...when the door": Leon Gellert, "Case of Private 19022", *Herald*, 13 March 1948.

239 "troublesome"and ff.: FM/AH, 15 August 1925.

239 "He is conscious" and ff.: "A French Criticism of Newman", 25–26. Eliot had originally asked Manning to translate the Fernandez article, but he declined for lack of time. FM/TSE, 8 September 1924. Fernandez would later reply to Manning's criticism with "The Experiences of Newman: Reply to Frederic Manning", *Criterion*, 4 (October 1926).

240 "ease and precision" and ff.: *ibid*. 19.

240 "the idlest" and ff.: FM/WR, 9 October 1925.
240 "I want": FM/John Murray, 23 October 1925. Murray Archive. Manning came very close to selling Buckstone in September of 1924. FM/TSE, 8 September 1924.
240 "before deciding": FM/AH, 28 December 1925.
241 "extraordinary": FM/TSE, 17 February 1926.
241 "exhausted": FM/AH, 16 February 1926.
241 "Animae Suae": *Irish Statesman*, 20 February 1926, 736. Reprinted in *Literary Digest*, 3 April 1926, 32.
242 "religious controversy": Æ/FM, 23 March 1926. Bibliothèque Nationale, nouvelles acquisitions françaises, 15722, f. 436.
242 "I hope": FM/AH, 26 February 1926.
243 "I prefer music": FM/Sybil Gowthorpe, 6 July 1926.
243 "Why has no one": FM/John Murray, 13 May 1926. Murray Archive.
243 "that courage for dreams": FM/WR, 9 October 1924. Manning was here referring to Ramsay MacDonald, whose "trace of weakness under an apparent strength" he thought Rothenstein had captured very well in a recent drawing.
243 "I had one": FM/Sybil Gowthorpe, 6 July 1926.
243 "deplorable": FM/AH, 3 July 1926.
243 "rather small": FM/AH, 21 June 1926.
243 "very tiring": FM/AH, 3 July 1926.
243 "You would not believe": FM/Sybil Gowthorpe, 6 July 1926.
244 "later" and ff.: FM/RA, 8 August 1921.
244 "...the most": *Epicurus*, xxi.
244 "could discern": *ibid*. vi.
244 "sometimes rather difficult": John Murray/FM, 4 February 1926. Murray Archive.
245 "He had no interest": *Epicurus*, xxxiv-xxxv.
245 "To the Epicurean": *ibid*. xli.
246 *written: Andrew Birkin, *J. M. Barrie and the Lost Boys* (London, 1979). A television series relying on the same

material was produced in 1978.

246 "What's in a name": *ibid*. 196.

246 "I am sorry": Peter Davies/Eudo C. Mason (1901–1969), 7 June 1939. Peter Davies Archive. Mason, then at Leipzig, went on to become Professor of German at Edinburgh University. I found no evidence of his ever having written anything on Manning.

246 "It is quite": Peter Davies/Henry Manning, 22 February 1938.

248 "I can't": Nicholas Davies/author, 1 July 1977.

249 "to understand": *Men at War*, edited by Ernest Hemingway (New York, 1942), xvi.

249 "two best books": Peter Davies/Shakespear and Parkyn, 3 February 1955. Mitchell Library. Davies's good fortune with Manning led him to publish some other Australians, notably Christina Stead. See Rodney Wetherell, "Interview with Christina Stead", *Australian Literary Studies*, 9 (October 1980), 433–34.

249 "to pay": FM/WR, 6 November 1926.

249 "but I have really": FM/Sybil Gowthorpe, 27 May 1926.

249 "he dallied": William Rothenstein, *Since Fifty* (London, 1939), 83.

249 "In due course": Sybil Gowthorpe/author, 11 January 1979.

250 "with my mother": FM/John Murray, 5 May 1927. Murray Archive.

251 "On my arrival": Hanbury Davies/Henry Manning, 28 February 1935.

252 "I wish I had roots": FM/Sybil Gowthorpe, 6 June 1928.

253 "Mr Peter Davies": FM/John Murray, 5 May 1927. Murray Archive.

253 *1920s: *The Daily Mirror*, 26 February 1930.

253 "long-neglected" and ff.: FM/John Murray, 5 May 1927. Murray Archive.

253 "only attempted": *John O'London's Weekly*, 22 March 1930, 964.

254 "It was wilful": FM/TEL, 11 February 1930. *Letters to TEL*, 129.

254 "obstinately averse": This is from Rothenstein's obituary notice on Manning. That the season might be short for war books was intimated in the fact that *Punch* was already running a parody of them early in 1930. *Punch*, 12 February 1930, 174–75.

254 "lured" and ff.: *The Daily Mirror*, 26 February 1930.

254 "Peter took it": FM/TEL, 11 February 1930. *Letters to TEL*, 129.

254 "even during the war": FM/TEL, 14 March 1930. *Letters to TEL*, 130.

255 "In recording": *Middle Parts*, prefatory note.

255 "The Gilded Coach": "Madame de Sainte Claire has become an obsession. She rules me now as effectively as she ruled His Grandeur years ago; and I can't persuade myself that she has never existed. She exists now. She will read and fold up this letter at once, if I don't; I can almost see her hand coming over my shoulder to take it. One can get away from real people, but imaginary people haunt us more especially when they are female." FM/JGF, 18 June 1912.

255 "I really want": FM/Sybil Gowthorpe, 11 February 1930.

255 "unique interest": *The Publisher and Bookseller*, 30 August 1929, cover advertisement.

257 *Davies/Lawrence dialogue: Houghton Library.

257 "an adept": FM/TEL, 14 March 1930, *Letters to TEL*, 130.

257 "pure *Scenes*": TEL/FM, 25 February 1930. Garnett, *Letters of TEL*, 682. Lawrence had a liking for such constructions. See his introduction to the illustrated edition of Richard Garnett's *The Twilight of the Gods* (London, 1924).

257 "practically certain": Aldington, "An Introduction", 27.

The review that Aldington wrote of the book in 1930 (*Sunday Referee*, 2 March 1930) does not indicate any suspicion of the writer's identity. In the 1959 article Aldington says that such details as the hero being named "Bourne", and his incessant smoking, contributed to his earlier assumption. E. M. Forster, another admirer of *Scenes*, did not connect the two books.

257 "Life was a hazard": *Middle Parts*, 76.

257 "interminable": FM/AH, 5 January 1924.

257 "I shall not": FM/AH, 21 January 1924. See also letter of 28 December 1923.

258 *Arnold: Gellert, the admiring journalist who met him in Sydney in 1925, saw him in this way, and so did Dorothy Pound when questioned about him in 1962–63. Hergenhan, "Two Expatriates", 93.

258 "only that of the average": FM/A. V. Moore, 24 March 1930. Mitchell Library.

258 "hurriedly": FM/TEL, 11 February 1930. *Letters to TEL*, 129.

258 "a record": *Middle Parts*, prefatory note.

258 "scenes, times": Peter Davies/Eudo C. Mason, 7 June 1939. Peter Davies Archive.

258 *History of the King's Shropshire Light Infantry*: The book, edited by Major Walter deBurley Wood, gives a detailed account of the 7th battalion's movements. See especially 229–34.

259 "She bore no malice": *Middle Parts*, 60.

259 *presence: *The History of the Corps of the King's Shropshire Light Infantry* (Shrewsbury, 1971), 3, 139. One former member of the regiment told me that a comrade "recognised most of the characters referred to in the book". Arthur Allwood/author, 20 January 1978.

259 "Actual experience": FM/John Murray, 5 May 1927. Murray Archive.

260 "His impassive": *Middle Parts*, 227.

260 "delicate sensibility": *ibid*. 44.

260 "solitary and": *ibid.* 23.
260 "the faculty": *ibid.* 92.
261 "What they really needed": *ibid.* 165.
261 "I have drawn": *ibid.* Prefatory Note.
261 "moral effort": *ibid.* 92.
262 "Bourne sometimes": *ibid.* 205. Cf. *Scenes*, 253–54.
262 "Power is measured": *Middle Parts*, 10.
263 "part of the natural order": *ibid.* 193.
263 "a little less": *ibid.* 39.
263 "We're fightin'": *ibid.* 150–51. Not all readers have been impressed by Manning's skill with dialect. See John Douglas Pringle, "*Her Privates We*", in *On Second Thought* (Sydney, 1971), 93.
265 "Je t'aime": *Middle Parts*, 117–18.
266 "always treated women": *ibid.* 107.
266 "And they said good-bye": *ibid.* 120.
267 "like the fish-pools": *ibid.* 14.
268 "He was a reticent": *ibid.* 133.
268 "Bourne flung himself": *ibid.* 216–17.
269 "always see" and ff.: *ibid.* 252.
269 "a sense of triumph" and ff.: *ibid.* 246–47.
270 *dead: For an extended comparison of the two books see Holger M. Klein, "Dazwischen Niemandsland: *Im Western Nichts Neues* und *Her Privates We*", in *Grossbritannien und Deutschland. . . Festschrift fur John W. P. Bourke*, edited by Ortwin Kuhn (Munich, 1974), 487–512.
270 "Anyway, he argued": *Middle Parts*, 241.
271 "the sergeant-major": *ibid.* 247.
271 **For Whom the Bell Tolls*: *For Whom the Bell Tolls* (New York, 1940), 414. Echoes of Manning can be also heard in other works of Hemingway, most recently in the name (David Bourne) given to the hero of the posthumously published novel, *The Garden of Eden* (New York, 1986). Of the several dozen selections he chose to include in *Men at War*, the selection from Manning's novel is one of the

few Hemingway discussed in his introduction.

271 "I thought": FM/A. V. Moore, 24 March 1930. Mitchell Library.

272 "fuckin'": *Middle Parts*, 6.

272 "blind forces": *ibid*. 42.

272 "love story": *Daily Telegraph*, 16 December 1930. Forster's phrase may have been picked up from Lawrence, who described the novel as a "love poem" in a letter to Manning of 25 February 1930. He had presumably said something of the same order to Forster when he wrote him "enthusiastically" about the novel on 8 February. This earlier letter is not published, and I owe my knowledge of its existence (and tone) to Forster's biographer. P. N. Furbank/author, 21 July 1979.

272 "most intensely himself": This is a phrase from a letter Manning wrote to Rothenstein, 1 July 1918. "In every 'show' one undergoes a kind of katharsis (as Aristotle described the function of tragedy); or what St. Paul called an 'emptying of oneself'; and curiously enough it is precisely at such moments that a man becomes most intensely himself."

273 "It is a fine book": *New Republic*, 23 July 1930, 296.

273 *1930: It was to have been ready in November, but "an unforseen circumstance" slowed its appearance until 15 January. *The Middle Parts of Fortune*, sold only by subscription, was supposed to have been ready in October, but was delayed until "probably...December 15th, and will be immediately distributed". *Publisher and Bookseller*, 8 November 1929, 920. In the last stages of production Davies was evidently uncertain of precisely when the special edition, already "heavily over-subscribed", would be available, for while the title page carries the date MCMXXIX, stamped on the spine of each of the two volumes is "1930".

273 *doubters: See exchange of letters in the *New Statesman*, 29 March and 5, 12 April 1930.

273 *received: An indirect example of admiration is in Henry Williamson's *Patriot's Progress*, published in April of 1930: the hero's army number is 19023. Williamson regarded *Her Privates We* as "a masterpiece". *Patriot's Progress* (London, 1968 edition), unpaginated preface. A more whimsical example of how other writers paid respect to (or cashed in on) the novel's fame is *WAAC Demobilised: Her Private Affairs 1918–1930*, which came out in July 1930 as a sequel to *WAAC: The Woman's Story of the War* (March 1930). Both books were published anonymously by T. W. Laurie.

274 *sold: Eric Partridge, "The War Continues", *The Window*, 1 (April 1930), 70. In his Autumn and Christmas catalogue for 1931 Peter Davies announced that the book had thus far sold 30,000 copies. By the terms of the contract, drawn up 11 April 1929, Manning received from the "ordinary" edition (*Her Privates We*) 10% on the first thousand copies, 12½% on the next two thousand, and 15% on all copies beyond three thousand. He received a flat 15% on all copies of the "special" edition (*The Middle Parts of Fortune*). Peter Davies Archive.

274 German and Swedish editions: A Swedish translation was published in 1930 (by Wahlstrom and Widstrand, Stockholm), but there was no German edition until 1966 (Rainer Wunderlich Verlag, Tubingen).

274 "I am not puffed": FM/Sybil Gowthorpe, 11 February 1930.

274 "the work we live by": FM/WR, 22 December 1922.

274 *the book: *Sunday Referee*, 2 February 1930. A photo of the Selfridge window appears in *Publisher and Bookseller*, 28 March 1930, 699.

274 "Peter Davies is trying": TEL/FM, 25 February 1930. Garnett, *Letters of TEL*, 682–83.

274 "*Her Privates We* and Women": *Time and Tide*, 21 February 1930, 247.

275 "a little terrified": FM/TEL, 14 March 1930, *Letters to TEL*, 130.

275 "Private 19022": *Daily Mirror*, 26 February 1930.

275 "greedy enough": FM/TEL, 14 March 1930. *Letters to TEL*, 130.

275 "You, and Polly" and ff.: FM/Frieda Lynch Bernard, 1 February 1930.

275 *acquaintances alike: Ryllis Hacon, A. V. Moore, Olivia Shakespear.

275 "and am now deliberately": TEL/FM, 25 February 1930. Garnett, *Letters of TEL*, 682.

276 "I had your address": FM/TEL, 11 February 1930, *Letters to TEL*, 129.

276 "That would have been". TEL/FM, 15 May 1930, Garnett, *Letters to TEL*, 691. Lawrence owned copies of all of Manning's books except *Epicurus*, and he had read that as well. *T. E. Lawrence by his Friends*, edited by A. W. Lawrence (New York, 1937), 447; Garnett, *Letters of TEL*, 688.

276 "It is perfectly clear": JGF/Henry Manning, 1 December 1936.

277 "I did not want": FM/TEL, 26 March 1930. *Letters to TEL*, 131–32.

277 "practically" and ff.: FM/TEL, 9 May 1930. *ibid*, 136.

277 "magnificent book": *ibid*. 134.

277 "You took me": *ibid*. 134–35.

278 "smooth" and "ironical": FM/TEL, 28 August 1931. *ibid*. 141. Manning is here talking about a recent meeting with Feisal.

279 "in a more modern" and ff.: FM/John Murray, 11 March 1930. Murray Archive.

279 "You will realize": John Murray/FM, 10 March 1930. Murray Archive.

279 "rights" and ff.: FM/John Murray, 15 March 1930. Murray Archive.

279 "disclose": John Murray/FM, 14 March 1930. Murray

Archive.

279 "The newspapers": FM/John Murray, 21 March 1930. Murray Archive.

280 "merely in a tentative": FM/John Murray, 11 March 1930. Murray Archive.

280 "new matter": John Murray/FM, 19 March 1930. Murray Archive. Manning responded on 21 March.

280 "I hope": John Murray/FM, 24 March 1930. Murray not only released to Manning the remaining 80 copies of *Scenes* at ordinary authors' rates, but surrendered to him as well all rights on his volumes of poems.

280 "rather melancholy": FM/John Murray, 7 April 1930. Murray Archive.

281 "young man": FM/Arnold Bennett, 12 December 1930. La Fayette Butler Collection of Arnold Bennett, Pennsylvania State University Libraries.

281 "voluntary exile": *Scenes* (1930), 269.

281 "simply endless" and ff.: *ibid*. 270.

281 "wishes to become": *ibid*. 274.

281 "Sometimes I have pity": *ibid*. 289.

281 "the metaphysical": FM/WR, 19 December 1930.

281 "difficult": FM/TEL, 13 August 1930. *Letters to TEL*, 139.

281 "The child": FM/TEL, 29 October 1930. *ibid*.

282 "poor Charles Whibley": FM/TEL, 26 March 1930. *ibid*. 131. The earliest I can put them together is at a houseparty at Pixton in 1912. Pixton Visitors Book.

282 "scholarship" and ff.: Arthur Galton, *Acer in Hostem* (Windermere, 1913), 43–44. This is a privately printed book consisting of brief notices that Galton originally wrote for Christmas circulars for Cornish Brothers, booksellers in Birmingham. The dedication is worth quoting: "To Dorothy Shakespear, In Memory of Dreaming Hours at Oxford, With a Hope of More Golden Realities in ROME."

282 "He was distinct": FM/TSE, 27 May 1930.

282 "I don't fancy" and ff.: FM/Sybil Gowthorpe, 6 July 1926.

282 "I like or dislike": FM/TEL, 26 March 1930. *Letters to TEL*, 131.

282 "I was very glad": Charles Whibley/FM, 22 June 1917.

282 *blind man: Penelope Hughes-Hallett (secretary at Faber & Faber)/author, 13 September 1979.

283 "close and unpleasant" and ff.: FM/Dot Manning, 26 June 1930.

283 "some future time" and ff.: FM/TSE, 27 May 1930.

283 "As I put": FM/TEL, 29 October 1930. *Letters to TEL*, 140.

283 **Her Privates We*: *Spectator*, 22 November 1930, 796; *Times Literary Supplement*, 20 November 1930, 966.

283 *heard of?: Contract. Peter Davies Archive.

283 "the earlier book": *Publisher and Bookseller*, 28 November 1930, 1199.

283 "satisfactory": The firm has no record of sales. This was Manning's judgment: FM/WR, 19 December 1930. In Davies's Autumn and Christmas catalogue for 1931 there is mention that "a few copies" of the limited edition were still available.

284 *15 June 1947: Mrs Jacqueline Kavanagh (Written Archive Officer)/author, 15 January 1981.

284 "First published": *Times Literary Supplement*, 25 December 1930, 1102.

284 "*Scenes and Portraits*": *Dublin Magazine*, 6 (July-September 1931), 76.

284 "It is a portrait": *Everyman*, 4 December 1930, 598.

284 *American edition: Scribners no longer has any record of the book, and the *National Union Catalogue* lists only three libraries with the American edition. Peter Davies used a cellophane dust jacket which was stamped with Manning's name in large red type. One such copy is still held by John Rothenstein and his wife.

285 *20 years earlier: Putnam's records on the book were destroyed by fire several years ago. But in the archive of

Peter Davies there is a note to the effect that the book did not sell very well in America.

285 "thin juice": *Outlook*, 25 March 1931, 439.

285 "beyond reach" and ff.: *New York Herald Tribune*, 12 April 1931.

285 *its difficulty: FM/J. M. Barrie, 28 December 1930, Lilly Library, Indiana University; FM/WR, 19 December 1930.

285 "I have always": FM/TEL, 12 January 1931. *Letters to TEL*, 140.

285 "I heard": FM/WR, 3 January 1931. Actually Manning had already arranged for a copy of *Scenes* to be sent to Bennett, with whom he had exchanged a few notes since first writing him in March to thank him for his review of *Middle Parts*. Bennett ultimately noticed *Scenes* "as well worth reprinting" (*Evening Standard*, 18 December 1930), but said nothing else about a book that ten years before he had dismissed: "I got F. Manning's *Scenes and Portraits* on the strength of high praise of it from people who ought to be able to judge. Well, I couldn't read it. The author is very clever and original, and sometimes suggestive; but he does not know his job. He is an amateur. He cannot hold the thing together and his literary sense is very defective." *London Mercury*, 2 (October 1920), 680. Bennett, in 1930, denied ever having written in the *Mercury*, "about either you or anybody else". Manning was willing to let the matter pass, but his hope of meeting Bennett was broken by the latter's death. For Bennett's opinion of the war novel see the *Evening Standard*, 23 January, 11 September, and 18 December 1930. All of these articles are reprinted in Mylett, *Arnold Bennett: The Evening Standard Years*.

285 "I feel": FM/WR, 23 March 1931.

285 "to write my romance": FM/TEL, 12 January 1931. *Letters to TEL*, 141.

286 "insatiable appetite": FM/TEL, 4 January 1932. *ibid*. 144.

286 "I want to get" and ff.: FM/TEL, 21 December 1931. *ibid.* 142.

286 "The air here": FM/WR, 19 July 1931.

286 "any satisfactory work" and ff.: FM/TEL 21 December 1931. *Letters to TEL*, 142.

286 "nearly died": FM/WR, 29 April 1932.

286 "style and form" and ff.: FM/TEL, 13 August 1930. *Letters to TEL*, 139.

287 "relapse": FM/Mrs de Mestre, 12 October 1934.

Chapter 8

288 *to withstand: *Herald*, 31 December 1932. Four days earlier the *Herald* had carried a small notice of Manning's coming "on a health trip".

288 "one of the finest": caption attached to photo printed in a magazine. The clipping, found in Eleanor Manning's home, unfortunately lacks a title or date.

288 "in the front" and ff.: *Bulletin*, 22 March 1933, 5.

289 "You want": *Middle Parts*, 191.

289 *anyone else: FM/Mrs de Mestre, 12 October 1934.

289 "I think" and ff.: FM/Henry Manning, 25 June 1934.

290 *his brother: It was not the first time he had suggested arguments to a practising politician. FM/Aubrey Herbert, 24 February 1912.

290 "Ultimately": draft in Manning's land, Manning's home, Sydney.

290 "I am not working": FM/Henry Manning, 31 July 1934.

291 "most": AG/Laurence Binyon, 27 January 1890.

291 "Unfortunately": FM/TEL, 20 June 1930. *Letters to TEL*, 137.

292 "Mr Manning has the genius": *The Dublin Magazine*, 6 (July-September 1931), 76.

292 "a man in the flesh" and ff.: Untitled parody, Mitchell Library.

294 "this coster-monger age": FM/TEL, 26 July 1934. *Letters to TEL*, 146.

294 "I shall leave": FM/TEL, 26 March 1934. This part of the letter is left out of the printed version.
294 "quite spoilt": FM/Mrs de Mestre, 12 October 1934.
294 "You might let me": FM/Agnes Gelsthorpe, 25 March 1934.
294 "succession of colds" and ff.: FM/Henry Manning, 25 June 1934.
294 "I don't know": FM/Mrs de Mestre, 12 October 1934.
295 "a dreadful old house" and ff.: FM/Olivia Shakespear, 22 July 1934. Library State University of New York, Stony Brook.
295 "magnificent Rolls": FM/Henry Manning, 20 September 1934.
296 "modern and comfortable": FM/Olivia Shakespear, 22 July 1934. Library State University of New York, Stony Brook.
296 "as a book": FM/Henry Manning, 31 July 1934.
297 "Peter Davies wrote": TEL/FM, 16 November 1934. Mitchell Library. This letter is printed in L. T. Hergenhan, "Some Unpublished Letters from T. E. Lawrence to Frederic Manning", *Southerly*, 23 (1963), 250.
297 "getting on quite well": FM/Henry Manning, 31 July 1934.
297 "I have not": FM/Henry Manning, 20 September 1934.
297 "If you come": FM/TEL, 17 July 1934, *Letters to TEL*, 145.
297 "One can't of course" and ff.: FM/William Manning, 18 December 1934.
297 "I thought it might": FM/Henry Manning, 30 September 1931.
297 "within call": FM/William Manning, 18 December 1934.
298 **Her Privates We*: Gladys Gelsthorpe heard this from "Pen".
298 "Food, hotels" and ff.: FM/William Manning, 18 December 1934.
298 "Not that I shall": FM/TEL, 21 December 1934. *Letters to*

TEL, 148.

299 "I shall be delighted":Dr J. A. Galletly/author, 27 June 1977.

300 *mother: In possession of Mrs Gelsthorpe.

300 "I am so dreadfully": Peter Davies/Lady Manning, 22 February 1935.

301 "Strange to think": TEL/Peter Davies, 28 February 1935. Garnett, *Letters of TEL*, 859–60.

301 *Manning's mother: Rothenstein, *Since Fifty*, 264.

301 *brief paragraphs: *Herald*, 25 February 1935; *Telegraph*, 25, 26 February 1935.

301 "If the death": *Saturday Review of Literature*, 18 May 1935, 15.

301 "News does not": *Poetry*, 46 (July 1935), 219.

301 "happening": Robert Speaight, *William Rothenstein* (London, 1962), 405.

302 "very generous" and ff.: Fr George Gallagher, S. J./Lady Manning, 11 March 1935.

302 "my own private": JGF/Henry Manning, 1 December 1936. The poem, then unpublished, was enclosed in the letter to Harry Manning where Fairfax compared Manning to T. E. Lawrence. In 1982 I sent a copy of the letter to Fairfax's daughter and received a poignant reply: "When I read my father's letter to Harry Manning I must admit I burst into tears — I remembered him writing it at my great-aunt's home when we were in Sydney on holiday. I was 12! The poem I know well, of course, but leaping out at me from the past, as it were, made it far more real to me." Benita Biso/author, 15 July 1982.

302 "The dead leaves": "Demeter Mourning", *Eidola*.

303 "looked again": William Roscoe/author, 29 September 1977.

303 "quite delightful": TSE/A. V. Moore, 30 November 1954. Mitchell Library.

Acknowledgements

I owe this book to the many people who appear within it, and to many more who do not.

The essential assistance of Eleanor Manning will be clear. She helped in every way she could, and I deeply regret that she and her cousin, William O. Manning, did not live to see the book.

The considerable assistance given by Patricia Dickson, Nellie Bates, Dr J. A. Galletly, Agnes Gelsthorpe, Lady Cynthia Sandys, Eva Sumner, Rachel Rothenstein Ward, and Ivor and Victor Woolmer will also be clear from the text. I hope that I have come near to finding the man they remember.

Other individuals shared with me important letters, papers, and information. I wish to thank Benita Biso, Dr J. Burrows, Nicholas Davies, Ruthven Davies, Dr George Day, Margaret Fitzherbert, Ian Fletcher, P. N. Furbank, Nicolete Gray, Bill Holmes, Patricia Hope, Michael Lane, A. W. Lawrence, Joseph McLeod, John and Mary Nettle, Arthur Patrick, Reverend G. T. Roberts, William Roscoe, K. M. Sexby, and Joan Waldegrave. Special thanks go to Omar Pound for providing so much.

Archives, libraries, and record offices in America, Australia, England, and France contributed generously to this book. My great debt to the firm of John Murray will be apparent. I am indebted as well to the Beinecke Rare Book and Manuscript Library, Houghton Library, the Harry Ransom Humanities Research Center at the University of Texas, the Mitchell Library, the Australian National Library, the British Library, the Army Records Centre, the library of the *Spectator,* and the Bibliothèque Nationale.

A number of other institutions also provided me with materials: the Bodleian Library, the BBC Archives, the Brotherton Library (Leeds), Girton College Library (Cambridge), Merton College Library (Oxford), New College Library (Oxford), the Public Record Office, the DMS Watson Library (University College, London), the West Sussex Record Office, Lilly Library (Indiana University), Northwestern University Library, Pennsylvania State University Libraries, the Joseph Regenstein Library (University of Chicago), Southern Illinois University Library, the Library of the State University of New York (Stony Brook), the University of Michigan Library, the University Research Library, UCLA, and the State Library of South Australia.

While the staffs of all of these institutions were invariably helpful, I must single out for special mention the efforts of Caroline Dalton of New College Library, Catherine Santamaria of the Australian National Library, and C. A. Seaton of the *Spectator.*

A number of friends read the manuscript: Peter Heydon, David Hughes, William Ingram, David P. Jordan, Richard and Linnea Levy, and Peter Quint. I hope they will see how I have profited from their comments. I also want to thank James Gindin for an early and perceptive reading, and A. Walton Litz for a later one.

Special thanks go to Hubert Cohen, Raymond and Daphne Grew, and John Shy for extended discussions about the book, and to Thomas and Leslie Tentler who assisted in too many ways to name or thank adequately.

Finally, I would like to thank Richard Walsh, the publisher at Angus & Robertson until 1986, for his belief that an unorthodox book about a little known writer deserved to be published.

Pound and Dorothy Shakespear, Their Letters 1909–1914, edited by Omar Pound and A. Walton Litz, are reprinted by permission of Faber & Faber and New Directions.

Acknowledgement is also due to Faber & Faber and New Directions for permission to print from previously unpublished and uncollected work of Ezra Pound © Ezra Pound Literary Trust 1982, 1985.

Extracts from the published letters of T. E. Lawrence appear by permission of the Trustees of his estate.

Extracts from Frederic Manning, *The Middle Parts of Fortune,* New York, 1977, are reprinted by permission of William Heinemann Ltd and St Martin's Press, Inc.

Bibliography

BOOKS

The Vigil of Brunhild, London, John Murray, 1907.

Scenes and Portraits, London, John Murray, 1909.

Poems, London, John Murray, 1910.

Eidola, London, John Murray, 1917.

The Life of Sir William White, London, John Murray, 1923.

The Middle Parts of Fortune, London, The Piazza Press, issued by Peter Davies, 1929.

Her Privates We, London, Peter Davies, 1930.

Scenes and Portraits, New Edition, London, Peter Davies, 1930.

POETRY PUBLISHED IN MAGAZINES

''Bal Masque'', *Outlook,* 19 May 1906, p. 686.

''The Secret'', *Outlook,* 16 June 1906, p. 814.

''Noon'', *Atlantic Monthly,* July 1909, p. 101. Reprinted in *Poems*.

''Persephone'', *The English Review,* December 1909, p. 6. Reprinted as ''Kore'' in *Poems.*

''Hecate'', *Spectator,* 12 March 1910, p. 423. Reprinted as ''Canzone'' in *Poems.*

''Hera Parthenia'', *English Review,* May 1910, p. 196.

''To Artemis the Destroyer'', *English Review,* May 1910, p. 197.

''Danae's Song'', *Forum,* February 1911, p. 151. Reprinted as ''Danae'' in *Eidola.*

''The Vision of Demeter'', *English Review,* April 1911, p. 7.

"The Mother", *Spectator,* 6 January 1912, p. 512. Reprinted in *Eidola*.

"Ganhardine's Song", *Country Life,* 19 October 1912, p. 512. Reprinted in *Eidola.*

"Winter", *Windsor Magazine,* February 1913, p. 357. Reprinted in *Eidola.*

"Passe-Pied", *Spectator,* 26 April 1913, p. 715. Reprinted as "Hurleywane" in *Eidola.*

"Simaetha", *Poetry,* June 1913, p. 99. Reprinted in *Eidola*.

"At Even", *Poetry*, June 1913, p. 100.

"From Demeter (The Faun's Call)", *Poetry,* June 1913, p. 100. Reprinted as "The Faun" in *Eidola.*

"Sacrifice", *Poetry,* July 1916, pp. 181–82. Reprinted in *Eidola.*

"The Choosers", *Spectator,* 8 July 1916, pp. 44–45. Reprinted in *Eidola.*

"Anacreontic", *Poetry,* January 1917, p. 186. Reprinted as "The Cup" in *Eidola*.

"Bois de Mametz: August 16", *The Quest,* January 1917, pp. 333–35. Reprinted as "Bois de Mametz" in *Eidola*.

"Echo", *The Chapbook,* July 1919, p. 29.

"Animae Suae", *Irish Statesman,* 20 February 1926, p. 736.

Miscellaneous Prose

"Ibsen", *Sydney Daily Telegraph,* 3 November 1900, p. 11.

"The Organ Monkey",[?], *Outlook,* 16 July 1904, p. 609.

"An Interlude", *Westminster Gazette,* 18 November 1905, p. 4.

"Some Contemporary Poets", *Cornish Brothers Catalogue,* 1911, pp. 58–59.

"Greek Genius and Greek Democracy", *Edinburgh Review,* April 1913, pp. 334–51.

"M. de Gourmont and the Problem of Beauty", *Little Review,* February/March, 1919, pp. 19–26.

"An Unionist's *Apologia", Nation,* 29 March 1919, pp. 773–74.

"The Poetry of Mr Binyon", *Piccadilly Review,* 23 October 1919, p. 7.

"Three Fables", *Coterie,* Easter 1920, pp. 17–19.

"Dean Inge", *Twenty-Four Portraits,* William Rothenstein, 1920, n. p.

"Poetry in Prose", *The Chapbook,* April 1921, pp. 10–15.

"Libertinism and St Évremond", *New Statesman,* 3 September 1921, pp. 593–94.

"The Port of London", *New Statesman,* 24 September 1921, pp. 682–83.

"Critic and Aesthetic", *Quarterly Review,* July 1924, pp. 123–44.

Introductory Essay, *Epicurus, His Morals,* translated by Walter Charleton (1651), London, Peter Davies, 1926.

REVIEWS IN THE *CRITERION*

"Le Père Hyacinthe", July 1924, pp. 460–67.

Greek Historical Thought; *Greek Civilization and Character,* Arnold J. Toynbee; *Greek Literary Criticism,* T. D. Denniston, October 1924, pp. 134–37.

Courte Histoire du Christianisme, Albert Houtin; *Le Mystère du Jésus,* S. L. Couchond; *Propos sur le Christianisme,* Alain; *La Sibylle,* Th. Zielinski, January 1925, pp. 320–21.

"A French Criticism of Newman", January 1926, pp. 19–31.

Un Prêtre Symboliste: Marcel Hébert; *Une Vie de Prêtre: Mon Expérience*, Albert Houtin, June 1926, pp. 590–93.

Catullus: The Complete Poems, translated and edited by F. A. Wright, June 1926, pp. 603–04.

"A Note on Sir James Frazer", September 1927, pp. 198–205.

Carmen, et quelques autres nouvelles de Prosper Mérimée, Introduction de M. Valéry Larbaud, November 1927, pp. 448–55.

REVIEWS IN THE *SPECTATOR*

"Shakespearean Criticism", 18 December 1909, pp. 1055–56.
"Milton", 16 April 1910, pp. 625–26.
"Southey's Poems", 2 July 1910, pp. 22–23.
"The Genius of Swift", 23 July 1910, pp. 134–35.
"A French Critic on Lyly", 10 September 1910, pp. 391–92.
"George Sand", 8 October 1910, pp. 560–61.
"The Etruscans", 22 October 1910, pp. 651–52.
"Balzac and the *Comédie Humaine*", 29 October 1910, pp. 694–95.
"Two Books of Italian Verse", 28 January 1911, p. 119.
"The Correspondence of Swift", 18 March 1911, pp. 402–03.
"The Work of J. M. Synge", 1 April 1911, pp. 482–83.
"The Influence of Greece", 22 April 1911, pp. 602–03.
"Mr Zangwill's Fantasies", 20 May 1911, p. 772.
"The Memoirs of Countess Golovine", 17 June 1911, pp. 930–31.
"Molière Malgré Lui", 24 June 1911, pp. 969–70.
"William Morris", 8 July 1911, pp. 69–71.
"Samuel Rogers", 19 August 1911, pp. 283–84.
"Lafcadio Hearn in Japan", 2 September 1911, pp. 346–47.
"Coleridge", 23 September 1911, pp. 458–59.
"Robert Louis Stevenson", 7 October 1911, pp. 549–50.
"On Translating Dante", 14 October 1911, pp. 599–600.
"French Poetry", 23 December 1911, p. 1123.
"Shelley", 30 December 1911, pp. 1154–55.
"The Symposiarch", 27 January 1912, pp. 153–54.
"French Literature", 16 March 1912, pp. 444–45.
"The Elizabethans", 30 March 1912, pp. 514–15.
"Gray", 13 April 1912, pp. 586–87.
"De Contemptu Mundi", 27 April 1912, pp. 647–48.
"John Andrew Doyle", 1 June 1912, pp. 874–75.
"The Literature of Power", 22 June 1912, pp. 991–92.
"Travel and Pilgrimage", 13 July 1912, pp. 59–60.
"William Langland", 27 July 1912, pp. 130–31.

''Novels of Character and Environment'', 7 September 1912, pp. 335–37.

''English Prose Rhythm'', 28 September 1912, pp. 453–54.

''The Borgia Family'', 19 October 1912, pp. 601–02.

''Tales of Autolycus'', 9 November 1912, pp. 752–53.

''Letters to William Allingham'', 23 November 1912, pp. 861–62.

''Meredith's Poems'', 7 December 1912, pp. 931–32.

''The Poetry of Coleridge'', 21 December 1912, pp. 1063–64.

''Richelieu'', 11 January 1913, pp. 64–65.

''The Crock of Gold'', 15 March 1913, pp. 453–54.

''Swift's Friendships'', 12 April 1913, pp. 618–19.

''Lyric Poetry'', 1 November 1913, p. 683.

''Frederick Tennyson'', 1 November 1913, p. 721.

''Formal Poetry'', 10 January 1914, pp. 58–59.

''The Poetry of Blake'', 4 April 1914, p. 567.

''Cesare Borgia'', 25 April 1914, pp. 702–03.

''Spenser's Sonnets in French'', 16 May 1914, p. 835.

''The Age of Johnson'', 27 June 1914, pp. 1091–92.

''A Life of Francis Thompson'', 4 July 1914, pp. 18–19.

''The Poet as Virtuoso'', 24 July 1915, pp. 114–15.

''Rhythm in Verse'', 20 December 1919, p. 864.

''Some Winchester Letters'', 10 January 1920, pp. 51–52.

''Prosody and Shakespeare'', 3 April 1920, pp. 459–60.

Index